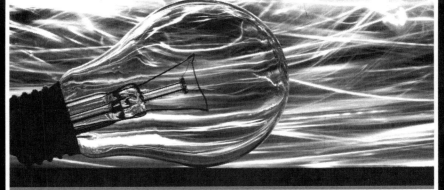

SPARKS

A Reader to Energize Writing

Third Edition

Donna Barnard

Orange Coast College

Kendall Hunt
publishing company

Kendall Hunt
publishing company

www.kendallhunt.com
Send all inquiries to:
4050 Westmark Drive
Dubuque, IA 52004-1840

Dedicated to

Barbara Underwood

in admiration of her courage; and

Bonnie Garcia;

I miss you both.

| SECTION ONE | Remembering: Personal Voices   1 |

| SECTION TWO | Contemplations: Essays that Explain and Explore   71 |

| SECTION THREE | Essays that Argue and Define   177 |

| SECTION FOUR | Writing Strategies   283 |

| SECTION FIVE | Research   319 |

| SECTION SIX | Basic Punctuation Rules and Practice   331 |

SECTION ONE

Remembering: Personal Voices   1

SECTION TWO

Contemplation: Essays that Explain and Explore   71

SECTION THREE   ## Essays that Argue and Define   177

SECTION FOUR   ## Writing Strategies   283

| SECTION SIX | **Basic Punctuation Rules and Practice 331** |

Essays by Rhetorical Mode

NARRATION

"A Voice for the Lonely by Stephen Corey
"City Out of Breath" by Ken Chen
"Mortality" by Bailey White
"Turbulence" by David Sedaris
"Burl's" by Bernard Cooper
"Learning to Read and Write" by Frederick Douglas
"Meat" by Brian Doyle
"Reading the River" by Mark Twain

DESCRIPTION

"Museum Piece" by David Huddle
"Joyas Voladoras" by Brian Doyle
"Mute Dancers: How to Watch a Hummingbird" by Diane Ackerman
"Hair" by Diane Ackerman
Burl's" by Bernard Cooper
"A Tree Beyond Imagining" by Reg Sanger
"The Courage of Turtles" by Edward Hoagland
"American Children" by John Updike

ILLUSTRATION/EXEMPLIFICATION

"The Little Mermaid" by Pauline Kael
"Naps" by Barbara Holland
"Joyas Voladoras" by Brian Doyle
"Hair" by Diane Ackerman
"Mute Dancers: How to Watch a Hummingbird" by Diane Ackerman
"Roll Over Bach, Too!" by Jack Kroll
"Monster Mash" by Jack Kroll

"Musical Awakenings" by Clayton Collins
"Black Widow" by Gordon Grice
"The Content of Our Character" by Shelby Steele
"Disposable Rocket" by John Updike
"The Courage of Turtles" by Edward Hoagland
"The Chemist's War" by Deborah Blum
"Somebody's Baby" by Barbara Kingsolver

DEFINITION

"On the Uncertainty of the Future" by Yoshida Kenko
"Hair" by Diane Ackerman
"Joyas Voladoras" by Brian Doyle
"The Content of Our Character" by Shelby Steele
"The Culture of Celebrity" by Joseph Epstein
"Truth" by J. Ruth Gendler
"The Surfing Savant" by Paul Solotaroff
"On Boxing" by Joyce Carol Oates

PROCESS

"Mute Dancers: How to Watch a Hummingbird" by Diane Ackerman
"Disposable Rocket" by John Updike
"Black Widow" by Gordon Grice
"Learning to Read and Write" by Frederick Douglass

COMPARISON/CONTRAST

"The Little Mermaid" by Pauline Kael
"City Out of Breath" by Ken Chen
"Mortality" by Bailey White
"Disposable Rocket" by John Updike
"Somebody's Baby" by Barbara
    Kingsolver
"The Tree Beyond Imagining" by Reg
    Saner

CAUSE AND EFFECT

"Drugs" by Gore Vidal
"Letter to His Master" by Fredrick
    Douglass
"Nourishing Awareness in Each
    Moment" by Thich Nhat Hanh
"The Courage of Turtles" by Edward
    Hoagland
"The Writing Life: The Point of the
    Long and Winding Sentence" by
    Pico Iyer
"The Tree Beyond Imagining" by Reg
    Saner

ARGUMENTATION

"The Little Mermaid" by Pauline Kael
"Drugs" by Gore Vidal
"Naps" by Barbara Holland
From "How to Drive Fast" by P.J.
    O'Rourke

"Nourishing Awareness in Each
    Moment" by Thick Nhat Hanh
"About Men" by Gretel Ehrlich
"The Content of Our Character" by
    Shelby Steele
"Letter to His Master" by Frederick
    Douglass
"The Writing Life: The Point of the
    Long and Winding Sentence" by
    Pico Iyer
"Roll Over, Bach, Too!" by Jack Kroll
"Somebody's Baby" by Barbara
    Kingsolver
"The Chemist's War" by Deborah Blum
"Prince: The Fargodome" by Chuck
    Klosterman
"On Boxing" by Joyce Carol Oates

ANALYSIS

"Museum Piece" by David Huddle
"On the Uncertainty of the Future" by
    Yoshida Kenko
"Nourishing Awareness in Each
    Moment" by Thich Nhat Hanh
"Prince: The Fargodome" by Chuck
    Klosterman
From "The Culture of Celebrity" by
    Joseph Epstein
"American Children" by John Updike
"About Men" by Gretel Ehrlich
"Disposable Rocket" by John Updike
"Monster Mash" by Jack Kroll

Sub

HUMOR AND SATIRE

See specific page numbers in the index for exercises on these style techniques. For brief explanations—including common errors such as fragments, comma splices, and run-on sentences—see the glossary.

ALLITERATION: "Naps," "Mute Dancers: How to Watch a Hummingbird," "Prince."

APPOSITIVES: "Modern Times."

CONCLUSIONS: "Joyas Voladoras."

COLONS: "American Children," "City Out of Breath," "Drugs," "The Content of Our Character," "The Writing Life: The Point of the Long and Winding Sentence."

DASHES: "Modern Times," "Museum Piece," "How to Drive Fast," "Black Widow."

DESCRIPTION AND SENSORY WRITING: "A Voice for the Lonely," "Burl's."

DETAILS AND WORD CHOICE: "Joyas Voladoras," "American Children," "The Little Mermaid," "Mortality."

DIALOGUE: "Turbulence."

EXAMPLES: "The Little Mermaid."

INTRODUCTIONS: "Mute Dancers: How to Watch a Hummingbird" (Teaming Up #1), "Roll Over Bach, Too!" "Truth," "The Chemist's War," "Somebody's Baby."

LISTING: "American Children," "Disposable Rocket," "The Content of Our Character."

QUESTIONS: "Nourishing Awareness in Each Moment," "Roll Over Bach, Too."

PERIODIC AND LOOSE SENTENCES:
    PERIODIC—"Mute Dancers: How to Watch a Hummingbird."
    LOOSE—"Meat," "Letter to His Master," "How to Drive Fast," "Advice to Youth," "A Voice for the Lonely."

SEMICOLONS: "City Out of Breath," "Hair."

TITLES: "Monster Mash."

TRANSITIONS: "About Men."

WORD PLAY (SIMILE, METAPHOR, PERSONIFICATION, HYPHENATED WORDS): "The Courage of Turtles," "Joyas Voladoras" (Teaming Up #2), "Musical Awakenings," "The Culture of Celebrity," "A Tree Beyond Imagining," "Truth," "Reading the River."

Refer to specific readings under "Writing Ideas" for writing assignments using one or more of these rhetorical modes.

ANALYZING AND EXPLAINING: "A Voice for the Lonely," "Modern Times," "Burl's," "The Courage of Turtles," "Museum Piece," "Mute Dancers: How to Watch a Hummingbird," "Roll Over Bach, Too," "Monster Mash," "Musical Awakenings," "Disposable Rocket," "Black Widow," "The Culture of Celebrity," "Fiddling While Africa Starves," "About Men," "How to Drive Fast," "Turbulence," "Somebody's Baby."

ARGUMENTATION: "City Out of Breath," "Black Widow," "The Little Mermaid," "Drugs," "Naps," "The Content of Our Character," "Letter to His Master," "The Chemist's War," "The Writing Life: The Point of the Long and Winding."

CAUSE/EFFECT: "Nourishing Awareness in Each Moment," "Hair," "How to Drive Fast," "Advice to Youth."

COMPARISON/CONTRAST: "On the Uncertainty of the Future," "Museum Piece," "Nourishing Awareness in Each Moment," "Roll Over Bach, Too!" "Prince," "Monster Mash," "City Out of Breath," "Hair," "Joyas Voladoras," "American Children," "Disposable Rocket," "The Little Mermaid," "Naps," "Letter to His Master," "The Tree Beyond Imagining," "Meat," "Drugs,""Reading the River," "Somebody's Baby."

CLASSIFICATION: "Mortality," "Turbulence."

DEFINITION: "The Culture of Celebrity," "About Men," "The Content of Our Character," "Truth."

DESCRIPTION: "Museum Piece," "Toys," "Prince," "Monster Mash," "City Out of Breath," "Hair," "American Children," "Graven Images," "About Men," "How to Drive Fast," "Mortality," "Turbulence," "Burl's."

NARRATION: "A Voice for the Lonely," "Burl's," "The Courage of Turtles," "On the Uncertainty of the Future," "American Children," "On the Content of Our Character," "Turbulence," "Advice to Youth," "Meat."

PROCESS ANALYSIS: "Mute Dancers: How to Watch a Hummingbird," "Graven Images," "Cat Bathing as Martial Art," "Advice to Youth."

RESEARCH: "A Voice for the Lonely," "Modern Times," "Burl's," "The Courage of Turtles," "Toys," "Mute Dancers: How to Watch a Hummingbird," "Hair," "Musical Awakenings," "Graven Images," "Black Widow," "Drugs," "Naps," "Fiddling While Africa Starves," "The Content of Our Character," "Advice to Youth."

Acknowledgments

In memory of Ed Dornan, I'll always be grateful for his help getting me started in writing, teaching, and publishing. This book wouldn't have happened without him.

And I can't forget Steve Rigolosi—a belated thanks for your guidance, quick responses, and hard work on the first edition of *Sparks*.

A special thanks to those extraordinary professors Alice Brekke and Eileen Lothamer—colleagues, friends, mentors—for setting me on my life's path, helping me achieve my goals, and encouraging me throughout this endeavor. You changed my life.

Muchas gracias to Gary and Glynis Hoffman and their book *Adios, Strunk and White* for helping me find my writer's voice and transforming my writing. A gal couldn't have better office mates or friends. Thank you for always being there.

And what would I have done without fellow writer, friend, track buddy, and idea man Gene Garofolo? Thanks for those brainstorming sessions during painful workouts but pleasant coffee sessions.

A nod to Jen and the crew at The Neighborhood Cup in Aliso Viejo for keeping me supplied with tea and homemade scones while I took up space in their coffee shop writing this second edition.

A big thanks to Janice Samuels, Ryan L. Schrodt, and Renae Horstman at Kendall Hunt for the hard work on the second edition. You helped make the process smooth.

Ray Wood and Lara Sanders—you were both such a big help brainstorming ideas and talking me through the third edition changes. Thank you for your patience, Lara, with my queries and follow-up questions, the pleasant phone calls and conferencing. And Amanda Smith, kudos to you for keeping my panic in check. Your cheery replies to my numerous emails kept me sane.

To all of you at Kendall/Hunt, you are the best in the business.

Finally, my thanks to reviewer colleagues for their many insightful suggestions on the first edition. Your advice was invaluable. You'll find many of your suggestions incorporated into this second edition:

Teresa Gibbons, Grand Valley State University, Michigan
Beth Hash, Bluefield State College, West Virginia
Greg Kemble, Yuba College, California
Rick Ladonsi, Grand Valley State University, Michigan
Richard Levesque, Fullerton College, California
Dr. Gary Sligh, Lake-Sumter Community College, Florida
Dr. Melanie Wagner, Lake-Sumter Community College, Florida

WHY THIS BOOK?

Today's students are, in general, technology savvy and media-saturated. They deserve a reader that speaks their language, sparks their interest, challenges their assumptions, incites their passions. Online research in academic databases, photographs for writing prompts, film connections, and a smorgasbord of essays should all be a part of a 21st-century reader if teachers want to help motivate developmental writing students—in an increasingly visual culture—to want to read and write.

I've kept the diverse classroom—the different backgrounds and age groups—in mind, and while I can't promise students will like every essay, I think they'll find something that will interest and challenge them, perhaps shock them. Donald Murray in "What Is a Practical Education?" wrote that a good college "must be an uncomfortable place, a threatening place, a challenging place." He believes students should be offered ideas and theories that shake them up, make them think, maybe even frighten them; the more students are shocked and challenged in college, according to Murray, the more prepared they'll be for life. I chose the essays with Murray's philosophy in mind, arranging essays from easiest to most complex within each section, offering students readings they can feel comfortable with and ones that will test their abilities.

In addition to essays and the exercises that go with them, the book offers sections on surviving college, writing strategies for different essay styles, and basic tools for researching and documenting sources. The "User's Guide" gives tips on negotiating the text as well as alternative tables of contents; in the "Survival Kit" section, students will discover tips for succeeding in college, advice for becoming better readers, diplomacy for working in groups, and ways to respond to their classmates' work.

Essay topics range from music and film to celebrities and automobiles, hummingbirds and turtles to war and technology. Section One, "Remembering: Personal Voices" includes a diversity of writers writing in the personal voice, sharing stories about their lives and experiences: topics include war and technology, nature, sexual identity, and culture; in "Contemplations: Essays that Explain and Explore," the writers attempt to make sense of the world by explaining and analyzing art, music, film, sports, the media, history, and social issues; "Essays That Argue and Define" contains opinion essays on technology, social issues, and racism.

Not everyone reacts to humor in the same way—what's funny to one person may leave another wondering what the laughter is all about—but the "Essays that Argue and Define" section attempts to provide a diversity of humorous styles from P. J. O'Rouke's outrageous satire on teens drinking and driving to the more subtle humor of Bailey White's "Mortality," the satire of Mark Twain to the modern humor of David Sedaris.

After the essay sections, there are strategies for writing essays and an introduction to research and documentation using the Modern Language Association (MLA) style.

I've tried to keep the book as jargon-free as possible, using terminology only when necessary. Instead of confusing students with the different names for clauses and phrases, I've labeled most of them dependent or independent word groups. When I do mention a term, it will be in **bold; students can turn to the glossary for an explanation.**

The styling exercises that accompany the essays are designed to make students think about how good writers accomplish good writing. Some students think good writers are born that way, but writing—as teachers know—like any skill, can be learned with diligence, patience, and desire. Focusing on style—especially sentence structures—not only spices writing, but teaches correctness: modeling advanced sentences reinforces punctuation and grammar.

The assignments and style techniques are tried and true. I thank my students for sometimes double-acting as guinea pigs. While some of the techniques may seem advanced or difficult (some may seem too simple, depending on your students' level), I assure you that with some practice my students mastered at least some—if not all—of them.

From the more advanced student to the struggling writer, the book attempts to interest and challenge students, make them better thinkers and writers, and help them find their voices.

HOW TO USE THIS BOOK

Because most essays are hybrids, blending various modes and themes, I've not organized the book in the strictly traditional rhetorical or thematical arrangement, though I've added alternative tables of contents to help you find your way around the book if you're more comfortable with those systems. A narrative can present an argument and almost always contains description; an exemplification essay might also define; a classification essay may explain and so forth, so I've divided the book into four sections: In "Remembering Personal Voices," you'll find a diversity of voices telling their stories, relating their experiences, making their points through memories. "Contemplations: Essays that Explain and Explore" contains essays that attempt to make sense of the world, of history, nature, art, and the human mind. "Essays that Argue and Define," while containing some traditional arguments, also presents viewpoints in a variety of forms, and the "Essays that Argue and Define" section offers narration, satirical arguments, process analysis, and other styles. Within each section, I've attempted to arrange the essays, questions, and assignments from simpler to more complex, an arrangement I owe to my students; they've illustrated to me through their writing, questions, and class discussion which assignments and readings present more challenges.

Because I cover style as it relates to the essays, you might find a technique covered in different spots in the book, which might seem repetitive, but techniques need practice for mastery, and it's possible to read many of the essays and not run across a particular technique even though it's offered several times in the book. The **periodic** and **loose** sentences might accompany several essays because the sentences themselves take on many forms. Colons and semicolons can be used in a variety of ways. I've focused on these styles because students often come to college without some of the tools that spark writing—or haven't practiced them since early high school. Modeling good writers improves writing.

If you're working from a rhetorical mode perspective, the assignment arrangement, too, may be unfamiliar because you might find narrative assignments, for example, in every section. The Assignment Guide at the beginning of the book will tell you where to find writing ideas compatible with narration, description, argumentation, cause/effect, and so forth.

Two other features of this book attempt to help you understand the essays. The "Dustbin of History and Culture" (meant ironically) preceding each essay explains references to history, culture, literature, or other areas that might be unfamiliar (the "dustbin of history" is a phrase Greil Marcus borrowed from Leon Trotsky for his book of the same title; Greil argues that history *does not* belong only to the past, relegated to the dustbin). Though some of the references may seem obvious to you, they may not to others, and the allusions are there because my students have asked me, "What's that mean?" While a feather quill might seem obvious to most, I've had several students ask me about it, students unfamiliar with cultures or historical periods where feather quills might be common, and some students might be embarrassed to ask about a reference that the rest of the class takes for granted. At other times, I list cultural references that might be familiar but detail and context of time and place might be elusive.

The second feature, the "Exploring Language" section, defines words and gives ideas for usage. Practice using the words, as they'll do you little good otherwise. The more words your students add to your vocabulary arsenal, the more complex their reading, thinking, and writing skills become.

I've tried to make it easy for students and instructors to navigate the book, but let me know if there's something I didn't think of that might make it easier for you. I welcome your comments.

NAVIGATING THE COLLEGE QUAGMIRE

Many students have a tough time adjusting to college. Others glide. Even the best students fumble at times, so consider these tips to help navigate the system.

TIPS FOR SUCCESS

First, find out what resources your college has to help. Is there a tutoring center? A writing lab? Learning disabled center? Financial aid? Make use of these resources. Students might not know that schools often offer free health care on campus. If reading skills need polish, find out if the college offers reading courses. See if there's a spelling course or computer lab with a spelling tutor. The same goes for weaknesses in grammar, math, or any area. Seek and ye shall find.

Consider the workload. Talk to a counselor about your schedule and whether it's too much. Working full time and taking five or six classes, may be overdoing it, if you're struggling in classes, it may be time to reconsider.

Get organized. Some schools have classes in surviving college, often offered through counseling. Be sure to have a good notebook with a section for each class, and take notes. Unless you have a photographic mind, you can't possibly remember everything important the teacher says. Write it down, especially if it's on the board, PowerPoint, document cam, or other electronic source. If a teacher repeats an idea, write it down. If you must be absent, get someone in class to take notes for you. Offer to return the favor. While this may seem obvious, I often see students neglect note taking and then wonder why their grades suffer.

Homework can be overwhelming. Set aside time each day to study. Budget your time: study, work, play. We all need time away from work to do the things we enjoy. The word *recreation* means to re-create, so budget time to recreate yourself. The general rule for studying is to budget two hours of study time for each hour spent in class, so a three-hour class requires six hours a week of studying.

Don't be afraid to ask questions. Raise your hand. If the teacher has an office and office hours, make use of them. Be sure you understand the homework assignments. If not, get clarification. If you miss class, find out what you missed. Assume you missed something.

Read the syllabus and know the teacher's rules. Know how many absences each teacher allows, and keep track. Don't assume a teacher will take late homework because of illness. If you must miss class, get your homework to school somehow, by friend, relative, courier.

Turn off all electronics unless instructed otherwise. Buy the books or find out if the library has them or if the teacher has placed them on reserve. Don't sit in silence, not understanding lectures and failing tests because you don't have the books. Find out what help is available. You might be eligible for financial aid.

Many students don't realize the abundance of resources available on campus, often for free. Surviving college means balancing your time, staying organized, and seeking help when you need it. Ask. Your college wants to help.

READING TIPS

In a visual culture where most of our stories come in the form of movies or television and our news from the Internet and television, where films make it easy for us to avoid reading difficult classic literature like Shakespeare and Homer why, then, should we bother to read, other than learning basic communications skills so we can surf the net, play online games, catch up with friend on social networks, and fill out job applications?

Reading does more than provide information. It hones intelligence, forces interaction with the text, teaches vocabulary through context, sharpens critical thinking skills, improves verbal and written communication, and illustrates punctuation and difficult sentence structure. You think in language. The more you read, the more language you learn, and the more sophisticated your thinking and analysis become. What you get from reading versus viewing is incalculable.

To be a successful college student, read actively. When you sit down to read, do so with a highlighter, notepad, and dictionary, paper or electronic. Looking up words in a dictionary can be tedious—but to learn, to improve reading, to be able to think more complexly, then a dictionary is a must. Don't stop to look up every unfamiliar word; mark the words and reach for the dictionary later. Don't just find the words and jot down their meanings; figure out the context and match the proper definitions. Practice using the words in daily conversations and writings. If you look up the meaning but never use the word, you probably won't remember it.

Highlight passages meaningful or unclear and passages the teacher points out. Try to figure out the writer's main idea and key supporting points. Write questions about difficult passages in the margin as they occur to you.

Here are some points to consider when **annotating** (see the glossary) the text:

1. Ask a question about a difficult concept, and then attempt to answer it.
2. Compliment the writer on style: strong word choices, description, specific detail, **metaphor and simile**, **personification**, use of punctuation, sentence structure (for example, **loose** and **periodic** sentences), a hook in the introduction, a snazzy title or complain about any of these techniques.
3. Point out the main idea or thesis of the essay and the supporting evidence.
4. Comment on the strength of the argument or point. Agree or disagree.
5. Look for smooth transitions between paragraphs or ideas within paragraphs.
6. Pinpoint the tone or mood of the essay: academic/analytical, casual, melancholy, contemplative, humorous, cynical, joyful, poignant, and so on.
7. Mention the essay's organization. Is it chronological (order of events), point-by-point (one point in each paragraph), or some other method?

Sometimes you read a passage only to find you have no idea what you just read. It's normal for the mind to drift, but make every effort to get back on task. Read the passage again, highlighter and pencil ready. If you're highlighting and making notes, looking up words and thinking about definitions, you'll be an active reader, more likely to absorb material.

Textbooks usually suggest reading an assignment or essay at least three times: once through quickly to survey, a second time to question the content, and a third time to review. Although that's the best approach, crowded schedules don't always permit this type of diligence, but you should at least highlight, question, and look up words. Try to read a difficult piece at least twice. Don't give up in frustration if the reading is particularly hard. It's tough at times—I sloughed through some pretty leathery Anglo-Saxon literature as a graduate student—but sticking it out is the only way.

If you're not convinced as to the benefits of reading, think about what it would be like to be denied the privilege. Frederick Douglass, an American slave, tells his story in the following essay, "Learning to Read and Write," from his famous work, *Narrative of the Life of Frederick Douglass.*

LEARNING TO READ AND WRITE

Frederick Douglass—an American slave—escaped from cap-
tivity to Massachusetts, becoming a famous writer and lec-
turer, speaking out against the evils of slavery, and advising
Abraham Lincoln. In this essay, he recounts how he learned
to read and write despite laws forbidding slaves an education.

1   I lived in Master Hugh's family about seven years. During this time, I succeeded in learning to read and write. In accomplishing this, I was compelled to resort to various stratagems. I had no regular teacher. My mistress, who had kindly commenced to instruct me, had, in compliance with the advice and direction of her husband, not only ceased to instruct, but had set her face against my being instructed by any one else. It is due, however, to my mistress to say of her, that she did not adopt this course of treatment immediately. She at first lacked the depravity indispensable to shutting me up in mental darkness. It was at least necessary for her to have some training in the exercise of irresponsible power, to make her equal to the task of treating me as though I were a brute.

2   My mistress was, as I have said, a kind and tender-hearted woman; and in the simplicity of her soul she commenced, when I first went to live with her, to treat me as she supposed one human being ought to treat another. In entering upon the duties of a slave-holder, she did not seem to perceive that I sustained to her the relation of a mere chattel, and that for her to treat me as a human being was not only wrong, but dangerously so. Slavery proved as injurious to her as it did to me. When I went there, she was a pious, warm, and tender-hearted woman. There was no sorrow or suffering for which she had not a tear. She had bread for the hungry, clothes for the naked, and comfort for every mourner that came within her reach. Slavery soon proved its ability to divest her of these heavenly qualities. Under its influence, the tender heart became stone, and the lamblike disposition gave way to one of tiger-like fierceness. The first step in her downward course was in her ceasing to instruct me. She now commenced to practise her husband's precepts. She finally became even more violent in her opposition than her husband himself. She was not satisfied with simply doing as well as he had commanded; she seemed anxious to do better. Nothing seemed to make her more angry

than to see me with a newspaper. She seemed to think that here lay the danger. I have had her rush at me with a face made all up of fury, and snatch from me a newspaper, in a manner that fully revealed her apprehension. She was an apt woman; and a little experience soon demonstrated, to her satisfaction, that education and slavery were incompatible with each other.

3   From this time I was most narrowly watched. If I was in a separate room any considerable length of time, I was sure to be suspected of having a book, and was at once called to give an account of myself. All this, however, was too late. The first step had been taken. Mistress, in teaching me the alphabet, had given me the *inch,* and no precaution could prevent me from taking the *ell.*

4   The plan which I adopted, and the one by which I was most successful, was that of making friends of all the little white boys whom I met in the street. As many of these as I could, I converted into teachers. With their kindly aid, obtained at different times and in different places, I finally succeeded in learning to read. When I was sent on errands, I always took my book with me, and by going one part of my errand quickly, I found time to get a lesson before my return. I used also to carry bread with me, enough of which was always in the house, and to which I was always welcome; for I was much better off in this regard than many of the poor white children in our neighborhood. This bread I used to bestow upon the hungry little urchins, who, in return, would give me that more valuable bread of knowledge. I am strongly tempted to give the names of two or three of those little boys, as a testimonial of the gratitude and affection I bear them; but prudence forbids;—not that it would injure me, but it might embarrass them; for it is almost an unpardonable offence to teach slaves to read in this Christian country. It is enough to say of the dear little fellows, that they lived on Philpot Street, very near Durgin and Bailey's shipyard. I used to talk this matter of slavery over with them. I would sometimes say to them, I wished I could be as free as they would be when they got to be men. "You will be free as soon as you are twenty-one, *but I am a slave for life!* Have not I as good a right to be free as you have?" These words used to trouble them; they would express for me the liveliest sympathy, and console me with the hope that something would occur by which I might be free.

5   I was now about twelve years old, and the thought of being *a slave for life* began to bear heavily upon my heart. Just about this time, I got hold of a book entitled "The Columbian Orator." Every opportunity I got, I used to read this book. Among much of other interesting

matter, I found in it a dialogue between a master and his slave. The slave was represented as having run away from his master three times. The dialogue represented the conversation which took place between them, when the slave was retaken the third time. In this dialogue, the whole argument in behalf of slavery was brought forward by the master, all of which was disposed of by the slave. The slave was made to say some very smart as well as impressive things in reply to his master—things which had the desired though unexpected effect; for the conversation resulted in the voluntary emancipation of the slave on the part of the master.

6   In the same book, I met with one of Sheridan's mighty speeches on and in behalf of Catholic emancipation. These were choice documents to me. I read them over and over again with unabated interest. They gave tongue to interesting thoughts of my own soul, which had frequently flashed through my mind, and died away for want of utterance. The moral which I gained from the dialogue was the power of truth over the conscience of even a slaveholder. What I got from Sheridan was a bold denunciation of slavery, and a powerful vindication of human rights. The reading of these documents enabled me to utter my thoughts, and to meet the arguments brought forward to sustain slavery; but while they relieved me of one difficulty, they brought on another even more painful than the one of which I was relieved. The more I read, the more I was led to abhor and detest my enslavers. I could regard them in no other light than a band of successful robbers, who had left their homes, and gone to Africa, and stolen us from our homes, and in a strange land reduced us to slavery. I loathed them as being the meanest as well as the most wicked of men. As I read and contemplated the subject, behold! that very discontentment which Master Hugh had predicted would follow my learning to read had already come, to torment and sting my soul to unutterable anguish. As I writhed under it, I would at times feel that learning to read had been a curse rather than a blessing. It had given me a view of my wretched condition, without the remedy. It opened my eyes to the horrible pit, but to no ladder upon which to get out. In moments of agony, I envied my fellow-slaves for their stupidity. I have often wished myself a beast. I preferred the condition of the meanest reptile to my own. Any thing, no matter what, to get rid of thinking! It was this everlasting thinking of my condition that tormented me. There was no getting rid of it. It was pressed upon me by every object within sight or hearing, animate or inanimate. The silver trump of freedom had roused my soul to eternal wakefulness. Freedom

now appeared, to disappear no more forever. It was heard in every sound, and seen in every thing. It was ever present to torment me with a sense of my wretched condition. I saw nothing without seeing it, I heard nothing without hearing it, and felt nothing without feeling it. It looked from every star, it smiled in every calm, breathed in every wind, and moved in every storm.

7   I often found myself regretting my own existence, and wishing myself dead; and but for the hope of being free, I have no doubt but that I should have killed myself, or done something for which I should have been killed. While in this state of mind, I was eager to hear any one speak of slavery. I was a ready listener. Every little while, I could hear something about the abolitionists. It was some time before I found what the word meant. It was always used in such connections as to make it an interesting word to me. If a slave ran away and succeeded in getting clear, or if a slave killed his master, set fire to a barn, or did any thing very wrong in the mind of a slaveholder, it was spoken of as the fruit of *abolition*. Hearing the word in this connection very often, I set about learning what it meant. The dictionary afforded me little or no help. I found it was "the act of abolishing"; but then I did not know what was to be abolished. Here I was perplexed. I did not dare to ask any one about its meaning, for I was satisfied that it was something they wanted me to know very little about. After a patient waiting, I got one of our city papers, containing an account of the number of petitions from the north, praying for the abolition of slavery in the District of Columbia, and of the slave trade between the States. From this time I understood the words *abolition* and *abolitionist*, and always drew near when that word was spoken, expecting to hear something of importance to myself and fellow-slaves. The light broke in upon me by degrees. I went one day down on the wharf of Mr. Waters; and seeing two Irishmen unloading a scow of stone, I went, unasked, and helped them. When we had finished, one of them came to me and asked me if I were a slave. I told him I was. He asked, "Are ye a slave for life?" I told him that I was. The good Irishman seemed to be deeply affected by the statement. He said to the other that it was a pity so fine a little fellow as myself should be a slave for life. He said it was a shame to hold me. They both advised me to run away to the north; that I should find friends there, and that I should be free. I pretended not to be interested in what they said, and treated them as if I did not understand them; for I feared they might be treacherous. White men have been known to encourage slaves to escape, and then, to get the reward, catch them and return them to their mas-

ters. I was afraid that these seemingly good men might use me so; but I nevertheless remembered their advice, and from that time I resolved to run away. I looked forward to a time at which it would be safe for me to escape. I was too young to think of doing so immediately; besides, I wished to learn how to write, as I might have occasion to write my own pass. I consoled myself with the hope that I should one day find a good chance. Meanwhile, I would learn to write.

8   The idea as to how I might learn to write was suggested to me by being in Durgin and Bailey's ship-yard, and frequently seeing the ship carpenters, after hewing, and getting a piece of timber ready for use, write on the timber the name of that part of the ship for which it was intended. When a piece of timber was intended for the larboard side, it would be marked thus—"L." When a piece was for the starboard side, it would be marked thus—"S." A piece for the larboard side forward, would be marked thus—"L.F." When a piece was for starboard side forward, it would be marked thus—"S.F." For larboard aft, it would be marked thus—"L.A." For starboard aft, it would be marked thus— "S. A." I soon learned the names of these letters, and for what they were intended when placed upon a piece of timber in the ship-yard. I immediately commenced copying them, and in a short time was able to make the four letters named. After that, when I met with any boy who I knew could write, I would tell him I could write as well as he. The next word would be, "I don't believe you. Let me see you try it." I would then make the letters which I had been so fortunate as to learn, and ask him to beat that. In this way I got a good many lessons in writing, which it is quite possible I should never have gotten in any other way. During this time, my copy-book was the board fence, brick wall, and pavement; my pen and ink was a lump of chalk. With these, I learned mainly how to write. I then commenced and continued copying the Italics in Webster's Spelling Book, until I could make them all without looking on the book. By this time, my little Master Thomas had gone to school, and learned how to write, and had written over a number of copy-books. These had been brought home, and shown to some of our near neighbors, and then laid aside. My mistress used to go to class meeting at the Wilk Street meeting-house every Monday afternoon, and leave me to take care of the house. When left thus, I used to spend the time in writing in the spaces left in Master Thomas's copy-book, copying what he had written. I continued to do this until I could write a hand very similar to that of Master Thomas. Thus, after a long, tedious effort for years, I finally succeeded in learning how to write.

ADVICE FOR WORKING IN GROUPS

Your instructor has just asked you to break into groups to work together on a project—perhaps one of the Teaming Up exercises in this book—or for peer evaluations or discussion. You may dislike this idea, feeling that you always get stuck with the bulk of the work, or perhaps you just prefer to work alone; or you might relish the idea, enjoying the group interaction and break from routine (regardless of your viewpoint, many instructors and businesses consider group work essential practice for the work place). Whether you love or loathe it, you may be asked to participate, so here are a few guidelines to help your group get along, split up the work fairly, stay focused on the task, and get the most out of the session.

1. Introduce yourselves and perhaps exchange phone numbers in case you have questions later.
2. Draw up some rules of civility. How will you handle discussion to ensure that each member gets a chance to speak? What will you do about an unruly or rude student? What will you do if a member of the group doesn't show up with a crucial part of the project? What happens if a team member slacks off, bringing shoddy work or none at all?
3. Consider assigning each member a daily task: discussion director, note taker, reader (someone to read passages or directions to the group), typist, spokesperson. You can alternate the jobs each time you split into groups or keep the same tasks.
4. Split up the work fairly. If the project involves research, be sure that each person is responsible for a portion. If you're writing a group essay, assign each person a paragraph to work on at home.
5. Stay focused. If you notice your group deteriorating into discussion of the latest football score or concert attended, try to steer the members back to work. It's natural to get sidetracked, but if it happens too frequently, you're in danger of not completing the work, irritating the teacher, and embarrassing yourselves in front of the rest of the class.
6. Keep noise to a minimum.
7. If you give it a good try and feel you just can't work with your group, it's okay to ask the teacher if you can switch teams, but do it diplomatically. Tell your group that you plan to ask for a transfer, citing philosophical differences. Or say something polite like "I've really enjoyed working with you but would like to try another group, get to know some new people." Don't leave the group with ill feelings.

In general, be courteous to your group and the rest of the class. Follow that golden rule to treat others as you would like to be treated.

PEER EVALUATIONS: RESPONDING TO YOUR CLASSMATES' WORK

Reading and responding honestly to your peer's writing can be difficult. Afraid to offend, you offer only positive remarks, ignoring the flaws, sending the poor soul home with the mistaken impression he or she has written a masterpiece. Or perhaps you're the critical type, finding fault with everything, not offering a kind word, demoralizing your classmate into giving up. Neither response is ideal, but perhaps a balance between the two will help the student discover the positive aspects of his or her work as well as what might need revision. Following are some questions that might help you evaluate another's work kindly but constructively. You'll need a separate sheet of paper, a pen, and a highlighter.

Note: Do not edit another student's work by correcting grammar, punctuation, and spelling. That's the student's job. It's all right to point out that an essay contains several **comma splices** or other errors, but leave the detective work to your peer.

1. Start out positive. What do you like best about the paper? Be specific. Instead of "I really like how you describe things," write "The line in your essay *A thick layer of snow covers the road, and the leafless trees impose a sinister feel; our steps on the crunchy snow break the silence* is so vivid I feel like I'm there. Well done!"

2. Does the essay have a title that grabs your interest? If not, make suggestions or refer the student to the index of this book to look up strategies for creating snappy titles.

3. Does the introduction hook the reader? If not, again refer the student to the index to look up strategies for writing introductions.

4. Does the essay have a thesis or make a point? What is the point? If you are not sure, ask the writer. Does the thesis address the prompt?

5. Does the writer use vivid detail so that you see, hear, smell, feel, taste the experience? If not, tell the writer where you think more detail or description is needed.

6. Is the writing specific, using strong verbs and nouns? ("Joe ambled along the rocky shore" is stronger than "The boy walked along the beach.") Point out sentences that could be more specific.

7. Does the writer provide enough examples to support his or her point? Are the examples appropriate, or would others be stronger?

8. Is the paper well organized? Does the writer make clear paragraph breaks with **transitions** (see the glossary)? Is each paragraph organized around a central idea, or do details wander away from the topic? Does each paragraph support the main idea of the essay?

9. Are there any mechanical errors that detract from the paper, like frequent misspellings, punctuation problems, fragments, run-on sentences, shifts in tense or person, or other errors?

10. How is the writing style? Are the sentence patterns varied (short, medium, long sentences)? Can some sentences be combined? Does the writer use **figurative language** (see the glossary)? Does the writer rely on too many "to be" verbs (is, are, was, were, be, being, been, am)? Use your highlighter to highlight each "to be" verb. More than three or four per page signals weak verb use. Is the writing clear? Are there spots where you're not sure of the meaning?

Remembering: Personal Voices

INTRODUCTION

Sharing personal experiences motivates some of the finest writing; many writers use the first person point of view to explain, to argue, to reflect, to analyze. The narrative voice, once considered the lightweight of academia, has gained acceptance as a legitimate form of expression for argument, research, and other essay strategies. Whether writing about nature, science, medicine, history, psychology, education, or any topic, writers know that engaging the reader with personal experience, description, figurative language, and other style techniques engage readers and make otherwise dry material digestible.

Most of the essays in this book rely in part on the personal voice, even if it isn't the primary mode of expression, whether an introduction, an anecdote, or a conclusion: Shelby Steele's personal experiences growing up black and middle class in "On the Content of Our Character" strengthen his argument and help define the dilemma; Gretel Ehrlich's stories of growing up around cowboys in Wyoming help bust a stereotype; and so on.

The essays in this section lean on narration more than others, though their arguments and analysis are just as strong and convincing: Bernard Cooper's beautifully written struggle with sexual identity; Edward Hoagland's fable-like stories of turtles and their plight; Brian Doyle's tribute to a fallen friend in the 9/11 attacks and its subtext; "We all churn inside" as Doyle writes before the conclusion of "Joyas Voladoras."

A VOICE FOR THE LONELY

Stephen Corey

Stephen Corey is an editor and author of poetry and essays. In this piece, he reminisces about the death of singer Roy Orbison of "Pretty Woman" fame, speculating on friendship, the impact of music, and "forces of circumstance and the fate of inches."

DUSTBIN OF HISTORY AND CULTURE

TRANSISTOR RADIO: a small, often pocket-sized, portable radio receiver developed in 1954, becoming popular in the 1960's and 1970's, especially with teenagers, not unlike today's IPods and other devices with portable music.

1   The right silence can be a savior, especially in these days of motor-cycles, leaf blowers, and malls that thrum with a thousand voices and dozens of sundry machines. Five or six days a week, I get up pretty early—generally around 4 A.M.—and one of the things I like most about those last hours of darkness is their stillness. The house is quiet, the streets are quiet, and (except on weekends, when some of the serious drunks are hanging on) the all-night restaurants are quiet. Reading and writing and thinking come more easily when you know you won't be interrupted, and over the past 20 years I've never found a better mental bodyguard than the hours before dawn.

2   I got my first serious training as an early riser when I acquired a newspaper delivery route in seventh grade: three miles of widely scattered houses on the edge of Jamestown, New York, and beyond—just me, the moon, darkness, and the various faces of silence. I recall stopping my brisk walk sometimes, especially in winter when every step squeaked and crunched on the snow that nearly always covered the ground, and marveling at how there were no sounds except those of my own making. But just as often, that quiet made me nervous, even though my hometown was awfully safe in those days. I learned to offset the urge to look over my shoulder by carrying a pocket-sized transistor radio.

3   The music helped me to cope with more than just the empty morning streets—I was, as I said, in seventh (and then eighth, and finally ninth) grade during those lone marches. In short, I was just

learning something of what much of that music was about: love—lost, found, hoped for, and despaired of.

4   Most habits die hard, and old ones can seem immortal. Last week, I was up as usual at 4 A.M., and I headed out in the car toward the nearest newspaper box. As always during these quick runs, I flipped on the radio for some wake-up rhythms to jolt my system for the solitary work time soon to come back at the house.

5   Instead of music, I caught the voice of the all-night deejay just as she was saying, "We have tragic news in over the wire: singer Roy Orbison is dead . . ." She gave a quick flurry of details (heart attack, Hendersonville, North Carolina, hospital), repeated the central fact— "Roy Orbison, dead at 52"—and then (my heart applauds her still for this) said not a word but cut straight into "Only the Lonely."

6   There I was, cruising down the abandoned city street with the radio now up as loud as I could stand it, mouthing the rising and falling words, rocking side to side as I held the wheel, and riding Orbison's wailing, nearly-cracking voice back 24 years to the passenger seat of Jon Cresanti's Volkswagen beetle.

7   We're told these days that the hottest and fastest wire into memory is our sense of smell, but music must run a close second. Some songs carry us into a certain mood, some to a general region of our past lives, and some to a very particular moment and situation in time. Jon and I were brought together by chance and loneliness for a couple of months during our sophomore year in high school. The alphabetical seating in our homeroom put us next to each other in the back row, and Jon was a talker. We hadn't known each other before: we came from different parts of town, had different friends, and moved through different sequences of classes. But for a while we found a bond: my girlfriend had recently dropped me after more than a year of going steady, and Jon had eyes for a girl who had none for him.

8   I had time—all the time I was no longer spending with my girl. John had a car and was old enough to drive it, having failed a grade and thereby become a crucial year older than the typical sophomore. I signed on board, and we cruised day after day, weekend after weekend, killing time and eating at the wondrous new "fast food restaurant" that had just opened. We sat in his car eating 15-cent hamburgers and 12-cent french fries near the real golden arches, the kind that curved up and over the entire little structure (no inside seating, no bathrooms)—and, naturally, listening to the radio. The Four Seasons were with us, as were The Beach Boys, Nat King Cole, The Supremes.

9   But in those two desperate months of shotgunning for Jon, there was only one song that really mattered, one song we waited for, hoped for, and even called the radio station and asked for: Roy Orbison's "Pretty Woman."

10   That opening handful of heavy guitar notes (a lovesick teenager's equivalent of Beethoven's Fifth) carried us into a world of possibility, a world where a moment's fancy could generate love, where losers could be winners just by wishing for success. The pretty woman walks on by, and another failure has occurred—but suddenly, the downward sweep of the wheel is reversed as the woman turns to walk back; and there is nothing in the world but fulfillment of one's dreams.

11   Pop songs are full of such stuff, of course, and have been for as long as the phonograph record and the radio have been with us; we get all kinds of talk about the importance of television in modern life, but I think we need more examination of the ways we have been encompassed by music. I'm not talking about ranting "discussions" of the immorality of certain strains of pop music, but some real studies of the much wider and deeper implications of growing up in a world awash with radio waves.

12   Needless to say, I wasn't concerned about such matters there in the McDonald's parking lot. I wouldn't even have thought about what it was in Orbison's singing that made him so important to me. I took the words of the song's story for their relevance to my own emotional state, and I floated with those words inside a musical accompaniment that both soothed and roused my fifteen-year-old body.

13   When I heard of Orbison's death, I found myself wanting to figure out just what it was in that strange voice that might have been so compelling for me and others across the years. I think it might be in the way the voice itself often seems about to fail: in Orbison's strange and constant modulations, from gravelly bass-like sounds to strong tenor-like passages to piercing falsetto cries, there is the feeling for the listener that the singer is always about to lose control, about to break down under the weight of what he is trying to sing. Never mind that this is not true, that Orbison's style was one carefully achieved; what we are talking about here is emotional effect, the true stuff of pop and country music.

14   If Roy could make it, we could make it. And if Roy could stand failing, so could we.

15   This feeling of camaraderie with the faraway record star increased for me, I think, the first time I saw him. He was so ordinary-looking—no, he was so *homely*, so very contrary to what one expects romantic musical heroes to look like. He was *us*.

16   The right singer, the right sadness, the right silence. The way I heard the story of the death of Orbison's wife in 1966 (and the way I'll keep believing it) was that the two of them were out motorcycling when an errant car or truck hit them from an angle. She was riding just a few feet to the side of and behind him, so the other vehicle clipped the back of his cycle but caught hers full force. I've never gotten over this chilling illustration of the forces of circumstance and the fate of inches, so much so that over the years I have regularly found the story called to mind for retelling in classrooms or at parties.

17   I graduated from high school the year of the accident, and Orbison disappeared from the national music scene. (It wasn't until recently that I heard how the death of two sons by fire in 1967 compounded Orbison's private tragedies.) Oddly, there is a way in which the disappearance or the death of a singer these days doesn't really matter to his or her listeners, since that person is still present in exactly the same way as before. All the songs take on a slightly new cast, but the singer still lives in a way that one's own deceased relatives and friends cannot.

18   When my girl wanted me back, I dropped Jon's friendship and never tried to regain it—a not-very-commendable way to be. But we were glued for a while by those banging Orbison notes and those erratic vocals, and maybe that was enough, or at least all that one could hope for.

19   . Music can block out silence, on dark scary roads and in moments of loneliness. But there's also a sense or two in which a song can create silence: when we're "lost in a song" the rest of the world around us makes, for all practical purposes, no sound. And in an even more strange way, a song we love goes silent as we "listen" to it, leaving us in that rather primitive place where all the sounds are interior ones—sounds which can't be distinguished from feelings, from pulsings and shiverings, from that gut need to make life stronger than death for at least a few moments.

20   When "Only the Lonely" faded, that wonderful deejay still knew enough not to say a word. She threw us straight forward, 4:15 A.M., into "Pretty Woman."

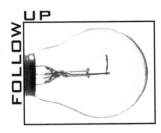

A VOICE FOR THE LONELY

Exploring Language

camaraderie: a feeling of getting along, friendship, or kinship.
erratic: irregular or unpredictable.
falsetto: a high-pitched voice, usually referring to a male.
modulations: changes in tone or pitch.
sundry: various or miscellaneous.
tenor: in this context , a music term referring to an adult male voice
    whose pitch falls between the bass (low pitch) and alto (high pitch).
thrum: strum, as in playing a stringed musical instrument.
Note: For pronunciation, go to dictionary.com, search the word, and
click on the speaker icon.

USAGE   Notice how Corey uses *thrum* in his opening paragraph to describe
noises not related to music. Consider other words connected to music
that might be used in unusual ways.

Thinking and Talking Points

1. Corey writes, "We're told these days that the hottest and fastest wire
   into memory is our sense of smell, but music must run a close second." Find examples of how music helps Corey wire into his memory. Think about the other senses like smell, touch, taste, sight and
   discuss whether they have a similar ability to conjure up memory.
   Rate them as to their effectiveness. Why do you think music has been
   proven to be such a powerful memory invoker?
2. Reread paragraph #17. What does Corey mean by "the songs take on
   a slightly new cast"?
3. Reread paragraph #19. How does a song create silence for Corey? Explain
   how music leaves the listener in a "primitive" place of "pulsings and shiverings." What other entertainment might create this type of silence?
4. What is the purpose of Corey's essay? Is it just a tribute to Roy
   Orbison, or does he have another purpose?
5. Corey writes, "I've never gotten over this chilling illustration of the
   forces of circumstance and the fate of inches." Look up fate and destiny. Though used as synonyms, there are some subtle differences

between these two words. What do you discover when comparing the definitions? In your own words, describe the differences. What is your definition of fate and destiny?

Styling

A **loose sentence** begins with a main (complete) sentence followed with a series of add-ons—using commas to separate them—all describing or providing more information about the same subject in the main sentence, similar to items or actions in a series but more detailed.

In "A Voice for the Lonely," Stephen Corey uses this style to write about music transporting him back in time:

> There I was, *cruising* down the abandoned city street with the radio now up as loud as I could stand it, *mouthing* the rising and falling words, *rocking* side to side as I held the wheel, and *riding* Orbison's waiting, nearly-cracking voice back 24 years to the passenger seat of Jon Cresanti's Volkswagen Beetle.

The sentence breaks down into a main plus three add-ons:

> (Main) There I was, cruising down the abandoned city street with the radio now up as loud as I could stand it,
> (Add-on) mouthing the rising and falling words,
> (Add-on) rocking side to side as I held the wheel,
> (Add-on) and riding Orbison's waiting, nearly-cracking voice back 24 years to the passenger seat of Jon Cresanti's Volkswagen Beetle.

Notice that the add-ons cannot stand alone as complete sentences. They depend on the main sentence to make them complete. All three describe Corey's action, staying on the same subject. Each add-on begins with an "ing" action word.

PRACTICE   Add-on three dependent word groups beginning with "ing" to the main sentence below. Try to be detailed and specific so that your sentence doesn't look like a simple list. Strive for the same length as Corey's sentence. Use a comma after each "ing" group.

Maria sat under the oak tree,

YOU TRY IT   Write five sentences of your own based on the above model, making sure that each one begins with a complete sentence (the main sentence) followed by three or four "ing" add-ons.

Warning: Edit your sentences for run-on, comma splice, and fragment errors (see the glossary or the rules in the "Basic Punctuation Rules and Practice" section if you are not familiar with these terms).

Teaming Up

1. **Warm-up for Writing Idea #3.** Bring in an article on a favorite singer, alive or dead. Before you come to class, write a summary of the article. In your group, do a **freewrite** on why you like this particular singer or group. Read your freewrites aloud in your group. Who has the most convincing freewrite? You can use your summary and freewrite for Writing Idea #3.

2. **Warm-up for Writing Idea #2.** At home, freewrite on the idea of fate. To what degree do you think fate controls our lives? Why? What's your experience with fate? Read your freewrites in your group, comparing responses, debating the issue.

Writing Ideas

(For more writing ideas on music, see "Prince," "Musical Awakenings," and "Roll Over Bach, Too").

1. Write an essay about a friend who was once very close to you. Explain what made the friendship special and why the friendship broke off. If music played a role in the memories, describe it, modeling Corey when he writes about his memories of John, making use of the sense of sound.

2. Corey writes about the death of Roy Orbison's wife, stating, "I've never gotten over this chilling illustration of the forces of circumstance and the fate of inches." Write an essay about a time when you first realized you were—to some degree—at the mercy of fate. Use at least one of the senses in your essay: sight, sound, smell, touch, taste.

3. Use your school or local library's online periodicals database and find an article on a singer you admire. Use the information to write a tribute, as Corey does, to this singer. Write about the music's impact on you, either emotionally or as a memory link. If the singer has died, write about where you were when you heard the news and your reaction.

Essay Connections

In "Musical Awakenings," Clayton Collins writes about music's ability to heal, and Jack Kroll, in "Roll Over Bach, Too," writes an essay about the Beatles and their tremendous impact on music and culture. "Prince" by Chuck Klosterman expresses the author's admiration of Prince as a genius.

TURBULENCE

David Sedaris

Essayist and funny man David Sedaris has several collections to his credit: Me Talk Pretty One Day, Naked, Holidays on Ice, and Dress Your Family in Corduroy and Denim (a grammy winner for best spoken-word album). He's also a frequent contributor to The New Yorker magazine, where "Turbulence" appeared.

1   On the flight to Raleigh, I sneezed, and the cough drop I'd been sucking on shot from my mouth, ricocheted off my folded tray table, and landed, as I remember it, in the lap of the woman beside me, who was asleep and had her arms folded across her chest. I'm surprised that the force didn't wake her—that's how hard it hit—but all she did was flutter her eyelids and let out a tiny sigh, the kind you might hear from a baby.

2   Under normal circumstances, I'd have had three choices, the first being to do nothing. The woman would wake up in her own time, and notice what looked like a shiny new button sewn to the crotch of her jeans. This was a small plane, with one seat per row on Aisle A, and two seats per row on Aisle B. We were on B, so should she go searching for answers I would be the first person on her list. "Is this yours?" she'd ask, and I'd look dumbly into her lap.
"Is what mine?"

3   Option No. 2 was to reach over and pluck it from her pants, and No. 3 was to wake her up and turn the tables, saying, "I'm sorry, but I think you have something that belongs to me." Then she'd hand the lozenge back and maybe even apologize, confused into thinking that she'd somehow stolen it.

4   These circumstances, however, were not normal, as before she'd fallen asleep the woman and I had had a fight. I'd known her for only an hour, yet I felt her hatred just as strongly as I felt the stream of cold air blowing into my face—this after she'd repositioned the nozzle above her head, a final fuck-you before settling down for her nap.

5   The odd thing was that she hadn't looked like trouble. I'd stood behind her while boarding and she was just this woman—forty at most—wearing a T-shirt and cutoff jeans. Her hair was brown, and

fell to her shoulders, and as we waited she gathered it into a ponytail and fastened it with an elastic band. There was a man beside her, who was around the same age and was also wearing shorts, though his were hemmed. He was skimming through a golf magazine, and I guessed correctly that the two of them were embarking on a vacation. While on the gangway, the woman mentioned a rental car, and wondered if the beach cottage was far from a grocery store. She was clearly looking forward to her trip, and I found myself hoping that, whichever beach they were going to, the grocery store wouldn't be too far away. It was just one of those things that go through your mind. Best of luck, I thought.

6   Once on board, I realized that the woman and I would be sitting next to one another, which was fine. I took my place on the aisle, and within a minute she excused herself and walked a few rows up to talk to the man with the golf magazine. He was at the front of the cabin, in a single bulkhead seat, and I recall feeling sorry for him, because I hate the bulkhead. Tall people covet it, but I prefer as little leg room as possible. When I'm on a plane or in a movie theatre, I like to slouch down as low as I can, and rest my knees on the seat back in front of me. In the bulkhead, there is no seat in front of you, just a wall a good three feet away, and I never know what to do with my legs. Another drawback is that you have to stow all of your belongings in the overhead compartment, and these are usually full by the time I board. All in all, I'd rather hang from one of the wheels than have to sit up front.

7   When they announced our departure, the woman returned to her seat, and hovered a half foot off the cushion, so she could continue her conversation with the man she'd been talking to earlier. I wasn't paying attention to what they were saying, but I believe I heard him refer to her as Becky, a wholesome name that matched her contagious, almost childlike enthusiasm.

8   The plane took off and everything was as it should be until the woman touched my arm, and pointed to the man she'd been talking to earlier. "Hey," she said, "see that guy up there?" Then she called out his name—Eric, I think—and the man turned and waved. "That's my husband, see, and I'm wondering if you could maybe swap seats so that me and him could sit together."

9   "Well, actually—" I said, and before I could finish her face hardened, and she interrupted me, saying, "What? You have a problem with that?"

10   "Well," I said, "ordinarily I'd be happy to move, but he's in the bulkhead, and I just hate that seat."

11   "He's in the what?"

12   "The bulkhead," I explained. "That's what you call that front row."

13   "Listen," she said, "I'm not asking you to switch because it's a bad seat. I'm asking you to switch because we're married." She pointed to her wedding ring, and when I leaned in closer to get a better look at it she drew back her hand, saying, "Oh, never mind. Just forget it."

14   It was as if she had slammed a door in my face, and quite unfairly, it seemed to me. I should have left well enough alone, but instead I tried to reason with her. "It's only a ninety-minute flight," I said, suggesting that in the great scheme of things it wasn't that long to be separated from your husband. "I mean, what, is he going to prison the moment we land in Raleigh?"

15   "No, he's not going to prison," she said, and on the last word she lifted her voice, mocking me.

16   "Look," I told her, "if he was a child I'd do it." And she cut me off saying, "Whatever." Then she rolled her eyes and glared out the window.

17   The woman had decided that I was a hard-ass, one of those guys who refuse under any circumstances to do anyone a favor. But it's not true. I just prefer that the favor be my idea, that it leaves me feeling kind rather than bullied and uncomfortable. So, no. Let her sulk, I decided.

18   Eric had stopped waving, and signalled for me to get Becky's attention. "My wife," he mouthed. "Get my wife."

19   There was no way out, and so I tapped the woman on the shoulder.

20   "Don't touch me," she said, as if I had thrown a punch.

21   "Your husband wants you."

22   "Well, that doesn't give you the right to touch me." Becky unbuckled her seat belt, raised herself off the cushion, and spoke to Eric in a loud stage whisper: "I asked him to swap seats, but he won't do it."

23   He cocked his head, sign language for "How come?," and she said, much louder than she needed to, " 'Cause he's an asshole, that's why."

24   An elderly woman across the aisle turned to look at me, and I pulled a Times crossword puzzle from the bag beneath my seat. That always makes you look reasonable, especially on a Saturday, when the words are long and the clues are exceptionally tough. The problem is that you have to concentrate, and all I could think of was this woman.

25   Seventeen across. A fifteen-letter word for enlightenment. "I am not an asshole," I wrote, and it fit.

26   Five down. Six-letter Indian tribe. "You are."

27   Look at the smart man, breezing through the puzzle, I imagined everyone thinking. He must be a genius. That's why he wouldn't swap seats for that poor married woman. He knows something we don't.

28   It's pathetic how much significance I attach to the Times puzzle, which is easy on Monday and gets progressively harder as the week advances. I'll spend fourteen hours finishing the Friday, and then I'll wave it in someone's face and demand that they acknowledge my superior intelligence. I think it means that I'm smarter than the next guy, but all it really means is that I don't have a life.

29   As I turned to my puzzle, Becky reached for a paperback novel, the kind with an embossed cover. I strained to see what the title was, and she jerked it closer to the window. Strange how that happens, how you can feel someone's eyes on your book or magazine as surely as you can feel a touch. It only works for the written word, though. I stared at her feet for a good five minutes, and she never jerked those away. After our fight, she'd removed her sneakers, and I saw that her toenails were painted white, and that each one was perfectly sculpted.

30   Eighteen across: "Not impressed."

31   Eleven down: "Whore."

32   I wasn't even looking at the clues anymore.

33   When the drink cart came, we fought through the flight attendant.

34   "What can I offer you folks?" she asked, and Becky threw down her book saying, "We're not together." It killed her that we might be mistaken for a couple, or even friends. "I'm travelling with my husband," she continued. "He's sitting up there. In the bulkhead."

35   You learned that word from me, I thought.

36   "Well, can I offer—"

37   "I'll have a Coke," Becky said. "Not much ice."

38   I was thirsty, too, but more than a drink I wanted the flight attendant to like me. And who would you prefer, the finicky baby who cuts you off and gets all specific about her ice cubes, or the thoughtful, nondemanding gentleman who smiles up from his difficult Saturday puzzle saying, "Nothing for me, thank you"?

39   Were the plane to lose altitude and the only way to stay aloft was to push one person out the emergency exit, I now felt certain that the flight attendant would select Becky rather than me. I pictured her clinging to the door frame, her hair blown so hard it was starting to fall out. "But my husband—" she'd cry. Then I would step forward saying, "Hey, I've been to Raleigh before. Take me instead." Becky

would see that I am not the asshole she mistook me for, and in that instant she would lose her grip, and be sucked into space.

40   Two down: "Take that!"

41   Its always so satisfying when you can twist someone's hatred into guilt—make them realize that they were wrong, too quick to judge, too unwilling to look beyond their own petty concerns. The problem is that it works both ways. I'd taken this woman as the type who arrives late at a movie, then asks me to move behind the tallest person in the theatre so that she and her husband can sit together. Everyone has to suffer just because she's sleeping with someone. But what if I was wrong? I pictured her in a dimly lit room, trembling before a portfolio of glowing X-rays. "I give you two weeks at the most," the doctor says. "Why don't you get your toenails done, buy yourself a nice pair of cutoffs, and spend some quality time with your husband. I hear the beaches of North Carolina are pretty nice this time of year."

42   I looked at her then, and thought, No. If she'd had so much as a stomach ache, she would have mentioned it. Or would she? I kept telling myself that I was within my rights, but I knew it wasn't working when I turned back to my puzzle and started listing the various reasons I was not an asshole

43   Forty across: "I give money to p—"

44   Forty-six down: "—ublic radio."

45   While groping for reason No. 2, I noticed that Becky was not making a list of her own. She was the one who had called me a name, who had gone out of her way to stir up trouble, but it didn't seem to bother her in the least. After finishing her Coke, she folded up the tray table, summoned the flight attendant to take her empty can, and settled back for a nap. It was shortly afterward that I put the throat lozenge in my mouth, and shortly after that that I sneezed, and it shot like a bullet onto the crotch of her shorts.

46   Nine across: "Fuck!"

47   Thirteen down: "Now what?"

48   It was then that another option occurred to me. You know, I thought. Maybe I will swap places with her husband. But I'd waited too long, and now he was asleep as well. My only way out was to nudge this woman awake, and make the same offer I sometimes make to Hugh. We'll be arguing, and I'll stop in mid-sentence and ask if we can just start over. "I'll go outside and when I come back in we'll just pretend this never happened, O.K.?"

49   If the fight is huge, he'll wait until I'm in the hall, then bolt the door behind me, but if it's minor he'll go along, and I'll reenter the apartment saying, "What are you doing home?" Or "Gee, it smells good in here. What's cooking?"—an easy question, as he's always got something on the stove.

50   For a while, it feels goofy, but eventually the self-consciousness wears off, and we ease into the roles of two decent people, trapped in a rather dull play. "Is there anything I can do to help?"

51   "You can set the table if you want."

52   "All-righty then."

53   I don't know how many times I've set the table in the middle of the afternoon, long before we sit down to eat. But the play would be all the duller without action, and I don't want to do anything really hard, like paint a room. I'm just so grateful that he goes along with it. Other people's lives can be full of screaming and flying plates, but I prefer that my own remains as civil as possible, even if it means faking it every once in a while.

54   I'd gladly have started over with Becky, but something told me she wouldn't go for it. Even asleep, she broadcast her hostility, each gentle snore sounding like an accusation. Ass-hole. Ass-ho-ole. The landing announcement failed to wake her, and when the flight attendant asked her to fasten her seat belt she did it in a drowse, without looking. The lozenge disappeared beneath the buckle, and this bought me an extra ten minutes, time spent gathering my things, so that I could make for the door the moment we arrived at our gate. I just didn't count on the man in front of me being a little bit quicker, and holding me up as he wrestled his duffelbag from the overhead bin. Had it not been for him, I might have been gone by the time Becky unfastened her seat belt, but as it was I was only four rows away, standing, as it turned out, right beside the bulkhead.

55   The name she called me was nothing I hadn't heard before, and nothing that I won't hear again, probably. Eight letters, and the clue might read, "Above the shoulders, he's nothing but crap." Of course, they don't put words like that in the Times crossword puzzle. If they did, anyone could finish it.

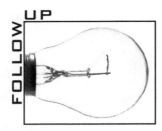

TURBULENCE

Thinking and Talking Points

1. Analyze the behavior of both people. Should he have moved his seat? Why or why not? If the woman were to tell the story, how would she tell it? Outline both points of view.
2. Though not everyone has the same sense of humor, the essay has intended humor. Whether or not you think the essay is funny, discuss strategies Sedaris uses to convey humor.
3. What is the main point of the story?
4. Much of the story is told using dialogue. Rewrite a section of the dialogue into prose. What does the story lose by this change?
5. What is the purpose of the example of how he resolves conflicts with Hugh?

Styling

You might come across a writing situation where dialogue is appropriate or necessary to get across your point, tone, or characterization. Dialogue can liven up a section of otherwise dull prose.

Notice that in Sedaris's essay, whenever the speaker changes, a new paragraph begins (the proper format for dialogue). Punctuation goes inside the quotation marks:

"Well," I said, "ordinarily I'd be happy to move, but he's in the bulkhead, and I just hate the bulkhead."
"He's in the what?"
"The bulkhead," I explained. "That's what you call that front row."

Also note that when an interruption like "I said" or "said Rob" occurs in the middle of the sentence being quoted, a comma goes after it, and you would not capitalize "ordinarily" because it's part of the sentence containing the word "well."

PRACTICE Put the following exchange between Alice and the Caterpillar —from *Alice 's Adventures in Wonderland* by Lewis Carroll—in dialogue form, using correct punctuation, quotation marks, and a new line when the speaker changes.

What do you mean by that? said the Caterpillar, sternly. Explain yourself! I can't explain myself, I'm afraid Sir, said Alice because I'm not myself, you see. I don't see said the Caterpillar. I'm afraid I can't put it more clearly Alice replied, very politely for I can't understand it myself, to begin with; and being so many different sizes in a day is very confusing. It isn't said the Caterpillar.

You can see how confusing it is when each speaker is not clarified with punctuation, quotation marks, and a new paragraph.

YOU TRY IT   In dialogue form, write down a recent conversation, or rewrite a section of your last essay to include dialogue. You can also write down an exchange from a favorite film.

Teaming Up

1. Discuss the situation in the essay, and how you think the woman, Becky, would tell her side of the story. After brainstorming, rewrite the situation from Becky's point of view. Use proper dialogue form. Be prepared to read your paper to the rest of the class.

2. Individually, make a list of Pet Peeves (minor, annoying things that other people do that bother you). Next share your list. Chances are that at least one item on someone else's list is something that you're guilty of doing. Discuss ways to resolve such conflicts or control the behavior in ways acceptable to all in the group.

Writing Ideas

1. Write a narrative essay about a ridiculous, embarrassing, or otherwise unpleasant encounter you've experienced. Describe the situation and use dialogue. Explain how you resolved—or wish you had resolved—the conflict.
2. Write an essay about everyday annoyances, social niceties that people sometimes ignore, and the conflicts or misunderstandings they can cause. Give advice on how these situations might be peaceably resolved. Consider splitting types of annoyances into classifications (see Writing Strategies for Classification in Section Five), perhaps from minor offenses to more major ones.
3. Think of something to which you attach a significance (for Sedaris, it's the *New York Times* crossword puzzle); it can be an object, a ritual, anything that has meaning for you in some small way. Avoid

major social rituals like attending church or getting married. Find something that you do on a regular basis that has significance. Write an essay describing the object or ritual, and explain its significance and perhaps analyze whether or not there's anything absurd in your attachment.

Essay Connections

P. J. O'Rourke's "How to Drive Fast" and Mark Twain's "Advice to Youth," both have themes of bad behavior. "Somebody's Baby" by Barbara Kingsolver also recounts a rude encounter on an airplane.

Lawrence Weschler

Lawrence Weschler, on the first day after Desert Storm, is both fascinated and repelled by a war fought with technology. He recounts the coldness of the news media, which celebrates the clean aerial strikes, but ignores the carnage left behind. Think about his connection of the war with the victims of the San Francisco earthquake.

DUSTBIN OF HISTORY AND CULTURE

DESERT STORM: The Persian Gulf War between the United States and Iraq in 1991. *MODERN TIMES*: a 1936 film by Charlie Chaplin, a social protest against the dehumanization caused by the Industrial Age with its assembly lines and machines.

1 The morning after the launching of Desert Storm, a group of us at my office were talking about this awesome new thing that has entered the world, these awesome new things: this unprecedented kind of warfare with its truly precision, pinpoint aerial bombing; this unprecedented kind of war where, thanks to the various satellite technologies, you get to hear the results of that bombing instantaneously, as it's happening. Modern, we said, high-tech, uncanny, eerie, futuristic. And yet, of course, at another level, there's nothing new here. On the ground, the carnage of war, the gore, the frantically desperate attempts at rescue, the bitterly expiring hopes—they're all the same as they've ever been.

2 One of my friends there at the office that day commented on the way he'd been haunted all morning by the memory of an article he'd read last year—he couldn't remember where—about the San Francisco earthquake. About this young couple who'd been buried alive together in a small room in their collapsed apartment, their bones crushed in debris up to their waists, the two of them huddled together in this narrow air pocket. And of how the rescuers finally got to them—but at that very moment the wreckage caught fire; they were able to free up the husband, but he was forced to leave his wife behind and she perished in the flames.

3   We were all silent for a moment—CNN in the background was cross-cutting between the latest Pentagon briefing and live coverage of a speech by the Turkish prime minister in Ankara.

4   "Wait a second," my friend said. "I remember: it was in the *Whole Earth Review*. In fact, I bet we can even access it over Nexus." Our office is tied into one of those computerized data bases which offers continuously updated access to the complete back-contents of hundreds of newspapers and periodicals. My friend set himself down before the system's console, revved up the machine, punched in a few key words—*earthquake* and *fire* and *rescue* and *couple*—and instantaneously that very article appeared on the screen. He punched a few more buttons and the console's neighboring printer revved up and began spewing out a copy. The whole process didn't take more than a few moments.

5   The account, by Stewart Brand, was every bit as compelling as our colleague had remembered it. It turned out that Brand himself had happened to be visiting the neighborhood at the moment the earthquake struck and that he'd played an impromptu part in the volunteer rescue attempts: he'd been one of those on the outside, scrambling through the wreckage. "Of course, it wasn't as direct and purposeful as this brief account makes it seem," he records. "A real rescue is dreamy and hesitant, full of false starts and conflicting ideas, at times frantic and focused, at times diffuse. It is a self-organizing process, neither quick nor tidy. . . ." Much later, weeks after the disaster, he'd gone back and interviewed several of the principals from that evening's incident, including Bill Ray, the husband, who was still recovering at a hospital. In his article, Brand interwove their stories, and his account climaxed as the firemen were being driven back by the flames:

> "I told Janet," [this is Ray talking] "I told her 'I'm going to get free, and we're both going to get free.' I assumed that I was binding her and that if I could get loose, then she could get loose. You just start pulling with everything you've got. You reach up and you pull on the lathe and the plaster, and it's breaking off in your hand. . . . Janet was screaming because it was a lot of pain and her arms were trapped, and a picture frame of glass was cutting her.
>
> "Then I got free, but she still wasn't. I tried to pull her out. Smoke was coming in. You could hear the flames cracking and popping. She couldn't pull herself loose, and I couldn't get to her."
>
> What they said to each other then, Bill Ray prefers to keep private. "Then I left," [Ray recalls] "I crawled out that hole. . . ."

6   And so forth. That terrible lacuna—the private moment, what they possibly could have said to each other—has haunted me, too, ever since I read it. And, of course, I've been imagining the hundreds of variations of that scene being played out half a globe away; the fact that accidental strikes on civilian targets are purportedly being kept to a minimum doesn't comfort me in the least. I envision seventeen-year-old boys scrambling desperately to rescue their buddies, having to abandon the attempt in the face of further bombardments, and the image is in no way softened by the allegedly mitigating circumstance that the boys in question may be wearing uniforms.

7   But, strangely, the image that really haunts me, and the one I just can't shake, is that of my colleague in the eerie glow of his Nexus console, calmly punching that set of keys, activating the machine—the machine silently humming away, surveying the veritable continents of information before it, instantaneously targeting its quarry, yanking it out of the endless field and delivering it up to us whole. The surgical precision of the whole process. For a moment that morning, my colleague seemed to me like one of those amazing young officers strapped to his battle station aboard the AWACs control planes circling high above Saudi Arabia—coolly surveying his console, punching in the coordinates, splaying out the information, directing the entire battle.

8   CNN, Nexus, AWACs—they're all of a piece. And the carnage on the ground is something entirely else, almost infinitely removed.

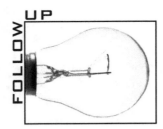

MODERN TIMES

Exploring Language

camaraderie: a feeling of getting along; friendship or kinship.

carnage: the leftovers from slaughter, usually referring to dead people, especially after a battle.

diffuse: to scatter or spread.

eerie: ghostly or spooky.

impromptu: spontaneous or unrehearsed.

lacuna: break or interruption; cavity.

mitigating circumstances: special situations that allow for tolerance when leniency might not otherwise be permitted.

quarry: the victim or prey that one is hunting or focusing on.

splaying: spreading out.

uncanny: strange, weird, extraordinary.

unprecedented: never seen before; new, unrivaled.

Note: For pronunciation, visit dictionary.com, search the word, and click on the speaker icon.

USAGE   Examine the author's use of *mitigating* and *eerie.* Why do you think he made these particular choices? Here's a vocabulary challenge: use *uncanny, eerie,* and *quarry* in the same sentence.

Thinking and Talking Points

1. Why do you think the piece is called "Modern Times"? Give examples from the essay.

2. Explain the connection between the war and the earthquake. Why is Weschler's friend "haunted all morning" by the memory of an earthquake incident? What's significant about the friends' silence after hearing the earthquake story in paragraph #2 and the CNN coverage in the background?

3. What is Weschler's point? Do you think he's saying that war is not justified? Or is he just lamenting the need for war? Find evidence in the article to support your response.

4. Why is Weschler haunted by the image of his colleague at the console of the computer?
5. How do you think this highly technological war differs from previous wars like Vietnam and War World II? What does Weschler indicate he thinks? What's the emotional or psychological difference for the soldiers? Can you relate his ideas on war and technology to the Iraq war or the war in Afghanistan?

Styling

Weschler uses variations of **loose** and **periodic** sentence styles and dashes for writing spice (for more on using dashes, see the Styling section with David Huddle's "Museum Piece"). But let's take a look at a sentence with dashes that set off an **interrupting clause** called an **appositive**. Appositives rename, describe, or give more information about **nouns** (subjects) and help eliminate clunky clauses using *who* and *which*. Here's Weschler's sentence:

> My friend set himself down before the system's console, revved up the machine, punched in a few key words—*earthquake* and *fire* and *rescue* and *couple*—and instantaneously that very article appeared on the screen.

The group of words set off by dashes is an appositive because it renames *key words*. Notice that Weschler's sentence would be complete without the appositive:

> My friend set himself down before the system's console, revved up the machine, punched in a few key words, and instantaneously that very article appeared on the screen.

You have a choice of setting off interrupters with commas, dashes, or parentheses. When interrupting a sentence with a list, as Weschler does, it's a good idea to use dashes, especially when the list contains commas. Dashes will help avoid misreading. If Weschler had used commas instead of the dashes and conjunctions, and if the key words had not been italicized, the sentence would be confusing:

> My friend set himself down before the system's console, revved up the machine, punched in a few key words, earthquake, fire, rescue, couple, and instantaneously that very article appeared on the screen.

Weschler also uses appositives with commas to rename nouns:

Much later, weeks after the disaster, he'd gone back and interviewed several of the principals from that evening's incident, including Bill Ray, the husband, who was still recovering at a hospital.

The husband renames the noun *Bill Ray.*

Identity the appositives in the following sentences; notice which ones require dashes for clarity.

Her acupuncturist, Jerry, moved to Thailand.

The orchids—dendrobiums, oncidiums, cymbidiums, and cattleyas—bloomed a riot of colors.

My dog, a lazy Golden Retriever, is loveable but useless.

PRACTICE   Fill in the blanks below with words or phrases that describe, rename, or give extra information about the nouns.

My college, _____, changes to a sixteen-week semester next spring.

Her car, _____, sat crumpled in the corner of the police impound yard.

The band, _____, drew a large crowd at the county fair.

The vegetable garden— _____ —grew despite neglect.

YOU TRY IT   Create five sentences of your own with appositives, using dashes and a list in at least two of them. Use this technique in one of the Writing Ideas below.

Teaming Up

1. Have each group member bring in some information about the reasons behind the Persian Gulf War (or another war), half of the group finding arguments justifying the war, half against it. Discuss these reasons and whether or not you think the war was justified.

2. **Warm-up for Writing Idea #2.** In your group, make a list of technological advances that have had an impact on people's lives. Discuss the positive and negative aspects of these technologies. Compare your results with those of the other groups in your class.

Writing Ideas

1. Using a list from "Teaming Up" activity #2, choose one technological advance to explore. Write an essay that discusses the advantages and disadvantages of the technology, proposing a solution to minimize the disadvantages.
2. Research the public's reaction to the Persian Gulf War; then research the reaction to the Vietnam War or Iraq. Write an essay describing these reactions and the reasons behind them. What has changed culturally or socially to cause a change in attitude?
3. Watch the silent Charlie Chaplin film *Modern Times* and discuss its relevance to Weschler's ideas in his essay. How is Weschler's essay a social protest? What is he protesting? How might his point, and Charlie Chaplin's, be relevant today? Draw direct parallels between the film, the essay, and current events.

MORTALITY

Bailey White

In this excerpt from her book Mama Makes Up Her Mind and Other Dangers of Southern
Living, *Bailey White—a first grade teacher, writer, radio commentator—writes about her life in
the South, where she lives with her eccentric mother. Here, with gentle humor, she compares her
aging car to her new car as well as her aging body.*

DUSTBIN OF HISTORY AND CULTURE

GRACIE ALLEN: (1906–1964) American film and TV comedian, married to comedian George Burns.

VIVALDI: (1678–1741) Italian composer and violinist.

1   It really makes you feel your age when you get a letter from your
insurance agent telling you that the car you bought, only slightly
used, the year you got out of college, is now an antique. "Beginning
with your next payment, your insurance premiums will reflect this
change in classification," the letter said.

2   I went out and looked at the car. I thought back over the years. I
could almost hear my uncle's disapproving voice. "You should never
buy a used car," he had told me the day I brought it home. Ten years
later I drove that used car to his funeral. I drove my sister, Louise, to
the hospital in that car to have her first baby, and I drove to Atlanta
in that car when the baby graduated from Georgia Tech with a degree
in physics.

3   "When are you going to get a new car?" my friends asked me.

4   "I don't need a new car," I said. "This car runs fine."

5   I changed the oil often, and I kept good tires on it. It always got
me where I wanted to go. But the stuffing came out of the backseat
and the springs poked through, and the dashboard disintegrated. At
300,000 miles the odometer quit turning, but I didn't really care to
know how far I had driven.

6   A hole wore in the floor where my heel rested in front of the accelerator, and the insulation all peeled off the fire wall. "Old piece of

junk," my friends whispered. The seat-belt catch wore out, and I tied on a huge bronze hook with a fireman's knot.

7   Big flashy cars would zoom past me. People would shake their fists out the windows. "Get that clunker off the road!" they would shout.

8   Then one day on my way to work, the car coughed, sputtered, and stopped. "This is it," I thought, and I gave it a pat. "It's been a good car."

9   I called the mechanic. "Tow it in," I said. "I'll have to decide what to do." After work I went over there. I was feeling very glum. The mechanic laughed at me. "It's not funny," I said. "I've had that car a long time."

10   "You know what's wrong with that car?" he said. "That car was out of gas." So I slopped a gallon of gas in the tank and drove ten more years. The gas gauge never worked again after that day, but I got to where I could tell when the gas was low by the smell. I think it was the smell of the bottom of the tank.

11   There was also a little smell of brake fluid, a little smell of exhaust, a little smell of oil, and after all the years a little smell of me. Car smells. And sounds. The wonderful sound when the engine finally catches on a cold day, and an ominous tick tick in July when the radiator is working too hard. The windshield wipers said "Gracie Allen Gracie Allen Gracie Allen." I didn't like a lot of conversation in the car because I had to keep listening for a little skip that meant I needed to jump out and adjust the carburetor.

12   I kept a screwdriver close to hand—and a pint of brake fluid, and a new roter, just in case. "She's strange," my friends whispered. "And she drives so slow."

13   I don't know how fast I drove. The speedometer had quit working years ago. But when I would look down through the hole in the floor and see the pavement, a gray blur, whizzing by just inches away from my feet, and feel the tremendous heat of internal combustion pouring back through the fire wall into my lap, and hear each barely contained explosion just as a heart attack victim is able to hear his own heartbeat, it didn't feel like slow to me. A whiff of brake fluid would remind me just what a tiny thing I was relying on to stop myself from hurtling along the surface of the earth at an unnatural speed, and when I finally arrived at my destination, I would slump back, unfasten the seat-belt hook with trembling hands, and stagger out. I would gather up my things and give the car a last look. "Thank you, sir," I would say. "We got here one more time."

14   But after I got that letter, I began thinking about getting a new car. I read the newspaper every night. Finally I found one that sounded good. It was the same make as my car, but almost new. "Call Steve," the ad said.

15   I went to see the car. It was parked in Steve's driveway. It was a fashionable wheat color. There was carpet on the floor, and the seats were covered with a soft, velvety-feeling stuff. It smelled like acrylic and vinyl and Steve. The instrument panel looked like what you would need to run a jet plane. I turned a knob. Mozart's Concerto for Flute and Harp poured out of four speakers. "But how can you listen to the engine, with music playing?" I asked Steve.

16   I turned the key. The car started instantly. No desperate pleadings, no wild hopes, no exquisitely paired maneuvers with the accelerator and the choke. Just instant ignition. I turned off the radio. I could barely hear the engine running, a low, steady hum. I fastened my seat belt. Nothing but a click.

17   Steve got in the passenger seat, and we went for a test drive. We floated down the road. I couldn't hear a sound, but I decided it must be time to shift gears. I stomped around on the floor and grabbed Steve's knee before I remembered it had automatic transmission. "You mean you just put it in 'Drive' and drive?" I asked.

18   Steve scrunched himself way over against his door and clamped his knees together. He tested his seat belt. "Have you ever driven a car before?" he asked.

19   I bought it for two thousand dollars. I rolled all the windows up by mashing a button beside my elbow, set the air-conditioning on "Recirc," and listened to Vivaldi all the way home.

20   So now I have two cars. I call them my new car and my real car. Most of the time I drive my new car. But on some days I go out to the barn and get in my real car. I shoo the rats out of the backseat and crank it up. Even without daily practice my hands and feet know just what to do. My ears perk up, and I sniff the air. I add a little brake fluid, a little water. I sniff again. It'll need gas next week, and an oil change.

21   I back it out and we roll down the road. People stop and look. They smile. "Neat car!" they say.

22   When I pull into the parking lot, my friends shake their heads and chuckle. They amble into the building. They're already thinking about their day's work. But I take one last look at the car and think what an amazing thing it is, internal combustion. And how wonderful to be still alive!

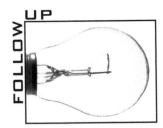

MORTALITY

Thinking and Talking Points

1. Why does White title her essay "Mortality"?
2. Find sensory details in the essay. How do these details enhance the humor?
3. Most people are excited about the prospect of owning a new car. Why is White so reluctant to relinquish her old clunker?
4. How is White's old car a metaphor? What clues are there in the essay to support a metaphorical subtext?
5. Is White simply trying to entertain her reader or is she making a point?

Styling

In Thinking and Talking Points #2, you located sensory details, a strong tool writers use to enhance writing, to make the reader feel, hear, taste, smell, and see the experience.

PRACTICE Sit in your car or another spot and **freewrite** on each of the senses for five minutes.

YOU TRY IT Use the best details from your freewrite above to write a paragraph describing your car or other spot. You can use your description in Writing Idea #1.

Teaming Up

1. **Warm-up for Writing Idea #2.** Bring in photos of various styles of cars. In your group, co-write a paragraph describing and comparing each car and the type of person who would drive each vehicle. Make a list of the stereotypes you created about each person. Then debunk each stereotype (noting how each stereotype might be refuted).

2. Before class, write a paragraph describing an object or place—your car or perhaps your room—and what it reveals about your personality. In class—without yet revealing your writing—team up with

another person and tell each other what object you chose. Now write what you think the other person's choice reveals about his or her personality. Compare. Did your speculations match?

Writing Ideas

1. What you drive—like hairstyle and clothing—can reveal personality. Write an essay describing your car—or dream car—and what it says about your identity.
2. Observe several people and their cars, and write an essay that classifies people and the types of cars they drive, illustrating how what we drive can reveal something about our personalities. Admit that you are generalizing and there are always exceptions to your classification; otherwise, you might get accused of committing a logic error.
3. Write an essay that discusses what the automobile says about American culture. If you like, you can restrict your discussion to the culture of a particular region like New York or California.

Note: See Writing Idea #3 with "Disposable Rocket."

Essay Connections

Diane Ackerman's "Hair" is about other revealing aspects of culture: hairstyle and identity. Joseph Epstein explores America's obsession with celebrities in "The Culture of Celebrity."

READING THE RIVER

From Life on the Mississippi, Mark Twain

Mark Twain (Samuel L. Clemens, 1835-1910, born in Florida, Missouri), best known for his novels The Adventures of Huckleberry Finn *and* Tom Sawyer—*as well as his tall tales—grew up in Hannibal, Missouri, along the Mississippi River, and worked as steamboat pilot for five years, where he heard the riverboat term "mark twain," meaning two fathoms (12 feet deep), a safe depth for navigation. In this excerpt from his book* Life on the Mississippi, *he recounts his experiences learning to navigate the river, lamenting that though a pilot gains knowledge and skill, he loses much of the appreciation of the "beauty and romance," much like a doctor who no longer sees a woman's beauty, only the telltale signs of illness.*

DUSTBIN OF HISTORY AND CULTURE

MISSISSIPPI RIVER: The third longest river in North America, flowing approximately 2,350 miles from Lake Itasca in Minnesota to the Gulf of Mexico.

1   It turned out to be true. The face of the water, in time, became a wonderful book—a book that was a dead language to the uneducated passenger, but which told its mind to me without reserve, delivering its most cherished secrets as clearly as if it uttered them with a voice. And it was not a book to be read once and thrown aside, for it had a new story to tell every day. Throughout the long twelve hundred miles there was never a page that was void of interest, never one that you could leave unread without loss, never one that you would want to skip, thinking you could find higher enjoyment in some other thing. There never was so wonderful a book written by man; never one whose interest was so absorbing, so unflagging, so sparklingly renewed with every reperusal. The passenger who could not read it was charmed with a peculiar sort of faint dimple on its surface (on the rare occasions when he did not overlook it altogether); but to the pilot that was an italicized passage; indeed, it was more than that, it was a legend of the largest capitals, with a string of shouting exclamation points at the end of it, for it meant that a wreck or a rock was buried there that could tear the life out of the strongest vessel that ever floated. It is the faintest and simplest expression the water ever makes, and the most hideous to a pilot's eye. In truth, the passenger who could not read this book saw nothing but all manner of pretty pictures in it, painted by the sun and shaded by the clouds, whereas

to the trained eye these were not pictures at all, but the grimmest and most dread-earnest of reading matter.

2   Now when I had mastered the language of this water, and had come to know every trifling feature that bordered the great river as familiarly as I knew the letters of the alphabet, I had made a valuable acquisition. But I had lost something, too. I had lost something which could never be restored to me while I lived. All the grace, the beauty, the poetry, had gone out of the majestic river! I still kept in mind a certain wonderful sunset which I witnessed when steamboating was new to me. A broad expanse of the river was turned to blood; in the middle distance the red hue brightened into gold, through which a solitary log came floating, black and conspicuous; in one place a long, slanting mark was broken by boiling, tumbling rings, that were as many-tinted as an opal; where the ruddy flesh was faintest, was a smooth spot that was covered with graceful circles and radiating lines, ever so delicately traced; the shore on our left was densely wooded, and the somber shadow that fell from this forest was broken in one place by a long, ruffled trail that shone like silver; and high above the forest wall a clean-stemmed dead tree waved a single leafy bough that glowed like a flame in the unobstructed splendor that was flowing from the sun. There were graceful curves, reflected images, woody heights, soft distances; and over the whole scene, far and near, the dissolving lights drifted steadily, enriching it every passing moment with new marvels of coloring.

3   I stood like one bewitched. I drank it in, in a speechless rapture. The world was new to me, and I had never seen anything like this at home. But as I have said, a day came when I began to cease from noting the glories and the charms which the moon and the sun and the twilight wrought upon the river's face; another day came when I ceased altogether to note them. Then, if that sunset scene had been repeated, I should have looked upon it without rapture, and should have commented upon it, inwardly, after this fashion: "This sun means that we are going to have wind tomorrow; that floating log means that the river is rising, small thanks to it; that slanting mark on the water refers to a bluff reef which is going to kill somebody's steamboat one of these nights, if it keeps on stretching out like that; those tumbling 'boils' show a dissolving bar and a changing channel there, the lines and circles in the slick water over yonder are a warning that troublesome place is shoaling up dangerously; that silver streak in the shadow of the forest is the 'break' from a new snag, and

he has located himself in the very best place he could have found to fish for steamboats; that tall dead tree, with a single living branch, is not going to last long, and then how is a body ever going to get through this blind place at night without the friendly old landmark?

4   No, the romance and the beauty were all gone from the river. All the value any feature of it had for me now was the amount of usefulness it could furnish toward compassing the safe piloting of a steamboat. Since those days, I have pitied doctors from my heart. What does the lovely flush in a beauty's cheek mean to a doctor but a 'break' that ripples above some deadly disease? Are not all her visible charms sown thick with what are to him the signs and symbols of hidden decay? Does he ever see her beauty at all, or doesn't he simply view her professionally, and comment upon her unwholesome condition all to himself? And doesn't he sometimes wonder whether he has gained most or lost most by learning his trade?

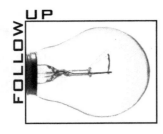

READING THE RIVER

Exploring Language

acquisition: something acquired or gained.
conspicuous: easily seen or noticed.
opal: a gem that comes in a variety of colors.
ruddy: a healthy red, as in a ruddy complexion.
rapture: ecstatic joy or delight.
reperusal: perusal means to survey or read; reperusal means to survey or read again.
shoaling: shoals are shallow places in a body of water.
somber: dark, gloomy; dimly lit.
trifling: insignificant; of very little importance.
wrought: worked or embellished.
yonder: over there; the thing more distant, or farther.
Note: For pronunciation, visit dictionary.com, search the word, and click on the speaker icon.

USAGE Look up other forms of the word *rapture* (rapturous, enraptured) and use each in a sentence. Use *somber* to describe the tone or mood of an inanimate object, perhaps a particular artwork like a film, painting, or novel. Look up the words *further* and *farther*, noting the differences and using each in a sentence.

Thinking and Talking Points

1. Discuss the implications of the title, the many ways Twain reads the river.
2. Study the repetition of the word "never" in paragraph #1. How does repetition work in his favor? How does it underscore his point? When would a writer avoid such repetition? (See **"Teaming Up" #1** for practice using this technique.) Also study the first line of the introduction. How does this simple declarative sentence hook the reader?
3. List--from paragraph #1—each comparison of the river to reading and writing, explaining the meaning. For example, he compares "faint

dimples" on the river's surface to italicized passages. What do italics signal to the reader?

4. In paragraphs #2 and #3, Twain describes the river before and after he learned to pilot a riverboat. Study the word choices and phrases he uses to create **tone**. Discuss the tone in each paragraph and how Twain achieves the desired contrast.

5. Twain combines two techniques in his conclusion: extended comparison and the question style paragraph. Why is the analogy appropriate to his subject? How do the questions build up to a concluding thought? Rewrite the questions into statements. Is anything lost in the translation? (See **Teaming Up #2** for practice with the question paragraph.)

Styling

In his conclusion, Mark Twain uses an extended comparison, or **metaphor**, of a doctor examining a beautiful woman to a riverboat pilot navigating the river. Notice that he breaks down different aspects of the features considered beautiful in a woman and directly compares them to what the doctor might see, moving from specific to general:

Beautiful Features	**Doctor's View**
lovely blush in a beauty's cheek	break that ripples above some deadly disease
visible charms	signs and symbols of decay
beauty	unwholesome condition

Joyce Carol Oates, in her essay "On Boxing," uses this technique, comparing the boxing match to a story: the dialogue is the unspoken language between the boxers; the setting is the ring, lights, ropes, and stained canvas; the spectators are the audience; ringside announcers are narrators. By breaking down both the elements of the boxing ring and the elements of story, she matches them up, creating an extended metaphor.

PRACTICE   List the qualities and activities associated with the seasons of the year. For example, under winter the list might contain bleak, cold, hibernation, snow, rain, bare trees, storms, death, warm fires, snow skiing, ice skating, short days and long nights.

Next, list the qualities of particular people in your life: family members, friends, spouses, or co-workers. Pick one to match up with one of the seasons you listed. For example, a brother might be compared to winter: has a temper, doesn't care for your feelings, is sharp-tongued, but in the right mood, perhaps he's warm and fun loving.

YOU TRY IT   Write an extended metaphor using your practice list. Begin the comparison mentioning the person and the season: "My brother is a cold winter day, bleak and barren." Then go on to match up items from your list in the season with the qualities of the person.

Note: If the season activity doesn't result in a good extended comparison, try breaking down other items or activities like cooking, a zoo, baseball, a clock, state of mind, and so on.

Teaming Up

1. The style activity works well in groups with small adjustments: brainstorm the qualities of the seasons together, help each other with word choices for the people-in-your-life lists, write paragraphs separately, and peer review the finished products. Revise and edit at home.
2. Most paragraphs with statements can be turned into strong questions, creating a thought-provoking introduction or conclusion. A paragraph of questions—like Mark Twain's conclusion—stands out. Read the following question style paragraphs:

From an introduction to an essay titled "No Wonder They Call Me a Bitch" by Ann Hodgman:

"I've always wondered about dog food. Is a Gaines-burger really like a hamburger? Can you fry it? Does dog food 'cheese' taste like real cheese? Does Gravy Train actually make gravy in the dog's bowl, or is that brown liquid just dissolved crumbs? And exactly what are by-products?"

From *An Almanac for Moderns* by Donald Culross Peattie:

"But of what use, pray, is man? Would anybody, besides his dog, miss him if he were gone? Would the sun cease to shed its light because there were not human beings here to sing the praises of sunlight? Would there be sorrow among the little hiding creatures of underwood, or loneliness in the hearts of the proud and noble beasts?

Would the other simians feel that their king was gone? Would God, Jehovah, Zeus, Allah, miss the sound of hymns and psalms, the odor of frankincense and flattery?"

Rewrite each paragraph into statements and discuss whether or not the paragraphs work better as questions or statements. What do the questions imply about the writer's attitude toward the topic?

Choose one of the styles to imitate. For the first example, think of a product to target, and begin "I've always wondered about _____." Some topics to consider for the second example: lawyers, CEO's, vice-presidents, politicians, infomercials, reality television. You might begin your writing, "Of what use is _____."

Note: Adjust the verb as needed for singular or plural subjects. "Of what use are politicians?"

Writing Ideas

1. Write an essay contrasting and/or comparing the style (word choice, sentence structure, figurative language, organization, description, and other techniques) in "Reading the River" and Ken Chen's "City Out of Breath." Consider the two cultures and time periods and how they may or may not impact the writer's viewpoint. Express an opinion.

2. Describe a place or activity from two points in time and how your perspective changed. You might describe it first as you knew it as a child and how, as an adult, your view has changed. Often, a place or activity we enjoy when young loses its charm as we mature. Describe each view of the place in detail. Try using an extended comparison in one of the paragraphs. Use the senses—sight, sound, smell, touch, taste—in both descriptive sections and zoom in on details.

Essay Connections

Parts of "The Courage of Turtles" by Edward Hoagland (the pond before and after) provide contrast for the second writing idea. Ken Chen's "City Out of Breath" gives a glimpse of China. Reg Saner's "The Tree Beyond Imagining" uses extended comparison to describe Utah conifers.

MEAT

Brian Doyle

Brian Doyle's work—short stories, poems, essays—have appeared in numerous publications, including Best American Essays, The American Scholar, The Atlantic Monthly, Harper's, and many anthologies. He's also written several essay collections and a novel, Mink River. "Meat" appeared in The Sun Magazine, March 2012. Like "Joyas Voladoras," his essay surprises the reader with its not-what-it-appears-on-the-surface conclusion.

DUSTBIN OF HISTORY AND CULTURE

ABBOTABAD: a city in Pakistan.

1   My friend Tommy Crotty, who was a terrific basketball player in New York and went on to play college ball and be a cheerful husband and excellent dad before the idiot who just died in Abbottabad murdered him and thousands of people on September Eleventh, used to call every big guy he ever played with *Meat*.

2   Hey, Meat, he would say to the lumbering earnest centers he played with, and hey, Meat, he would say to his tree-trunk power forwards, and even his high-strung small forwards were all leaner Meat to Tommy, except in cases like mine; I started at small forward because guys who were bigger than me couldn't score if you locked them in the gym for a week, and guys who could shoot better wouldn't go into the lane to rebound without a helmet and crowbar, and I could at least convert easy shots and grab uncontested rebounds. So I started up front alongside two Meats, and Tommy ran the point with a succession of reckless gunners at shooting guard, which was a misnamed position on any team Tommy ran unless he trusted the other guard to take decent shots and hit half of them, in which case he would deliver the ball to him like a cake on a silver platter.

3   He was a most amazing point guard, Tommy Crotty, his name often all one word in the mouths of the coaches and refs and parents and fans who came to watch him slide like a grinning knife through what seemed like every Catholic-school team in the greater New York

metropolitan area: *tommycrotty!* You would even hear this odd word in churches and bars and one time at a police station, where there was a misunderstanding about an automobile until the sergeant realized that we played with *tommycrotty*, the word reverential in his mouth like he was talking about one of the lesser Apostles. It turned out one of his kids was a ballplayer, and his kid's team had gone up against our team, and, total respect for you other guys, said the sergeant, but our guys had your number except for that kid at the point, that kid is a magician, I never seen a kid do things like that with a basketball, and he is not the most athletic kid I ever seen either, which was true, Tommy was never going to be six feet tall, not in this life, and he was what even his mom called husky.

4   One time I asked Tommy why he called all the big guys Meat and he said it was just easier that way, learning their names was pointless because they all responded to the same simple stimuli. They want the ball early, you know, said Tommy. I think to reassure themselves that they exist. So I get each Meat a basket early, and then they're *happy*, man. They are not the brightest bulbs in the galaxy. Once they score they are good for long stretches. Meat has short memory. Later in the half I get them another bucket or two each, just to be sure they're awake. Otherwise I want them *working*, you know? Not worrying about scoring. I'll take care of the score, but I need work done out there, and *you're* not going to do it, prancing around like a hairy ballerina. At least *you* don't yell for the ball, which is why I give it to you when you're open. Some guys actually *yell at me* for the ball, can you imagine? Once in a while a Meat will set up his tent in the hole and wave for the ball. I wave back, man. Can you imagine signaling *me* to give *you* the ball? You don't think *I* know where the ball should go? Jesus. I had a Meat once who was waving for the ball, and I waved back, and his face lit up, and he says *hey Tommy!* This is why I call them Meat, man. They are not the brightest bulbs who ever lived.

5   This was how Tommy talked to us in the gym and the playground, but when he was talking to the coaches and refs and parents and fans who called him *tommycrotty* he used his Altar Boy Voice, all polite and reasonable and thanking the Madonna for what small gifts he had been given, and stuff like that. You could melt butter in the mouth that otherwise pretty much had only the words *meat* and *good game* in it. He didn't talk on the floor at all during the game but afterwards he was one of the few guys I ever knew who made a point of shaking every guy's hand on both teams and saying *good game* and actually

meaning it, which is rare, most guys don't mean it at all and they would give you the finger if people weren't watching.

6   But what I really want to tell you about Tommy isn't how he called all big guys Meat; it's about the time I absolutely hammered a guy on a blind pick in a game, and Tommy said something to me afterwards that I've thought about a lot since he was murdered by the idiot in Abbottabad. The guy I clocked had been fouling Tommy the whole game, because basically Tommy was killing his team and the rest of us weren't and this guy figured he would cut the head off the snake, you know? So he bashed Tommy every chance he got, setting mean picks, cracking Tommy's hands and arms while supposedly going for the ball, really dropping the hammer on him twice when he drove to the basket, and one time accidentally on purpose whipping a pass right in Tommy's face like the ball slipped but it didn't. Finally the rest of us had had enough, and me and the Meat set up a blind back pick, which is an evil basketball way to exact vengeance on a guy. The guy you are trying to nail comes flying around the Meat pick, a standard high pick he expects and has seen all game, and then runs smack into a second vicious pick which he did *not* expect, the second pick being me with an elbow aimed at his eye. Well, the guy went down in a heap, and there was a ruckus with coaches and dads yelling, but the ref had seen the way the guy was bashing Tommy, and he figured an eye for an eye, so that was that.

7   But that *wasn't* that, as it turned out, because after the game Tommy read me the riot act, and told me never to do that again, not on his floor, or I would never see the ball again except in the windows of sports stores. He said he understood why we had done it, and he appreciated the thought, but there was a right way and a wrong way to play, and he would be damned if anyone on his team played the wrong way. I asked what about the other guy hammering him and he said screw the other guy, with a guy like that you just play harder and show him the error of his ways. I said that was stupid, that guys like that were idiots, and would never see the error of their ways, and the best way to deliver a message to guys like that was with your elbow in his eyeball, maybe both elbows. You are not listening to me, said Tommy patiently, which is disappointing, you are not Meat, try to pay attention, and remember I have the ball and you do not. There is a right way and a wrong way to play. We play the right way. Guys who play the wrong way will lose in the end. Are you listening to me? Do I have to write this down? The way to teach a guy who plays the

wrong way is to play the right way. *They want you to play the wrong way.* Get it? They are not the brightest bulbs in the galaxy. So the way to really drive them bonkers and make them go home and punch the wall is to play the right way. Firstly it is the only way to play, and secondly it gives them a chance to wake up, although personally I would not bet the house on that. Are you listening to me?

8   Yes, I was. Yes.

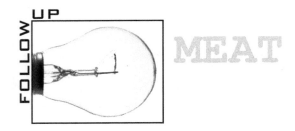

Exploring Language

reverential: to show reverence (respect, awe).

ruckus: commotion, uproar.

Note: For pronunciation, visit dictionary.com, search the word, and click on the speaker icon.

USAGE   For practice with different forms of words, write one sentence using the word *reverence* and one using *reverent*.

Thinking and Talking Points

1. Doyle begins his essay with a long sentence, clauses connected with the conjunction "and." The main sentence is "My friend Tommy Crotty used to call every big guy he ever played with *Meat*." The rest of the material interrupts the main sentence. Most students have been taught not to connect a series of clauses or phrases with too many conjunctions. Why would an award-winning author like Doyle break this so-called rule?

2. Look for other casual writing elements or rule-breaking (comma splices, clichés, word choices, sentence structures) in "Meat" and discuss their use. How do they work in the author's favor?

3. Make a list of the similes and identify the ones that do not fall into the **cliché** category.

4. What is the essay's **subtext** (underlying message), Doyle's real purpose? How does that purpose relate to the opening of the essay? How do Tommy's thoughts on the right and wrong way to play—especially since Tommy's death—hint at this subtext, especially when related to the opening lines of the essay and Doyle's last line?

5. In the beginning of paragraph #6, Doyle writes that it isn't Tommy calling all the big guys Meat that he wants to share, but something he's thought a lot about since Tommy was murdered. How do the first five paragraphs set the reader up for his real topic?

Styling

This **loose sentence** conveys a sense of action that would be lost if broken into a series of sentences:

> So he bashed Tommy every chance he got, setting mean picks, cracking Tommy's hands and arms while supposedly going for the ball, really dropping the hammer on him twice when he drove to the basket, and one time accidentally on purpose whipping a pass right in Tommy's face like the ball slipped but it didn't.

The main sentence, "So he bashed Tommy every chance he got," functions independently and could end with a period but continues with a series of actions using commas:

> *setting* mean picks,
> *cracking* Tommy's hands and arms while supposedly going for the ball,
> really *dropping* the hammer on him twice when he drove to the basket,
> and one time accidentally on purpose *whipping* a pass right in
>   Tommy's face like the ball slipped but it didn't.

Commas separate each action; these actions cannot function alone, relying on the first main sentence to be complete. Notice that turning these actions into complete, separate sentences sounds stilted and simplistic:

> So he bashed Tommy every chance he got. He set mean picks. He cracked Tommy's hands and arms while supposedly going for the ball. He really dropped the hammer on him twice when he drove to the basket. One time he accidentally on purpose whipped a pass right in Tommy's face like the ball slipped but it didn't.

By simply turning the verbs (set, cracked, dropped, whipped) into the "ing" form (setting, cracking, dropping, whipping) and omitting the subject "he," the writer creates a sentence packed with action that flows, underscoring the abuse heaped upon Tommy by the other basketball player.

PRACTICE   Combine the following sentences into one by changing the verbs (in italics) to the "ing" form, omitting the subject, connecting them to the first sentence with commas, but leaving the first sentence as it is to avoid writing a long fragment:

The boxer jabbed at his opponent. He hit him with a vicious right hook. He slammed him with a mind-numbing left. He backed him into the corner of the ropes. He pummeled him with a series of unforgiving blows. He finished him with an uppercut for the win.

YOU TRY IT Write five loose sentences with a series of at least four actions using the "ing" form.

Teaming Up

1. Brainstorm a list of five social issues. Discuss ideas that might be used as narrative (story) to imply or illustrate each issue. Use one of the ideas—or one of your own—for Writing Idea #2.

Writing Ideas

1. Drawing on the answers to Thinking and Talking Points 1-3, write an essay analyzing Brian Doyle's style, perhaps comparing/contrasting it to other essays with casual style like "Prince" by Chuck Klosterman; or compare/contrast "Meat" to an essay with more traditional style like "The Chemist's War" by Deborah Blum.
2. After reading other essays that are metaphor or contain subtext for a larger point—"Disposable Rocket" by John Updike, "Mortality" by Bailey White, "The Tree Beyond Imagining" by Reg Sanger—write an essay that uses a narrative (like Doyle) or metaphor to make a point about a larger issue.

Essay Connections

For essays with subtext or metaphor, see the list in Writing Idea #2. Other essays that include sports are "The Surfing Savant" by Paul Solotaroff and "On Boxing" by Joyce Carol Oates.

BURL'S

Bernard Cooper

Bernard Cooper is a writing teacher whose work has been published in Harper's Magazine, The Paris Review, and Best American Essays. "Burl's" appeared in the Los Angeles Times Magazine and Best American Essays. In this essay, a young Bernard Cooper discovers that things aren't always as they appear; life is more complex and ambiguous than he thought. He ponders this idea using a series of incidents that contribute to or lead up to this realization, as well as an epiphany about his own sexual identity and "the hazy border between the sexes."

DUSTBIN OF HISTORY AND CULTURE

MUSES: Greek goddesses of inspiration—prompted memory and presided over the arts and sciences; calling on the muse was a standard literary convention in epic poetry like Milton's *Paradise Lost*.

1   I loved the restaurant's name, a compact curve of a word. Its sign, five big letters rimmed in neon, hovered above the roof. I almost never saw the sign with its neon lit; my parents took me there for early summer dinners, and even by the time we left—father cleaning his teeth with a toothpick, mother carrying steak bones in a doggie bag—the sky was still bright. Heat rippled off the cars parked along Hollywood Boulevard, the asphalt gummy from hours of sun.

2   With its sleek architecture, chrome appliances, and arctic temperature, Burl's offered a refuge from the street. We usually sat at one of the booths in front of the plate-glass windows. During our dinner, people came to a halt before the news-vending machine on the corner and burrowed in their pockets and purses for change.

3   The waitresses at Burl's wore brown uniforms edged in checked gingham. From their breast pockets frothed white lace handkerchiefs. In between reconnaissance missions to the table, they busied themselves behind the counter and shouted "Tuna to travel" or "Scorch that patty" to a harried short-order cook who manned the grill. Miniature pitchers of cream and individual pats of butter were extracted from an industrial refrigerator. Coca-Cola shot from a glinting spigot. Waitresses dodged and bumped one another, frantic as atoms.

4   My parents usually lingered after the meal, nursing cups of coffee while I played with the beads of condensation on my glass of ice water, tasted Tabasco sauce, or twisted pieces of my paper napkin into mangled animals. One evening, annoyed with my restlessness, my father gave me a dime and asked me to buy him a *Herald Examiner* from the vending machine in front of the restaurant.

5   Shouldering open the heavy glass door, I was seared by a sudden gust of heat. Traffic roared past me and stirred the air. Walking toward the newspaper machine, I held the dime so tightly it seemed to melt in my palm. Duty made me feel large and important. I inserted the dime and opened the box, yanking a *Herald* from the spring contraption that held it as tight as a mousetrap. When I turned around, paper in hand, I saw two women walking toward me.

6   Their high heels clicked on the sun-baked pavement. They were tall, broad-shouldered women who moved with a mixture of haste and defiance. They'd teased their hair into nearly identical black beehives. Dangling earrings flashed in the sun, brilliant as prisms. Each of them wore the kind of clinging, strapless outfit my mother referred to as a cocktail dress. The silky fabric—one dress was purple, the other pink—accentuated their breasts and hips and rippled with insolent highlights. The dresses exposed their bare arms, the slope of their shoulders, and the smooth, powdered plane of flesh where their cleavage began.

7   I owned at the time a book called *Things for Boys and Girls to Do.* There were pages to color, intricate mazes, and connect-the-dots. But another type of puzzle came to mind as I watched those women walking toward me: What's Wrong With This Picture? Say the drawing of a dining room looked normal at first glance; on closer inspection, a chair was missing its leg and the man who sat atop it wore half a pair of glasses.

8   The women had Adam's apples.

9   The closer they came, the shallower my breathing was. I blocked the sidewalk, an incredulous child stalled in their path. When they saw me staring, they shifted their purses and linked their arms. There was something sisterly and conspiratorial about their sudden closeness. Though their mouths didn't move, I thought they might have been communicating without moving their lips, so telepathic did they seem as they joined arms and pressed together, synchronizing their heavy steps. The pages of the *Herald* fluttered in the wind. I felt them against my arm, light as batted lashes.

10   The woman in pink shot me a haughty glance and yet she seemed pleased that I'd taken notice, hungry to be admired by a man, or even

an awestruck eight-year-old boy. She tried to stifle a grin, her red lipstick more voluptuous than the lips it painted. Rouge deepened her cheekbones. Eye shadow dusted her lids, a clumsy abundance of blue. Her face was like a page in *Things for Boys and Girls to Do*, colored by a kid who went outside the lines.

11   At close range, I saw that her wig was slightly askew. I was certain it was a wig because my mother owned several; three Styrofoam heads lined a shelf in my mother's closet; upon them were perched a Page-Boy, an Empress, and a Baby-Doll, all in shades of auburn. The woman in the pink dress wore her wig like a crown of glory.

12   But it was the woman in the purple dress who passed nearest me, and I saw that her jaw was heavily powdered, a half-successful attempt to disguise the telltale shadow of a beard. Just as I noticed this, her heel caught on a crack in the pavement and she reeled on her stilettos. It was then that I witnessed a rift in her composure, a window through which I could glimpse the shades of maleness that her dress and wig and makeup obscured. She shifted her shoulders and threw out her hands like a surfer riding a curl. The instant she regained her balance, she smoothed her dress, patted her hair, and sauntered onward.

13   Any woman might be a man. The fact of it clanged through the chambers of my brain. In broad day, in the midst of traffic, with my parents drinking coffee a few feet away, I felt as if everything I understood, everything I had taken for granted up to that moment—the curve of the earth, the heat of the sun, the reliability of my own eyes—had been squeezed out of me. Who were those men? Did they help each other get inside those dresses? How many other people and things were not what they seemed? From the back, the impostors looked like women once again, slinky and curvaceous, purple and pink. I watched them disappear into the distance, their disguises so convincing that other people on the street seemed to take no notice, and for a moment I wondered if I had imagined the whole encounter, a visitation by two unlikely muses.

14   Frozen in the middle of the sidewalk, I caught my reflection in the window of Burl's, a silhouette floating between his parents. They faced one another across a table. Once the solid embodiments of woman and man, pedestrians and traffic appeared to pass through them.

15   There were some mornings, seconds before my eyes opened and my senses gathered into consciousness, that the child I was seemed to hover above the bed, and I couldn't tell what form my waking would take—the body of a boy or the body of a girl. Finally stirring, I'd blink

against the early light and greet each incarnation as a male with mild surprise. My sex, in other words, didn't seem to be an absolute fact so much as a pleasant, recurring accident.

16   By the age of eight, I'd experienced this groggy phenomenon several times. Those ethereal moments above my bed made waking up in the tangled blankets, a boy steeped in body heat, all the more astonishing. That this might be an unusual experience never occurred to me; it was one among a flood of sensations I could neither name nor ignore.

17   And so, shocked as I was when those transvestites passed me in front of Burl's, they confirmed something about which I already had an inkling: the hazy border between the sexes. My father, after all, raised his pinky when he drank from a teacup, and my mother looked as faded and plain as my father until she fixed her hair and painted her face.

18   Like most children, I once thought it possible to divide the world into male and female columns. Blue/Pink. Rooster/Hens. Trousers/ Skirts. Such divisions were easy, not to mention comforting, for they simplified matter into compatible pairs. But there also existed a vast range of things that didn't fit neatly into either camp: clocks, milk, telephones, grass. There were nights I fell into a fitful sleep while trying to sex the world correctly.

19   Nothing typified the realms of male and female as clearly as my parents' walk-in closets. Home alone for any length of time, I always found my way inside them. I could stare at my parents' clothes for hours, grateful for the stillness and silence, haunting the very heart of their privacy.

20   The overhead light in my father's closet was a bare bulb. Whenever I groped for the chain in the dark, it wagged back and forth and resisted my grasp. Once the light clicked on, I saw dozens of ties hanging like stalactites. A monogrammed silk bathrobe sagged from a hook, a gift my father had received on a long-ago birthday and, thinking it fussy, rarely wore. Shirts were cramped together along the length of an aluminum pole, their starched sleeves sticking out as if in a halfhearted gesture of greeting. The medicinal odor of moth-balls permeated the boxer shorts that were folded and stacked in a built-in drawer. Immaculate underwear was proof of a tenderness my mother couldn't otherwise express; she may not have touched my father often, but she laundered his boxers with infinite care. Even back then, I suspected that a sense of duty was the final erotic link between them.

21   Sitting in a neat row on the closet floor were my father's boots and slippers and dress shoes. I'd try on his wingtips and clomp around, slipping out of them with every step. My wary, unnatural stride made me all the more desperate to effect some authority. I'd whisper orders to imagined lackeys and take my invisible wife in my arms. But no matter how much I wanted them to fit, those shoes were as cold and hard as marble.

22   My mother's shoes were just as uncomfortable, but a lot more fun. From a brightly colored array of pumps and slingbacks, I'd pick a pair with the glee and deliberation of someone choosing a chocolate. Whatever embarrassment I felt was overwhelmed by the exhilaration of being taller in a pair of high heels. Things will look like this someday, I said to myself, gazing out from my new and improved vantage point as if from a crow's nest. Calves elongated, arms akimbo, I gauged each step so that I didn't fall over and moved with what might have passed for grace had someone seen me, a possibility I scrupulously avoided by locking the door.

23   Back and forth I went. The longer I wore a pair of heels, the better my balance. In the periphery of my vision, the shelf of wigs looked like a throng of kindly bystanders. Light streamed down from a high window, causing crystal bottles to glitter, the air ripe with perfume. A makeup mirror above the dressing table invited my self-absorption. Sound was muffled. Time slowed. It seemed as if nothing bad could happen as long as I stayed within those walls.

24   Though I'd never been discovered in my mother's closet, my parents knew that I was drawn toward girlish things—dolls and jump rope and jewelry—as well as to the games and preoccupations that were expected of a boy. I'm not sure now if it was my effeminacy itself that bothered them as much as my ability to slide back and forth, without the slightest warning, between male and female mannerisms. After I'd finished building the model of an F-17 bomber, say, I'd sit back to examine my handiwork, pursing my lips in concentration and crossing my legs at the knee.

25   One day my mother caught me standing in the middle of my bedroom doing an imitation of Mary Injijikian, a dark, overeager Armenian girl with whom I believed myself to be in love, not only because she was pretty but because I wanted to be like her. Collector of effortless A's, Mary seemed to know all the answers in class. Before the teacher had even finished asking a question, Mary would let out a little grunt and practically levitate out of her seat, as if her hand were filled with helium. "Could we please hear from someone else today besides Miss

Injijikian," the teacher would say. *Miss Injijikian*. Those were the words I was repeating over and over to myself when my mother caught me. To utter them was rhythmic, delicious, and under their spell I raised my hand and wiggled like Mary. I heard a cough and spun around. My mother froze in the doorway. She clutched the folded sheets to her stomach and turned without saying a word. My sudden flush of shame confused me. Weren't boys supposed to swoon over girls? Hadn't I seen babbling, heartsick men in a dozen movies?

26   Shortly after the Injijikian incident, my parents decided to send me to gymnastics class at the Los Angeles Athletic Club, a brick relic of a building on Olive Street. One of the oldest establishments of its kind in Los Angeles, the club prohibited women from the premises. My parents didn't have to say it aloud: they hoped a fraternal atmosphere would toughen me up and tilt me toward the male side of my nature.

27   My father drove me downtown so I could sign up for the class, meet the instructor, and get a tour of the place. On the way there, he reminisced about sports. Since he'd grown up in a rough Philadelphia neighborhood, sports consisted of kick-the-can or rolling a hoop down the street with a stick. The more he talked about his physical prowess, the more convinced I became that my daydreams and shyness were a disappointment to him.

28   The hushed lobby of the athletic club was paneled in dark wood. A few solitary figures were hidden in wing chairs. My father and I introduced ourselves to a man at the front desk who seemed unimpressed by our presence. His aloofness unnerved me, which wasn't hard considering that no matter how my parents put it, I knew their sending me here was a form of disapproval, a way of banishing the part of me they didn't care to know.

29   A call went out over the intercom for someone to show us around. While we waited, I noticed that the sand in the standing ashtrays had been raked into perfect furrows. The glossy leaves of the potted plants looked as if they'd been polished by hand. The place seemed more like a well-tended hotel than an athletic club. Finally, a stoop-shouldered old man hobbled toward us, his head shrouded in a cloud of white hair. He wore a T-shirt that said "Instructor"; his arms were so wrinkled and anemic, I thought I might have misread it. While we followed him to the elevator, I readjusted my expectations, which had involved fantasies of a hulking drill sergeant barking orders at a flock of scrawny boys.

30   The instructor, mumbling to himself and never turning around to see if we were behind him, showed us where the gymnastics class took place. I'm certain the building was big, but the size of the room

must be exaggerated by a trick of memory, because when I envision it, I picture a vast and windowless warehouse. Mats covered the wooden floor. Here and there, in remote and lonely pools of light, stood a pommel horse, a balance beam, and parallel bars. Tiers of bleachers rose into darkness. Unlike the cloistered air of a closet, the room seemed incomplete without a crowd.

31   Next we visited the dressing room, empty except for a naked middle-aged man. He sat on a narrow bench and clipped his formidable toenails. Moles clotted his back. He glistened like a fish.

32   We continued to follow the instructor down an aisle lined with numbered lockers. At the far end, steam billowed from the doorway that led to the showers. Fresh towels stacked on a nearby table made me think of my mother; I knew she liked to have me at home with her—I was often her only companion—and I resented her complicity in the plan to send me here.

33   The tour ended when the instructor gave me a sign-up sheet. Only a few names preceded mine. They were signatures, or so I imagined, of other soft and wayward sons.

34   When the day of the first gymnastics class arrived, my mother gave me money and a gym bag and sent me to the corner of Hollywood and Western to wait for a bus. The sun was bright, the traffic heavy. While I sat there, an argument raged inside my head, the familiar, battering debate between the wish to be like other boys and the wish to be like myself. Why shouldn't I simply get up and go back home, where I'd be left alone to read and think? On the other hand, wouldn't life be easier if I liked athletics, or learned to like them?

35   No sooner did I steel my resolve to get on the bus than I thought of something better: I could spend the morning wandering through Woolworth's, then tell my parents I'd gone to the class. But would my lie stand up to scrutiny? As I practiced describing phantom gymnastics, I became aware of a car circling the block. It was a large car in whose shaded interior I could barely make out the driver, but I thought it might be the man who owned the local pet store. I'd often gone there on the pretext of looking at the cocker spaniel puppies huddled together in their pen, but I really went to gawk at the owner, whose tan chest, in the V of his shirt, was the place I most wanted to rest my head. Every time the man moved, counting stock or writing a receipt, his shirt parted, my mouth went dry, and I smelled the musk of sawdust and dogs.

36   I found myself hoping that the driver was the man who ran the pet store. I was thrilled by the unlikely possibility that the sight of

me, slumped on a bus bench in my T-shirt and shorts, had caused such a man to circle the block. Up to that point in my life, lovemaking hovered somewhere in the future, an impulse a boy might aspire to but didn't indulge. And there I was, sitting on a bus bench in the middle of the city, dreaming I could seduce an adult. I showered the owner of the pet store with kisses and, as aquariums bubbled, birds sang, and mice raced in a wire wheel, slipped my hand beneath his shirt. The roar of traffic brought me to my senses. I breathed deeply and blinked against the sun. I crossed my legs at the knee in order to hide an erection. My fantasy left me both drained and changed. The continent of sex had drifted closer.

37   The car made another round. This time the driver leaned across the passenger seat and peered at me through the window. He was a complete stranger, whose gaze filled me with fear. It wasn't the surprise of not recognizing him that frightened me, it was what I did recognize—the unmistakable shame in his expression, and the weary temptation that drove him in circles. Before the car behind him honked, he mouthed "hello" and cocked his head. What now, he seemed to be asking. A bold, unbearable question.

38   I bolted to my feet, slung the gym bag over my shoulder, and hurried toward home. Now and then I turned around to make sure he wasn't trailing me, both relieved and disappointed when I didn't see his car. Even after I became convinced that he wasn't at my back— my sudden flight had scared him off—I kept turning around to see what was making me so nervous, as if I might spot the source of my discomfort somewhere on the street. I walked faster and faster, trying to outrace myself. Eventually, the bus I was supposed to have taken roared past. Turning the corner, I watched it bob eastward.

39   Closing the kitchen door behind me, I vowed never to leave home again. I was resolute in this decision without fully understanding why, or what it was I hoped to avoid; I was only aware of the need to hide and a vague notion, fading fast, that my trouble had something to do with sex. Already the mechanism of self-deception was at work. By the time my mother rushed into the kitchen to see why I'd returned so early, the thrill I'd felt while waiting for the bus had given way to indignation.

40   I poured out the story of the man circling the block and protested, with perhaps too great a passion, my own innocence. "I was just sitting there," I said again and again. I was so determined to deflect suspicion away from myself, and to justify my missing the class, that I portrayed the man as a grizzled pervert who drunkenly veered from lane to lane as he followed me halfway home.

41 My mother cinched her housecoat. She seemed moved and shocked by what I told her, if a bit incredulous, which prompted me to be more dramatic. "It wouldn't be safe," I insisted, "for me to wait at the bus stop again."

42 No matter how overwrought my story, I knew my mother wouldn't question it, wouldn't bring the subject up again; sex of any kind, especially sex between a man and a boy, was simply not discussed in our house. The gymnastics class, my parents agreed, was something I could do another time.

43 And so I spent the remainder of that summer at home with my mother, stirring cake batter, holding the dustpan, helping her fold the sheets. For a while I was proud of myself for engineering a reprieve from the athletic club. But as the days wore on, I began to see that my mother had wanted me with her all along, and forcing that to happen wasn't such a feat. Soon a sense of compromise set in; by expressing disgust for the man in the car, I'd expressed disgust for an aspect of myself. Now I had all the time in the world to sit around and contemplate my desire for men. The days grew long and stifling and hot, an endless sentence of self-examination.

44 Only trips to the pet store offered any respite. Every time I went there, I was too electrified with longing to think about longing in the abstract. The bell tinkled above the door, animals stirred within their cages, and the handsome owner glanced up from his work.

45 I handed my father the *Herald*. He opened the paper and disappeared behind it. My mother stirred her coffee and sighed. She gazed at the sweltering passersby and probably thought herself lucky. I slid into the vinyl booth and took my place beside my parents.

46 For a moment, I considered asking them about what had happened on the street, but they would have reacted with censure and alarm, and I sensed there was more to the story than they'd ever be willing to tell me. Men in dresses were only the tip of the iceberg. Who knew what other wonders existed—a boy, for example, who wanted to kiss a man—exceptions the world did its best to keep hidden.

47 It would be years before I heard the word "transvestite," so I struggled to find a word for what I'd seen. "He-she" came to mind, as lilting as "Injijikian." "Burl's" would have been perfect, like "boys" and "girls" spliced together, but I can't claim to have thought of this back then.

48 I must have looked stricken as I tried to figure it all out, because my mother put down her coffee cup and asked if I was O.K. She

stopped just short of feeling my forehead. I assured her I was fine, but something within me had shifted, had given way to a heady doubt. When the waitress came and slapped down our check—"Thank You," it read, "Dine out more often"—I wondered if her lofty hairdo or the breasts on which her nametag quaked were real. Wax carnations bloomed at every table. Phony wood paneled the walls. Plastic food sat in a display case: fried eggs, a hamburger sandwich, a sundae topped with a garish cherry.

Exploring Language

akimbo: hands on the hips and elbows turned outward.

askew: in this context, crooked or out of line.

cloistered: secluded or sheltered from the world.

conspiratorial: suggestive of having a conspiracy, which means having a secret or plot.

elongated: stretched out or lengthened.

ethereal: delicate or rare; otherworldly.

fraternal: in this context, brotherly union or affection.

frothed: bubbled or foamed.

garish: tasteless and/or flashy; excessively ornate.

haughty: arrogant or scornful.

incredulous: astounded, shaken, shocked, surprised.

insolent: bold, rude, discourteous.

periphery: on the edge or border.

pretext: misleading behavior or appearance, intentionally to conceal a true purpose.

reconnaissance: an information-gathering mission. The military often sends reconnaissance missions made up of a few people (sometimes only one) into enemy territory to gather information about the other side.

scrupulously: carefully, exactly, meticulously; honestly.

stalactite: an icicle-shaped deposit of calcium carbonate hanging from the roof of a cave.

synchronizing: happening at the same time.

telepathic: being able to communicate through the mind rather than words or gestures.

transvestite: a person, usually a male, who adopts the clothing and manner of the opposite sex for emotional or sexual gratification.

voluptuous: suggesting fullness of form and beauty; sensual.

USAGE Create **personification** using the words *insolent* and *haughty* to describe an object. For example, Cooper writes, "The silky fabric—one dress was purple, the other pink—accentuated their breasts and hips and rippled with insolent highlights." The word *insolent* is a human quality, but he uses it to describe the highlights in their dresses. Make a list of as many objects as you can, and then try *insolent* and *haughty* in front of each one. Choose your best combination and write a sentence.

Thinking and Talking Points

1. Examine Cooper's word choices, particularly how he uses strong **verbs** like *hovered* and *rippled*. What other style techniques does Cooper use in his essay? Find *similes* and *metaphors* and explain what they add to the essay.

2. At what point in the essay did you first suspect Cooper is leading up to a realization about his own sexual identity? What clues can you find early in the essay?

3. Discuss Cooper's parents and their reaction to their son's not-so-masculine qualities. How do they cope with the situation? Is their reaction typical of many parents? Do you think they ever accept young Bernard's sexual orientation? What clues in the essay lead you to this conclusion?

4. Cooper writes, "Like most children, I once thought it possible to divide the world into male and female columns." What blurs this line for young Bernard? To what extent do you divide the world along gender lines? What other situations can you think of where things aren't always what they appear?

5. Analyze the structure of this essay. Why does Cooper begin and end with the restaurant? In what way are the series of events he describes related? Why does he put them in the order he does? What conclusion do they lead to about the world?

Styling

Slowing down time like a slow motion camera, Cooper takes a slice of time—a few seconds—and describes it in minute detail, stretching a few seconds onto a canvas, creating a vivid portrait of the two women who walk by him on the sidewalk outside of Burl's. He could have written, "Two women dressed as men walked by me on the sidewalk." We wouldn't be nearly as intrigued nor surprised. He teases the reader, leading up to realization that these two women are men, recreating the experience he had as a young boy, puzzling over it, finally astounding himself and the reader with the line—set off by itself—"The women had Adam's apples." His slow motion technique creates a sense of reality, pulling the readers into the piece, making them see the event through young Bernard's eyes.

PRACTICE   Reread the section where Cooper describes seeing the two women on the sidewalk. Examine how he slows down time, zooming in on the details. Make a lists of word choices and phrases he uses to accomplish this goal. Underline or list strong verb choices and **figurative language** (see the glossary).

Next, think of a meaningful event in your life, perhaps one that led you to some realization about the world. Choose something that happened in a short period of time so you can zoom in close on the details. If you can't recreate a scene, sit in a public place and people-watch until you see an interesting person or event to describe. Make a list of details. Pay close attention. If you're writing about a person, you might list things like this: frayed collar, cracked toenails, lipstick-smeared mouth. Think about fabrics, accessories, expressions. If you get stuck, reread Cooper's piece for ideas.

YOU TRY IT   Using your list of details, write a paragraph or two describing a person or event. If it's a person, he or she should be in motion. Use slow-motion-camera writing to zoom the reader in on the action. Use at least one *simile* or *metaphor*, strong *verbs,* and lots of details. Make use of the senses: touch, taste, smell, sound, sight.

Teaming Up

1. In your group, make a list of big things (a whale, for example). Think of at least ten items. Next, replace the word *continent* in Cooper's sentence, "The continent of sex had moved closer." Try out each word on the list. Do any of them work as well as Cooper's metaphor? Discuss Cooper's use of *continent* to describe sex. Why does it work so well? What word choices on your list flopped?

2. **Warm-up for Writing Idea #2.** Before class, brainstorm and do a **freewrite** about a time you had a child-to-adult epiphany, a time when you realized that appearances can be deceiving. Now share your freewrites.

Writing Ideas

1. Write an essay about an awareness you had as a child that things aren't always what they seem. Think of several events that led to, contributed to, or confirmed this epiphany (a sudden, illuminating discovery), and use them to lead the reader to your realization.

2. Visit an online database that subscribes to periodicals, such as Infotrac, available at your public, college, or university library. Do some research on the controversy surrounding the genetic link to sexual orientation. Look at both sides of the issue. Write an essay explaining the controversy.

Essay Connections

"Oranges and Sweet Sister Boy" by Judy Ruiz—not in this text, but in *Best American Essays* college edition—makes a good companion essay to "Burl's."

THE COURAGE OF TURTLES

Edward Hoagland

Edward Hoagland is best known for his nature and travel essays, with several collections to his credit, among them Walking the Dead Diamond River, The Final Fate of Alligators, and The Courage of Turtles. In this essay from the book of the same title, Hoagland expresses his admiration of these creatures through anthropomorphizing and a series of stories resembling fables.

DUSTBIN OF HISTORY AND CULTURE

BERET: French, a cap with no visor, usually made of wool.
BON MOTS: French, literally meaning "good word"; clever remark or witticism.
IDÉE FIXE: French meaning fixed idea; obsession.
MARGAY CAT: A small, spotted, forest-dwelling cat of Central and South America, closely resembling the ocelot.

1   Turtles are a kind of bird with the governor turned low. With the same attitude of removal, they cock a glance at what is going on, as if they need only to fly away. Until recently they were also a case of virtue rewarded, at least in the town where I grew up, because, being humble creatures, there were plenty of them. Even when we still had a few bobcats in the woods the local snapping turtles, growing up to forty pounds, were the largest carnivores. You would see them through the amber water, as big as greeny wash basins at the bottom of the pond, until they faded into the inscrutable mud as if they hadn't existed at all.

2   When I was ten I went to Dr. Green's Pond, a two-acre pond across the road. When I was twelve I walked a mile or so to Taggart's Pond, which was lusher, had big water snakes and a waterfall; and shortly after that I was bicycling way up to the adventuresome vastness of Mud Pond, a lake-sized body of water in the reservoir system of a Connecticut city, possessed of cat-backed little islands and empty shacks and a forest of pines and hardwoods along the shore. Otters, foxes, and mink left their prints on the bank; there were pike and perch. As I got older, the estates and forgotten back lots in town were parceled out and sold for nice prices, yet, though the woods had shrunk, it seemed that fewer people walked in the woods. The new

residents didn't know how to find them. Eventually, exploring, they did find them, and it required some ingenuity and doubling around on my part to go for eight miles without meeting someone. I was grown by now, I lived in New York, and that's what I wanted to do on the occasional weekends when I came out.

3   Since Mud Pond contained drinking water I had felt confident nothing untoward would happen there. For a long while the developers stayed away, until the drought of the mid-1960s. This event, squeezing the edges in, convinced the local water company that the pond really wasn't a necessity as a catch basin, however; so they bulldozed a hole in the earthen dam, bulldozed the banks to fill in the bottom, and landscaped the flow of water that remained to wind like an English brook and provide a domestic view for the houses which were planned. Most of the painted turtles of Mud Pond, who had been inaccessible as they sunned on their rocks, wound up in boxes in boys' closets within a matter of days. Their footsteps in the dry leaves gave them away as they wandered forlornly. The snappers and the little musk turtles, neither of whom leave the water except once a year to lay their eggs, dug into the drying mud for another siege of hot weather, which they were accustomed to doing whenever the pond got low. But this time it was low for good; the mud baked over them and slowly entombed them. As for the ducks, I couldn't stroll in the woods and not feel guilty, because they were crouched beside every stagnant pothole, or were slinking between the bushes with their heads tucked into their shoulders so that I wouldn't see them. If they decided I had, they beat their way up through the screen of trees, striking their wings dangerously, and wheeled about with that headlong, magnificent velocity to locate another poor puddle.

4   I used to catch possums and black snakes as well as turtles, and I kept dogs and goats. Some summers I worked in a menagerie with the big personalities of the animal kingdom, like elephants and rhinoceroses. I was twenty before these enthusiasms began to wane, and it was then that I picked turtles as the particular animal I wanted to keep in touch with. I was allergic to fur, for one thing, and turtles need minimal care and not much in the way of quarters. They're personable beasts. They see the same colors we do and they seem to see just as well, as one discovers in trying to sneak up on them. In the laboratory they unravel the twists of a maze with the hot-blooded rapidity of a mammal. Though they can't run as fast as a rat, they improve on their errors just as quickly, pausing at each crossroads to look left and right. And they rock rhythmically in place, as we often

do, although they are hatched from eggs, not the womb. (A common explanation psychologists give for our pleasure in rocking quietly is that it recapitulates our mother's heartbeat *in utero.*)

5   Snakes, by contrast, are dryly silent and priapic. They are smooth movers, legalistic, unblinking, and they afford the humor which the humorless do. But they make challenging captives; sometimes they don't eat for months on a point of order—if the light isn't right, for instance. Alligators are sticklers too. They're like war-horses, or German shepherds, and with their bar-shaped, vertical pupils adding emphasis, they have the *idée fixe* of eating, eating, even when they choose to refuse all food and stubbornly die. They delight in tossing a salamander up towards the sky and grabbing him in their long mouths as he comes down. They're so eager that they get the jitters, and they're too much of a proposition for a casual aquarium like mine. Frogs are depressingly defenseless: that moist, extensive back, with the bones almost sticking through. Hold a frog and you're holding its skeleton. Frogs' tasty legs are the staff of life to many animals— herons, raccoons, ribbon snakes—though they themselves are hard to feed. It's not an enviable role to be the staff of life, and after frogs you descend down the evolutionary ladder a big step to fish.

6   Turtles cough, burp, whistle, grunt and hiss, and produce social judgments. They put their heads together amicably enough, but then one drives the other back with the suddenness of two dogs who have been conversing in tones too low for an onlooker to hear. They pee in fear when they're first caught, but exercise both pluck and optimism in trying to escape, walking for hundreds of yards within the confines of their pen, carrying the weight of that cumbersome box on legs which are cruelly positioned for walking. They don't feel that the contest is unfair; they keep plugging, rolling like sailorly souls—a bobbing, infirm gait, a brave, sea-legged momentum—stopping occasionally to study the lay of the land. For me, anyway, they manage to contain the rest of the animal world. They can stretch out their necks like a giraffe, or loom under-water like an apocryphal hippo. They browse on lettuce thrown on the water like a cow moose which is partly sub- merged. They have a penguin's alertness, combined with a build like a brontosaurus when they rise up on tiptoe. Then they hunch and ponderously lunge like a grizzly going forward.

7   Baby turtles in a turtle bowl are a puzzle in geometrics. They're as decorative as pansy petals, but they are also self-directed building blocks, propping themselves on one another in different arrange- ments, before up-ending the tower. The timid individuals turn fear-

less, or vice versa. If one gets a bit arrogant he will push the others off the rock and afterwards climb down into the water and cling to the back of one of those he has bullied, tickling him with his hind feet until he bucks like a bronco. On the other hand, when this same milder-mannered fellow isn't exerting himself, he will stare right into the face of the sun for hours. What could be more lionlike? And he's at home in or out of the water and does lots of metaphysical tilting. He sinks and rises, with an infinity of levels to choose from; or, elongating himself, he climbs out on the land again to perambulate, sits boxed in his box, and finally slides back in the water, submerging into dreams.

8   I have five of these babies in a kidney-shaped bowl. The hatchling, who is a painted turtle, is not as large as the top joint of my thumb. He eats chicken gladly. Other foods he will attempt to eat but not with sufficient perseverance to succeed because he's so little. The yellow-bellied terrapin is probably a yearling, and he eats salad voraciously, but no meat, fish, or fowl. The Cumberland terrapin won't touch salad or chicken but eats fish and all of the meats except for bacon. The little snapper, with a black crenelated shell, feasts on any kind of meat, but rejects greens and fish. The fifth of the turtles is African. I acquired him only recently and don't know him well. A mottled brown, he unnerves the greener turtles, dragging their food off to his lairs. He doesn't seem to want to be green—he bites the algae off his shell, hanging meanwhile at daring, steep, head-first angles.

The snapper was a Ferdinand until I provided him with deeper water.

9   Now he snaps at my pencil with his downturned and fearsome mouth, his swollen face like a napalm victim's. The Cumberland has an elliptical red mark on the side of his green-and-yellow head. He is benign by nature and ought to be as elegant as his scientific name (*Pseudemys scripta elegans*), except he has contracted a disease of the air bladder which has permanently inflated it; he floats high in the water at an undignified slant and can't go under. There may have been internal bleeding, too, because his carapace is stained along its ridge. Unfortunately, like flowers, baby turtles often die. Their mouths fill up with a white fungus and their lungs with pneumonia. Their organs clog up from the rust in the water, or diet troubles, and, like a dying man's, their eyes and heads become too prominent. Toward the end, the edge of the shell becomes flabby as felt and folds around them like a shroud.

10   While they live they're like puppies. Although they're vivacious, they would be a bore to be with all the time, so I also have an adult

wood turtle about six inches long. Her top shell is the equal of any seashell for sculpturing, even a Cellini shell; it's like an old, dusty, richly engraved medallion dug out of a hillside. Her legs are salmon-orange bordered with black and protected by canted, heroic scales. Her plastron—the bottom shell—is splotched like a margay cat's coat, with black ocelli on a yellow back-ground. It is convex to make room for the female organs inside, whereas a male's would be concave to help him fit tightly on top of her. Altogether, she exhibits every camouflage color on her limbs and shells. She has a turtleneck neck, a tail like an ele-phant's, wise old pachydermous hind legs, and the face of a turkey—except that when I carry her she gazes at the passing ground with a hawk's eyes and mouth. Her feet fit to the fingers of my hand, one to each one, and she rides looking down. She can walk on the floor in per-fect silence, but usually she lets her plastron knock portentously, like a footstep, so that she resembles some grand, concise, slow-moving id. But if an earthworm is presented, she jerks swiftly ahead, poises above it, and strikes like a mongoose, consuming it with wild vigor. Yet she will climb on my lap to eat bread or boiled eggs.

11   If put into a creek, she swims like a cutter, nosing forward to inter-cept a strange turtle and smell him. She drifts with the current to go downstream, maneuvering behind a rock when she wants to take stock, or sinking to the nether levels, while bubbles float up. Getting out, choosing her path, she will proceed a distance and dig into a pile of humus, thrusting herself to the coolest layer at the bottom. The hole closes over her until it's as small as a mouse's hole. She's not as aquatic as a musk turtle, not quite as terrestrial as the box turtles in the same woods, but because of her versatility she's marvelous, she's everywhere. And though she breathes the way we breathe, with scarcely percepti-ble movements of her chest, sometimes instead she pumps her throat ruminatively, like a pipe smoker sucking and puffing. She waits and blinks, pumping her throat, turning her head, then sets off like a lop-ing tiger in slow motion, hurdling the jungly lumber, the pea vine and twigs. She estimates angles so well that when she rides over the rocks, sliding down a drop-off with her rugged front legs extended, she has the grace of a rodeo mare.

12   But she's well off to be with me rather than at Mud Pond. The other turtles have fled—those that aren't baked into the bottom. Creeping up the brooks to sad, constricted marshes, burdened as they are with that box on their backs, they're walking into a setup where all their enemies move thirty times faster than they. It's like the night-mare most of us have whimpered through, where we are weighted

down disastrously while trying to flee; fleeing our home ground, we try to run.

13   I've seen turtles in still worse straits. On Broadway, in New York, there is a penny arcade which used to sell baby terrapins that were scrawled with bon mots in enamel paint, such as KISS ME BABY. The manager turned out to be a wholesaler as well, and once I asked him whether he had any larger turtles to sell. He took me upstairs to a loft room devoted to the turtle business. There were desks for the paper work and a series of racks that held shallow tin bins atop one another, each with several hundred babies crawling around in it. He was a smudgy-complexioned, bespectacled, serious fellow and he did have a few adult terrapins, but I was going to school and wasn't actually planning to buy; I'd only wanted to see them. They were aquatic turtles, but here they went without water, presumably for weeks, lurching about in those dry bins like handicapped citizens, living on gumption. An easel where the artist worked stood in the middle of the floor. She had a palette and a clip attachment for fastening the babies in place. She wore a smock and a beret, and was homely, short, and eccentric-looking, with funny black hair, like some of the ladies who show their paintings in Washington Square in May. She had a cold, she was smoking, and her hand wasn't very steady, although she worked quickly enough. The smile that she produced for me would have looked giddy if she had been happier, or drunk. Of course the turtles' doom was sealed when she painted them, because their bodies inside would continue to grow but their shells would not. Gradually, invisibly, they would be crushed. Around us their bellies—two thousand belly shells—rubbed on the bins with a mournful, momentous hiss.

14   Somehow there were so many of them I didn't rescue one. Years later, however, I was walking on First Avenue when I noticed a basket of living turtles in front of a fish store. They were as dry as a heap of old bones in the sun; nevertheless, they were creeping over one another gimpily, doing their best to escape. I looked and was touched to discover that they appeared to be wood turtles, my favorites, so I bought one. In my apartment I looked closer and realized that in fact this was a diamondback terrapin, which was bad news. Diamondbacks are tidewater turtles from brackish estuaries, and I had no seawater to keep him in. He spent his days thumping interminably against the baseboards, pushing for an opening through the wall. He drank thirstily but would not eat and had none of the hearty, accepting qualities of wood turtles. He was morose, paler in color, sleeker and more Oriental in the carved ridges and rings that formed his shell. Though

I felt sorry for him, finally I found his unrelenting presence exasperating. I carried him, struggling in a paper bag, across town to the Morton Street Pier on the Hudson River. It was August but gray and windy. He was very surprised when I tossed him in; for the first time in our association, I think, he was afraid. He looked afraid as he bobbed about on top of the water, looking up at me from ten feet below. Though we were both accustomed to his resistance and rigidity, seeing him still pitiful, I recognized that I must have done the wrong thing. At least the river was salty, but it was also bottomless; the waves were too rough for him, and the tide was coming in, bumping him against the pilings underneath the pier. Too late, I realized that he wouldn't be able to swim to a peaceful inlet in New Jersey, even if he could figure out which way to swim. But since, short of diving in after him, there was nothing I could do, I walked away.

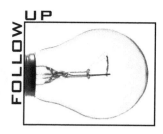
Exploring Language

amicably: friendly, peaceable.

apocryphal: doubtful, false; can also imply mythical.

benign: gentle, gracious; of mild character.

brackish: salty or not appealing to the taste; repulsive.

canted: slanted or tilted.

carapace: protective shell or shell-like covering.

convex: a surface that curves outward; concave curves inward.

crenelated: dented or notched.

elongating: lengthening or extending.

estuaries: where rivers—fresh water—meet the sea.

forlorn: in despair or depressed.

giddy: light-hearted or silly.

gimpy: with a limp; handicapped.

governor: in this context, an attachment to a machine or engine to regulate or control speed, like on a car.

id: psychological term referring to the part of the unconscious that embodies the instinctual need and desires, like pleasure.

humus: decomposed animal or vegetable material in soil.

ingenuity: inventive or skillful.

inscrutable: in this context—inscrutable mud—not able to see through it; unfathomable.

interminably: seemingly unending.

lush: luxuriant, abundant vegetation.

metaphysical: abstract thought; sometimes refers to the supernatural.

menagerie: a collection of varied and usually unusual animals, though can refer to people or things.

morose: gloomy, sullen.

napalm: a jellylike, inflammable substance used in bombs.

nether: lower or under; below the surface.

ocelli: a simple eye or an eye-like spot as on a peacock's feathers.

parceled: a quantity or unit of something bundled or packaged up for sale.

portentous: ominous or threatening; momentous.

priapic: phallic, or penis-like.
perambulate: walk or stroll about.
rapidity: quickness.
recapitulate: to repeat in a summarized form.
ruminatively: to meditate or ponder.
stickler: perfectionist; an unyielding person.
untoward: improper; unfavorable or unfortunate.
vivacious: lively, spirited.
voracious: consuming large quantities, as in "voracious appetite" or "voracious reader."
wane: to fade or come near an ending; the moon wanes when it is past its full part.
wax: the period between the new and full moon.
Note: For pronunciation, go to dictionary.com, search the word, and click on the speaker icon.

USAGE Use three of the words from the list to describe an animal in one of the Writing Ideas or in Teaming Up #3.

Thinking and Talking Points

1. Hoagland uses **anthropomorphizing** (assigning human characteristics or personality traits to animals) of turtles throughout the essay. An example would be the quality of courage, a trait generally associated with humans. How do the turtles display courage? Locate other human characteristics like courage and then discuss why you think he relies so heavily on this technique.
2. Examine where Hoagland compares turtles to other animals. What is his purpose with these comparisons?
3. In addition to anthropomorphizing, Hoagland uses other style devices: simile, metaphor, vivid description, sentence variety—long, medium, and short sentences—and punctuation marks such as dashes and semicolons. Choose at least one of each style and discuss how the style enhances the essay.
4. Several stories—often compared to fables—concerning turtles connect to make a point in this essay. What do you think is the overall purpose? Identify the moral of each story and the order in which he arranges them. Discuss why he chooses to end the essay with the story of the Diamondback turtle.
5. What does the essay imply about human interference with animal habitat? Is there an environmental commentary embedded here?

Styling

Adding comparisons in the form of **simile** and **metaphor** to your essay helps your reader envision size, shape, swiftness, slowness, facial features—almost anything. It goes beyond mere description, elevating your writing to sharpness and clarity. Edward Hoagland, instead of using boring measurements for size, describes snapping turtles "as big as greeny wash basins" and a hatchling as "not as large as the top joint of my thumb." For other details, he describes baby turtles "as decorative as pansy petals," for movement "rolling like sailorly souls" and "hunch and ponderously lunge like a grizzly going forward." Students sometimes complain that they're not creative enough to write **figurative language**, but you can learn to write strong comparisons by using simple techniques and remembering a golden rule—if you've heard it before, don't use it. It has become a **cliché**. Strive for originality.

Here is how to get started. To describe, for example, how fast an animal moves, think of all the things that move swiftly and make a list: shooting stars, a magician's sleight of hand, bottle rockets, a jet fighter. The list could go on and on, but when choosing which comparison to use, think about the tone, the feeling you want the reader to experience about the animal. A shooting star might imply fading-into-the-background; a magician's sleight of hand may lend mystery; a jet fighter a fierce or battle-like tone; a bottle rocket, a sudden burst of speed. Then pick the best one and write a sentence about it. One student wrote about dolphins riding in the wake of the boat, "Suddenly, they were off like bottle rockets."

Practice

Think of an animal or person to write about. Make a list of features you'd like to describe. Following the instructions above, brainstorm a list for each feature. Then create a fill-in-the-blank comparison, something like the following:

As fast as (or as slow as) _____

A nose like _____

As big as (or as small as) _____

A body like (choose a shape to compare, for example a football)

_____

Don't limit yourself to these examples. Try to come up with some of your own.

YOU TRY IT Create sentences for each of your best comparisons. You might also try dropping *like* or *as* for a more direct metaphor.

Teaming Up

1. **Anthropomorphizing: Warm-up for Writing Idea #1:** In small groups (or as a class with the teacher writing suggestions on the board), brainstorm a list of human character—or personality—traits like humility, patience, greed. Write down at least twenty. Next, individually write a type of animal at the top of a sheet of paper. Take three minutes to write down any human character traits (you can use them from the list or create your own) that might be associated with that animal. At the end of three minutes, pass the paper to the right. Each person must then continue the list they have received. For the second round, work for two minutes. Repeat this process a third time, working for one minute. Give the list back to its original owner. Now each person has a brainstorming list to use for Writing Idea #1.

2. **Warm-up for Writing Ideas #2 and #3:** Each student brings one of *Aesop 's Fables* to class (available online with a Google search. Edu sites are best). In small groups, read each fable and choose one to present to the class. Identify and discuss the elements of fables listed in Writing Idea #3 and summarize and outline the chosen fable. Decide who will present which element to the class (each student should be responsible for at least one of the elements). For the presentation, each team member explains to the class how one element functions in the story. You might choose one student to summarize the story.

Writing Ideas

1. Research a wild animal you admire and write an essay that uses **anthropomorphizing** to humanize the creature. The essay can be humorous, mourn the plight of the animal, argue whether or not the animal should be kept as a pet (no giraffes, rhinos, or other animals that would not make reasonable pet choices; consider ferrets, snakes, racoons, wild birds, or other small creatures), or admire the animal's

ability to survive, either in the wild or in an environment encroached on by development.

2. Write an essay that uses a series of stories (from your own experience) with morals. Before writing, find a copy of *Aesop's Fables* (some available online) and read a few stories to help you understand the format. All stories should connect to illustrate an overall point. Be sure to use proper **transition**.

3. Write your own **fable** (a story where animals represent humans to teach lessons or morals concerning humans; "The Ant and the Grasshopper" in *Aesop's Fables* is a good example). Involve at least two animals using the elements of fables: characters and setting, action/dialogue, conflict, events that result from the conflict, and a moral. Read several fables—some available online—to warm-up.

Essay Connections

Several animal essays in *Sparks* include "Mute Dancers: How to Watch a Hummingbird" by Diane Ackerman, "Black Widow" by Gordon Grice, and "Joyas Voladoras" by Brian Doyle.

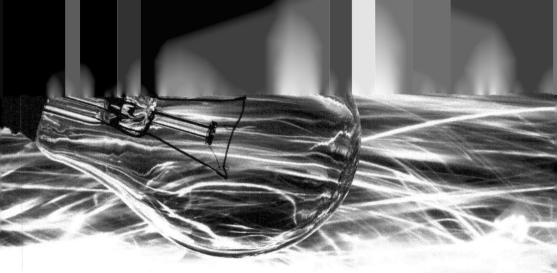

Contemplations: Essays that Explain and Explore

INTRODUCTION

Visit an art museum and gaze at a Jan Vermeer painting through David Huddle's eyes. Learn about the secret lives of hummingbirds with Diane Ackerman. Discover Music's healing power with Clayton Collins. Explore Hong Kong with Ken Chen. Get a new perspective on truth in Ruth Gendler's personification. Analyze two painter's views of children with John Updike. Crawl into the world of the black widow spider with Gordon Grice. In this section, writers attempt to explain some aspect of the world, from hair to hearts, naps to meditation.

These essays—like most—are hybrids, often blending rhetorical modes, not always fitting into a classic argument, narrative, definition, or other organizational box. Some contemplate, like Brian Doyle in "Joyas

Voladoras," a seemingly on-the-surface meditation of animal facts, but the heartbreaks in the conclusion give the piece another subtext to consider; others marvel at the wonder of nature while explaining its inner workings, as do Reg Saner in "A Tree Beyond Imagining" and Diane Ackerman in "Mute Dancers: How to Watch a Hummingbird"; John Updike amuses with his exploration of the male body, but at the end sobers with its allusions to death; Jack Kroll looks at our darker motivations for watching horror films in "Monster Mash." All analyze.

Trying to light some aspect of the complex world invites critical thinking, research, and rumination. Analysis, an important skill in college and throughout life, explores the many facets of a subject.

As you read, study how these writers organize their essays, but also pay attention to the thinking process evident in the writing. How do they arrive at their conclusions? What evidence do they use for support? *How* writers write is as important as what, so examine style—figurative language (metaphor, simile, personification), sentence variety, punctuation, transition. Studying others' writings teaches us by example how to become better writers and thinkers.

ON THE UNCERTAINTY OF THE FUTURE

Yoshida Kenko

In this short essay, Japanese poet, essayist, and Buddhist priest Yoshida Kenko (approximately 1283–1350) ruminates on how uncertainty, to some extent, controls our lives. Kenko, a prominent literary figure in his day, is still an important part of Japanese education.

1   You may intend to do something today, only for pressing business to come up unexpectedly and take up all of your attention the rest of the day. Or a person you have been expecting is prevented from coming, or someone you hadn't expected comes calling. The thing you have counted on goes amiss, and the thing you had no hopes for is the only one to succeed. A matter which promised to be a nuisance passes off smoothly, and a matter which should have been easy proves a great hardship. Our daily experiences bear no resemblance to what we had anticipated. This is true throughout the year, and equally true for our entire lives. But if we decide that everything is bound to go contrary to our anticipations, we discover that naturally there are also some things which do not contradict expectations. This makes it all the harder to be definite about anything. The one thing you can be certain of is the truth that all is uncertainty.

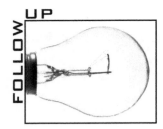

ON THE
UNCERTAINTY
OF THE FUTURE

Thinking and Talking Points

1. Summarize Kenko's purpose in this short meditation. What support does he use?
2. To what extent does the author think uncertainty plays a role in our lives?
3. How relevant is this essay to modern life? Give examples to support your view.
4. What point does the essay make about contrary expectations (expecting things will go wrong)?
5. What tone does Kenko take when addressing his readers? Study his **point of view** for help discerning his tone.

Teaming Up

1. Each member of the group make a list of expectations—things that you are reasonably certain will go smoothly. The list can be composed of anything from technology expectations (cell phones, computers, DVRs) to more meaningful expectations (medical test results, a job interview, a marriage proposal). Hand your list to the person on your right. Each person, on a scale of one to ten (ten being absolutely certain, one being will never happen) rate each item on the list. Discuss the results. Are the results in favor of optimism or pessimism?

2. **Warm-up for Writing Idea #1:** Individually, write a paragraph about a time you had an expectation that turned out the opposite, something you thought would happen but didn't (you can brainstorm ideas first with the group). After writing your paragraph, read them aloud and decide who has the best one to read to the class.

Writing Ideas

1. Write an essay about a time you had an expectation that turned out to be a disappointment (or a time you had a negative expectation that turned out positive). Describe the anticipation leading up to the expectation, the event itself, and your feelings afterward.

2. Compare the writing style and philosophy of Yoshida Kenko's essay to Thich Nhat Hanh's piece "Nourishing Awareness in Each Moment." Is there a similarity in the thought of these two Buddhists from very different time periods?

3. Write your own meditation on something from your daily life: an emotion (anger, joy, depression, grief, humility), a philosophy or belief (destiny, solitude, death), an institution (marriage, education, medicine), nature (many essays in the book provide examples of reflections on nature, and pair well with Thich Nhat Hanh's essay, "Nourishing Awareness in Each Moment").

Essay Connections

Thich Nhat Hanh's "Nourishing Awareness in Each Moment" (a rumination on television and mood by a modern Vietnamese monk) pairs up with Kenko's essay. Joseph Epstein's "The Culture of Celebrity" comments on our obsession with famous people, connecting to Hanh's piece. Many reflective nature essays appear in this book, teaming up with Hanh's ideas of solitude and meditation rather than noisy television that can affect mood.

MUSEUM PIECE

David Huddle

David Huddle is a university professor and writer of fiction and nonfiction. He's written a collection of essays titled "The Writing Habit" as well as a novella, three collections of poetry, and four collections of short stories. In this short piece, he describes three paintings by Jan Vermeer, focusing on "A Lady Writing," proclaiming, "All those art history courses, all these visits to the museum, attending lectures, reading catalogs: nothing teaches you just to look the way you're doing it now!"

DUSTBIN OF HISTORY AND CULTURE

JAN VERMEER: Dutch painter who lived from 1632–1675.
FEATHER QUILL: A feather with a hollow reed used as a pen.

1   Jan Vermeer's *The Girl with the Red Hat* always appealed to you because of that hat. Incredible scarlet aura spinning around her head like pure energy. Mouth open. Delicate coating of light that makes you think she's just licked her lips. Got to appreciate the composition. Lively and precise at the same time. The face of the girl isn't much. You like the look of her hat. You know it excites her to be wearing that hat. But there's nothing about the actual person. What she has to say wouldn't be much. Features are crude. Common girl all dressed up.

2   Another Vermeer here you've gotten to know. *Maiden with a Flute.* Little sister of *The Girl with the Red Hat.* Not nearly as flamboyant, but it's another composition that makes you smile. They're both paintings that have some wit.

3   This one day, instead of passing with a quick pause-and-look, the way you always have before—maybe because the room is empty, and you have plenty of time—you take one step closer to the third of those Vermeers: *A Lady Writing.* One step closer to a picture you've seen dozens of times before.

4   The lady of the picture isn't really writing. She's stopped writing. Her pen—it's a small feather quill—is still in place on the paper. Her other hand is holding the page down. She's just looked up. You've

interrupted her. Her face has this expression that is warm and so complex. But that expression is not for you—it's left over from the moment before she saw you. She looks that way because of whatever it was she was writing. It has to be a letter: this lady is writing to her good friend—or maybe to her sister—about something that really pleases her. You wonder what it could be. You can almost sense the pleasure flying away from her as she stops her writing.

5   She isn't beautiful. The way her hair is fixed, it looks like she's put it up in curlers. But you get her whole life out of this picture. All those art history courses, all these visits to the museum, attending lectures, reading catalogs: nothing teaches you just to look the way you're doing it now! Thousands of days of this lady's living click into this single instant. Across three hundred years of time, she looks you straight in the eyes. *Look,* she says. *Go ahead and look. My life feels to me the same as yours feels to you—so full I could burst with it. Please let me get back to my letter. You go on with whatever you're doing out there in the twentieth century.*

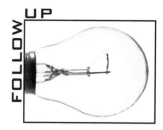

MUSEUM PIECE

Thinking and Talking Points

1. Study the painting of *A Lady Writing* (available online), and then reread Huddle's description. What is your reaction? Is it similar to Huddle's or do you have a different response?
2. As a student, you've probably been told to avoid "you" when writing essays. Why do you think Huddle uses "you" to address the reader? In what situations might it be acceptable to address the reader so casually?
3. Huddle breaks another general writing rule: don't use sentence **fragments**. Sometimes, though, fragments can work to the writer's advantage. Examine the fragments. Why do you think Huddle uses them?
4. In the last paragraph, what point does Huddle make about enjoying versus studying paintings? Rewrite his point in your own words. What other subjects might apply to his point?

CAUTION While writers often use **fragments** for a particular effect, I caution beginning writers against using them until they have mastered **complete sentences**.

Styling

This short essay pops with style, making it difficult to focus on just one technique. In addition to breaking writing rules in favor of style, Huddle also uses **simile**: "Incredible scarlet aura spinning around her head like pure energy." His detailed descriptions and lively word choices draw you into the essay. But look more closely at how he uses dashes (—), a writing tool that students aren't often taught. Dashes can be used in place of commas around groups of words called **interrupters** because they interrupt the main sentence to add information or detail:

> Her pen—it's a small feather quill—is still in place on the paper.

Huddle could write, "Her pen is still in place on the paper." The clause "it's a small feather quill" interrupts the main sentence with extra information. The writer could use commas or parentheses instead of dashes, but he chose the stronger dashes to draw attention to the feather quill. Study the other dashes in the essay. Notice that dashes can also be used to set off a phrase, clause, or another sentence at the end of a sentence.

SAMPLE SENTENCE WITH DASHES   The Okapi—like a creature out of a fairy tale—is an animal that looks half giraffe, half zebra.

PRACTICE   Fill in the blank between the dashes with a descriptive or informational phrase.

The child— _____ —shoved cake into her mouth.

YOU TRY IT   Create three sentences of your own using dashes. It might help to write a simple sentence first, inserting the interrupting words and dashes later.

Tip: parentheses whisper, commas talk, dashes shout.

Teaming Up

1. Bring to class a picture of a painting or other artwork that appeals to you. One place to look is the Metropolitan Museum website—you can visit almost any museum online and print pictures. Before coming to class, **freewrite** about the picture. What does the picture make you think about? What feeling do you get from looking at it? What details stand out the most? Group up in teams of three to five members. Pass the pictures to the right. Study the picture and freewrite about it. Pass pictures to the right and freewrite two more times so that each person has written about three pictures plus his or her own. Pull out the freewrite written at home. Group all of the freewrites with the picture they are about. Read the freewrites and discuss the reactions. What details or reactions seem to be the same in the majority of freewrites? Did feelings differ significantly on the same picture? Which picture got the most varied reactions?

2. Go to the library (or search the online databases) and find art criticism on some of Jan Vermeer's paintings. You'll find books on art criticism in the reference section as well as the regular book stacks. Sister Wendy's criticisms of art are a good place to start—her writing is not muddled with overblown language. If you have trouble finding an article, ask the librarian. In groups, read the criticisms and compare them to Huddle's essay. Which piece did you enjoy the most? Which one gives the most insight into the painting? Study the style in each

article. Do the writers of these articles use strong style, as Huddle did?

CAUTION Avoid the Web when looking for criticism. The Web is full of dubious articles. You can search for hours without finding anything. You're better off visiting the library at your college or in your community or accessing a reputable library's online databases.

Writing Ideas

1. Find a painting or photograph of an historical event: *Third of May* by Francisco Goya; *Washington Crossing the Delaware* by Emanuel Gottlieb Leutze; *Death of Socrates* by Jacques-Louis David. You can also use photographs—try visiting an online photography exhibit or a book like the *History of Rock and Roll;* possibilities are endless. Next, study the picture and imagine yourself there: sights, sounds, smells, feelings, tastes. Choose a point of view: who will you be, an observer of the scene or one of the characters in the picture? Be sure to look up the historical facts. Facts must be accurate, but you can invent the sensory details. Now, write an essay narrating the event. Stick to the picture as much as possible. Practice using dashes.

2. Browse through some art books and choose an artist who interests you. Choose three paintings by the same artist. Following Huddle's model, write an essay discussing the three paintings. Notice that Huddle saves the painting that he most strongly reacts to discuss last, spending two full paragraphs on it. Use **simile** and strong description.

3. Find a painting—a portrait—of a person who seems to be speaking to you. You can use the website or visit the library. After studying the portrait, write an essay using details to describe the painting and what you imagine the person is thinking. Write in the present tense and address the reader as "you."

Essay Connections

John Updike's essay "American Children," like Huddle's essay, analyzes art in an easy-to-understand manner.

NOURISHING AWARENESS IN EACH MOMENT

Thich Nhat Hanh

Spiritual leader and Zen monk Thich Nhat Hanh has many achievements: he founded a Buddhist university in Vietnam and a social services school for youth, taught at the Sorbonne and Columbia University, chaired the Buddhist delegation in the Paris Peace Talks, was nominated by Martin Luther King Jr. for the Nobel Peace Price, has helped refugees all over the world, founded a meditation in south of France (where he lives as an exile from his native country), and written many books on Buddhist thought and meditation, including The Art of Power, Anger, The Miracle of Mindfulness, and Peace is Every Step, where "Nourishing Awareness in Each Moment" appears. In this essay, he wonders why people will watch bad television programs rather than cherish solitude, believing that when we watch bad television, "we become the TV program."

1   One cold, winter evening I returned home from a walk in the hills, and I found that all the doors and windows in my hermitage had blown open. When I had left earlier, I hadn't secured them, and a cold wind had blown through the house, opened the windows, and scattered the papers from my desk all over the room. Immediately, I closed the doors and windows, lit a lamp, picked up the papers, and arranged them neatly on my desk. Then I started a fire in the fireplace, and soon the crackling logs brought warmth back to the room.

2   Sometimes in a crowd we feel tired, cold, and lonely. We may wish to withdraw to be by ourselves and become warm again, as I did when I closed the windows and sat by the fire, protected from the damp, cold wind. Our senses are our windows to the world, and sometimes the wind blows through them and disturbs everything within us. Some of us leave our windows open all the time, allowing the sights and sounds of the world to invade us, penetrate us, and expose our sad, troubled selves. We feel so cold, lonely, and afraid. Do you ever find yourself watching an awful TV program, unable to turn it off? The raucous noises, explosions of gunfire, are upsetting. Yet you don't get up and turn it off. Why do you torture yourself in this way? Don't you want to close your windows? Are you frightened of soli-

tude—the emptiness and the loneliness you may find when you face yourself alone?

3   Watching a bad TV program, we *become* the TV program. We are what we feel and perceive. If we are angry, we are the anger. If we are in love, we are love. If we look at a snow-covered mountain peak, we are the mountain. We can be anything we want, so why do we open our windows to bad TV programs made by sensationalist producers in search of easy money, programs that make our hearts pound, our fists tighten, and leave us exhausted? Who allows such TV programs to be made and seen by even the very young? We do! We are too undemanding, too ready to watch whatever is on the screen, too lonely, lazy, or bored to create our own lives. We turn on the TV and leave it on, allowing someone else to guide us, shape us, and destroy us. Losing ourselves in this way is leaving our fate in the hands of others who may not be acting responsibly. We must be aware of which programs do harm to our nervous systems, minds, and hearts, and which programs benefit us.

4   Of course, I am not talking only about television. All around us, how many lures are set by our fellows and ourselves? In a single day, how many times do we become lost and scattered because of them? We must be very careful to protect our fate and our peace. I am not suggesting that we just shut all our windows, for there are many miracles in the world we call "outside." We can open our windows to these miracles and look at any one of them with awareness. This way, even while sitting beside a clear, flowing stream, listening to beautiful music, or watching an excellent movie, we need not lose ourselves entirely in the stream, the music, or the film. We can continue to be aware of ourselves and our breathing. With the sun of awareness shining in us, we can avoid most dangers. The stream will be purer, the music more harmonious, and the soul of the filmmaker completely visible.

5   As beginning meditators, we may want to leave the city and go off to the countryside to help close those windows that trouble our spirit. There we can become one with the quiet forest, and rediscover and restore ourselves, without being swept away by the chaos of the "outside world." The fresh and silent woods help us remain in awareness, and when our awareness is well-rooted and we can maintain it without faltering, we may wish to return to the city and remain there, less troubled. But sometimes we cannot leave the city, and we have to find the refreshing and peaceful elements that can heal us right in

the midst of our busy lives. We may wish to visit a good friend who can comfort us, or go for a walk in a park and enjoy the trees and the cool breeze. Whether we are in the city, the countryside, or the wilderness, we need to sustain ourselves by choosing our surroundings carefully and nourishing our awareness in each moment.

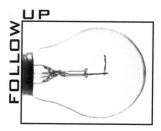
Exploring Language

hermitage: a place where one can live in solitude; a retreat.
raucous: rough-sounding, harsh.
Note: For pronunciation, go to dictionary.com, search the word, and click on the speaker icon.

USAGE Use *raucous* in a sentence to describe one of the following: laughter, sporting event, specific television program, particular music or song, or something mechanical (for example, a machine, tool, or musical instrument).

Thinking and Talking Points

1. Hanh writes, "Sometimes in a crowd we feel tired, cold, and lonely." What evidence does he give for this statement? How do you interpret his statement?
2. Another statement Hanh writes, "Our senses are our windows to the world, and sometimes the wind blows through them and disturbs everything within us," is a **metaphor** (see the glossary). Explain the comparison. What other metaphors does he use?
3. What connection does he make between our fear of solitude and bad television programs? Do you agree that bad television programs affect our mood? How might it negatively "guide us, shape us, and destroy us"? Are some people afraid of being alone and need noise to distract them? What do you think they fear?
4. Bad television, according to Hanh, is not the only thing that affects our mood. What other "lures" do you think pull us away from "ourselves"? What examples does he mention?
5. What solution does Hanh propose to the problem he presents? Do you agree or disagree with his ideas? Provide evidence to support your view.

Styling

This essay uses several thought-provoking questions that speak directly to the reader. Though often students are taught not to use questions, this style—when done well—can create moments of hesitation, causing the reader to think and attempt to answer.

In paragraph #2, Hanh writes, "Do you ever find yourself watching an awful TV program, unable to turn it off?" and, "Why do you torture yourself this way? Don't you want to close your windows? Are you frightened of solitude—the emptiness and loneliness you may find when you face yourself alone?"

Hanh asks questions that he believes most people will—if they're honest with themselves—have to answer yes. Notice that the first question asks something that most of us have found ourselves doing, so we nod, almost smiling in agreement. But the second question catches us off guard: we've probably not thought of it as torturing ourselves. The question stops us momentarily, making us wonder why we watch such bad programs. It's a gentle reprimand. The third question, "Don't you want to close your windows?" applies to an earlier metaphor of the senses being windows to the world; in other words, he's asking, "Don't you want to stop the torture?" The final question gets to the heart of his point: we're afraid of solitude, of being alone with ourselves, so we'll use any device to distract us from ourselves. These statements wear a costume, disguised as questions.

PRACTICE   Make a list of other negative behaviors people participate in to ward off loneliness or to procrastinate.

YOU TRY IT   Take one behavior from your list and create a series of thought-provoking questions that are really statements in disguise. Follow the above example, building your questions to a conclusion about the behavior.

Teaming Up

1. **Warm-up for Writing Idea #1:** The Styling makes a good Teaming Up activity. Make a group brainstorming list; select one item and have each member of the team write as many questions as possible in five minutes. Next, read all of the questions and decide which ones to use to create the Styling paragraph. Build your questions to a conclusion about the behavior.

2. **Warm-up for Writing Idea #2:** As a group, brainstorm a list of television programs that you consider bad by Hanh's standards. Next to each one, write why you think each program has a negative impact. Co-write a paragraph about these programs, describing the programs and their effects, and attempt to explain why you watch them.

Writing Ideas

1. Write an essay that explores another distraction people use as an avoidance technique. Examine the causes (what, how, and why people are avoiding) and effects (what long-term harm this behavior does to the individual or to others). Some examples might be the boss who never delegates (or delegates too much), a sibling who avoids family confrontations, or the spouse or partner who always agrees or backs down to avoid conflict.
2. Write an essay about the effect of bad television programs on our minds and moods. Explore and explain why people watch such programs and how they're harmful (or write a defense of such programs).
3. Compare the style and Buddhist thought in Hanh's essay to Yoshida Kenko's "On the Uncertainty of the Future." Though of vastly different centuries, what do these two essays have in common?

Essay Connections

Yoshida Kenko's "On the Uncertainty of the Future" is an obvious choice. Another commentary on modern life is Joseph Epstein's "The Culture of Celebrity."

TRUTH

J. Ruth Gendler

Multifaceted—artist, teacher, author—J. Ruth Gendler, in addition to her numerous poems, essays, and nationally exhibited artwork, has written three books: Notes on the Need for Beauty, Changing Light: The Eternal Cycle of Night and Day, and The Book of Qualities where she personifies 100 human emotions in sometimes humorous and often close-to-the-bone ways.

1   Truth is tall and rather unconventional looking. He has golden hair and a short beard. He does not like statistics and is not particularly concerned about fact, but he loves a good story. He chronicled the contemporary film scene for a while. He quit when his reviews started being quoted out of context. Though he never hides what he feels, by nature he is gentle and not at all sarcastic. However, he does have a fierce temper. He has observed that people who only listen with one ear when he says something in a kind way are always impressed by his anger.

2   Truth has been employed as a thief stealing illusions. He can climb over any security fence we have constructed to keep out disturbing influences. Although he can unlock any window or door, he is no longer interested in breaking in or getting away. No longer thrilled by the chase nor by defying authorities, he has given up on the challenge of trying to find new ways to escape.

3   X-rays, photographs of cells, and the history of plants fascinate Truth. When Truth's fingers touch my shoulder, I hear bone touching bone. Truth has set down his bundle of needs, and his shoulders are soft and spacious, outlined by light.

4   Truth learned to act in the theater of qualities, and his studies in mime continue. He lingers in the long pauses between the questions and the answers. He has made an altar to his loneliness. Certainty and Uncertainty are both welcome at his table. Truth is willing to wait for a long time with little attentions or visible encouragement. Truth is not willing to live without Love.

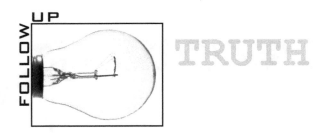

Thinking and Talking Points

1. Gendler writes that Truth is unconventional looking, isn't concerned much with facts, but "he loves a good story." How do these details make the reader think about truth in a new way? Explain the implications of these details.

2. Examine Truth's jobs—reviewing contemporary film, a thief stealing illusions, and acting and studying mime: how are these jobs appropriate for this quality? Reread the paragraphs that include his employment and then explain the implied meaning.

3. Why might Truth be fascinated by "X-rays, photographs of cells, and the history of plants"?

4. Why might people construct a security fence to keep out a "disturbing influence" like Truth?

5. Why would Truth make "an altar to his loneliness" and welcome Certainty and Uncertainty at his table?

Styling

Gendler's *personification* of truth shows the many sides of this quality, the ways we twist it, often not welcoming it for forcing reality. In other personifications in her book, Gendler has Rage as Depression's only friend, and Confusion is Patience's nephew; Doubt camps out in the living room; Patience "carries sacks of peace and purses filled with small treasures." She develops each quality into a mini story, revealing often-not-thought-about aspects of the word.

PRACTICE Choose an emotion or human personality trait to personify and freewrite for five minutes, focusing on other feelings that might occur with the trait like depression with anger, fear and anxiety, or guilt with manipulation. Decide on gender, what the word might look like, what jobs or hobbies it might have, what its favorite food might be, where it hangs out. Use the other qualities as friends or relatives (see the "Introductions" section of your text for a list to get started).

YOU TRY IT   Write a one to two paragraph personification using your ideas from the practice. Capitalize each of the qualities used as characters, like a proper name, and avoid using the word to describe itself (for example, don't write that Depression is depressed).

Teaming Up

1. Each person in the group answers the "Thinking and Talking Points." Compare answers and discuss differing opinions.

2. Do the Styling as a group, choosing one quality to develop together. Brainstorm ideas and decide which ones to use. Co-write a paragraph.

Writing Ideas

1. Use the Styling as an introduction to a larger definition essay. The rest of the essay should use the "Strategies for Defining Terms," perhaps building a paragraph around each strategy.
2. Use personification to write an essay defining a human quality or emotion. Sustain the personification throughout, but try to blend the "Strategies for Defining Terms" into the personification.

Essay Connections

Joseph Epstein's "The Culture of Celebrity" clarifies the difference between fame and celebrity, a good essay for modeling definition strategies, as does "On the Content of Our Character" by Shelby Steele. "A Tree Beyond Imagining" uses personification, and "The Courage of Turtles" **anthropomorphizes**.

MUTE DANCERS

How to Watch a Hummingbird

Diane Ackerman

Diane Ackerman's fascination with nature and the senses combine in this essay. Using mythology and fact, she heightens the reader's awareness of the wonder of hummingbirds. She's the author of "A Natural History of the Senses," a national bestseller made into a PBS special.

DUSTBIN OF HISTORY AND CULTURE

BELTANE: Ancient Celtic feast/celebration with bonfires and rites of purification observed in May.

LI'L ABNER: A comic strip by cartoonist Al Capp introduced in 1934 and continuing until 1977. The strip satirically commented on public figures and current events through hillbilly characters in a place called Dogpatch.

NORTHERN LIGHTS: A spectacular atmospheric light show also known as the aurora borealis or polar lights. Lights of various hues shift and dance.

1   A lot of hummingbirds die in their sleep. Like a small fury of iridescence, a hummingbird spends the day at high speed, darting and swiveling among thousands of nectar-rich blossoms. Hummingbirds have huge hearts and need colossal amounts of energy to fuel their flights, so they live in a perpetual mania to find food. They tend to prefer red, trumpet-shaped flowers, in which nectar thickly oozes, and eat every 15 minutes or so. A hummingbird drinks with a W-shaped tongue, licking nectar up as a cat might (but faster). Like a tiny drum roll, its heart beats at 500 times a minute. Frighten a hummingbird and its heart can race to over 1,200 times a minute. Feasting and flying, courting and dueling, hummingbirds consume life at a fever pitch. No warm-blooded animal on earth uses more energy, for its size. But that puts them at great peril. By day's end, wrung-out and exhausted, a hummingbird rests near collapse.

2   In the dark night of the hummingbird, it can sink into a zombielike state of torpor; its breathing grows shallow and its wild heart slows to only 36 beats a minute. When dawn breaks on the fuchsia

and columbine, hummingbirds must jump-start their hearts and fire up their flight muscles to raise their body temperature for another all-or-nothing day. That demands a colossal effort, which some can't manage. So a lot of hummingbirds die in their sleep.

3   But most do bestir themselves. This is why, in American Indian myths and legends, hummingbirds are often depicted as resurrection birds, which seem to die and be reborn on another day or in another season. The Aztec god of war was named Huitzilopochtli, a compound word meaning "shining one with weapon like cactus thorn," and "sorcerer that spits fire." Aztec warriors fought, knowing that if they fell in battle they would be reincarnated as glittery, thuglike hummingbirds. The male birds were lionized for their ferocity in battle. And their feathers flashed in the sun like jewel-encrusted shields. Aztec rulers donned ceremonial robes of hummingbird feathers. As they walked, colors danced across their shoulders and bathed them in a supernatural light show.

4   While most birds are busy singing a small operetta of who and what and where, hummingbirds are virtually mute. Such small voices don't carry far, so they don't bother much with song. But if they can't serenade a mate, or yell war cries at a rival, how can they perform the essential dramas of their lives? They dance. Using body language, they spell out their intentions and moods, just as bees, fireflies or hula dancers do. That means elaborate aerial ballets in which males twirl, joust, sideswipe and somersault. Brazen and fierce, they will take on large adversaries—even cats, dogs or humans.

5   My neighbor Persis once told me how she'd been needled by hummingbirds. When Persis lived in San Francisco, hummingbirds often attacked her outside her apartment building. From their perspective she was on *their* property, not the other way round, and they flew circles around her to vex her away. My encounters with hummingbirds have been altogether more benign. Whenever I've walked through South American rain forests, with my hair braided and secured by a water-proof red ribbon, hummingbirds have assumed my ribbon to be a succulent flower and have probed my hair repeatedly, searching for nectar. Their touch was as delicate as a sweat bee's. But it was their purring by my ear that made me twitch. In time, they would leave unfed, but for a while I felt like a character in a Li'l Abner cartoon who could be named something like "Hummer." In Portuguese, the word for hummingbird (*Beija flor*) means "flower kisser." It was the American colonists who first imagined the birds humming as they went about their chores.

6   Last summer, the historical novelist Jeanne Mackin winced to see her cat, Beltane, drag in voles, birds and even baby rabbits. Few things can compete with the blood lust of a tabby cat. But one day Beltane dragged in something rare and shimmery—a struggling hummingbird. The feathers were ruffled and there was a bit of blood on the breast, but the bird still looked perky and alive. So Jeanne fashioned a nest for it out of a small wire basket lined in gauze, and fed it sugar water from an eye dropper. To her amazement, as she watched, "it miscarried a little pearl." Hummingbird eggs are the size of coffee beans, and females usually carry two. So Jeanne knew one might still be safe inside. After a quiet night, the hummingbird seemed stronger, and when she set the basket outside at dawn, the tiny assault victim flew away.

7   It was a ruby-throated hummingbird that she nursed, the only one native to the East Coast. In the winter they migrate thousands of miles over mountains and open water to Mexico and South America. She may well have been visited by a species known to the Aztecs. Altogether, there are 16 species of hummingbirds in North America, and many dozens in South America, especially near the equator, where they can feed on a buffet of blossoms. The tiniest—the Cuban bee hummingbird—is the smallest warm-blooded animal in the world. About two and one-eighth inches long from beak to tail, it is smaller than the toe of an eagle, and its eggs are like seeds.

8   Hummingbirds are a New World phenomenon. So, too, is vanilla, and their stories are linked. When the early explorers returned home with the riches of the West, they found it impossible, to their deep frustration, to grow vanilla beans. It took ages before they discovered why—that hummingbirds were a key pollinator of vanilla orchids— and devised beaklike splinters of bamboo to do the work of birds.

9   Now that summer has come at last, lucky days may be spent watching the antics of hummingbirds. The best way to behold them is to stand with the light behind you, so that the bird faces the sun. Most of the trembling colors aren't true pigments, but the result of light staggering through clear cells that act as prisms. Hummingbirds are iridescent for the same reason soap bubbles are. Each feather contains tiny air bubbles separated by dark spaces. Light bounces off the air bubbles at different angles, and that makes blazing colors seem to swarm and leap. All is vanity in the end. The male's shimmer draws a female to mate. But that doesn't matter much to gardeners, watching hummingbirds patrol the impatiens as if the northern lights had suddenly fallen to earth.

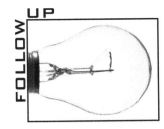

FOLLOW UP

MUTE
DANCERS

Exploring Language

benign: gentle, kind.

bestir: get moving. Impress your friends with this one by saying, "Bestir yourself," instead of "Hey, get off the couch, let's go."

colossal: huge, enormous. A good word to replace humongous, which has been banished to the realm of slang.

iridescence: glistening, shimmering, rainbow colors that change with movement. Use *iridescence, glisten,* or *shimmer* in one of the Writing Ideas below.

mania: enthusiasm taken to the extreme; can also refer to a mental illness.

torpor: sluggishness; couch-potato mode.

voles: small rodents resembling rats or mice but with shorter tails and limbs and heavier bodies.

wince: to flinch or draw back as if in pain.

Note: For pronunciation, go to dictionary.com, search the word, and click on the speaker icon.

USAGE   See *bestir, colossal, iridescence.*

Thinking and Talking Points

1. Though the essay is subtitled "How to Watch a Hummingbird," Ackerman gives very little advice on how to watch these creatures. How, then, does the essay teach you to watch hummingbirds?

2. Ackerman uses lively **verbs** in her essay to create action, words like *jump-start* and *fire up* (paragraph #2) and *needled* (paragraph #5). Find other action words in the essay and discuss their effectiveness. Try changing these words to more common ones, *needled* to *bothered,* for example. Does the essay lose anything by these changes?

3. Ackerman uses **simile** and **metaphor** to give spark to her essay: "And their feathers flashed in the sun like jewel-encrusted shields" (paragraph #3). Go on a hunt for other similes and metaphors and make a list. Discuss why metaphor might be an important style tool in aca-

demic essays—a research paper, for example—rather than just poetry and other fiction. For more on **figurative language**, see the Styling section with "Musical Awakenings."

4. Ackerman writes that hummingbirds communicate through dance, "they spell out their intentions and moods just as bees, fireflies or hula dancers do." What other creatures communicate silently? In what ways do humans communicate nonverbally?

5. What is Ackerman's purpose for writing this essay? Is it merely to inform, or can you find another reason? State her purpose in your own words.

Styling

Many writers use this easy-to-model sentence style.

> Feasting and flying, courting and dueling, hummingbirds consume life at a fever pitch.

Ackerman introduces her complete sentence—*hummingbirds consume life at a fever pitch*—with two sets of words that describe *how* the hummingbirds consume life. She links two words ending in *ing* with *and*: *feasting* and *flying.* Then she uses a comma followed by two more words ending in *ing: courting* and *dueling.* Notice the comma before the beginning of the complete sentence (beginning with *hummingbirds*). Also notice that the words linked with *and* go together in some way: feasting and flying both begin with *f.* Courting and dueling, while seemingly opposite activities, often connect in the animal world as males duke it out for the attention of a female.

   Note: This type of sentence is called a **periodic sentence**.

PRACTICE   Fill in the blanks with two sets of words ending with *ing.*

_____ and _____, _____ and _____, the cat tortured the mouse.

_____ and _____, _____ and _____, the dancer charmed the audience.

YOU TRY IT   Now write three sentences of your own in the above style. Use this technique in your next essay.

Teaming Up

1. Bring in pictures of animals (the more unusual the better). Form groups of three to five students and study the pictures. Choose one you're all familiar with or find intriguing. Brainstorm a list of characteristics unique to that creature. For ideas, reread Ackerman's piece or visit the Natural History Museum website and click on *Amazing Facts*. Next, co-write a riddle paragraph, using the characteristics as clues, saving the more obvious hints for the end. You can write from the first person point of view—*I*—or the third person—*he, she, it.* Here's an example of a riddle by bird writer George Hollister:

   > He's half tail and half feet. The rest of him is head and beak. When he runs, he moves on blurring wheels. He can turn on a dime and leave change. He doesn't need to fly because he can run faster. He kicks dirt in a snake's face, and then eats the snake.

   You'd want to reveal the answer—a roadrunner—at the end of the riddle. Notice that Hollister uses short sentences and metaphoric language while saving the more obvious clue—he doesn't need to fly because he can run faster—for near the end.

   After you've written your riddle, read it to the rest of the class and let them guess. Use this technique in one of the Writing Ideas below. Riddles work nicely as introductions to essays. (For more on how to write riddles, see the "Masquerading" section in *Adios, Strunk and White*—where the roadrunner riddle appears—by Gary and Glynis Hoffman, available through Amazon.com.)

2. In your group, discuss the controversy surrounding animals and emotions: to what extent do animals have feelings? What is your own experience? If there are any vegetarians in the group, have their experiences with animals influenced their decision to give up meat?

Writing Ideas

1. Observe an animal closely—a bird, an insect (you can sometimes buy a praying mantis at the local plant nursery), an animal at a zoo—and take notes about the animal's behavior. Write an essay explaining how to watch this animal. If necessary, look up information about the creature's behavior.

2. Choose a bird you think interesting or unusual. Research and write an essay which attempts to answer this question: what problem or problems did adaptation or evolution help the bird solve? For example,

Ackerman explains how hummingbirds solved the problem of being mute (see paragraph #14). Use a riddle introduction (see Teaming Up activity #1) to hook the reader.

3. Ackerman mentions that hummingbirds are often depicted as resurrection birds in mythology. Explore another animal that's often represented in myth or legend. For example, Native American myths and legends often depict eagles and wolves. Read the myth and then look up scientific information on the animal. Write an essay which attempts to explain—as Ackerman does—why the animal achieved its mythic or legendary status.

Essay Connections

Several animal-themed essays include "The Courage of Turtles" by Edward Hoagland; "Black Widow" by Gordon Corice; "Joyas Voladoras" by Brian Doyle.

FROM "THE SURFING SAVANT"

Paul Solotaroff

Paul Solotaroff is a contributing editor to Rolling Stone *and* Men's Journal, *with articles appearing in* Vanity Fair, GQ, Vogue, *and* The New York Times Magazine. *Books include* The House of Purple Hearts *(1995),* Group *(1999), and his latest,* The Body Shop *(2010), a memoir chronicling his use of steroids in the 1970's. His writing has also appeared several times in* Best American Sports Writing. *"The Surfing Savant," first published in* Rolling Stone *in 2010 and the 2011 edition of* Best American Sports Writing, *tells the story of surfing champion Clay Marzo and his struggle with Asperger's syndrome, a high-functioning form of autism.*

DUSTBIN OF HISTORY AND CULTURE

CHA CHA: a Latin ballroom dance with a quick three-step movement.

SHAUN WHITE: American champion snowboarder and two-time Olympic gold medalist.

1   Put him in the water and Clay Marzo is magic, a kid with so much grace and daring that you laugh in disbelief to watch him surf. Every day he's out there in the South Pacific, shredding huge swells till he's faint with hunger and near the verge of dehydration. He doesn't really ride waves as much as fly them, soaring above the sea foam upside down and spinning the nose of his board in whiplash twists. Just two years out of high school, Marzo is remaking a sport held hostage by rules and hack judges, turning it into a cross between aquatic parkour and X Games stunt work. Call it what you want, it's a sight to behold. *Sorry, but humans can't do that*, you keep thinking. Then he goes and does it all morning long.

2   But if you sit and list the things that Marzo has trouble doing, they quickly outrun the things he finds easy. He's unable, for instance, to eat a simple meal without much of it ending up on his shirt or the floor. Out of water, he has trouble interacting with other people, either staring in bafflement at their grins and jokes or avoiding casual contact altogether. He blurts things out, chants rap songs to himself, and pulls out clumps of his hair when anxious. When he speaks, which isn't often, he seems younger than his 20 years, mumbling like a bash-

ful eighth-grader. For years, the rap on Marzo has been that, for all his talents, he's a pothead who chokes in competitions. And then there are the even-nastier names he's had to deal with, slurs that burned deep: retard, moron, slacker, zombie. In middle school, Marzo was treated so badly that his mother, Jill, had to pull him out and teach him at home, where he wouldn't be punched for staring at wannabe thugs. His agonizing shyness has fractured his family and sparked ugly set-tos with his father, Gino, an old-school hard-hat striver who accused him of flaking off and screwing up his shot at stardom. That charge hurts Clay more than the others combined: when your own father misconceives you so badly, how can you hope that strangers will understand?

3   Now, pushing back from lunch at a Maui fish stand, bits of ahi po'boy dotting his face and lap, Marzo wears the grin of a birthday boy who gets to eat as much cake as he wants. To see him like this, hands clasped across his belly, is to encounter a kid whose first and last directive is pure, physical joy. But the facts are more complex and less happy. Marzo has Asperger's syndrome, a form of high-functioning autism that causes no end of social confusion and anguish, and that commonly burdens those afflicted with a single, smothering obsession: bird songs or train routes or the history of naval warfare. "Though Asberger's teens are typically bright and verbal, they can't connect with kids their age or with people they don't know well," says Dr. Michael Linden, an autism specialist who diagnosed Marzo at the age of 18, after a dozen years of botched assessments. "Feelings are a foreign language to them, and they're unable to pick up social cues. A lot of them retreat from relationships and get stuck in a special activity or interest that they devote themselves to intensely."

4   Like a lot of adult Aspies, as some with the diagnosis have taken to calling themselves, Marzo is a baffling mix of powers and deficits. He has no interest in the written word (and has read few of the dozens of stories about him in sports magazines, which regularly anoint him one of surfing's saviors) but is brilliant, even clairvoyant, in the water. Looking at the horizon, Marzo can read waves that others can't and intuit where they'll break before they crest. Traveling fills him with such dread that he's sick with nausea days before boarding a plane, but he gets up each day and surfs lethal points on Maui's western shore. The kinds of waves he lives on don't crash near sandy beaches; instead, he climbs down lava cliffs to reach breaks rife with boulders and a seafloor of spear-tipped coral reefs that can turn a surfer's chest

to chum. His body is a travelogue of scars and welts, but it bores him to talk about the dangers he courts—the boards he routinely snaps taking hellish falls; the waves that hold him down till his lungs scream, half a minute or more during really heavy sets. Only once, he says, has he been afraid of the surf. "There were tiger sharks behind me," he says, wiping a quarter-size splotch of mayo off his cheek. "They were pretty big, so I bailed quick."

5   After lunch, Marzo pays a visit to Adam Klevin, a muscular, bald-shaved man who's seen more of Clay in water than anyone besides his mother. For the past five years, Klevin has risen at dawn to film every wave that Marzo catches and compile the highlights. Today, on one of the flatscreens in the unkempt room that Klevin uses as an editing suite, Marzo is up and riding a 12-foot swell. Dancing on the wave front with cha-cha turns that brace him for a bigger move, he whips the back of the board into a savage 360 that surfers call a throw-tail reverse. It's a common trick, but there are few people on the planet who can successfully nail it in Maui after a recent storm has raised waves the size of houses. Marzo is barely upright as he exits the spin, his mouth a perfect O of exaltation. He bangs a hard left into the next section of wave and throws a front-side snap that lifts him clean out of the water, arms and knees in vehement opposition. He can't possibily make it—his rear end's gone, and God knows what he's looking at over his shoulder as he grabs the rail of the board for dear life. The wave collapses on the jagged floor, blowing up a squall of white-capped spray in which the boy and board go missing. For a moment there's nothing, just the chaos of foam. Then the chop parts, and here he somehow comes, half off the board but still in charge. This isn't surfing, this is sorcery, a kid so alive and electrically good that he makes this look like the world's one true religion.

6   But when I turn to say as much, Marzo is somewhere else, head down and eyes fixed on some inner shore. He has everything he needs to be his sport's Shaun White—the face, the body, the game-changing skill—and a chance to be a beacon for the 1.5 million kids in this country with autism-related disorders. But Marzo has neither the drive nor the nervous system to handle being famous. No, if it's all the same, he'd rather be alone, paddling back out, through the churn and boulders, to where the big waves break. It's the one place on Earth he feels safe.

7   For an island synonymous with God-sent waves and the goofy-foot cool of surf kitsch, Maui has produced shockingly few riders driven enough to compete with the sport's name-brand stars. "There's

a small-tow vibe here that's held guys back when they surfed the bigger stages," says Erik Aeder, a surf photographer and Maui native who has shot every local kid who showed much promise. "Plus, the trade winds make the waves choppy, which made it hard to learn the elegant moves that used to win tournaments."

8   But in the late eighties, a new breed of riders stood the game on end. Inspired by the halfpipe pyrotechnics of skate and snowboarders, surfers like Kelly Slater and Christian Fletcher started to approach waves differently, shooting over the top of the lip, using the wave's speed to do airs and inverts and sudden, violent turns. "Those guys made their style a global phenomenon through videos and photo spreads," says Matt Warshaw, author of the forthcoming *The History of Surfing* and former editor of *Surfer* magazine. "Kids everywhere went to school on their hi-fi moves, and that next generation went bigger and faster, trying for stunt-show things in junior contest."

9   Among that contingent was a brood from Maui of exceptionally gifted boys. Raised within an hour's drive of each other, they came up together through the Pee-Wee ranks and traveled as extended family, becoming stars before they were in their teens. Dusty Payne was the first to join the pro-surfer tour after winning an international juniors competition in 2008. Kai Barger and Granger Larsen are right behind him, and all three, according to an industry insider, "should be solid fixtures" on the top-money list of years to come.

10   But the best of that bunch, from boyhood on, was Marzo. With his bottomless hunger for hugh maneuvers and unsinkable sense of balance and intuition, he looked, to all who saw him, like the future of the sport while he was still in grade school. He was fiercely competitive at tournaments, racked up wins in every age division, and seemed an inevitable heir to Slater, the great soul surfer with nine world titles. "When he showed up for the national championships and put down perfect 10s at age 15, the media declared him the next great icon," says Warshaw. "Other kids could do some of the things he did, but not with his power and naturalness and skill at getting out of tight spots."

11   Though tournaments aren't as crucial to surfing fans as they are in other sports—there's a widespread sense that the rules are too archaic, favoring cautious riders over hellions—the hope was that Marzo and his class of big-air starlings would push the game up the board-sport totem and land it in the mainstream. (Surfing, eclipsed by X Games theatrics, remains virtually invisible on TV.)

12   Marzo seemed made to order for the thresher of pro surfing, which has cut down many kids with outsize talent. It begins with the year-

long World Qualifying Series, a continent-hopping gauntlet of contests against hundreds of amateur riders, all of them vying for 16 slots on the World Tour. Once Marzo turned pro and moved on to the big leagues, he would compete against the world's top 44 surfers in a globe-spanning season that lasts 10 months.

13   But it's one thing to rule the scholastic circuit, where no one's really watching but the families of other surfers, and a kid with Marzo's gifts could crush opponents by going bigger, faster, and braver. It's another to dominate the junior tour, where Marzo encountered battle-tested surfers with three or four years on him, most of them versed in the mind games and sly mechanics of contest strategy. The fake-outs on the waves, the jockeying for position—it was a language his Aspie brain couldn't process, blind as it is to tacit cues. Add in the crowds of fans, the announcers blaring scores over the PA system, and the cam-eramen in the water shooting action footage, and Marzo was sabotaged by his own senses. Nor did he fully grasp the rudiments of tourna-ment rules, which give riders a half-hour to produce two scoring runs. Often, Marzo would land a hellfire move on an early wave, then bob like a buoy as time ran out, waiting for the perfect swell. "He had a couple of years of brilliance, but then something happened," says Warshaw. "We figured maybe it was the pressure of the travel or—well, no one really knew at the time."

14   Including Clay. Almost from birth, he's had a sizable gift for con-founding expectations. Born in San Diego, he moved at nine months to the small town of Lahaina, steps from the sea in Maui; his mom and dad, both avid surfers, wanted to be closer to the waves. "Clay was wading before he could walk, and he walked at seven and a half months," recalls Jill. "At three months, he swam with his head under water, and by one he was on the front of his dad's surfboard, riding waves all the way in." Both parents were fine, if workaday, athletes—Jill, a massage therapist, loved volleyball as a kid; Gino, a carpenter, played baseball in college—and they organized their lives around the care and feeding of not one but two surf prodigies. Clay's half-brother, Cheyne, who is seven years older, was signed by sponsors at the age of 13. "Clay adored Cheyne and wanted to be like him, right up to the stickers on his board," says Jill. "And it went both ways: Cheyne bragged him up to sponsors, saying, "Wait'll you get a load of my younger brother."

15   Clay entered his first contest at the age of five, and took home a trophy for finishing fourth. By seven, he'd joined the kiddie corps of

local prodigies, sharing sleepovers, picnics, and family trips with Payne, Barger, and Larsen. "We were doing bigger, wilder stuff because we always had waves to play with," Clay recalls. "It's the Maui style: trying to top each other and look like we weren't even trying." There'd be half a dozen boys in the back of Jill's van, burping and farting the 15 miles to surf the North Shore breaks. "That was a magical time for Clay, the best years of his life," says Jill. "They were wonderful with him, really treated him like a brother, though even then they could see that he was different."

16   But even with the fact of his diagnosis, the surf world expects things of Marzo. Tierney thinks he should "bite the bullet" and do the Qualifying Series, which can now be completed in a "doable" six months instead of a hellish year. "It would be a tough haul, but he'd get to join the World Tour and surf against his idols in great waves," Tierney insists. "He's one of the five best on the planet in terms of talent, and with focus and a couple of years' experience he could be one of the best who ever did it." Marzo's manager is pinning hopes on a prospective new pro tour for big-air, balls-out riders. "Just 16 guys, the best progressive surfers, and an hour, not a half-hour, for heats. No one knows if it'll go yet—there's no sponsor attached—but it would be perfect for Clay," says Varnes. Even Marzo is prone to grand ambitions, though they change each time you ask him. "The new tour would be cool—I could deal," he says. But the next day he's talking about the free-surf option, in which the great alternative riders—Dane Reynolds, Bruce Irons—command big money to travel the globe for films and photo shoots.

17   Still, as I stand on the rise overlooking the beach in Maui, it's hard to imagine how a kid like Marzo could manage any of those options. I think back on our first—and last—sit-down chat, in which he all but fled the room, screaming. It began well enough, with Marzo talking about his childhood and name-checking his heroes, Bruce Irons and Kalani Robb. "Those guys invented the moves," he says. "We were just trying to take them farther." Then, out of the blue, he announces that surfing is the thing that "saved" him. "It's the best drug ever," he says, "and I'm lucky to have it."

18   I gently ask what it saved him from. He stares out the window and starts to yank his forelock. "I just...see things different, from the back of my brain," he says. "Other people see'em from the front, I guess. It's not good or bad, just how I am. Sort of makes it harder, though, you know?"

19   "How so?"

20   His free hand paws the side of his trunks, damp in the air-chilled room. "Well, I need people's help to get stuff done. Telling me where to go and what to say, and sometimes I don't like that, or I'm tired and don't want..."

21   The sentence just hangs there, whirring in space. I hold off, giving him room to work through the tangle of half-formed thoughts. Instead, he tugs his hair so hard that a clump comes off in his fingers. Panicked, I ask about the feeling he gets when he does something splendid on a wave. "I can't describe it," he says, slouching so low that he burrows into his chest. "Just pleasure, I guess. Where you want it over and over, and do anything to get it...Are we almost done?"

22   "Just one more," I say, looking at a poster-size photo on the wall. In it, Marzo is stock-still on his board, raising his arms in benediction as a 20-foot wave hulks above him. In the undepicted instant after the photo was taken, he paddled coolly around the edge of the wave before it smashed him to bits on the rocks. "What do you think when you see that picture?" I ask.

23   He mashes his lower lip, but releases the hair he's wrapped around a clenched index finger. "I was stoked," he says. "That wave was bombing, and there was another, even bigger, right behind it."

24   What he doesn't add is that he had just returned from a nightmare trip and felt blessed to be home again. Marzo is a creature of waves, but of these waves, the rocky, shark-toothed waters of Maui that he knows by heart. Look at him now, out beyond the reef, doing tricks to raise his flagging spirits. In surf no bigger than a picket fence, he's positioned himself above the swell, skimming like a coin from crest to crest. Just as each dies, he spies a new section to carve his name upon, hurling his board up the short-sleeve face to ride the foam again. He's forgotten the guys watching from their pickup trucks, and the small crowd up here with our mouths agape, and the father he can't please, and the brother who cut him dead—all of that's gone now, carried away by the hunchbacked westerly waves. He'll surf until lunchtime, then come back after a nap, and if not for the tiger sharks that hunt these waters once the sun goes down, he might never get out of the bliss machine, which makes no claim, only grants them.

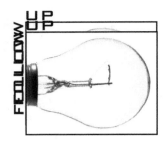

THE SURVING SAVANT

Exploring Language

agape: mouth wide open in surprise or amazement.

archaic: an older form, commonly used in an earlier time, though rare today.

exaltation: in praise; euphoric; elated.

intuit: to know or discover by intuition.

kitsch: tasteless or sentimental junk-art.

parkour: also known as freerunning, running through city streets, jumping or climbing to get around obstacles as quickly as possible.

rife: of common occurrence; plentiful or abundant.

rudiments: the first or basic principles of a subject.

striver: someone who strives (strive meaning to try hard or exert; with much effort).

thresher: a machine (or flail, a handheld stick-like instrument) that separates grains and seeds from plants like wheat.

vehement: intense or passionate; strongly emotional.

Note: For pronunciation, visit dictionary.com, search the word, and click on the speaker icon.

Thinking and Talking Points

1. In paragraph #11, Solotaroff writes, "Marzo seemed made to order for the thresher of pro surfing, which has cut down many kids with out-size talent." Explain the metaphor (see the definition for "thresher" on the Exploring Language list if unfamiliar with it).

2. List other metaphors and similes in the essay and discuss how the comparisons help the reader visualize or understand the subject.

3. How does the writer gain the reader's empathy for Marzo? Find word choices, sentences, and paragraphs from the essay to illustrate.

4. How is Asperger's syndrome both a help and a hindrance for Marzo? What are the symptoms?

5. In paragraph #4, the author uses contrasts, juxtaposing them with the conjunction "but." Study the paragraph and explain how these contrasts help the reader better understand Marzo.

Styling

Reread paragraph #5, the description of Clay Marzo surfing. Notice how the writer zooms into the scene, breaking down each motion, slowing the action so the reader sees each movement. Study each sentence for word choices and comparisons.

PRACTICE Think of a familiar action—a sport, dance, race, skateboarding, snowboarding, almost anything with action will work—and break it down into smaller parts, focusing on less than a minute of the action, visualizing each movement, making notes on each. The project works better if you can either watch the action live or view on TV or the internet.

YOU TRY IT Write the action into a paragraph, using detailed description of each movement with comparisons for at least one. For paragraph structure, see the "Writing Strategies" section of the text.

Teaming Up

1. **Warm-up for Writing Idea #1.** Clay Marzo had been diagnosed with attention deficit disorder as a child, before Dr. Linden correctly confirmed that Clay has Asperger's. Have each group member bring in articles on both disorders, as well as listing Clay's symptoms from the essay. Make a list of similarities and differences of symptoms between attention deficit disorder and Asperger's. Compare your findings. Why did it take until Clay was 18 before he got an accurate diagnosis? How similar/different are the disorders? Are they that easy to mistake?
2. The essay contains numerous dashes. Have each member work on a section of the essay, writing down the sentences with dashes. Using the "Styling" with "Black Widow" by Gordon Grice and the rules for "Dashes" in the "Basic Punctuation Rules and Practice" section in the text, individually write a sentence for each type of dash usage in the essay. Compare sentences and peer edit for correctness.

Writing Ideas

1. Using the warm-up from "Teaming Up" #1, write a mini-research paper that discusses these two disorders, comparing symptoms. Research statistics as to how many Asperger's children initially get a

misdiagnosis. In the conclusion, make some recommendations to help people more easily recognize Asperger's. **Or** write about two other disorders that often are mistaken, like bi-polar disorder and depression.

2. Using the "Styling" practice, write an essay that examines in depth another sport, arguing for it as an art form, using artistic terms to describe it. For examples, reread the descriptions in "The Surfing Savant" and read the short piece "On Boxing" by Joyce Carol Oates. Use figurative language, comparing the sport to an art, like Solotaroff does with describing one of Clay's moves as the Cha Cha. Tip: break down an art like dance, music, painting, or an animal in nature, and so on, listing the movements and actions to find comparisons to the sport.

Essay Connections

Joyce Carol Oates's "On Boxing" argues that boxing is an art; Brian Doyle in "Meat" describes basketball, with a surprising subtext to the story.

MONSTER MASH

Jack Kroll

Jack Kroll was an award-winning journalist and drama critic for Newsweek. He died at age 74 on June 8, 2000. This article appeared in a special edition of Newsweek (summer 1998). Kroll explores our fascination with horror, chronicling the development of the genre, lamenting the newer horror films like Scream that "[make] the genre seem to be regressing."

DUSTBIN OF HISTORY AND CULTURE

FREUDIAN: A reference to the ideas of Sigmund Freud (1856–1939), an Austrian psychiatrist and founder of psychoanalysis.

IONIANS: Greeks who lived toward the end of the second millennium B.C., some emigrating to what is now Turkey and the west coast of Asia Minor, giving the region the name Ionia.

1   "Then his teeth flew out; from two sides, blood came to his eyes; the blood that from lips and nostrils he was spilling, open-mouthed; death enveloped him in its black cloud."

2   Is this from the script for *The Texas Chain Saw Massacre? Friday the 13th, Part VIII?* No, it's from Homer's *Iliad,* which opened 3,000 years ago, performed to a preliterate audience by bards who were the ancestors of theater and film. The terror inspired in those ancient Ionians by such passages must have been something to see.

3   Terror may have been the first feeling that human beings ever experienced, in a world that threatened their very survival. The horror genre is a way for humans to revisit that primal fear, to turn it into pleasure, the pleasure of being safely scared. Horror lets us die vicariously, producing an artificial orgasm of mortality. Horror films came in with the very birth of the movies. Thomas Edison couldn't wait to get *Frankenstein* into his newly invented medium, turning out a 16-minute version of Mary Shelley's novel in 1910. Frankenstein's monster, Dracula and the Wolf Man are the unholy three of horror movies. Frankenstein's collage of body parts is the embodiment of

man's arrogant desire to write his own Book of Genesis. The monster has new meaning in our age of genetic splicing and artificial intelligence. Dracula is Death as seducer; he sucks our blood to take us to a perverse immortality. The Wolf Man wrenches us back to our origins in the animal world of pure instinct, reversing evolution with its burden of consciousness and responsibility.

4   Boris Karloff's burlap-suited, screw-necked creature in James Whale's 1931 *Frankenstein* is still the greatest of all incarnations of monsterhood, an amazing blend of bewilderment, despair and savage rage beyond anything human. Bela Lugosi, a much more limited actor, nonetheless achieved vampiric perfection in Tod Browning's *Dracula* (also 1931). The best-dressed of all monsters, Lugosi's Dracula is also the most erotic, surveying the necks of various lily-skinned maidens with a connoisseur's libidinous leer before puncturing them with his miniphalic incisors. Lon Chaney Jr. as the Wolf Man (1941) is such a clumsy galoot of an actor that he is believably hapless in his vulpine transformation, giving his soul-saving death at the hands of his father an affectingly Freudian pathos.

5   The '30s were a golden age for horror movies: Fredric March convulsing between virtue and vice as Dr. Jekyll and Mr. Hyde (1932), mad scientist Charles Laughton turning innocent animals into screwed-up humans in *The Island of Lost Souls* (1932) and, perhaps the most nightmarish of all horror films, Tod Browning's *Freaks,* in which a troupe of real sideshow freaks takes revenge on a beautiful trapeze artist and turns her into a monstrous half-human, half-bird. These films had a special resonance in the Depression, especially *King Kong,* in which the giant ape rampaging in a New York split between bread lines and skyscrapers seemed to symbolize a society at the mercy of Darwinian forces.

6   When men went off to war in the '40s, horror movies gave equal time to the unconscious sado-sexual yearnings of women in Jacques Tourneur's *Cat People* movies, with the enigmatic Simone Simon playing a feline version of the Wolf Man. The postwar '50s closed with a masterpiece, Alfred Hitchcock's *Psycho,* the *Citizen Kane* of horror movies in its far-ranging influence. Hitchcock's ironic genius mixed themes of cross-gendering, straightforward and perverse sexuality, Oedipal conflict and schizophrenia. Janet Leigh's last moments of life in the shower turned a bathtub into a mini-Transylvania of ordinary life. Horror provided a counterpoint to the disruptions of the '60s when George Romero created splatter movies with *Night of the*

Living Dead (1968), in which a militia of corpses left their graves to attack those who dared to live. Splatter pics mutated like killer amoebas, targeting young people as both protagonists and audiences. In endlessly sequeled series like *Halloween* and *Nightmare on Elm Street*, the hockey-masked Jason and razor-gloved Freddy were like demonized parental surrogates punishing kids for their newfound sexual freedom.

7   But the flood of teen horror makes the genre seem to be regressing. In Wes Craven's recent box-office smashes, *Scream* and *Scream 2*, it's as if the horror movie were engaged in autoerotic worship of itself. The kids in *Scream* talk incessantly about horror flicks, with a faux hipness that makes you wish all of them would be killed by some self-respecting monster. Horror movies need to return to good old guilt-ridden grown-up panic. The apocalyptic dangers in our time should give new life to the pure horror film. It's doubtful that the Americanization of Godzilla will do the job.

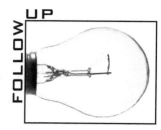

FOLLOW UP

MONSTER MASH

Exploring Language

autoerotic: self-satisfaction of sexual desire.

connoisseur: an expert or judge of taste, usually in a specific area, like a wine connoisseur.

enigmatic: puzzling or paradoxical (contradictory).

galoot: a clumsy person.

hapless: unfortunate or unlucky.

leer: to look at with lustful intent or in a lewd way; lascivious.

libidinous: lustful.

pathos: arousing pity, sympathy.

preliterate: a culture that hasn't developed writing.

vicariously: through the experience of another. Kroll means that moviegoers experience death through the characters in horror films.

vulpine: resembling a fox; crafty. Which definition do you think Kroll means?

Note: For pronunciation, go to dictionary.com, search the word, and click on the speaker icon.

USAGE   Write a sentence or two explaining how you (or someone you know) live vicariously, either through films, reading, or television.

Thinking and Talking Points

1. How does Kroll organize the essay?
2. What point does he make about modern horror films? If you've seen any of the films he mentions, do you agree with him?
3. Kroll comments, "Horror movies need to return to good old guilt-ridden grown-up panic." What does he mean? Why does he think guilt-ridden films offer more to the viewer?
4. "The monster has new meaning in our age of genetic splicing and artificial intelligence." In what way? Can you think of examples from film and life that support Kroll's observation?

5. How is the horror genre "a way for humans to revisit that primal fear, to turn it into pleasure, the pleasure of being safely scared"? How does horror let us "die vicariously"?

Styling

Jack Kroll knew that hooking the reader with a spirited title is a valuable tool, and he often uses lines or titles from old rock and roll songs. His essay "Roll Over, Bach, Too" borrows its title from a Beatles song titled "Roll Over, Beethoven." He lifts "Monster Mash" from another old rock and roll song of the same title. Many writers borrow from music, literature, and pop culture for lively titles.

PRACTICE Think of a possible essay topic for each of the following song titles (or brainstorm your own list of song titles to practice with):

"Mr. Pitiful" (from the soundtrack of the film *The Commitments*).

"Cupid's Dead" (from the CD *III Sides to Every Story* by Extreme).

"Only the Lonely" (Roy Orbison).

YOU TRY IT For your next essay, find a title off a CD or a line from a song to use as your essay title.

Note: For more ideas on creating titles, see the titles section in "Writing Basic College Essays."

Teaming Up

1. Brainstorm favorite movie scenes from a **genre** like action/adventure (for example, the Indiana Jones series, *Star Wars,* or *Iron Man*), drama, or science fiction (or other genres), and discuss why you like the films. Have each person in the group choose their favorite from the list and write an individual paragraph explaining how someone lives or dies vicariously through that type of character, perhaps a former jock who relives his or her glory day vicariously through armchair football or sports films. You may use yourself as an example or someone you know.

Writing Ideas

1. Watch two horror films, one old and one new, and write an essay arguing whether or not Kroll's assessment of modern teen horror movies is true: "But the flood of teen horror makes the genre seem to be regressing."

2. Write an essay comparing Dracula—perhaps Bela Lugosi's portrayal (or Bram Stoker's book)—to the modern vampire Edward Cullen in the book (or film) *Twilight*. How has the image of the vampire changed to reflect modern culture?

3. Watch one of the films discussed in "Monster Mash" and write an essay analyzing the film and its "good old guilt-ridden, grown-up panic." Quote from Kroll's essay to make your points. Use strong description of film scenes.

Essay Connections

Pauline Kael's "The Little Mermaid" provides an example of film review writing. Kroll also writes a music analysis of the Beatles' influence on culture.

CITY OUT OF BREATH

Ken Chen

Ken Chen—poet, law school graduate, critic, essayist—has published work in Best American Essays 2006, Boston Review of Books, Satellite: The Berkeley Magazine of News and Culture (which he founded), and Arts and Letters Daily. "City Out of Breath," first published in Mánoa 2005, describes the author's impressions of Hong Kong on a visit there with his father, a Taiwanese immigrant, in 2000.

DUSTBIN OF HISTORY AND CULTURE

FILM NOIR: A film genre with usually dark lighting and bleak, cynical, shady characters; the term used by the French critics in the 1940s to describe certain American detective films or thrillers.

MILTONIC: Refers to the writing style or themes of John Milton (1608–1674); considered one of the greatest of English poets, Milton, a Puritan, wrote his epic *Paradise Lost*, while blind, dictating to his daughter.

SAMUEL JOHNSON (1709–1784): Also known as Dr. Johnson, a prominent English figure of the 18th century; poet, essayist, critic, biographer.

1   So all night, we walk in one direction: up.

2   This is really the only direction you can go in Hong Kong, a direction hinted at by skyscrapers and aspired to by the Hong Kong Stock Exchange. By "we," I mean my father, myself, and our guide— my stepgrandmother-to-be—who somehow possesses both our combined age and our combined speed. Trudging up the stairs behind her, my father and I are already panting. We stop and laugh—really only to catch our breath — but by the top of the stairs we're bent and sagging, our hands on our knees. And there, at the end of the street, she's waving at us to hurry up, almost as if to fan away whatever remains of our quaint Californian version of walking. When we catch up with her, she says, in what seems like an especially Chinese blend of ridicule and public affection, that we walk too slowly.

[handwritten annotation: Is Father getting married?]

"City Out of Breath" by Ken Chen first published in *Mánoa*, Vol 17, No. 1, 2005. Reprinted by permission of Ken Chen.

3   If an American city at night is film noir, then Hong Kong is just a camera blur. The residents of Kowloon speed around with the same look on their faces, as if they're irked at their bodies for not being cars. You feel that if you stood still, the city would just rotate past you, as if you have no other choice but motion. Hong Kong accelerates as though located on another, faster-spinning earth. Anyone who has been there knows that time and space can flick off their objectivity and instead pulse and jump, symphonic rather than metronomic. In Hong Kong the world stretches time until time—along with space and language— goes elastic. It's like a Chinese painting in which conflicting perspectives soak through the landscape like radiation. A McDonald's sits next to a vegetable cart tended by a woman who looks about five hundred years old. The all-Chinese police band plays bagpipes and marches in kilts for the St. Patrick's Day parade. Street markets are the opposite of flowers: opening up at night and closing at day. In Hong Kong, all times are contiguous. All times are simultaneous. This essay is an attempt to describe a city that is itself already a description—Hong Kong is a description of time. This essay is also an experiment in time travel—an artifact of memory from July 2000. Hong Kong is now the same city but a different place. Prosperity—once the city's one-word gloss—is slowly becoming synonymous with Shanghai. "I hear everyone's real depressed over there," I say at dinner to the mother of a friend of mine from Hong Kong. "That they're jealous, with all the jobs heading over to the mainland and all." She chews on a piece of lettuce and says, "Yes, they are jealous. But they have a right to be."

4   Five years later, we spend the next half-hour taking elevators that lead to stairs that lead to elevators. I don't have any idea where we're going and just follow my father, an immigrant from Taiwan whose Mandarin, I realize, makes him only a third less lost than I am. He's following our guide, who, like Hong Kong itself, is all energy and no conversation. "We're headed for Victoria Peak today," my dad announced this morning. The touristy lookout could be the only spot where Hong Kong can be made comprehensible.

5   Suddenly our guide stops. Are we lost? This possibility is not surprising. It feels like we've been going in spirals, victims of some kind of geographic hoax. Our guide decides to ask for directions in Cantonese. She stops a man with a dark complexion who reminds me of the vendors at the Taipei night market. He has short, wiry hair that resembles a scouring pad and is wearing a security guard's uniform. Chinese—I think—obviously. Probably a migrant from the

mainland. "Where is Victoria Peak?" she asks him in Cantonese. The security guard looks at her and says, "Do you speak English?"

6   Dad and I look at each other. He says, "This is a strange city," and I start laughing, relieved that I'm not the only one who thinks so. We seem to be fumbling through different languages, shifting, testing, trying to find one we can all stand in. A bus rocking through the northern hills speaks to its passengers in Miltonic English: *Do not board or alight whilst bus is in motion.* (Lucifer alights. Buses throttle.) And a week ago in Taiwan, my father had shed the most mundanely engrossing fear of any Chinese immigrant to America: his accent. He became a master of languages, all traces of self-consciousness suddenly gone from his voice. He chatted with taxi drivers and strangers about the drenching humidity or about which restaurants were good, casually code-switching to Taiwanese for jokes, Mandarin for information, and English for translation and one-word exclamations. When we showed up at the desk of the Taipei Hilton, the girls on staff spotted my dad and approached him in nervous English. He paused, got an odd look on his face—the fuzzy expression that Looney Tunes characters have when they're suspended in midair and about to fall—and said in Mandarin: "I'm Chinese!"

7   Back to searching for Victoria Peak, my father starts to ask the question in English, but someone interrupts. A Hong Kong yuppie standing thirty feet away muffles his cell phone in his blazer lapel and tells us the answer in rushed Cantonese. Some men in black blazers walk by, and some teens with blond spiky hair walk by, and some middle-aged men with grimy white aprons walk by—mostly Chinese, but otherwise unidentifiable. Indian? Polynesian? British? Hong Kong is an intensely international city. Every street in Kowloon is an intersection, not only of wet-walled alleys and futuristic buildings of glass, but also of the more transparent rays of cultures.

8   Somehow you are supposed to teach yourself how to comprehend Hong Kong's energy and flashy contradictions: Asian and Western; the encroaching Chinese mainland and the remnants of England; the greasy night markets of sticky-rice tamales and knockoff leather boots that slouch right across from Tiffany, Chanel, and Prada. The only things common to these are the offices sending air-conditioned blasts into the street, a kind of longing for money, and, most important, the sense of storytelling that the city seems to require as a visitor's pass. Hong Kong has a way of turning on your internal monologue. Walking becomes an act of silent storytelling, figuring people out. You feel like you are lost in some prelapsarian novel in which the plot has begun but the characters wait for you to

name them. In some time, at some place, we step into an underground Cantonese restaurant and I see a gray-suited, red-tied man act like a parody of the States. American, I say, with an American accent: good-natured smiles, occasionally the slow English dispatched on foreigners and children, and a slightly uncomfortable look, as though he's worried he's outnumbered.

9   Finally we find Victoria Peak, by which I mean that we find the gondola to get us there. We buy tickets and step in, waiting to be hoisted up into the humid nighttime atmosphere. The cab starts moving. At first, nothing in the windows but the ads on the sides of the tunnel, and then suddenly the city. Our gondola windows have become postcards. Hong Kong poses before us, bright, earnestly capitalist, electric, multiplying. A concrete wall blocks the view, and then the city is back again. Under us, a small red house sits on the cuff of the panorama. Light drops out of a pair of shutters, a door or window is open; someone is home. More stone, more wall. We hit the crest, reach our destination: Victoria Peak, the highest spot in Hong Kong and, for a tourist, the best. We have a God's-eye view of the skyline. The buildings shine yellow, white, orange, blue, all reflected in the dark bay waters; giant corporate logos shrink, sky-scrapers huddle, and the city glows with a brilliant coolness. My eye seems too small to hold it all in.

10   We take the bus back. I sit on the top of a double-decker bus, on the left side, in a city where they drive on the left side of the road. As we shake downhill, making acute turns, I begin to regret my seating preference: the wobbly tourists' corner. The bus hits a few branches, careens over double yellow lines, winds downhill. Whipped by full-motion vertigo, I grope for the metal railing, squeezing it as if for juice, and then laugh at my own cowardice. I gasp, then yawn in a slow, measured sort of panic, a civilized form of suffocation. Hong Kong—a city out of breath.

11   After we've been back from Victoria Peak for a few hours, I go to the front desk of the hotel. A Hong Kong–Chinese woman in her mid-twenties looks up the Internet rates for me. She reads the per-minute charges off a small white card, and her voice compresses Mandarin, English, and Cantonese into a linguistic diamond: the Chinese-British accent. There's the Merchant-Ivory sound, the lilt that movies tell us is cultured but that also seems austere and imperial, the way Chinese period films do. Yet the sound is also familiar, humble, and awkward: a Chinese voice wandering inside the English language. The sound of it reminds me of my parents. I can't get enough of it.

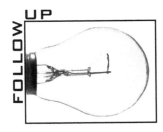
CITY OUT OF BREATH

Exploring Language

acute: serious or critical; intense; also a geometry term for angles less than 90 degrees. P9 116

austere: severe or stern; somber appearance or personality; also, lacking adornment.

careen: to rush carelessly.

contiguous: connected in space or time. 114

irked: irritated or annoyed.

lilt: sing or speak in a rhythmic or spirited manner; a lively sound or movement (as in "He walked into the room with a lilt in his step.").

linguistic: the study of language. 116

mundane: ordinary; unimaginative, common.

prelapsarian: relating to a time before the fall of Adam and Eve.

vertigo: dizziness; confusion.

Note: For pronunciation, go to dictionary.com, search the word, and click on the speaker icon.

USAGE   Make a list of mundane situations or thinking. Write three sentences using *mundane* and at least one other word from the list.

Thinking and Talking Points

1. Search through the essay for Chen's descriptions of people. What do you notice? How do these descriptions underscore his point about Hong Kong?
2. Study Chen's use of dashes. He could use commas. Why the choice to use dashes instead? Explain each instance, why it might be a stronger choice than commas.
3. Chen describes American cities at night as film noir. Explain what you think he means. What evidence does he use as support for Hong Kong as "a camera blur"?
4. Find additional metaphors and similes and explain how they clarify a point or help the reader visualize a person or situation. Also consider the title and what it conveys about the essay's meaning.

5. Chen writes, "In Hong Kong, all times are contiguous. All times are simultaneous." He goes on to make other references to time. What's his purpose? How do his comments on time help explain a city that he says is "out of breath"?

Styling

Most students know how to use a colon with a simple list, but when that list becomes complicated with details that might require commas, then the list can get confusing. Such lists require more sophisticated punctuation. Chen uses semicolons to separate pairs when describing the contradictions in Hong Kong. In paragraph #8, he writes, "Somehow you are supposed to teach yourself how to comprehend Hong Kong's energy and flashy contradictions: Asian and Western; the encroaching Chinese mainland and the remnants of England; the greasy night markets of sticky-rice tamales and knock-off leather boots that slouch right across from Tiffany, Chanel, and Prada." Each semicolon signals a new set of items at odds with each other in this eclectic city.

PRACTICE   Write a complete sentence that makes a statement about the contradictions in a city you are familiar with and add a colon. Next, make a list of contradictions and pair them up. Is there a modern glass and metal building next to an old, crumbling brick structure? Mansions next to shacks? An outdoor market next to a gleaming, modern mall? Be specific and detailed.

YOU TRY IT   Arrange each set of contradictions after your sentence with the colon. Add a semicolon after each set. Write three more sentences in this style, about any topic you think is rich with contradictions.

Note: You can also pair up items that have something in common (see the "Styling" with "Mute Dancers: How to Watch a Hummingbird.")

Teaming Up

1. **Warm-up for Writing Idea #1:** Bring in a photo of a town, city, or other place. Individually, write a description of the place in the photo, focusing on the mood the picture conveys and any details that would help the reader visualize the town without the photo. Read each other's

descriptions. Are their contradictory opinions of the town? Discuss any disparities in views. Choose one to read to the class.

2. **Warm-up for Writing Ideas #1 and #3:** Similar to Teaming Up #1, only this time describe the town or city where you are attending college. Share your impressions. If there are contradictions in views, discuss them and then write an argument against the views that differ from your own, attempting to convince your peers that they've misjudged the town, but be open to others' impressions. This activity also makes a good class brainstorm, with the teacher writing conflicting impressions on the board for discussion and writing possibilities.

Writing Ideas

1. Write about another city or place, one you're familiar with, describing its tone: is it rural, suburban, or urban? Naive or cynical? Snobby or friendly? Be specific, describing types of people, geography, buildings, the pace.

2. Compare two cities or towns that have something in common, but also exude different tones. For example, you might compare two small towns, one that's friendly, content, accepting; another that's nosey, judgmental, snobby. Use **personification** (see the glossary), describing each town as if it's a person.

3. Write an essay about the contradictions within a city, perhaps describing it during the day versus night, or consider contradicting the media's view of a particular city.

Essay Connections

"Somebody's Baby" by Barbara Kingsolver contrasts America's views of children with Spain.

THE TREE BEYOND IMAGINING

Reg Saner

Nature writer and poet Reg Sanger (born in 1931) has won numerous awards for his work, including a National Endowment of the Arts Fellowship, the Walt Whitman Award, and the Colorado's Governor Award. He studied as a Fulbright scholar in Florence, Italy, and has been published in over 140 magazines and 40 anthologies, with several books to his credit, mostly set in the American West: Living Large in Nature, The Dawn Collector: On My Way to the Natural World, Reaching Keel Seel: Ruin's Echo and the Anasazi, *and* The Three-Cornered Falcon: Essays on the Interior West and the Natural Scene.

1   Seeing is not believing. Any tree "acting out" in such hogwild and crazy ways—or so I used to feel—can't be truly arboreal. This one thinks it's a mad dog. Here's another trying to prove chaos might be a conifer. Yet another so riven, so warped, it looks like self-knowledge. Or is it just pretending to summarize World History? During our first acquaintance I ran across examples so willful and creaturely that my glance often boggled at believing what it saw. How could a juniper, I would ask myself, be throwing a fit?

2   Botanically speaking, of course, a juniper can't be perverse. As a dirt-common member of the cypress family it can at worst be only an oddball conifer. Other arboreal species may echo states we recognize in ourselves, but none I've run across seems so moody and emotional. Lifelong, we humans conceal our intimate histories, even while a version of them gets slowly written into our faces. This tree's neurotic past, however, appears at a glance, visible through no matter how many feigned identities. And though cone-bearing species may be tricky to tell, one from another, the one I have in mind is easy.

3   Beneath erstwhile needles that evolution has smoothed like snakeskin, and under cones shrunk to beads, a greyish-brown welter of wood appears. If it looks like tensed muscle and sinew, that illusion and the preceding traits do add up to generic juniper. But if the bark is shaggy as hanks of unbraided sisal; if the absolutely motionless trunk seems to be groveling in frenzy or twisting like smoke; and if in even the best-behaved specimen you see branches that mime

devastation having a temper tantrum, you know you're not only deal-ing with *Juniperus osteosperma*, Utah juniper. You know the example before your eyes is a special case: a high-desert strain of that species, one growing where it ought not to try.

4   If animal, such trees would be camels, and almost are. But what camel drinks sand? Hence the near-incredulity. On a sun-spattered, all-but-windless morning in Utah, for example, you stand smack in front of one, gasping at its self-tormented trunk fed by red sand; or fed by far less, a crevice in rock which that sand once was. Yet on naked stone those knotted roots have knuckled down to sipping a trunk and limbs into life. From a low writhing branch you might strip off a fibrous dangle of bark the creature seems clad in, all threads and shreds and tatters, like a beggar's rags. Obviously the bark's stringy hairs are real. Just as clearly, its tree as *tree* lacks full credibility. The riven trunk, the gesturing limbs in every style of passion, cannot be anything Nature approves, much less intended. So you're bound to wonder about botanical vandalism. Novice-like, you stand there in south-eastern Utah just staring and shaking your head: "Surely some-one has *done* this?"

5   Fact is, among Utah juniper of the high desert, flabbergasting abnormality is the norm only among individual trees defying limita-tion. Lots of rock, lots of sand, lots of wind, and very little rain can make juniper stands growing there, at the far end of possibility, an outpost of marginalized eccentrics. Not the whole species. No, the stressed-out examples I'm talking about, the trees you can see with-out quite believing, grow where they almost can't—at their ecological edge. We think timberline a question of mountain altitudes beyond which no conifer can rise. For desert junipers timberline may be a limit drawn in the sand, not by rarefied air but by rain, lower than which there is none, or as good as.

6   Thus, it's by taking root at the threshold of impossibility that this most irrational tree grows against all reason. A Utah juniper at the edge of its range is either so distraught or far gone in perplexity it can't make sense of itself. "Do you suppose I'd have grown this way," it seems to snort, "if I'd had any idea what I was getting into?"

7   Although the specimens I admire would indeed make more inter-esting museum pieces than many a prize now under glass, I realize that bringing just the tree inside wouldn't do. You'd need to bring along with it the thin air of its Southwestern plateau. You'd need too that powdery fine sand red as rust, rippled dunes sparsely tufted with

greasewood or Indian rice grass. And skies blue as chicory petals. Floating puffs of cumulus too, their undersides tinted by the red miles beneath them. Birdsong as well; rock wrens, horned larks, mocking-birds, vireos, piñon jays. And scrub jays, cowbirds, towhees. And vultures. Above all, you'd need desert sun with its glare, its incomparable clarities, deep shadows; its refusal to lie.

8   On the Grand Canyon's south rim, I have spent hours of clear weather, more intrigued by its pygmy forest of piñons and junipers than by the view. Happily roving among outcrops of chert and Kaibab limestone, well-content at being scolded by piñon jays, I have come upon deep depression and recovery—both alive in the same tree. How had it grown so depressed, I wondered. Through wrestling for its own affections? Or by being too much a shape-shifter ever to tire of dilemma? And how had recovery and relapse grown from the same trunk? Because its moods, like ours, don't believe in each other? There I found trees giving instructions in bravery. Found them more typical than not. To look at such lives and say "struggle" doesn't touch it.

9   During the same afternoon I stumbled upon a juniper who had once been a witch and couldn't quit practicing; then found countless others its bad example converted. As if they had used witchery to request eternal life and youth, they seemed the picture of what happens when only the first half is granted. The picture of how losers look when they win.

10   There amid the deranged and violent I also discovered "good" trees battening on the same rimrock; witnessed all the living optimism, all the hurt joy that can scuffle upward out of rock and suffer open. In wresting a living from limestone's long famines of rain they must sometimes have felt that enduring there was next to impossible, yet endure they had.

11   We admire most, I suppose, those virtues our souls utterly lack, or need more of. Even after twenty years, therefore, I'm apt to be spellbound by the drama of a particular trunk and limbs. Feeling sympathy and awe before such pure indomitability costs nothing, I know, because I've often stood that way a longish while, unaware that I was; as if hoping a touch of juniper courage might agree to come with me.

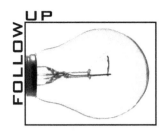
Exploring Language

arboreal: relating to trees or treelike.

battening: in this context, thriving or prospering.

boggled: overwhelmed or bewildered.

chert: a type of brittle rock primarily made up of microcrystalline quartz.

chicory: a blue-flowered plant, its leaves used in salads and the roots ground as a substitute for coffee.

distraught: agitated, upset, distracted.

eccentric: odd, erratic, or peculiar.

erstwhile: past or previous.

feigned: disguised or faked; pretend.

flabbergasting: astounding, bewildering, astonishing.

frenzy: extreme agitation or excitement; deranged.

groveling: complete submission; fawning in fear.

hank: in this context, a knot, loop, or coil.

incredulity: doubt, disbelief, skepticism.

indomitability: unconquerable.

marginalized: to place in a position of little importance, influence, or power.

novice: beginner or newcomer.

perverse: determined to go against what is right, expected, or desired; persistent or obstinate in what is wrong.

rarified: elevated in nature or style; of rare, high value.

rimrock: rock forming a natural boundary of a plateau or other rise.

riven: split apart (past participle form) or tear.

sinew: another name for tendon.

sisal: a fiber from the agave plant used to make ropes, rugs, and other items.

sparsely: thinly scattered; not thick (as in sparse hair or sparse population).

spattered: scattered or dashed in small particles ("Paint spattered the walls.")

tufted: threads, fibers, feathers, hair, etc. formed into a tight bunch at the bottom but loose at the top.
Note: For pronunciation, go to dictionary.com, search the word, and click on the speaker icon.

USAGE Choose two words from the above list that begin with the same sound and use them in a sentence, creating **alliteration** (see the glossary for definition).

Thinking and Talking Points

1. Make a list of comparisons to humans (personification) Saner uses to describe the Utah juniper; write a paragraph, in your own words, of the overall impression these personifications reveal about the writer's attitude toward these trees.
2. Saner writes, "Other arboreal species may echo states we recognize in ourselves, but none I've run across seems so moody and emotional." What other states of mind does he attribute to the Utah juniper? What other tree species might "echo states we recognize in ourselves"?
3. Explain how this essay's **subtext** contains a metaphor for the human mind and body. Pick out specific descriptive passages to prove the point. Study the conclusion—what is Saner's point?
4. What environment does this tree need to grow the way it does? How might this environment echo human emotional environment?
5. What other style—word choices, punctuation, sentence structure, specific detail, description—does the author use? Write down at least three and discuss how well—or not—the techniques work to improve the essay.

Styling

Personification of an object or state of being can lead to critical thinking about **subtext**: Saner's tree echoing human states; Hoagland's turtles (anthropomorphizing) mustering courage against the odds, the ministories becoming fables about the environment and our relationship with nature; Gendler's "Truth" is a thief stealing illusions.

PRACTICE Make a list of human personality traits (draw on #1 in Thinking and Talking Points or create a list from scratch). A thesaurus with synonyms can help (for example, look up the word happy and write down all of its synonyms, and do the same with other qualities on the list). A list of at least ten will make the project easier.

YOU TRY IT   Find pictures of different trees or other plant life. Choose one and read a little about it. Drawing from the list, write a paragraph personifying the plant. When finished, share the writing with others and determine what subtext you might have created.

Teaming Up

1. **Practice for Writing Idea #1:** The style exercise works well as a group activity. Everyone in the group brings in a picture of a tree or plant along with a little information. Brainstorm the list of qualities as a group, decide which qualities go with each plant (it's okay if they overlap), and then individually write the paragraphs—modeling Saner—using the human qualities to describe the plant or tree. Share the writing and discuss the subtext.

2. Each group member brings in pictures of the Utah juniper and other junipers. Study the photos and make a list of differences and similarities. Co-write a paragraph that describes the uniqueness of the Utah species in comparison to a more common juniper.

Writing Ideas

1. Research another plant or tree that grows in difficult conditions, perhaps desert flowers or certain types of orchids. Using the research and personification, write an essay that not only describes and personifies, but discusses how the plant or tree solves the problem of living in such an environment. For ideas, review Saner's essay and study where he talks about how the Utah Juniper survives in such a harsh place.
2. Read Brian Doyle's "Joyas Voladoras" and study it for subtext. Compare and/or contrast that essay to Saner's "The Tree Beyond Imagining." Discuss the use of subtext and style.

Essay Connections

Other essays containing subtext, comparisons (metaphor, simile), or personification include Ruth Gendler's "Truth"; Brian Doyle's "Joyas Voladoras"; Brian Doyle's "Meat"; Edward Hoagland's "The Courage of Turtles" (anthropomorphizing and subtext in the fable form); John Updike's "Disposable Rocket"; and Bailey White's "Mortality."

HAIR

Diane Ackerman

This essay is an excerpt from Diane Ackerman's book The Natural History of the Senses, which was made into a PBS special. Ackerman gives some fascinating facts and history about hair, as well as its connection with personal and group identity. She opens with the line, "Hair deeply affects people, can transfigure or repulse them."

DUSTBIN OF HISTORY AND CULTURE

GILGAMESH: An epic literary work from the Middle East written on clay tablets dating to about 2000 B.C. Gilgamesh is the name of the hero.

HAIR: A 1960s hippie musical.

RASTAFARIANS: People belonging to a Jamaican religious cult that forbids cutting off hair.

1   Hair deeply affects people, can transfigure or repulse them. Symbolic of life, hair bolts from our head. Like the earth, it can be harvested, but it will rise again. We can change its color and texture when the mood strikes us, but in time it will return to its original form, just as Nature will in time turn our precisely laid-out cities into a weedway. Giving one's lover a lock of hair to wear in a small locket around his neck used to be a moving and tender gesture, but also a dangerous one, since to spell-casters, magicians, voodooers, and necromancers of all sorts, a tuft of someone's hair could be used to cast a spell against them. In a variation on this theme, a medieval knight wore a lock of his lady's pubic hair into battle. Since one of the arch-tenets of courtly love was secrecy, choosing this tiny memento instead of a lock of hair from her head may have been more of a practical choice than a philosophical one, but it still symbolized her life-force, which he was carrying with him. Ancient male leaders wore long flowing tresses as a sign of virility (in fact, "kaiser" and "tsar" both mean "long-haired"). In the biblical story of Samson, the hero's loss of hair brings on his weakness and downfall, just as it did for the hero Gilgamesh before him. In Europe in more recent times, women who collaborated with the enemy in World War II were humiliated by having their hair cut short.

Among some orthodox Jews, a young woman must cut off her hair when she marries, lest her husband find her too attractive and wish to have sex with her out of desire rather than for procreation. Rastafarians regard their dreadlocks as "high-tension cables to heaven." These days, to shock the bourgeoisie and establish their own identity, as every generation must, many young men and women wear their hair as freeform sculpture, with lacquered spikes, close-cropped patterns that resemble a formal garden maze, and colors borrowed from an aviary or spray-painted alley. The first time a student walked into my classroom wearing a "blue jay," it *did* startle me. Royal-blue slabs of hair were brushed and sprayed straight up along the sides of his head, a long jelly roll of white hair fell forward over his eyebrows, and the back was shiny black, brushed straight up and plastered close to the head. I didn't dislike it, it just seemed like a lot to fuss with each day. I'm sure my grandmother felt that way about my mother's "beehive," and I know my mother feels that way about the curly weather system which is my own mane of long thick hair. One's hairstyle can be the badge of a group, as we've always known—look at the military's crew cut, or the hairstyles worn by some nuns and monks. In the sixties, wearing long hair, especially if you were a man, often fetched a vitriolic outburst from parents, which is why the musical *Hair* summed up a generation so beautifully. The police, who seemed so clean-cut and cropped then, were succeeded by a generation of police in long sideburns and mustaches. But I remember at the Boston Love-in in 1967, my first year away at college, hearing one young man say to a passing couple who ridiculed his ponytail: "Fuck you and fuck your hairdressers." I also remember, in the fifties, walking out of my bathroom with my hair sprayed into a huge bubble. "What have you done to your hair?" my father demanded. "I've just teased it," I said. To which he replied: "Teased? You've driven it insane." I wear my curly hair au naturel these days, in a shag cut the French call *la coupe sauvage* ("the savage cut"), but its volume and faintly erotic unruliness bother my mother's sense of propriety. To her generation, serious women have serious hairdos that are formal, sprayed, and don't move. A few weeks ago, she phoned to warn me that professional women aren't taken seriously if they don't have a "wet set" (rollers, hair dryer, setting lotion, hair spray). Loose ends on one's head signal loose ends in one's life. From this point of view, which has been popular for ages, a woman grows her hair long but keeps it tightly controlled in a bun, under a hat or scarf, or with hair spray, and lets her hair down only in private at night.

2   Most people have about 100,000 hair follicles on their head, and lose between fifty and a hundred hairs a day through normal combing, brushing, or fussing. Each hair grows for only about two to six years, at about five or six inches a year, and then its follicle rests for a few months, the hair falls out, and is eventually replaced by a new hair. So when you see a beautiful head of hair, you're looking at hairs in many different stages in a complex system of growth, death, and renewal. Fifteen percent of it is resting at any one time, the other 85 percent growing; many dozens of hairs are all set to die tomorrow, and deep in the follicles new hairs are budding.

3   Hair has a tough outer coating called the cuticle, and a soft interior called the cortex. People with coarse hair have larger follicles, and also a thin outer coat (10 percent of the hair) with a large inner cortex (90 percent). People with fine hair have smaller follicles, and almost the same amount of cuticle (40 percent) as cortex (60 percent). If the follicle cells grow in an even pattern, the hair will be straight; if they grow irregularly, the hair will be curly. Lice have a hard time attaching to thick hair, which is why black schoolchildren don't succumb to epidemics of head lice as often as their white classmates. Besides being sexy to most people, head hair protects the brain from the sun's heat and ultraviolet rays, helps to insulate the skull, softens impact, and constantly monitors the world only a hair's breadth away from our body, that circle of danger and romance we allow few people to enter.

4   Of course, hairs grow in many places around the body, even on the toes and inside the nose and ears. The Chinese, the American Indian, and some other peoples have very little hair on their face and body; those of Mediterranean descent can be so woolly and thickly haired they seem only a step away from our ape-man ancestors. Bald men are sexy men; they go bald from a high level of testosterone in the blood, which is why you don't see bald castrati or eunuchs. Men with thick mats of hair on their shoulders and backs used to scare me. A word like "carnivore" would form in my mind when I passed them on beaches. Women tend to be smoother-fleshed than men, so it makes sense that we would shave our legs and apply lotions to accentuate the gender difference. But despite efforts to remove hair from our bodies, quite a lot remains on the arms, faces, and heads of women, and the chest, arms, and legs of men, to do what it was intended to do.

5   Hair is special to mammals, although reptiles do form scales, which are related. Each hair grows from the papilla, a wad of tissue at the base of a follicle, where there is a nerve ending, and there may be a group of other nerve endings nearby. The average body has about five million hairs. Because hairy skin is thinner, it's more sensitive than smooth skin. One hair can be easily triggered: If something presses it or tugs at it, if its tip is touched, if the skin around it is pressed, the hair vibrates and sparks a nerve. Down is the most sensitive hair of all and only has to move 0.00004 of an inch to make a nerve fire. Still, it can't be firing all the time, or the body would go into sensory overload. There is an infinitesimally small realm in which nothing at all seems to be happening, a desert of sensation. Then the merest breeze starts to blow, nothing like a real disturbance. When it grows just strong enough to reach an electrical threshold, it fires an impulse to the nervous system. Hairs make wonderful organs of touch. "Breeze," our brain says without much fanfare, as a few hairs on our forearms lift imperceptibly. If a dust mote or insect brushes an eyelash, we know at once and blink to protect the eye. Though hairs can take shapes as various as down or antennae, some especially useful ones are *vibrissae*—the stiff hairs cats have as whiskers—which adorn many mammals, including whales and porpoises. A cat without its whiskers bumps into things at night, and can get its head caught in tight spaces. As we can. If we ever get a say-so in evolution, one of the things I'd vote for is whiskerlike feelers to keep us from bumping into furniture, friends, or raccoons in the dark.

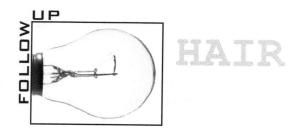

FOLLOW UP

HAIR

Exploring Language

aviary: a place to keep birds confined.

bourgeoisie: middle class.

castrati: those who have been castrated (had testicles or ovaries removed).

eunuch: a castrated man; usually refers to one put in charge of a harem.

infinitesimally: immeasurably small.

necromancers: those who practice magic or sorcery, often referring to raising dead spirits for the purpose of telling the future or influencing events.

Note: For pronunciation, go to dictionary.com, search the word, and click on the speaker icon.

Thinking and Talking Points

1. Ackerman writes that "one's hairstyle can be a badge of a group" and gives some examples. Think of other examples of a hairstyle being a badge of a group.

2. Ackerman makes good use of strong word choices. For example, she writes that hair "bolts" from the head. Find other strong word choices in the essay.

3. Ackerman writes, "Hair deeply affects people, can transfigure or repulse them." Discuss how hair transfigures or repulses people, giving examples. How is hair "symbolic of life"?

4. What does letting down one's hair symbolize? Find passages in the first paragraph where Ackerman discusses confining or loosening one's hair. Can you think of phrases from popular culture or literature that hint at this idea?

5. Reread paragraph #2. What might the "complex system of growth, death, and renewal" symbolize? Is she referring to more than just hair growth?

Styling

One way to create sentence variety is to use semicolons to connect two sentences (**independent clauses**). Ackerman writes:

> If the follicle cells grow in an even pattern, the hair will be straight; if they grow irregularly, the hair will be curly.

She could use a semicolon, a period, or a comma and conjunction:

> If the follicle cells grow in an even pattern, the hair will be straight. If they grow irregularly, the hair will be curly.

> If the follicle cells grow in an even pattern, the hair will be straight, but if they grow irregularly, the hair will be curly.

She chose the semicolon because the two sentences share the same structure and are closely related in thought. Each sentence contains an **introductory clause** (see the glossary) followed by a comma and complete sentence.

> *If the follicle cells grow in an even pattern* (introductory clause)
> *If they grow irregularly* (introductory clause)

These lead-ins introduce the main sentences. These two sentences balance each other like two children of equal weight on either side of a teeter-totter. Connecting them with a semicolon emphasizes that balance.

PRACTICE   For each of the following sentences, replace the period with a semicolon and add a complete sentence with an introductory clause.

> When Julia feeds her dachshund a Milk Bone treat, he rolls on the floor in ecstasy.

> If you feed and water orchids properly, they're easy to grow.

YOU TRY IT   Write three sentences following the above pattern. Try this style in one of the Teaming Up activities or Writing Ideas.

Teaming Up

1. Bring in photos of hairstyles and have each member of the group write a paragraph describing the hairdo and what it says about the person. Compare responses. Did you agree? What assumptions did you make about the person? What might be wrong with your assumptions?

2. **Warm-up for Writing Idea #3.** Have each member of the group bring in information on hairstyles from another culture. You might need to go to the library or access an online database through your library's web page. Try search terms like "hair and culture" or "hair and history." One example of a source would be *Hair: Its Power and Meaning in Asian Cultures* edited by Alf Hiltebeital et al. Share what you learned about the culture from your research. Write down the source information from each member. Now you have a start on Writing Idea #2.

Writing Ideas

1. Write an essay that describes your own hairstyle and how it reflects your identity. Consider how your hair has changed over the years—or not—and what those changes (or lack of) say about you.
2. Like hair, clothing can also reveal culture or personality. Visit your college or local library and use both an online database such as Infotrac and the book catalogue to research clothing from another time or culture; then, write an essay that explains how clothing reflects the cultural values.
3. Visit your college or local library and use both an online database such as Infotrac and the book catalogue to research hairstyles from another country. Write an essay comparing hairstyles from your own culture and the one you researched. What did you learn about each culture?

Essay and Film Connections

Three other essays analyze or reflect on cultural differences: "Naps" by Barbara Holland, "Somebody's Baby" by Barbara Kingsolver, and "City Out of Breath" by Ken Chen.

JOYAS VOLADORAS

Brian Doyle

Brian Doyle has several books of essays to his credit: Leaping: Revelations and Epiphanies, The Wet Engine: Exploring the Mad Wild Miracle of the Heart (where "Joyas Voladoras" appears), and Spirited Men. This essay also appeared in Best American Essays 2005. His collection of short stories is titled Epiphanies and Elegies.

1   Consider the hummingbird for a long moment. A hummingbird's heart beats ten times a second. A hummingbird's heart is the size of a pencil eraser. A hummingbird's heart is a lot of the hummingbird. *Joyas voladoras*, flying jewels, the first white explorers in the Americas called them, and the white men had never seen such creatures, for hummingbirds came into the world only in the Americas, nowhere else in the universe, more than three hundred species of them whirring and zooming and nectaring in hummer time zones nine times removed from ours, their hearts hammering faster than we could clearly hear if we pressed our elephantine ears to their infinitesimal chests.

2   Each one visits a thousand flowers a day. They can dive at sixty miles an hour. They can fly backward. They can fly more than five hundred miles without pausing to rest. But when they rest they come close to death: on frigid nights, or when they are starving, they retreat into torpor, their metabolic rate slowing to a fifteenth of their normal sleep rate, their hearts sludging nearly to a halt, barely beating, and if they are not soon warmed, if they do not soon find that which is sweet, their hearts grow cold, and they cease to be. Consider for a moment those hummingbirds who did not open their eyes again today, this very day, in the Americas: bearded helmetcrests and booted rackettails, violet-tailed sylphs and violet-capped woodnymphs, crimson topazes and purple-crowned fairies, red-tailed comets and amethyst woodstars, rainbow-bearded thornbills and glittering-bellied emeralds, velvet-purple coronets and golden-bellied star-frontlets, fiery-tailed awlbills and Andean hillstars, spatuletails and pufflegs, each the most amazing thing you have never seen, each thunderous wild

"Joyas Voladoras" by Brian Doyle from *The American Scholar,* Volume 73, No. 4, Autumn 2004. Copyright © 2004 by the author. Used by permission.

heart the size of an infant's fingernail, each mad heart silent, a brilliant music stilled.

3   Hummingbirds, like all flying birds but more so, have incredible enormous immense ferocious metabolisms. To drive those metabolisms they have racecar hearts that eat oxygen at an eye-popping rate. Their hearts are built of thinner, leaner fibers than ours. Their arteries are stiffer and more taut. They have more mitochondria in their heart muscles—anything to gulp more oxygen. Their hearts are stripped to the skin for the war against gravity and inertia, the mad search for food, the insane idea of flight. The price of their ambition is a life closer to death; they suffer more heart attacks and aneurysms and ruptures than any other living creature. It's expensive to fly. You burn out. You fry the machine. You melt the engine. Every creature on earth has approximately two billion heartbeats to spend in a lifetime. You can spend them slowly, like a tortoise, and live to be two hundred years old, or you can spend them fast, like a hummingbird, and live to be two years old.

4   The biggest heart in the world is inside the blue whale. It weighs more than seven tons. It's as big as a room. It is a room, with four chambers. A child could walk around in it, head high, bending only to step through the valves. The valves are as big as the swinging doors in a saloon. This house of a heart drives a creature a hundred feet long. When this creature is born it is twenty feet long and weighs four tons. It is waaaaay bigger than your car. It drinks a hundred gallons of milk from its mama every day and gains two hundred pounds a day, and when it is seven or eight years old it endures an unimaginable puberty and then it essentially disappears from human ken, for next to nothing is known of the mating habits, travel patterns, diet, social life, language, social structure, diseases, spirituality, wars, stories, despairs, and arts of the blue whale. There are perhaps ten thousand blue whales in the world, living in every ocean on earth, and of the largest mammal who ever lived we know nearly nothing. But we know this: the animals with the largest hearts in the world generally travel in pairs, and their penetrating moaning cries, their piercing yearning tongue, can be heard underwater for miles and miles.

5   Mammals and birds have hearts with four chambers. Reptiles and turtles have hearts with three chambers. Fish have hearts with two chambers. Insects and mollusks have hearts with one chamber. Worms have hearts with one chamber, although they may have as many as eleven single-chambered hearts. Unicellular bacteria have

no hearts at all; but even they have fluid eternally in motion, washing from one side of the cell to the other, swirling and whirling. No living being is without interior liquid motion. We all churn inside.

6   So much held in a heart in a lifetime. So much held in a heart in a day, an hour, a moment. We are utterly open with no one, in the end—not mother and father, not wife or husband, not lover, not child, not friend. We open windows to each but we live alone in the house of the heart. Perhaps we must. Perhaps we could not bear to be so naked, for fear of a constantly harrowed heart. When young we think there will come one person who will savor and sustain us always; when we are older we know this is the dream of a child, that all hearts finally are bruised and scarred, scored and torn, repaired by time and will, patched by force of character, yet fragile and rickety forevermore, no matter how ferocious the defense and how many bricks you bring to the wall. You can brick up your heart as stout and tight and hard and cold and impregnable as you possibly can and down it comes in an instant, felled by a woman's second glance, a child's apple breath, the shatter of glass in the road, the words "I have something to tell you," a cat with a broken spine dragging itself into the forest to die, the brush of your mother's papery ancient hand in the thicket of your hair, the memory of your father's voice early in the morning echoing from the kitchen where he is making pancakes for his children.

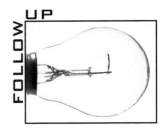

Exploring Language

inertia: resistance to motion, action, or change.
infinitesimal: extremely small; too small to be measured.
ken: knowledge or understanding.
mitochondria: simply put, it's part of the cell.
Note: For pronunciation, go to dictionary.com, search the word, and click on the speaker icon.

Thinking and Talking Points

1. Find several comparisons Doyle makes (like "heart the size of an infant's fingernail"). How do these comparisons help the reader visualize and/or relate to the animals he's describing?
2. How do the examples and points show our relationship to the creatures? What is Doyle's overall point?
3. Is the conclusion unexpected? If so, what is the expectation? How do the examples relate to the conclusion?
4. Usually, beginning writers are told not to repeat words too close together. How does Doyle use repetition to his advantage?
5. Other than comparison, what other style techniques liven up this essay? Examine the length of the sentences. What do you notice? Also consider punctuation in your examination.

Styling

In addition to brilliant and vivid comparisons (see the Styling with Hoagland's "The Courage of Turtles"), this essay's unexpected conclusion—shifting from the physical workings of hearts to the emotional—moves the reader in almost the same way as the specific heartbreaks he mentions. It's these powerhouse **specifics**—a woman's second glance, a child's apple breath, the shatter of glass in the road, the words "I have something to tell you," a cat with a broken spine dragging itself into the forest to die, the brush of your mother's papery ancient hand in the thicket of your hair, the memory of your father's voice early in the morning echoing from the kitchen where he is making pancakes for his children—that make this conclusion so utterly unforgettable.

Notice that these examples are detailed as well as specific: not just a cat with a broken spine, but dragging itself into the forest to die; instead of simply mother's hand, it's papery ancient hand; a child's *apple* breath. These details hammer the heart, right on target.

PRACTICE   Think of an issue that concerns you, whether personal, social, or political. For example, you might be concerned about the plight of abused and neglected children; the unnecessary deaths of pets at a local animal shelter that still kills for space; a politician's views; a relative's health, and so on. Brainstorm a list of at least ten specific, detailed examples.

YOU TRY IT   Make a point about the issue you brainstormed, and write a sentence modeled on Doyle's concluding sentence. Consider livening up the conclusion to your next essay with this technique.

Teaming Up

1. The above Styling technique works well as a group activity. Everyone contribute an idea; then vote on which idea to brainstorm. Decide which examples are the most vivid or memorable, and then co-write the sentence.

2. **Warm-up for Writing Idea #1:** Break down the parts of a machine—an automobile, an oven, washer or dryer, a computer, anything—or the anatomy of a particular animal (bird, insect, mammal). Have one person in the group list each part on a piece of paper. Discuss how each part might be a metaphor for a human emotion or personality trait, something like this:

    > beak = nagging
    > claws = jealousy
    > feathers = mothering

(You can use a particular animal or machine for your brainstorm: duck instead of bird; Volkswagen rather than car). List as many parts and traits as you can. Now examine the list for a tone: are the qualities mostly bitter, joyful, philosophical, sad, mean, humorous? Choose items from the list that seem similar in tone. Now co-write a paragraph comparing the animal parts to human behavior.

Writing Ideas

1. Using the warm-up in Teaming Up #2, write an essay that compares a person to either the parts of a machine or an animal. The person can be someone you know personally (a friend or relative, for example) or a public figure.

2. Compare and/or contrast Doyle's style and tone to Diane Ackerman's "Mute Dancers: How to Watch a Hummingbird." You might discuss a different style element—figurative language, sentence variety, word choice, punctuation—in each paragraph. Consider concluding with a contemplation of tone.

Essay Connections

See the Writing Ideas and Essay Connections with Hoagland's "The Courage of Turtles"; Ackerman's "Mute Dancers: How to Watch a Hummingbird"; Gordon Grice's "Black Widow."

AMERICAN CHILDREN

John Updike

John Updike was an American author of novels, poems, plays, essays, and frequent contributions to The New Yorker magazine. This essay, from his book Just Looking: Essays on Art, analyzes and compares two paintings of children, one by Winslow Homer and the other by John Singer Sargent. John Updike died in January, 2009.

DUSTBIN OF HISTORY AND CULTURE

Winslow Homer: (1836–1910) Often considered one of the best 19th-century American naturalist painters.

John Singer Sargent: (1856–1925) Primarily known for his portraits of wealthy and influential American families.

1   The boys and girls depicted here might not mix very well if they were released from their frames, but separately they compose two peaceful groups and two beautiful paintings. Winslow Homer's anonymous lads are taking their ease in a pasture; the daughters of the prosperous Edward Boit are scattered through two fine rooms, and all but one of them gaze with respectful curiosity at the busy bearded intruder into their home, the fashionable painter John Singer Sargent. The dashing impressionism of Sargent's technique carries a generation farther Homer's flickering grasses and dabs of sunny red, and the triangular pose of the little girl in the foreground mirrors the unified shape of the two country idlers. Both painters surround their childish subjects with large margins of environment. The effect is of silence: silent vases, silent sky, silent carpet and turf underfoot. A great hushed world waits around these children to be tasted, explored, grown into.

2   They take themselves seriously, and are taken seriously. Homer gives his little subjects a monumental dignity; there is something of Greek drapery in the color-gouged fold of the sunlit white sleeve, and something angelically graceful in the extended, self-shadowed feet. And Sargent, catching his subjects where they have alighted like white butterflies, displays deep spaces about them, and permits them all

the gravity their young femininity warrants. They recede, from youngest to oldest, toward a dark other room; beyond the toddler with her doll a girl no longer quite childish stands on the edge of shadow while her sister, a little taller and older still, is half-turned into it. The huge vase she leans against suggests a woman's shape. These young ladies are watching, not just the painter, but us, to see what we will do next, and whether what we do will be worthy of their responding. Like butterflies, they will elude us if we startle them.

3   Sargent's painting could have been a mere commission, an expert piece of toadying within the upper classes, but the jaunty eccentricity of its composition, and a daring within its deference, save it for art. Winslow Homer's could have been a bit of calendar art, falsely bucolic, but for the abstract power of a severe and stately composition that locks the barefoot pair as if forever into the center of the canvas and that lends solemn substance to a fleeting summer day. There is a mystery to the faces; the painter has declined all opportunity for easy anecdote within the ruddy shade of those hats.

4   Both artists have attempted honest portraits of children, as perhaps only Americans could have done. Though the Declaration of Independence nowhere promises a better deal for children, the American child does appear freer than his European counterpart and is taken more seriously—as a source of opinion, as a market for sales, and as not just a future inheritor but an independent entity now, while still a child. Childhood and then youth are seen in our democracy as classes that cut across class distinctions. Within their frames these two sets of children are similarly pensive. Responsible but powerless, childhood does not smile; it watches and waits, amid shadows and sun.

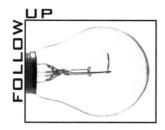

AMERICAN CHILDREN

Exploring Language

anecdote: a narrative account or story.

bucolic: relating to rural (country) life.

deference: respect or esteem for an elder or superior.

jaunty: carefree or high spirited.

pensive: thoughtful or meditative, in a dreamy sort of way, sometimes suggesting sadness.

toadying: brownnosing, flattering or, in modern slang, sucking up.

Note: For pronunciation, go to dictionary.com, search the word, and click on the speaker icon.

USAGE Practice using *pensive;* it's more descriptive than thoughtful. Look up thoughtful and pensive. What is the difference in meaning? Use each in a sentence that captures the subtle difference.

Thinking and Talking Points

1. What details in the essay help you understand the paintings or notice things you might otherwise have missed? Look up the paintings online and study the details.

2. Updike comments that American children "appear freer" than European children, and are "taken more seriously—as a source of opinion, as a market for sales, and as not just a future inheritor but an independent entity now, while still a child." Do you agree or disagree that American children are taken seriously? Be ready to support your response with examples.

3. At the end of his essay Updike writes, "Responsible but powerless, childhood does not smile; it watches and waits, amid shadows and sun." What do you think he means? In what way is childhood "responsible but powerless"?

4. Updike says of the children in the paintings that "there is a mystery to the faces" and "these two sets of children are similarly pensive." Study the paintings (available online). What features—facial, posture—make them look this way?

Styling

Updike uses a colon to list silent objects in the painting, an effective way to create sentence variety, establish a mood, and gather supporting details. He writes:

> The effect is of silence: silent vases, silent sky, silent carpet and turf underfoot.

Use a colon only after a complete sentence.

Usually, you don't want to repeat a word as Updike does with silent, but sometimes it's an effective tool to make a point. Though we're mostly concerned with practicing using the colon, try his repetition technique as a style bonus. You wouldn't want to do this in a paper too frequently, but one sentence like this can make an impact.

PRACTICE   Fill in the blanks with details that support the sentence. Here's an example:

> The concert radiated noise: *noisy drums, noisy bass,* and *noisy fans.*

Jerry's bedroom oozed dust: _____, _____, and _____.

After the storm, the old farmhouse leaked water: _____, _____, and _____.

The items in the refrigerator were covered in mold: _____, _____, and _____.

YOU TRY IT   Create five sentences of your own that begin with a complete sentence followed by a colon and a list of details. Try expanding your lists beyond three items.

Teaming Up

1. Bring in copies of the photos Updike discusses (available online). Discuss why you think Updike wrote that the children "might not mix very well if they were released from their frames." Co-write a dialogue between the two groups, what you imagine they would say to one another if they did meet.

2. Bring in a photograph of yourself (or someone else if you don't have a photo of yourself) as a child. Trade photos with another member of the group. Write a description of the picture of your classmate,

describing the mood of the child by giving details of facial expression, setting, and clothing, and what you think he or she might have been thinking at the time of the photograph.

Writing Ideas

1. Write an essay about a time you felt powerless but responsible when you were a child.
2. Find a painting that moves you in some way. Write an essay describing the painting and the feelings it evokes.
3. Find two paintings or photographs by different artists of the same subject: two landscapes, two women, two men, two dogs, any subject. Write an essay comparing the two pieces of art.

Essay Connections

Updike's book *Just Looking: Essays on Art* teems with essays full of style. David Huddle's essay "Museum Piece" journeys into the paintings of Jan Vermeer.

MUSICAL AWAKENINGS

Clayton S. Collins

This essay first appeared in Profiles: The Magazine of Continental Airlines. Clayton Collins discusses the work of neurologist and author Oliver Sacks, a strong believer in the healing power of music, and the essay contains fascinating case studies of people debilitated by stroke or other neurological diseases who are able to move once again when exposed to music.

DUSTBIN OF HISTORY AND CULTURE

FRIEDRICH NIETZSCHE: (1844–1900) A German philosopher, poet, and philologist (one who studies human speech, especially as it pertains to shedding light on culture). He coined the phrase "God is dead."

BIZET: (1838–1875) French composer best known for his operas, especially *Carmen.*

T. S. ELIOT: (1888–1965) British poet and critic. He won the Nobel prize for literature in 1948.

1   Oliver Sacks danced to the Dead. For three solid hours. At sixty. And with "two broken knees."

2   The Oxford-educated neurologist who likes to say, with an impish grin, that he doesn't like any music after Mozart's *Magic Flute,* wasn't particularly taken by the Grateful Dead concert in Friedrich Nietzsche's mnemonic sense, he explains (as only he would), "But in a tonic and dynamic sense they were quite overwhelming. And though I had effusions for a month after, it was worth it."

3   The power of music—not just to get an aging physician with classical tastes up and rocking, but also to "bring back" individuals rendered motionless and mute by neurological damage and disorders—is what's driving Sacks these days. The shyly brilliant and best-selling author of *The Man Who Mistook His Wife for a Hat* and *Awakenings*—the latter of which was made into a 1990 film starring Robin Williams—is working on another case-study book, one that deals in part with the role of music as a stimulus to minds that have thrown up stiff sensory barriers, leaving thousands of victims of stroke, tumors, Parkinson's

disease, Tourette's syndrome, Alzheimer's, and a wide range of less-publicized ailments alone, debilitated, and disoriented.

4   "One sees how robust music is neurologically," Sacks says. "You can lose all sorts of particular powers, but you don't tend to lose music and identity." His conviction regarding the role of music in helping the neurologically afflicted to become mentally "reorganized" runs deep: "Whenever I get out a book on neurology or psychology, the first thing I look up in the index is music," he says. 'And if it's not there, I close the book."

5   Born in London in 1933 and a permanent resident of the United States for the past thirty-four years, Sacks is a frequent public speaker, careening from stories about great composers and poets to a report about goldfish dancing to a Strauss waltz. However, Sacks is a reluctant celebrity. The fourth son (three of them doctors) of two physicians, he preferred solitary research early in his career, far more comfortable extracting myelin from earthworms than working with humans. But when he misplaced a vial of the white fatty substance in 1966, he was banished, in effect, to the less-prestigious realm of clinical medicine. Since then, Sacks has burrowed deep into the illnesses and the lives of persons in his care, a miner in the catacombs of the catatonic, chipping away at the walls around their neurological cores. . . .

6   Much of what he has encountered, particularly in working with patients at Beth Abraham Hospital, in the Bronx, is startling. Much of it relates to music.

7   "One saw patients who couldn't take a single step, who couldn't walk, but who could dance," he says. "There were patients who couldn't speak, but who could sing. The power of music in these patients was instantaneous . . . from a frozen Parkinsonian state to a freely flowing, moving, speaking state."

8   Sacks remembers a woman with Parkinson's who would sit perfectly still until "activated" by the music of Chopin, which she loved and knew by heart. She didn't have to hear a tune played. "It was sometimes sufficient to give her an opus number," Sacks says. "You would just say 'Opus 49,' and the F-minor *Fantasy* would start playing in her mind. And she could move."

9   Music is certainly cultural, acknowledges the doctor, but it is basically biological. "One listens to music with one's muscles," he says, quoting Nietzsche again. "The 'tonic' [the key] is mostly brainstem, an arousal response." The "dynamic"—how loud or forcefully the

music is played—registers in the basal ganglia. And the "mnemonic" aspect of songs speaks to the unique memories of individuals: from tribal chant to the blare of bagpipes to Bizet. The old cliché about music's universality, he says, has merit.

10   "Deeply demented people respond to music, babies respond to music, fetuses *probably* respond to music. Various animals respond to music," Sacks says. "There is something about the animal nervous system . . . which seems to respond to music all the way down.

11   "I don't know how it is with invertebrates. I think it's a desperately needed experiment to see how squids and cuttlefish respond," he says, his grin widening.

12   In 1974, Sacks was able to apply music therapy to himself to speed an orthopedic recovery. Hospitalized after a fall while climbing in Norway, he experienced neural damage and partial paralysis and sensed that he was, as a result, losing his "motor identity"—forgetting how to walk.

13   For weeks, flat on his back, he listened to a recording of a Mendelssohn violin concerto. One morning, awakened by the familiar piece, he got up and walked across the room to turn off the tape. He found that the concerto wasn't playing, except in his head. Then he realized he'd been walking, carried along by the tune. It was, he says, "the most dynamic experience in my life.

14   "I'm not normally all that fond of Mendelssohn," he jokes.

15   "I think the notion of music as being a prosthesis in a way, for neurological dysfunctions, is very fundamental," Sacks says, citing the case of a patient with damage to the frontal lobes of his brain.

16   "When he sings, one almost has the strange feeling that [music] has given him his frontal lobes back, given him back, temporally, some function that has been lost on an organic basis," Sacks says, adding a quote from T. S. Eliot: "You are the music, while the music lasts."

17   The key, says Sacks, is for patients to "learn to be well" again. Music can restore to them, he says, the identity that predates the illness. "There's a health to music, a life to music."

18   Those may not sound like the words of a typical clinician. But don't toss terms like "new age" and "holistic" at the good doctor. "I always tighten up a little bit when I hear the word 'holistic,'" he says, professing disdain for "Californian and Eastern" practices. For Sacks, who's been affiliated with a half-dozen neurological institutes and written dozens of seminal papers, medicine needs to be demonstrable, firmly grounded in physiology. Music's been healing for thousands of years, Sacks says. "It's just being looked at now more systematically and with these special populations."

19   So if the Grateful Dead moved Sacks to dance, it had been in the name of research. Seeking a clinical application, Sacks returned to Beth Abraham the next day and "kidnapped" one of his patients. "Greg" was an amnesiac with a brain tumor and no coherent memories of life since about 1969—but an encyclopedic memory of the years that came before, and a real love of Grateful Dead tunes.

20   Sacks took Greg to that night's show. "In the first half of the concert they were doing early music, and Greg was enchanted by everything," Sacks recalls. "I mean, he was not an amnesiac. He was completely oriented and organized and with it."

21   Between sets Sacks went backstage and introduced Greg to band member Mickey Hart, who was impressed with the depth of Greg's knowledge of the group but quite surprised when Greg asked after Pigpen. When told that the former band member had died twenty years before, "Greg was very upset," Sacks recalls. "And then thirty seconds later he asked, 'How's Pigpen?'"

22   During the second half, the band played its newer songs. And Greg's world began to fall apart. "He was bewildered and enthralled and frightened. Because the music for him—and this is an extremely musical man, who understands the idiom of the Grateful Dead—was both familiar and unfamiliar. . . . He said, 'This is like the music of the future.'"

23   Sacks tried to keep the new memories fresh. But the next day Greg had no memory of the concert. It seemed as if all had been lost. "But—and this is strange—when one played some of the new music, which he had heard for the first time at the concert, he could sing along with it and remember it."

24   It is an encouraging development. Amnesiacs have never been found capable of learning anything new. Children have been found to learn quickly lessons that are embedded in song. Sacks, the one-time quiet researcher, is invigorated by the possibilities. He wonders whether music could carry such information, to give his patient back a missing part of his life. To give Greg "some sense of what's been happening in the last twenty years, where he has no autobiography of his own."

25   That would have Sacks dancing in the aisles.

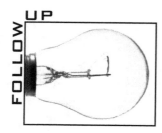

FOLLOW UP

MUSCIAL AWAKENINGS

Exploring Language

careening: leaning, swaying, or tipping to one side while in motion.
demonstrable: capable of being demonstrated.
effusions: look up this word and decide which context Collins is using.
enthralled: fascinated, absorbed.
holistic: looking at the whole thing rather than its parts; when applied to medicine, it means treating the mind and body as one.
invertebrates: animals with no backbone (no spine).
invigorated: energized; renewed; restored.
mnemonic: assisting memory—like the childhood learning songs mentioned in Thinking and Talking Points #3. Those tools help you remember information.
myelin: a fatty white goo that helps protect nerves.
neurological: having to do with the nervous system.
orthopedic: having to do with the bones, or skeletal system.
prosthesis: artificial limb.
seminal: creative; contributing to later development. In other words, Sacks wrote papers that got people thinking and developing his ideas.
Note: For pronunciation, go to dictionary.com, search the word, and click on the speaker icon.

USAGE Many of the words in the above list are medical and scientific terms which will be useful when reading and writing about those subjects. The words *effusions, invigorated, enthralled* beg to be used; they hop off the page. So in your essay, instead of writing "The song held my interest," write "The song enthralled me."

Thinking and Talking Points

1. According to Oliver Sacks, music is a powerful tool for healing. Go through the essay and list specific examples Sacks gives to support his view. What other powers can you attribute to music?
2. Collins writes that Sacks doesn't approve of "new age" or "holistic" therapies. But music therapy was once considered—and to some still

is—quack medicine. Find examples from the essay that support his point concerning therapy. What other once-considered-hogwash therapies can you think of that have become mainstream? What is your opinion about some of these therapies? Do you base your view on personal experience or what you've read or heard from others?

3. Collins writes that "children have been found to learn quickly lessons that are embedded in song." Do you remember any of these learning songs from childhood? Do you remember song lyrics better than test material? Explain.

4. Study the opening paragraph to this essay. How does it hook the reader's attention? Apply this technique of short, catchy sentences to your paragraph in Teaming Up #2.

Styling

In addition to a catchy opening and intriguing examples for support, Collins uses **metaphor** to spark life into his essay. He writes:

> Since then, Sacks has burrowed deep into the illnesses and the lives of persons in his care, a miner in the catacombs of the catatonic, chipping away at the walls around their neurological cores.

Collins compares Sacks to a miner and his patients' minds to catacombs. Look at this simple example from the Russell Sanders essay "Grub":

> Bloomington is ringed by the usual necklace of fast food shops.

The necklace image gives the reader a clearer picture of the town.

Here's an example based on the Sanders model: *Laguna Beach is the McDonald's of the art world.*

PRACTICE (For another technique for creating figurative language, see Teaming Up #1.) Fill in the blanks below with your town or a nearby community and an appropriate metaphor. Try brainstorming lists of toys, brand name foods, or retail shops to get ideas for metaphors. For example, Barbie Doll becomes this sentence: *Beverly Hills is the Barbie Doll of Southern California.* Your metaphor should convey a recognizable attitude about the city. The Barbie Doll example works because Beverly Hills has a reputation for being full of affluent people who drive expensive cars, drink Evian water, and get a lot of plastic surgery; not everyone in Beverly Hills fits this stereotype, but enough do to make the metaphor appropriate. And let's face it, Barbie must have had breast implants, and she has everything.

———————————————————— is the ———————————————————— of

————————————————————.

YOU TRY IT   Create three more sentences using metaphor. You can try this technique on other towns or cities you're familiar with, or describe friends or family members, your car, whatever sounds like fun: *My 1970 Chevy Vega is the Mr. Potato Head of the car world* (not very popular in our high-tech world, the Vega is seen as an oddity). Don't worry if some of the metaphors sound odd or silly. The idea is to practice creating metaphor.

Teaming Up

1. Here's a trick for creating a type of figurative language called **personification**. Form groups of three to five members and list some basic colors. Then list the various shades of that color. It helps if someone in the group has a set of colored pencils with various shades. Next, make a list of basic emotions. Think of as many words as you can that are similar for each emotion (synonyms). A thesaurus might help. Your lists might look like this:

Blue	*Happy*	*Sad*
navy	glad	unhappy
midnight	ecstatic	depressed
powder	cheerful	forlorn
peacock	delighted	melancholy
aquamarine	joyful	gloomy
royal	pleased	dejected

Brainstorm other emotions. Now replace each shade of color with an emotion that you think describes that color. For example, peacock blue is a shocking color, so you might label it *ecstatic blue*. Midnight blue might become *melancholy blue*. Now attach each emotion/color combination to an object: melancholy blue recliner; forlorn pink ribbon. Finally, build sentences for each emotion/color/object combination:

> The melancholy blue recliner sulked in the corner of the living room.

> My three-year-old sister's forlorn pink ribbon straggled limply through her tangled curls.

2. **Warm-up for Writing Idea #1.** Have your group decide on a song that you all agree you like. I know this may be difficult with the diver-

sity of tastes, but you can also use this activity to convince a dissenting member of the group that your song is worth listening to. Have one member bring in the lyrics, and if possible, have everyone listen to the song before class and write down their reactions. In groups, read and analyze the lyrics. Compare reactions. Co-write a paragraph reporting your findings.

Writing Ideas

1. Think of a song that has an emotional impact on you—or simply a song you like. Listen to it several times and try to identify why the music moves you. Is it the tone? The rhythm? The way a particular instrument sounds? Try to describe the music for your reader. Study the lyrics. Does the song contain metaphor? Hidden meanings or allusions like a poem? Write an essay analyzing the song's impact through its music and message. Use at least one metaphor and one word from the vocabulary list.

2. Some music performers take on almost mythic status in our culture—the Beatles, Elvis, Tupac Shakur—while others burst onto the music scene and quickly fade. The Grateful Dead—while not exactly mythic—has quite a cult following. There are Dead Head clubs, Web sites—even the death of Jerry Garcia hasn't squashed the group's allure. Write an essay that attempts to explain the cult phenomenon that surrounds certain music groups, movies, or TV shows. Focus on one such group like the Grateful Dead's Dead Heads, *Star Trek* Trekkies, *Rocky Horror Picture Show* groupies. Try to find a photo to generate accurate description. Use at least one metaphor or personification in your essay.

3. Do some research on another area of unconventional medicine: acupuncture, chiropractic, herbal remedies, laugh therapy, meditation. Look at arguments from both sides of the issue. Your library should have books in the reference section (or perhaps online) that have articles on both sides of various arguments. Decide whether or not you think the therapy is credible. Provide numerous examples—as Collins does—to support your view. For tips on researching, see the Research section of this book.

Essay Connections

"A Voice for the Lonely" by Stephen Corey also explores music's impact on mood and memory. "Monster Mash" by Jack Kroll and "Prince" by Chuck Klosterman argue particular musicians' influence on culture.

FROM "ON BOXING"

Joyce Carol Oates

One of America's most prolific contemporary writers, Joyce Carol Oates has written numerous novels, short stories, and essays. This excerpt is from her book On Boxing, *where she compares boxing to art: "Each boxing match is a story—a unique and highly condensed drama without words."*

DUSTBIN OF HISTORY AND CULTURE

FRIEDRICH NIETZSCHE: (1844–1900) A German philosopher, poet, and philologist (one who studies human speech, especially as it pertains to shedding light on culture). He coined the phrase "God is dead."

HELLENIC: Relating to Greece, especially ancient Greece and its art, culture, people, language.

Why are you a boxer, Irish featherweight champion Barry McGuigan was asked.

He said: "I can't be a poet. I can't tell stories."

1   Each boxing match is a story—a unique and highly condensed drama without words. Even when nothing sensational happens: then the drama is "merely" psychological. Boxers are there to establish an absolute experience, a public accounting of the outermost limits of their beings; they will know, as few of us can know of ourselves, what physical and psychic power they possess—of how much, or how little, they are capable. To enter the ring near-naked and to risk one's life is to make of one's audience voyeurs of a kind: boxing is so intimate. It is to ease out of sanity's consciousness and into another, difficult to name. It is to risk, and sometimes to realize, the agony of which agon (Greek, "contest") is the root.

2   In the boxing ring there are two principal players, overseen by a shadowy third. The ceremonial ringing of the bell is a summoning to full wakefulness for both boxers and spectators. It sets into motion, too, the authority of Time.

3   The boxers will bring to the fight everything that is themselves, and everything will be exposed—including secrets about themselves they cannot fully realize. The physical self, the maleness, one might say, underlying the "self." There are boxers possessed of such remarkable intuition, such uncanny prescience, one would think they were somehow recalling their fights, not fighting them as we watch. There are boxers who perform skillfully, but mechanically, who cannot improvise in response to another's alteration of strategy; there are boxers performing at the peak of their talent who come to realize, mid-fight, that it will not be enough; there are boxers—including great champions—whose careers end abruptly, and irrevocably, as we watch. There has been at least one boxer possessed of an extraordinary and disquieting awareness not only of his opponent's every move and anticipated move but of the audience's keenest shifts in mood as well, for which he seems to have felt personally responsible—Cassius Clay/Muhammad Ali, of course. "The Sweet Science of Bruising" celebrates the physicality of men even as it dramatizes the limitations, sometimes tragic, more often poignant, of the physical. Though male spectators identify with boxers no boxer behaves like a "normal" man when he is in the ring and no combination of blows is "natural." All is style.

4   Every talent must unfold itself in fighting. So Nietzsche speaks of the Hellenic past, the history of the "contest"—athletic, and otherwise—by which Greek youths were educated into Greek citizenry. Without the ferocity of competition, without, even, "envy, jealousy, and ambition" in contest, the Hellenic city, like the Hellenic man, degenerated. If death is a risk, death is also the prize—for the winning athlete.

5   In the boxing ring, even in our greatly humanized times, death is always a possibility—which is why some of us prefer to watch films or tapes of fights already past, already defined as history. Or, in some instances, art. (Though to prepare for writing this mosaic-like essay I saw tapes of two infamous "death" fights of recent times: the Lupe Pintor-Johnny Owen bantamweight match of 1982, and the Ray Mancini-Duk Koo-Kim lightweight match of the same year. In both instances the boxers died as a consequence of their astonishing resilience and apparent indefatigability—their "heart," as it's known in boxing circles.) Most of the time, however, death in the ring is extremely unlikely; a statistically rare possibility like your possible death tomorrow morning in an automobile accident or in next

month's headlined airline disaster or in a freak accident involving a fall on the stairs or in the bathtub, a skull fracture, subarachnoid hemorrhage. Spectators at "death" fights often claim afterward that what happened simply seemed to happen—unpredictably, in a sense accidentally. Only in retrospect does death appear to have been inevitable.

6   If a boxing match is a story it is an <u>always wayward story</u>, <u>one in which anything can happen</u>. And in a matter of seconds. Split seconds! (Muhammad Ali boasted that he could throw a punch faster than the eye could follow, and he may have been right.) In no other sport can so much take place in so brief a period of time, and so irrevocably.

7   Because a boxing match is a story without words, this doesn't mean that <u>it has no text or no language</u>, that it is somehow "brute," "primitive," "inarticulate," only that the text is improvised in action; the language a dialogue between the boxers of the most refined sort (one might say, as much neurological as psychological: a dialogue of split-second reflexes) in a joint response to the mysterious will of the audience which is always that the fight be a worthy one so that the crude paraphernalia of the setting—ring, lights, ropes, stained canvas, the staring onlookers themselves—be erased, forgotten. (As in the theater or the church, settings are erased by the way, ideally, of transcendent action.) Ringside announcers give to the wordless spectacle a narrative unity, yet boxing as performance is more clearly akin to dance or music than narrative.

8   To turn from an ordinary preliminary match to a "Fight of the Century" like those between Joe Louis and Billy Conn, Joe Frazier and Muhammad Ali, Marvin Hagler and Thomas Hearns is to turn from listening or half-listening to a guitar being idly plucked to hearing Bach's Well-Tempered Clavier perfectly executed, and that too is part of the story's mystery: so much happens so swiftly and with such heart-stopping subtlety you cannot absorb it except to know that something profound is happening and it is happening in a place beyond words.

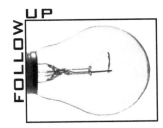

FROM

ON BOXING

Exploring Language

indefatigability: inability to be fatigued.
prescience: foresight or knowledge.
transcendent: overcoming or rising above the ordinary, often in reference to rising above the material to the spiritual.
voyeur: someone who likes to observe private or intimate acts, usually a sexual act or something sordid or scandalous.
Note: For pronunciation, go to dictionary.com, search the word, and click on the speaker icon.

Thinking and Talking Points

1. How does Oate's view of boxing differ from descriptions of this sport as brutal, almost animal-like? How does she support her belief?
2. In what way is boxing like dance and music?
3. What makes boxing intimate? How does that intimacy make the viewer—in a sense—a voyeur?
4. In what way does Oates mean that death is a prize? Does her essay give any insight into why some people engage in dangerous sports?

Styling

Opening an essay with a quote that underscores ideas in your writing is an effective way to get the reader's attention. To find a quote, use a dictionary of quotations, available at most libraries or on the Internet. Look up a topic and find several quotes by famous people; choose one to use as a hook in an essay. Notice, though, that Oates doesn't just dangle the quote at the top of the page with no connection to the first sentence; she transitions by picking up the word *story*. Another way to make the transition is to comment on the quote.

PRACTICE **Teaming Up #2** is a practice activity for using a dictionary of quotations, or use a dictionary of quotations on your own to find opening quotes for your next essay topic.

YOU TRY IT Use one of the quotes from the Practice or from **Teaming Up #2** as an opening to your next essay, blending it into the paragraph with a transition.

Teaming Up

1. **Warm-up for Writing Idea #1.** In groups, brainstorm a list of dangerous sports and discuss why people participate in activities that risk their lives.

2. Have each member of the group bring in quotes on boxing, either by visiting the library and copying a page from a dictionary of quotations or researching quotations online. Compare quotes and divide them according to whether they have a positive or negative view of boxing (put neutral ones aside). Divide the group into two teams, one team co-writing a paragraph in favor of boxing and the other against this sport. Use one of the quotations in each paragraph.

Writing Ideas

1. Write an essay describing another dangerous sport, either defending or condemning it. The **tone** of the description should reflect the attitude about the sport.
2. Watch *My Life as a Dog*, a Swedish film available in the foreign film section of most video stores. Write an essay that discusses the boxing theme in the film as a **metaphor** for Ingemar's life.
3. Compare the excerpt from *On Boxing* to Maya Angelou's "Champion of the World" from her autobiography *I Know Why the Caged Bird Sings* (not in this book). Write an essay that compares these two writers' styles, language, and ideas. Which writer has the more complex essay?

Essay Connections

"Disposable Rocket" by John Updike explores the male body and men's desire to participate in dangerous activities. Other sports essays include "The Surfing Savant" and "Meat."

DISPOSABLE ROCKET

John Updike

John Updike was an American author of novels, poems, plays, essays, and frequent contri-butions to The New Yorker magazine. In "Disposable Rocket," Updike reflects on the male body, traveling through several stages in a man's life from boyhood to old age, comparing the male and female body, writing, "Inhabiting a male body is much like having a bank account; as long as it's healthy, you don't think much about it. Compared to the female body, it is a low-maintenance proposition." John Updike died in January, 2009.

DUSTBIN OF HISTORY AND CULTURE

BYRON: Lord George Gordon Byron (1788–1824). A prominent writer of the English Romantic Period.

DIANA: Roman goddess of the moon and hunting, also the protector of women.

DIONYSUS: Greek god—known by the Romans as Bacchus—of wine and revelry.

DON JUAN: An epic satirical poem by Lord Byron chronicling the adventures of the hero—Don Juan—who becomes Byron's mouthpiece for his views on wealth, power, society, sex, poets, and politicians in England. In the dedication of the work, Byron insults Coleridge and Wordsworth, two of his contemporaries, also renowned poets.

MARS: The Roman god of war. The Greeks identified him with their god Ares.

VENUS: Roman goddess of love and beauty. The Greeks identified her with their goddess Aphrodite.

1   Inhabiting a male body is much like having a bank account; as long as it's healthy, you don't think much about it. Compared to the female body, it is a low-maintenance proposition: a shower now and then, trim the fingernails every ten days, a haircut once a month. Oh yes, shaving—scraping or buzzing away at your face every morning. Byron, in *Don Juan*, thought the repeated nuisance of shaving balanced out the periodic agony, for females, of childbirth. Women are, his lines tell us,

> *Condemn'd to child-bed, as men for their sins*
> *Have shaving too entail'd upon their chins, —*

> A *daily plague, which in the aggregate*
> *May average on the whole with parturition.*

From the standpoint of reproduction, the male body is a delivery system, as the female is a mazy device for retention. Once the delivery is made, men feel a faint but distinct falling-off of interest. Yet against the enduring female heroics of birth and nurture should be set the male's superhuman frenzy to deliver his goods: he vaults walls, skips sleep, risks wallet, health, and his political future all to ram home his seed into the gut of the chosen woman. The sense of the chase lives in him as the key to life. His body is, like a delivery rocket that falls away in space, a disposable means. Men put their bodies at risk to experience the release from gravity.

2   When my tenancy of a male body was fairly new—of six or so years' duration—I used to jump and fall just for the joy of it. Falling—backwards, downstairs—became a specialty of mine, an attention-getting stunt I was practicing into my thirties, at suburban parties. Falling is, after all, a kind of flying, though of briefer duration than would be ideal. My impulse to hurl myself from high windows and the edges of cliffs belongs to my body, not my mind, which resists the siren call of the chasm with all its might; the interior struggle knocks the wind from my lungs and tightens my scrotum and gives any trip to Europe, with its Alps, castle parapets, and gargoyled cathedral lookouts, a flavor of nightmare. Falling, strangely, no longer figures in my dreams, as it often did when I was a boy and my subconscious was more honest with me. An airplane, that necessary evil, turns the earth into a map so quickly the brain turns aloof and calm; still, I marvel that there is no end of young men willing to become jet pilots.

3   Any accounting of male-female differences must include the male's superior recklessness, a drive not, I think, toward death, as the darker feminist cosmogonies would have it, but to test the limits, to see what the traffic will bear—a kind of mechanic's curiosity. The number of men who do lasting damage to their young bodies is striking; war and car accidents aside, secondary-school sports, with the approval of parents and the encouragement of brutish coaches, take a fearful toll of skulls and knees. We were made for combat, back in the post-simian, East African days, and the bumping, the whacking, the breathlessness, the pain-smothering adrenaline rush, form a cumbersome and unfashionable bliss, but bliss nevertheless. Take your body to the edge, and see if it flies.

4   The male sense of space must differ from that of the female, who has such interesting, active, and significant inner space. The space that interests men is outer. The fly ball high against the sky, the long pass spiraling overhead, the jet fighter like a scarcely visible pinpoint nozzle laying down its vapor trail at forty thousand feet, the gazelle haunch flickering just beyond arrow-reach, the uncountable stars sprinkled on their great black wheel, the horizon, the mountaintop, the quasar—these bring portents with them, and awaken a sense of relation with the invisible, with the empty. The ideal male body is taut with lines of potential force, a diagram extending outward; the ideal female body curves around centers of repose. Of course, no one is ideal, and the sexes are somewhat androgynous subdivisions of a species: Diana the huntress is a more trendy body-type nowadays than languid, overweight Venus, and polymorphous Dionysus poses for more underwear ads than Mars. Relatively, though, men's bodies, however elegant, are designed for covering territory, for moving on.

5   An erection, too, defies gravity, flirts with it precariously. It extends the diagram of outward direction into downright detachability—objective in the case of the sperm, subjective in the case of the testicles and penis. Men's bodies, at this juncture, feel only partly theirs; a demon of sorts has been attached to their lower torsos, whose performance is erratic and whose errands seem, at times, ridiculous. It is like having a (much) smaller brother toward whom you feel both fond and impatient; if he is you, it is you in curiously simplified and ignoble form. This sense, of the male body being two of them, is acknowledged in verbal love play and erotic writing, where the penis is playfully given its own name, an individuation not even the rarest rapture grants a vagina. Here, where maleness gathers to a quintessence of itself, there can be no insincerity, there can be no hiding; for sheer nakedness, there is nothing like a hopeful phallus; its aggressive shape is indivisible from its tender-skinned vulnerability. The act of intercourse, from the point of view of a consenting female, has an element of mothering, of enwrapment, of merciful concealment, even. The male body, for this interval, is tucked out of harm's way.

6   To inhabit a male body, then, is to feel somewhat detached from it. It is not an enemy, but not entirely a friend. Our essence seems to lie not in cells and muscles but in the traces our thoughts and actions inscribe on the air. The male body skims the surface of nature's deep, wherein the blood and pain and mysterious cravings

of women perpetuate the species. Participating less in nature's processes than the female body, the male body gives the impression—false—of being exempt from time. Its powers of strength and reach descend in early adolescence, along with acne and sweaty feet, and depart, in imperceptible increments, after thirty or so. It surprises me to discover, when I remove my shoes and socks, the same paper-white hairless ankles that struck me as pathetic when observed them on my father. I felt betrayed when, in some tumble of touch football twenty years ago, I heard my tibia snap; and when, between two read-ing engagements in Cleveland, my appendix tried to burst; and when, the other day, not for the first time, there arose to my nostrils out of my own body the musty attic smell my grandfather's body had.

7   A man's body does not betray its tenant as rapidly as a woman's. Never as fine and lovely, it has less distance to fall; what rugged beauty it has is wrinkle-proof. It keeps its capability of procreation indecently long. Unless intense athletic demands are made on it, the thing serves well enough to sixty, which is my age now. From here on, it's chancy. There are no breasts or ovaries to admit cancer to the male body, but the prostate, that awkwardly located little source of seminal fluid, shows the strain of sexual function with fits of hysteri-cal cell replication, and all that beer and potato chips add up in the coronary arteries. A writer, whose physical equipment can be mini-mal, as long as it gets him to the desk, the lectern, and New York City once in a while, cannot but be grateful to his body, especially to his eyes, those tender and intricate sites where the brain extrudes from the skull, and to his hands, which hold the pen or tap the keyboard. His body has been, not himself exactly, but a close pal, pot-bellied and balding like most of his other pals now. A man and his body are like a boy and the buddy who has a driver's license and the use of his father's car for the evening; he goes along, gratefully, for the ride.

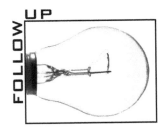

DISPOSABLE ROCKET

Exploring Language

aggregate: on the whole, or combined. Byron means that shaving for men—because it's a daily nuisance—on the whole may equal the agony of childbirth for women, which occurs less frequently.

androgynous: appearing partly male, partly female; of unclear gender.

chasm: a deep opening in the earth; sometimes refers to a wide difference in feelings, thoughts, or interests.

cosmogonies: theories about the origin of the universe.

ignoble: common, of low birth or origin; second rate; coarse; lacking refinement.

increments: stages of increasing number or value.

imperceptible: undetectable or unnoticeable; slight or minimal.

parturition: childbirth.

parapet: a balcony or low wall along the edge of a roof.

polymorphous: assuming or having many forms (*poly* means many or several).

portents: a sign of the future; an omen.

post-simian: after the apes (the prefix *post* means after).

tenancy: a tenant is someone who rents or occupies land or property, so tenancy means possession or status as a tenant.

quintessence: the most typical example or epitome; the purest or most perfect form.

Note: For pronunciation, go to dictionary.com, search the word, and click on the speaker icon.

USAGE Examine the passage where Updike uses the word *cosmogonies*. Why would he use this word in the same context with feminism?

Thinking and Talking Points

1. Updike writes, "The space that interests men is outer." How does he think it differs from female space? Do you agree or disagree? Why?
2. What other comparisons or contrasts—other than space—does Updike make between males and females? Do you agree with him? Explain.

3. Updike claims that "To inhabit a male body, then, is to feel somewhat detached from it." Are males detached from their bodies? How is that different from females' relationship with their bodies?
4. Look up information on the gods and goddess—Diana, Dionysus, Mars, and Venus—that Updike mentions, either on the Internet or in a dictionary of mythology. What point is he trying to make about our view of the human body? Think of the types of ads Updike mentions. Do you agree with his assertions? You might also search for images to help form a conclusion.
5. In what way is a rocket "disposable"? What qualities does the male body share with a disposable rocket? What other metaphors does Updike use? Do they tie together a common theme or idea in the essay?
6. Updike writes that his subconscious was "more honest" with him as a child. What do you think he means? Is your subconscious less honest now than when you were younger?

Styling

Many writers use lists of specific examples beaded together in one long sentence to give a feeling of continuity or chaos, excitement or enormity. In "Disposable Rocket," Updike creates a vivid list to illustrate what he calls male "space":

> The space that interests men is outer. The fly ball high against the sky, the long pass spiraling overhead, the jet fighter like a scarcely visible pinpoint nozzle laying down its vapor trail at forty thousand feet, the gazelle haunch flickering just beyond arrow-reach, the uncountable stars sprinkled on their great black wheel, the horizon, the mountaintop, the quasar—these bring portents with them, and awaken a sense of relation with the invisible, with the empty.

Notice the structure of this sentence. Updike first makes his list—each item in the series separated with a comma—followed by a dash, followed by a complete sentence.

PRACTICE   Fill in the blanks below with a list to go with each sentence. Don't resort to using all one-word objects. Notice that Updike sometimes describes or uses simile, "the jet fighter like a scarcely visible pin-point nozzle laying down its vapor trail at forty thousand feet."

_____ , _____ , _____ ,
_____ , _____ , _____ ,
_____ —these are a few of my favorite things.
_____ , _____ , _____ ,
_____ , _____ , _____ ,
_____ —all annoyances I've learned to live with.
_____ , _____ , _____ ,
_____ , _____ , _____ ,
_____ —that was the best summer of my life.

YOU TRY IT   Based on the Updike model, write five sentences of your own containing long lists. Use this sentence style in your next writing assignment.

Teaming Up

1. **Warm-up for Writing Idea #1.** Before class, do a quick freewrite or journal entry about a dream you had and what you think the dream means. You might consult a dream dictionary if you're stuck. In your group, describe your dream, and ask the other team members for their interpretations. Discuss whether your analysis matches your classmates'. What did you learn about yourself or other group members?

2. **Warm-up for Writing Idea #2.** Have each member of the group research the painting by Botticelli, *Birth of Venus* (available on the Internet), and do a freewrite describing her body type; then, write about what you think society considers the ideal female body type today. Compare your responses. Discuss how Botticelli's depiction of the ideal woman might differ from today's view. Who would be today's Venus?

Writing Ideas

1. Updike writes about the act of falling being prominent in his dreams when he was a boy. Think about a dream you had as a child—or maybe a more recent dream—and write an essay discussing what the dream meant, how it figured into events in your life. Explain in what way your subconscious might have been "more honest" with you as a child. You might compare a dream you had as a child to an adult dream.

2. Research visual depictions of the gods and goddesses Updike mentions in his essay—Venus, Diana, Mars, Dionysus. Write an essay comparing each god and goddess to today's popular models. Is there a big change in our view of the ideal male and female image as Updike indicates? Why might we be moving toward a more androgynous ideal?

3. Think of an object that makes a good metaphor for a member of your family. Write an essay explaining how this person is like the object, but give at least three qualities that the person shares with the object, explaining in detail what they have in common. For example, if your mother is old fashioned in her views, has a tarnished halo—meaning you discovered something shocking about her—but puts on a respectable or prudish front, you might use an antique silver teapot as the metaphor, explaining how she holds old-fashioned—antiquated—notions about gender roles (girls cook, boys take out the trash, for example), but you found out she paid her way through college working in a strip joint when you thought she was above reproach (tarnished like silver), yet she seems prudish (gets offended at an off-color joke or won't let you wear a mini-skirt).

THE BLACK WIDOW

Gordon Grice

Professor of English and humanities, spirolologist Gordon Grice eloquently explores the brutal world of the black widow spider, at the same time busting our misconceptions and urban legends about this misunderstood arachnid. His essays have been published in Harper's, High Plains Literary Review (the source of this essay), and Best American Essays 1996. He also has a book aptly titled The Red Hourglass.

DUSTBIN OF HISTORY AND CULTURE

BOUFFANT: A hairdo where the hair has been teased into a high, puffy dome on top of the head.

GARGOYLE: An architectural adornment that spouts water out of the rain gutters of buildings; the gargoyle, originally lion heads like those on the Parthenon in Athens, became associated with more grotesque beasts in the Middle Ages.

LYRE: A stringed instrument related to the harp, originating in ancient Greece.

1   I hunt Black Widow. When I find one, I capture it. I have found them in discarded wheels and tires and under railroad ties. I have found them in house foundations and cellars, in automotive shops and toolsheds, in water meters and rock gardens, against fences and in cinderblock walls. I have found them in a hospital and in the den of a rattlesnake, and once on the bottom of the chair I was sitting in.

2   Sometimes I raise a generation or two in captivity. The egg sacs produce a hundred or more pinpoint cannibals, each leaving a trail of gleaming light in the air, the group of them eventually producing a glimmering tangle in which most of them die, eaten by stronger sibs. Finally I separate the three or four survivors and feed them bigger game.

3   Once I let several egg sacs hatch out in a container about eighteen inches on a side, a tight wooden box with a sliding glass top. As I tried to move the box one day, the lid slid off and I fell, hands first, into the mass of young widows. Most were still translucent newborns, their bodies a swirl of brown and cream. A few of the females had eaten enough to molt; they had the beginnings of their blackness.

Their tangle of broken web clung to my forearms. They felt like trickling water in my arm hairs.

4   I walked out into the open air and raised my arms into the stiff wind. The widows answered the wind with new strands of web and drifted away, their bodies gold in the late sun. In about ten minutes my arms carried nothing but old web and the husks of spiderlings eaten by their sibs.

5   I have never been bitten.

6   The black widow has the ugliest web of any spider. The orb weavers make those seemingly delicate nets that poets have traditionally used as symbols of imagination, order, and perfection. The sheet web spiders weave crisp linens on the grass. But the widow makes messy-looking tangles in the corners and bends of things and under logs and debris. Often the web is littered with leaves. Beneath it lie the husks of insect prey, their antennae still as gargoyle horns, cut loose and dropped; on them and the surrounding ground are splashes of the spider's white urine, which looks like bird guano and smells of ammonia even at a distance of several feet. This fetid material draws scavengers—ants, sow bugs, crickets, roaches, and so on—which become tangled in vertical strands of silk reaching from the ground up into the web. The widow comes down and, with a bicycling of the hind pair of legs, throws gummy silk onto this new prey.

7   When the prey is seriously tangled but still struggling, the widow cautiously descends and bites the creature, usually on a leg joint. This is a killing bite; it pumps neurotoxin into the victim. The widow will deliver a series of bites as the creature dies, injecting substances that liquefy the organs. Finally it will settle down to suck the liquefied innards out of the prey, changing position two or three times to get it all.

8   Before the eating begins, and sometimes before the victim dies from the slow venom, the widow usually moves it higher into the web. It attaches some line to the prey with a leg-bicycling toss, moves up the vertical web strand that originally snagged the prey, crosses a diagonal strand upward to a higher point on a different vertical strand, and here secures the line. It has thus dragged the prey's body up off the ground. The whole operation is like that of a person moving a load with block and tackle. It occurs in three dimensions—as opposed to the essentially two-dimensional operations of orb weavers and sheet weavers.

9   You can't watch the widow in this activity very long without realizing that its web is not a mess at all but an efficient machine. It allows

complicated uses of leverage and also, because of its complexity of connections, lets the spider feel a disturbance anywhere in the web—usually with enough accuracy to tell the difference at a distance between a raindrop or leaf and viable prey.

10   The web is also constructed in a certain relationship to movements of air so that flying insects are drawn into it. This fact partly explains why widow webs are so often found in the face-down side of discarded car wheels—the wheel is essentially a vault of still air that protects the web, but the central hole at the top allows airborne insects to fall in. An insect that is clumsy and flies in random hops, such as a June beetle, is especially vulnerable to this trap. The widow often seems to choose her building sites according to indigenous smells rather than creating her own stinking waste pile from scratch. The webs turn up, for example, in piles of trash and rotting wood. A few decades ago, the widow was notorious for building its home inside the works of outdoor toilets. Scraping around with a stick before using the toilet was a common practice.

11   The architectural complexities of the widow web do not particularly impress the widows. They move around in these webs almost blind, yet they never misstep or get lost. In fact, a widow forcibly removed from its web and put back at a different point does not seem confused; it will quickly return to its habitual resting place. Furthermore, widows never snare themselves, even though every strand of the web is a potential trap. A widow will spend a few minutes every day coating the clawed tips of its legs with the oil that lets it walk the sticky strands. It secretes the oil from its mouth, coating its legs like a cat cleaning its paws.

12   The human mind cannot grasp the complex functions of the web but must infer them. The widow constructs it by instinct. A brain smaller than a pinhead contains the blueprints, precognitive memories the widow unfolds out of itself into actuality. I have never dissected with enough precision or delicacy to get a good specimen of the black widow brain, but I did glimpse one once. A widow was struggling to wrap a praying mantis when the insect's forelegs, like scalpels mounted on lightning, sliced away the spider's carapace and left exposed the clear droplet of bloody brain.

13   Widows reportedly eat mice, toads, tarantulas—anything that wanders into that remarkable web. I have never witnessed a widow performing a gustatory act of that magnitude, but I have seen them eat scarab beetles heavy as pecans; carabid beetles strong enough to

prey on wolf spiders; cockroaches more than an inch long; and hundreds of other arthropods of various sizes. Widows begin life by eating their siblings. An adult female will fight any other female; the winner often eats the loser. A popular game among Mexican children is to stage such fights and bet on the outcome. The children put the widows on a stick and pass it around so that everyone can see. Sometimes one female ties another up and leaves without killing her. I have come across such black pearls wrapped in silk and, upon peeling off the skin, seen the pearls unfold their legs and rush away.

14   The widow gets her name by eating her lover, though this does not always happen. He distinguishes himself from ordinary prey by playing her web like a lyre. Sometimes she eats him without first copulating; sometimes she snags him as he withdraws his palp from her genital pore. Sometimes he leaves unharmed after mating; in this case, he soon withers and dies on his own. I have witnessed male and female living in platonic relationships in one web. The males' palps, still swollen with sperm, proved that these relationships had not been sexual.

15   Many widows will eat as much as opportunity gives. One aggressive female had an abdomen a little bigger than an English pea. She snared a huge cockroach and spent several hours subduing it, then three days consuming it. Her abdomen swelled to the size of a largish marble, its glossy black stretching to a tight red-brown. With a different widow, I decided to see whether that appetite was really insatiable. I collected dozens of large crickets and grasshoppers and began to drop them into her web at a rate of one every three or four hours. After catching and consuming her tenth victim, this bloated widow fell from her web, landing on her back. She remained in this position for hours, making only feeble attempts to move. Then she died.

16   The first thing people ask when they hear about my fascination with the widow is why I am not afraid. The truth is that my fascination is rooted in fear.

17   I have childhood memories that partly account for my fear. When I was six my mother took my sister and me to the cellar of our farmhouse and told us to watch as she killed a widow. With great ceremony she produced a long stick (I am tempted to say a ten-foot pole) and, narrating her technique in exactly the hushed voice she used for discussing religion or sex, went to work. Her flashlight beam found a point halfway up the cement wall where two marbles hung together—one crisp white, the other a glossy black. My mother ran her stick

through the dirty silver web around them, and as it tore it sounded like the crackling of paper in fire. This sound is unique to the widow's powerful web—anybody with a little experience can tell a widow's work from another spider's by ear. The black marble rose on thin legs to fight off the intruder. As the plump abdomen wobbled across the wall, it seemed to be constantly throwing those legs out of its path. The impression it gave was of speed and frantic anger, but actually a widow's movements outside the web are slow and inefficient. My mother smashed the widow onto the stick and carried it up into the light. It was still kicking its remaining legs. Mom scraped it against the sidewalk, grinding it to a paste. Then she returned for the white marble—the widow's egg sac. This, too, came to an abrasive end.

18   My mother's stated purpose was to teach us how to recognize and deal with a dangerous creature we would probably encounter on the farm. But of course we also took the understanding that widows were actively malevolent, that they waited in dark places to ambush us, that they were worthy of ritual disposition, like an enemy whose death is not sufficient but must be followed with the murder of his children and the salting of his land and whose unclean remains must not touch our hands.

19   The odd thing is that so many people, some of whom presumably did not first encounter the widow in such an atmosphere of mystic reverence, hold the widow in awe. Various friends have told me that the widow always devours her mate, or that her bite is always fatal to humans—in fact, it almost never is. I have heard told for truth that goods imported from the Orient are likely infested with widows and that women with bouffant hairdos have died of widow infestation. Any contradiction of such tales is received as if it were a proclamation of atheism.

20   The most startling contribution to the widow's mythical status I have ever encountered was *Black Widow: America's Most Poisonous Spider,* a book that appeared in 1945. Between genuine scientific observations, the authors present the widow as a lurking menace with a taste for human flesh. They describe the experiments of other investigators; one involved inducing a widow to bite a laboratory rat on the penis, after which event the rat "appeared to become dejected and depressed." Perhaps the most psychologically revealing passage is the authors' quotation from another writer, who said the "deadliest Communists are like the black widow spider; they conceal their red underneath."

21   We project our archetypal terrors onto the widow. It is black; it avoids the light; it is a voracious carnivore. Its red markings suggest blood. Its name, its sleek, rounded form invite a strangely sexual discomfort; the widow becomes an emblem for a man's fear of extending himself into the blood and darkness of a woman, something like the legendary Eskimo vampire that takes the form of a fanged vagina.

22   The widow's venom is, of course, a soundly pragmatic reason for fear. The venom contains a neurotoxin that can produce sweats, vomiting, swelling, convulsions, and dozens of other symptoms. The variation in symptoms from one person to the next is remarkable. The constant is pain. A useful question for a doctor trying to diagnose an uncertain case: "Is this the worst pain you've ever felt?" A "yes" suggests a diagnosis of black widow bite. Occasionally people die from widow bites. The very young and the very old are especially vulnerable. Some people seem to die not from the venom but from the infection that may follow; because of its habitat, the widow carries dangerous microbes.

23   Some researchers hypothesized that the virulence of the venom was necessary for killing beetles of the scarab family. This family contains thousands of species, including the June beetle and the famous dung beetle the Egyptians thought immortal. All the scarabs have thick, strong bodies and unusually tough exoskeletons, and many of them are common prey for the widow. The tough hide was supposed to require a particularly nasty venom. As it turns out, the venom is thousands of times more virulent than necessary for this purpose. The whole idea is full of the widow's glamour: an emblem of eternal life killed by a creature whose most distinctive blood-colored markings people invariably describe as an hourglass.

24   No one has ever offered a sufficient explanation for the dangerous venom. It provides no evolutionary advantages: all of the widow's prey items would find lesser toxins fatal, and there is no particular benefit in killing or harming larger animals. A widow that bites a human being or other large animal is likely to be killed. Evolution does sometimes produce such flowers of natural evil—traits that are neither functional nor vestigial but utterly pointless. Natural selection favors the inheritance of useful characteristics that arise from random mutation and tends to extinguish disadvantageous traits. All other characteristics, the ones that neither help nor hinder survival, are preserved or extinguished at random as mutation links them with

useful or harmful traits. Many people—even many scientists—assume that every animal is elegantly engineered for its ecological niche, that every bit of an animal's anatomy and behavior has a functional explanation. This assumption is false. Nothing in evolutionary theory sanctions it; fact refutes it.

25   We want the world to be an ordered room, but in a corner of that room there hangs an untidy web. Here the analytical minds find an irreducible mystery, a motiveless evil in nature, and the scientist's vision of evil comes to match the vision of a God-fearing country woman with a ten-foot pole. No idea of the cosmos as elegant design accounts for the widow. No idea of a benevolent God is comfortable in a world with the widow. She hangs in her web, that marvel of design, and defies teleology.

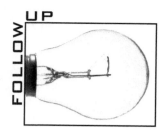

FOLLOW UP

THE BLACK WIDOW

Exploring Language

abrasive: in this context, harsh or rough. Can also refer to personality.

archetypal: an archetype is a recurrent character type, plot, symbol, or theme of seemingly universal significance; Carl Jung believed human beings have a collective subconscious and therefore have similar dreams. For example, dreams of flying or falling occur in almost every culture, as do literary archetypes like "Cinderella," which has variants in virtually every culture, going back as far as 500 B.C. China.

arthropods: a scientific term for animals with jointed limbs, segmented bodies (think ants), and exoskeletons (instead of skeletons, a hard outer shell), which includes insects, mollusks (snails), and crustaceans (lobster, shrimp).

carapace: protective shell or shell-like covering.

fetid: having a bad odor.

glamour: fascinating, attractive, or alluring; charm, enchantment.

gustatory: relating to the sense of taste.

indigenous: occurring naturally in a particular region or environment, as in "indigenous species."

insatiable: impossible to satisfy.

irreducible: cannot be made smaller or simpler.

malevolent: vicious ill-will.

neurotoxin: a toxin or poison that damages or destroys nerve tissue.

pragmatic: practical.

teleology: study of design in nature.

vestigial: body part left over from evolution that no longer has a purpose.

virulence: in this context, intensely poisonous.

voracious: eager to consume large quantities of food.

Note: For pronunciation, go to dictionary.com, search the word, and click on the speaker icon.

USAGE Look up "abrasive" for meanings other than the one in the Exploring Language list and use it in a sentence that implies one of those meanings.

172

Thinking and Talking Points

1. Reread the introduction to Grice's essay. Does the first sentence hook the reader? Why or why not? What is the effect of his listing all of the places where he has found black widows?
2. Find where the essay refutes our preconceived notions of the black widow. Did you hold these same ideas about the spider? How does Grice dispel these notions?
3. What is Grice's point in writing this essay? Is he trying to persuade you or merely inform? Defend your stand with evidence from the essay.
4. Hunt down the numerous **metaphors** and **similes** in this essay. How do they help convey an attitude about the black widow?
5. How does the essay provide information that helps the reader hunt for black widows (if desired)?
6. Grice writes in paragraph #23, "The whole idea is full of the widow's glamour: an emblem of eternal life killed by a creature whose most distinctive blood-colored markings people invariably describe an hourglass." What does the hourglass have to do with glamour? How is spider "glamorous"? See the definition under "Exploring Language."
7. What larger philosophical idea does Grice imply in his conclusion?

Styling

Many students—and non-students—think of punctuation as a mysterious code known only to English teachers that has very little purpose other than creating pause for the reader. While punctuation does create pause, it also helps strengthen your writer's voice, to say what you want to say, dramatically or demurely, simply or with complexity. Punctuation is style.

You might have noticed that Gordon Grice uses dashes in different ways for dramatic interruption or pause. Study the three ways he uses dashes: with a simple interruption, with a list that interrupts a sentence, and at the end of a sentence for emphasis.

Dashes with a simple interrupter:

> Many people—even many scientists—assume that every animal is elegantly engineered for its ecological niche, that every bit of an animal's anatomy and behavior has a functional explanation.

Notice that if you remove the words enclosed with dashes, the sentence still makes sense:

Many people assume that every animal is elegantly engineered for its ecological niche, that every bit of an animal's anatomy and behavior has a function explanation.

When practicing the use of dashes with an interrupter, test the sentence to see if you can remove the material within the dashes and still have a complete, coherent sentence. You might choose to use commas with an interrupter, or parentheses, but dashes draw attention to the interrupter "even many scientists," alerting the reader to the fact that even scientists—usually credited with logical thinking—make wrong assumptions.

Hint: Avoid using dashes with simple adjectives or prepositional phrases.

Dashes with an internal list that interrupts the sentence:

The fetid material draws scavengers—ants, sow bugs, crickets, roaches, and so on—which become tangled in vertical strands of silk reaching from the ground up into the web.

Again, you could take out the list and dashes and the sentence would still be grammatically correct and make sense: "The fetid material draws scavengers which become tangled in vertical strands of silk reaching from the ground up into the web."

CAUTION In the sentence above, dashes become essential; without the dashes, the word "scavengers" crashes into "ants," wreaking havoc with the sentence's meaning. If you use commas instead of dashes here, your reader might think "scavengers" is part of the list that includes ants rather than ants being an example of a scavenger in a list of other such bugs.

Dashes at the end for emphasis:

Widows reportedly eat mice, toads, tarantulas—anything that wanders into that remarkable web.

Then she returned for the white marble—the widow's egg sac.

Various friends have told me that the widow always devours her mate, or that her bite is always fatal to humans—in fact, it almost never is.

Her flashlight beam found a point halfway up the cement wall where two marbles hung together—one crisp white, the other a glossy black.

In these examples, Grice might have chosen to use a comma at the end of his sentence to connect non-essential or extra material, but the dash creates a bit of drama, a longer pause, lingering on those set-off words, both on the page and in the reader's mind.

PRACTICE   In each of the sentences below, fill in the blanks with appropriate material.

Simple Interrupter
> The bird— _____ —cautiously flitted down to the bird feeder.

List That Interrupts
> Those flowers— _____ , _____ , _____ , and _____ —do not grow well on that side of the house.

At the End for Emphasis
> Hummingbirds will attack almost anything— _____

YOU TRY IT   Write five of each type of dash sentence: five with simple interrupters, five with a list, and five with one dash at the end for emphasis.

Teaming Up

1. **Warm-up for Writing Idea #2:** Brainstorm urban legends you've heard about or read on the Internet. What fear does each legend prey on? Do you find these hoaxes helpful or harmful?

2. **Warm-up for Writing Idea #3:** Bring in a legend, fable, or story about an animal. Read all of the stories in your group and discuss what each story reveals about the culture. Choose one story to read to the rest of the class. Pick someone to read the story—or you can share the responsibility—and another member(s) to present your ideas. There are fables with "The Courage of Turtles" by Edward Hoagland. Many myths are available online.

Writing Ideas

1. Hunt another insect, perhaps one people usually think of as creepy or one that you fear: another type of spider, a preying mantis, a beetle, a centipede, or whatever you fancy. Be sure it's one that can be found in your immediate area. You might need to look up information on the creature's habits like what it eats, what habitat it likes, what time of year it can easily be located. Write an essay that attempts to persuade the reader of the creature's worthiness; maybe it's environmentally helpful or a friend to gardeners. Maybe it's simply fascinating. Use description, **figurative language**, and debunking of preconceived ideas about the critter.

2. A lot of urban legends get circulated on the Internet; you might have been victim to some of these untruths, usually sent as warnings to beware of some danger lurking around the next corner. Before the Internet, such stories circulated through word of mouth. Gather some of these stories, and write an essay that attempts to explain our fascination with these hoaxes and argues whether or not they're helpful, either warning of dangers that *could* occur or the opposite, that they incite fear and paranoia in an otherwise safe environment. Are they cautionary tales or fear-mongering?

3. Choose an animal and research myths and legends from different cultures about that animal. You might try Native American myths and legends, legends from around the world, *Aesop's Fables,* or a collection of animal myths from almost any country. Choose at least three different cultures and write an essay that explains how the culture views that creature and what that view reveals about the culture, its fears or hopes, its view about animals in general.

Essay Connections

Several animal essays in *Sparks* include "Mute Dancers: How to Watch a Hummingbird" by Diane Ackerman, "The Courage of Turtles" by Edward Hoagland, and "Joyas Voladoras" by Brian Doyle.

Essays that Argue and Define

INTRODUCTION

Argument and definition essays provoke controversy and stir debate, hopefully causing readers to consider the road-less-traveled angle of a topic or contemplate a word's meaning. They attempt to provide answers to provocative questions and broaden readers' viewpoints by breaking down stereotypes: Is our romantic view of the American cowboy accurate? What does it mean to grow up black and middle class? Are Americans anti-child compared to other countries? Are we afraid of naps? Does Disney butcher the original fairytales in favor of "vapid" family entertainment? Is it "possible to stop all drug addiction in the United States within a very short time"? Is there an epidemic of celebrity in America?

An argument doesn't have to be about the beat-into-the-ground issues like gun control, the death penalty, and mercy killing. There is very little left to say about these tired standards; good writers strive for originality, at least in the angle explored if not the topic itself. Gore Vidal writes about drugs, but with a bold approach that can shock some readers. As you read, study the writers' tactics, how they support their points and refute opposition, how they use style to their advantage—how they get the reader to at least think about the side of an issue he or she may not agree with. An essay that surprises or gets the reader to think is something worth writing.

THE LITTLE MERMAID

Pauline Kael

Pauline Kael (1919–2001) wrote film reviews for the The New Yorker magazine from the 1960s until her retirement in 1991. For a collection of her reviews, see the book For Keeps. In this short review, Kael lambastes Disney for turning Hans Christian Andersen's The Little Mermaid into "a bland reworking of old Disney fairy tales, featuring a teen-age tootsie in a flirty seashell bra."

DUSTBIN OF HISTORY AND CULTURE

HANS CHRISTIAN ANDERSEN: A Danish writer (1805–1875) credited with the creation of modern children's stories. He gained popularity writing literary fairy tales, *The Little Mermaid* being the original story that Disney "borrowed."

ROALD DAHL: A writer of children's books, *James and the Giant Peach* and *Charlie and the Chocolate Factory* are two of his most popular.

THE DARK CRYSTAL: A fantasy film for children, exploring the dark side of the soul.

KITSCH: A German word for tasteless or sentimental junk-art (sources: *The Concise Oxford Dictionary,* Ninth Edition, and *Merriam Webster's Collegiate Dictionary,* Tenth Edition).

FAUST: A man who sells his soul to the devil, in an old story made most famous by German poet and playwright Johann Wolfgang Goethe.

THE SECRET OF NIMH: A film based on the children's fantasy book *Mrs. Frisby and the Rats of Nimh* by Robert O'Brien.

WHERE THE WILD THINGS ARE: Children's fantasy picture book by Maurice Sendak about a boy named Max—angry at his mother and banished to his room without supper—who fantasizes sailing across the sea to a land of wild beasts.

1   Hans Christian Andersen's tear-stained *The Little Mermaid* is peerlessly mythic. It's the closest thing women have to a feminine Faust story. The Little Mermaid gives up her lovely voice—her means of expression—in exchange for legs, so she'll be able to walk on land and attract the man she loves. If she can win him in marriage, she will gain an immortal soul; if she can't, she'll be foam on the sea.

2   I didn't expect the new Disney *The Little Mermaid* to be Faust, but after reading the reviews ("everything an animated feature should

be," "reclaims the movie house as a dream palace," and so on) I expected to see something more than a bland reworking of old Disney fairy tales, featuring a teen-age tootsie in a flirty seashell bra. This is a technologically sophisticated cartoon with just about all the simpering old Disney values in place. (The Faust theme acquires a wholesome family sub-theme.) The film does have a cheerful calypso number ("Under the Sea"), and the color is bright—at least, until the mermaid goes on land, when everything seems to dull out.

3   Are we trying to put kids into some sort of moral-aesthetic safe house? Parents seem desperate for harmless family entertainment. Probably they don't mind this movie's being vapid, because the whole family can share it, and no one is offended. We're caught in a culture warp. Our children are flushed with pleasure when we read them *Where the Wild Things Are* or Roald Dahl's sinister stories. Kids are ecstatic watching videos of *The Secret of Nimh* and *The Dark Crystal*. Yet here comes the press telling us that *The Little Mermaid* is "due for immortality." People are made to feel that this stale pastry is what they should be taking their kids to, that it's art for children. And when they see the movie they may believe it, because this *Mermaid* is just a slightly updated version of what their parents took them to. They've been imprinted with Disney-style kitsch.

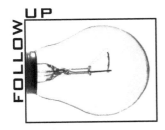

THE LITTLE MERMAID

Exploring Language

aesthetic: pleasing to the senses; often refers to artistic taste.
peerlessly: peerless means unrivaled, unequaled, unmatched.
simpering: smiling in a silly way.
tootsie: slang for female, akin to cutie-pie, but can also imply a
woman of ill repute (prostitute).
vapid: dull, flat, boring, unimaginative.
Note: For pronunciation, go to dictionary.com, search the word, and
click on the speaker icon.

USAGE Use at least one of the Exploring Language words in your next
writing assignment, or look one up in a thesaurus and choose a lively
substitute.

Thinking and Talking Points

1. Kael writes that in the original version of *The Little Mermaid,* the mermaid will gain an immortal soul if she marries the prince, a detail Disney left out. Even though you may not have read the original story or seen the film, what do you think might be lost in the story by omitting the idea of gaining an immortal soul?
2. How convincing is Kael's review? List specific evidence in the review that did or did not convince you.
3. Kael writes, "This is a technologically sophisticated cartoon with just about all the simpering old Disney values in place." What are Disney values? How are they simpering?
4. Kael asks, "Are we trying to put kids into some sort of moral-aesthetic safe house?" Are parents "desperate for harmless family entertainment"? Do children lose out, as Kael indicates, by being shielded from the classics in favor of blander cartoon versions?

Styling

Warm-up for Writing Idea #1. Specific examples are necessary in any
essay; if you don't support your point with specific examples, your

reader will think you don't know your subject. Kael cites several children's books and films, holding them up as standards, comparing them to Disney, illustrating Disney cartoons' inferiority. She didn't just write, "Other books and films are better." She reminds us of specific children's stories, hoping we'll remember and think, "I loved *Where the Wild Things Are* when I was a kid."

If you tell a friend, "I couldn't sleep all night because of the noises," your friend will mostly likely sympathize and ask, "What noises?" You would then proceed to give specific examples: somebody snoring, a barking dog, dripping faucet. Here's a paragraph from F. Scott Fitzgerald's *The Great Gatsby:*

> I couldn't sleep all night; a fog-horn was groaning incessantly on the Sound, and I tossed half sick between grotesque reality and savage frightening dreams. Toward dawn I heard a taxi go up Gatsby's drive and immediately I jumped out of bed and began to dress—I felt that I had something to tell him, something to warn him about and morning would be too late.

The groaning fog-horn, the frightening dreams, and the taxi breathe life into the paragraph.

PRACTICE   Think of a genre of films—action/adventure, comedy, science fiction, horror, drama—and make a list of titles from that genre.

YOU TRY IT   Using three or four of the items from your above list—you may have to alter the list to fit the **topic sentence**—write a paragraph with a topic sentence that makes a claim about that genre (something like "Most horror films attempt to scare the viewer with cheap gore-and-guts rather than a strong plot"). In a sentence or two, explain why each film title you chose from the list supports that topic sentence.

Teaming Up

1. In your group, discuss the children's literature and film examples Kael mentions in her essay, or other childhood favorites. What do you remember about the stories? What makes them literature rather than kitsch? If you have time, read one of these stories before discussion.

2. Kael writes, "They've been imprinted with Disney-style kitsch." In your group, make a list of all the places in our culture where you see Disney products or images and list companies you know Disney owns. Discuss in what ways a company like Disney might influence

society. Use your list and discussion to co-write a paragraph. The topic sentence should express an opinion; you might attempt to answer this question: have we been "imprinted with Disney-style kitsch"? Explain how the examples you use from the list support your opinion. If your group disagrees, it's okay to split up and write two paragraphs with different opinions.

Writing Ideas

1. Use the paragraph from the Styling section as a supporting paragraph of a larger essay.
2. Almost every culture has a version of the "Cinderella" fairy tale. Read several Cinderella versions. Choose two of the stories from different cultures and write a comparison/contrast essay. What do the differences tell us about the culture?
3. Watch another Disney fairy tale film and read the older version of the story—many of the written stories are from Grimms' fairy tales. Write an essay comparing the two, making a judgment about which story is more meaningful and why. Or read the original *The Little Mermaid* by Hans Christian Andersen and do a more in-depth comparison of it to the Disney version. (Available online.)

Essay Connections

Other essays critiquing culture include "The Culture of Celebrity" by Joseph Epstein, "City Out of Breath" by Ken Chen, and "Somebody's Baby" by Barbara Kingsolver.

DRUGS

Gore Vidal

Gore Vidal has written essays and novels, among them Myra Breckenridge (1968), one of his most famous. More recent works include The Golden Age, a novel, and The American Presidency, Vidal's view of the history of this highest office and the men who have served in it. In this essay, Vidal argues that we should legalize all drugs and provide warning labels, as we do for cigarettes. He states, "This will require heroic honesty. Don't say that marijuana is addictive or dangerous when it is neither, as millions of people know—unlike 'speed,' which kills most unpleasantly, or heroin, which is addictive and difficult to kick."

DUSTBIN OF HISTORY AND CULTURE

FU MANCHU: A Chinese villain with a long mustache who appears in stories by Sax Rohmer, later made into films—the character was usually played by a white man.

GNP: Gross National Product.

DR. SPOCK: Benjamin Spock, child pediatrician who wrote *The Common Sense Book of Baby and Child Care* (1946), a controversial book which advocated affection and more permissiveness toward children, and is believed to have had a major impact on child rearing.

DR. LEARY: Timothy Leary, identified with the hippie subculture. In a 1967 speech, he coined the phrase "you must turn on, tune in, and drop out."

1   It is possible to stop most drug addiction in the United States within a very short time. Simply make all drugs available and sell them at cost. Label each drug with a precise description of what effect—good and bad—the drug will have on the taker. This will require heroic honesty. Don't say that marijuana is addictive or dangerous when it is neither, as millions of people know—unlike "speed," which kills most unpleasantly, or heroin, which is addictive and difficult to kick.

2   For the record, I have tried—once—almost every drug and liked none, disproving the popular Fu Manchu theory that a single sniff of opium will enslave the mind. Nevertheless, many drugs are bad for certain people to take and they should be told why in a sensible way.

3   Along with exhortation and warning, it might be good for our citizens to recall (or learn for the first time) that the United States was the creation of men who believed that each man has the right to do what he wants with his own life as long as he does not interfere with his neighbor's pursuit of happiness (that his neighbor's idea of happiness is persecuting others does confuse matters a bit).

4   This is a startling notion to the current generation of Americans. They reflect a system of public education which has made the Bill of Rights, literally, unacceptable to a majority of high school graduates (see the annual Purdue reports) who now form the "silent majority"— a phrase which that underestimated wit Richard Nixon took from Homer, who used it to describe the dead.

5   Now one can hear the warning rumble begin: if everyone is allowed to take drugs everyone will and the GNP will decrease, the Commies will stop us from making everyone free, and we shall end up a race of Zombies, passively murmuring "groovy" to one another. Alarming thought. Yet it seems most unlikely that any reasonably sane person will become a drug addict if he knows in advance what addiction is going to be like.

6   Is everyone reasonably sane? No. Some people will always become drug addicts just as some people will always become alcoholics, and it is just too bad. Every man, however, has the power (and should have the legal right) to kill himself if he chooses. But since most men don't, they won't be mainliners either. Nevertheless, forbidding people things they like or think they might enjoy only makes them want those things all the more. This psychological insight is, for some mysterious reason, perennially denied our governors.

7   It is a lucky thing for the American moralist that our country has always existed in a kind of time-vacuum: we have no public memory of anything that happened before last Tuesday. No one in Washington today recalls what happened during the years alcohol was forbidden to the people by a Congress that thought it had a divine mission to stamp out Demon Rum—launching, in the process, the greatest crime wave in the country's history, causing thousands of deaths from bad alcohol, and creating a general (and persisting) contempt among the citizenry for the laws of the United States.

8   The same thing is happening today. But the government has learned nothing from past attempts at prohibition, not to mention repression.

9   Last year when the supply of Mexican marijuana was slightly curtailed by the Feds, the pushers got the kids hooked on heroin

and deaths increased dramatically, particularly in New York. Whose fault? Evil men like the Mafiosi? Permissive Dr. Spock? Wild-eyed Dr. Leary? No.

10   The Government of the United States was responsible for those deaths. The bureaucratic machine has a vested interest in playing cops and robbers. Both the Bureau of Narcotics and the Mafia want strong laws against the sale and use of drugs because if drugs are sold at cost there would be no money in it for anyone.

11   If there was no money in it for the Mafia, there would be no friendly playground pushers, and addicts would not commit crimes to pay for the next fix. Finally, if there was no money in it, the Bureau of Narcotics would wither away, something they are not about to do without a struggle.

12   Will anything sensible be done? Of course not. The American people are as devoted to the idea of sin and its punishment as they are to making money—and fighting drugs is nearly as big a business as pushing them. Since the combination of sin and money is irresistible (particularly to the professional politician), the situation will only grow worse.

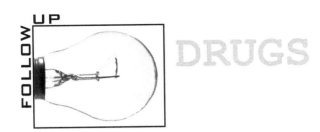

DRUGS

Exploring Language

exhortation: language intended to encourage, excite, or provoke.
perennially: permanently, enduringly, constantly.
Note: For pronunciation, go to dictionary.com, search the word, and click on the speaker icon.

USAGE   Locate *exhortation* in the essay and then look up synonyms. In what context does Vidal use the word? Now use the word in another context.

Thinking and Talking Points

1. Where in the essay does Vidal address and refute his opponents' views (those against drug legalization)? How well does he support his argument? Are there arguments from the other side he hasn't considered?
2. Reread paragraph #6. Do you think "forbidding people things they like or think they might enjoy only makes them want those things all the more"? Think of examples other than drugs.
3. Reread paragraphs #9 and #10. Explain what Vidal means by his statement, "The Government of the United States was responsible for those deaths." Do you agree or disagree with his reasoning? How does comparing the Bureau of Narcotics and the Mafia work in his favor?
4. Vidal writes, "The American people are as devoted to the idea of sin and its punishment as they are to making money—and fighting drugs is nearly as big a business as pushing them." Where in the essay does he support these statements? Do you agree or disagree with these ideas? Can you think of other examples that illustrate Americans are devoted to sin and its punishment?
5. Explain what Vidal means by his statement "we have no public memory of anything that happened before last Tuesday"? What examples does he use to support this statement?

Styling

You can use a colon to list items following a complete sentence or to give an explanation. Vidal writes:

> It's a lucky thing for the American moralist that our country has always existed in a kind of time-vacuum: we have no public memory of anything that happened before last Tuesday.

Notice that the phrase before the colon is a **complete sentence.** The phrase after the colon explains something in the complete sentence, in this instance, the time-vacuum. Although the sentence before the colon must be complete, what follows the colon can be either a complete or **incomplete sentence**. Here's another example of a sentence that uses a colon with an explanation; this is from Jamaica Kincaid's essay "On Seeing England for the First Time" (not in this book):

> I did not know then that this statement was meant to make me feel awe and small whenever I heard the word "England": awe at its existence, small because I was not from it.

Although the part before the colon forms a complete sentence, the phrase after the colon is incomplete, explaining "awe" and "small."

PRACTICE   After the colon in the following sentences, add a phrase or sentence that explains something in the main sentence.

> Gore Vidal claims the government could end most drug addiction in the United States: _____
>
> Some critics claim that *The Hunger Games* is not too far from current reality television shows: _____

YOU TRY IT   Create five sentences about your life—family members, hobbies, job—that use the colon with an explanation. Use this technique in your next writing assignment.

Teaming Up

1. Before coming to class, have each group member look up information on the Volstead Act. Share your information, and then compare what you've learned with the argument Vidal makes for legalizing drugs. Does he have a valid point? Can your group think of ways to refute him?

2. **Warm-up for Writing Idea #1.** Divide your group into two teams: one for legalizing drugs and one against. Don't worry about what side you really agree with. For critical thinking, you should be able to argue either side whether or not you agree. Do some research and prepare a debate. In class, debate the issue. Have an impartial judge— the teacher or another classmate—judge which side presents the strongest argument.

Writing Ideas

1. Gather information on the cost of the drug war—both economic and human—and write an essay that argues whether or not the Drug War is worth it. (See the Writing Strategies for Arguing section in this book.)
2. Throughout his essay, Vidal blames the government for the drug problem in America. Since this essay was written—1970—the drug war has raged on. Do some research to determine whether or not the drug problem has improved. Also gather information on the Iran-Contra affair. Write an essay that argues whether or not the drug situation in America has improved and to what degree the Iran-Contra affair supports Vidal's blaming the government.

Essay Connections

A more benign topic on America's "devotion to sin and its punishment" is "Naps" by Barbara Holland. P. J. O'Rourke's "How to Drive Fast" satirizes drinking and driving. "The Chemist's War" by Deborah Blum recounts the government's poisoning of alcohol during Prohibition.

HOW TO DRIVE FAST

P. J. O'Rourke

P. J. O'Rourke is a humorist and former foreign correspondent for Rolling Stone. The following is an excerpt from an essay in his book Republican Party Reptiles. O'Rourke satirizes young people who insist on drinking or taking drugs and then driving a car.

DUSTBIN OF HISTORY AND CULTURE

CHIVAS: A type of whiskey.

SIGMUND FREUD: A 19th-century doctor who founded psychoanalysis and the theory called the Oedipus Complex, which says that children will have an erotic attachment to the parent of the opposite sex.

CHERYL TIEGS: A supermodel in the 1970s and 1980s (O'Rourke's age is showing).

ALBERTO ASCARI: An Italian race-car driver who was killed in the 1950s during a race.

THE ILIAD: Epic poem by Homer written sometime around the 9th century B.C., set in the final year of the Trojan War.

ADIRONDACKS: Mountains in New York State.

1   When it comes to taking chances, some people like to play poker or shoot dice; other people prefer to parachute jump, go rhino hunting, or climb ice floes, while still others engage in crime or marriage. But I like to get drunk and drive like a fool. Name me, if you can, a better feeling than the one you get when you're half a bottle of Chivas in the bag with a gram of coke up your nose and a teenage lovely pulling off her tube top in the next seat over while you're going a hundred miles an hour down a suburban side street. You'd have to watch the entire Mexican air force crash-land in a liquid petroleum gas storage facility to match this kind of thrill. If you ever have much more fun than that, you'll die of pure sensory overload, I'm here to tell you.

2   But wait. Let's pause and analyze *why* this particular matrix of activities is perceived as so highly enjoyable. I mean, aside from the teenage lovely pulling off her tube top in the next seat over. Ignoring that for a moment, let's look at the psychological factors conducive to placing positive emotional values on the sensory-end product of expe-

rientially produced excitation of the central nervous system and smacking into a lamppost. Is that any way to have fun? How would your mother feel if she knew you were doing this? She'd cry. She really would. And that's how you know it's fun. Anything that makes your mother cry is fun. Sigmund Freud wrote all about this. It's a well-known fact.

3   Of course, it's a shame to waste young lives behaving this way—speeding around all tanked up with your feet hooked in the steering wheel while your date crawls around on the floor mats opening zippers with her teeth and pounding on the accelerator with an empty liquor bottle. But it wouldn't be taking a chance if you weren't risking *something.* And even if it is a shame to waste young lives behaving this way, it is definitely cooler than risking old lives behaving this way. I mean, so what if some fifty-eight-year-old butthead gets a load on and starts playing Death Race 2000 in the rush-hour traffic jam? What kind of chance is he taking? He's just waiting around to see what kind of cancer he gets anyway. But if young, talented *you,* with all of life's possibilities at your fingertips, you and the future Cheryl Tiegs there, so fresh, so beautiful—if the two of *you* stake your handsome heads on a single roll of the dice in life's game of stop-the-semi—now *that's* taking chances! Which is why old people rarely risk their lives. It's not because they're chicken—they just have too much dignity to play for small stakes.

4   Now a lot of people say to me, "Hey, P.J., you like to drive fast. Why not join a responsible organization, such as the Sports Car Club of America, and enjoy participation in sports car racing? That way you could drive as fast as you wish while still engaging in a well-regulated spectator sport that is becoming more popular each year." No thanks. In the first place, if you ask me, those guys are a bunch of tweedy old barf mats who like to talk about things like what necktie they wore to Alberto Ascari's funeral. And in the second place, they won't let me drive drunk. They expect me to go out there and smash into things and roll over on the roof and catch fire and burn to death when I'm sober. They must think I'm crazy. That stuff scares me. I have to get completely shit-faced to even think about driving fast. How can you have a lot of exciting thrills when you're so terrified that you wet yourself all the time? That's not fun. It's just *not fun* to have exciting thrills when you're scared. Take the heroes of the *Iliad,* for instance—they really had some exciting thrills, and were they scared? No. They were drunk. Every chance they could get. And so

am I, and I'm not going out there and have a horrible car wreck until somebody brings me a cocktail.

5   Also, it's important to be drunk because being drunk keeps your body all loose, and that way, if you have an accident or anything, you'll sort of roll with the punches and not get banged up so bad. For example, there was this guy I heard about who was really drunk and was driving through the Adirondacks. He got sideswiped by a bus and went head-on into another car, which knocked him off a bridge, and he plummeted 150 feet into a ravine. I mean, it killed him and every-thing, but if he hadn't been so drunk and loose, his body probably would have been banged up a lot worse—and you can imagine how much more upset his wife would have been when she went down to the morgue to identify him.

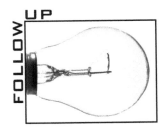

FOLLOW UP

HOW TO
DRIVE FAST

Exploring Language

conducive: helping or contributing.
experientially: relating to experience.
matrix: a mold or pattern from which something else originates or
   develops.
Note: For pronunciation, go to dictionary.com, search the word, and
click on the speaker icon.

USAGE   If you look matrix up in the dictionary, you'll see a collection of
meanings. Try to explain in a sentence or two how the meaning given
above applies to O'Rourke's phrase "matrix of activities."

Examine the sentence in which *conducive* appears (paragraph #2).
O'Rourke does something English teachers call a "shift in diction," meaning the writer mixes formal words with casual ones. Usually writers avoid
this shift. Why does O'Rourke purposely mingle dressed up words like
conducive with the phrase "smacking into a lamppost"?

Rewrite the sentence where *experientially* appears (paragraph #2)
using slang or casual language. Does the sentence lose some of its impact?

Thinking and Talking Points

1. This type of satire is tongue-in-cheek irony, which means the writer
   says the opposite of what he or she means. O'Rourke *says* he's in favor
   of drinking and driving, but he *means* just the opposite—drinking or
   taking drugs and driving are stupid activities that can get you killed.
   But how does he accomplish his goal? How do we know he's not serious? Look through the essay and find several (four or five) word
   choices and phrases that clearly tell the reader O'Rourke isn't in favor
   of drunk driving. Explain why you think these phrases show that
   O'Rourke isn't serious.

2. Some critics argue that satirical essays—while entertaining—are not
   "real" argument. Refute these critics by writing a paragraph arguing
   in favor of "How to Drive Fast" as a more effective argument for its
   intended audience (teens) than a finger-wagging straight lecture. Be

specific. Use examples and quotes from O'Rourke's essay and your own experience to support your stand. Even if you disagree, it's good critical thinking to take an opposing view.

3. Notice that O'Rourke organizes his essay in traditional structure: introduction with a **thesis**, body paragraphs with **transitions**, and a conclusion that slaps reality in the reader's face with the consequence of this type of behavior—death. Identify his thesis and transitions; find other areas where he uses *real* consequences of foolish behavior to keep the reader aware that drinking and driving is stupid.

4. Some readers object to O'Rourke's style of humor. What makes his essay controversial? Does the shock value of the essay work for or against him?

5. What is ironic about the Alberto Ascari example?

Styling

While satire is a style all its own, O'Rourke does use a variety of sentence patterns to add flow to his essay. Here's one example:

> Of course, it's a shame to waste young lives behaving this way— *speeding* around all tanked up *with* your feet hooked in the steering wheel *while* your date crawls around *on* the floor mats opening zippers *with* her teeth *and* pounding *on* the accelerator *with* an empty liquor bottle.

This pattern begins with a lead-in, "Of course," with a complete sentence followed by a dash with a series of add-ons that explain the behavior mentioned in the simple sentence. The first add-on begins with an "ing" word, *speeding*; the rest begin with prepositions and other connecting words (in italics in the example).

Note: For more discussion and practice on this sentence style (without the dash) see the "Styling" exercise with "A Voice for the Lonely."

PRACTICE   Complete the sentence below with at least three incomplete sentences. Start each with one of the connecting words or prepositions italicized above.

Fly fishing is a relaxing way to spend a vacation— _____,
_____, _____.

YOU TRY IT Create your own sentence. Start with a complete sentence followed by a dash. Next, write at least three that explain or describe the complete sentence.

The first incomplete sentence does not have to start with *ing*—you can use any of the linking words or prepositions.

CAUTION Edit and revise for **run-on sentences** and **fragments**. A **run-on sentence** consists of two or more sentences run together when instead they should be separated by a period, a semicolon, or a comma with a conjunction. For example, in paragraph #1, if O'Rourke had written "Some people like to play poker or shoot dice other people prefer to parachute jump," he would be guilty of creating a run-on sentence. Instead, he uses a semicolon to separate the statements.

O'Rourke does use several **fragments (incomplete sentences)** in his essay. Near the end of paragraph #4, for example, he writes: "Every chance they could get." While writers often use fragments for a particular effect, I caution beginning writers against using them until they have mastered **complete sentences**.

Teaming Up

1. In groups of three to five members, brainstorm a list of harmful or simply rebellious teen behavior. For the next class meeting, have each person bring in an article about one of these behaviors. Before coming to class, each person should prepare a summary of the article to present to the group. After discussing the articles, highlight passages from each that you all agree would be useful in writing an essay on that type of behavior. Practice incorporating these passages into writing by introducing them with the writer's name and words such as *states, shows, disagrees, agrees, argues, claims, according to.*

   EXAMPLE: Joe Brown states . . .

   Note: For the proper documentation of quotes, see the Basic Documentation section.

2. This activity works best with three people but can be adapted to larger groups. Read Writing Idea #2. Decide on a topic to satirize. Brainstorm a thesis and at least three paragraph ideas for support. Have each member of the group develop one idea into a satirical paragraph. Co-write an introduction and conclusion. Then decide how to organize the body paragraphs. Use transitions between paragraphs.

Writing Ideas

1. Find a copy of *The Onion*—a satirical newspaper (available at www.theonion.com)—and read one of the satirical news articles. Find a nonsatirical article on the same topic in a newspaper. Write an essay that analyzes the two pieces, explaining what's being satirized, why, and whether you agree that the topic deserves to be satirized.

2. Write a five-paragraph satirical essay using O'Rourke's strategy. Your target should be a behavior that you think is stupid, one where people usually ignore sensible arguments: steroid use, breast implants, political issues, drugs (narrow to a specific one like cocaine or amphetamines). Use the techniques explored in Thinking and Talking Points #1. This strategy is key to making the essay work.

Essay Connections

Jonathan Swift's "A Modest Proposal," one of the best satires in the English language, is easy to find on the Web.

NAPS

Barbara Holland

Barbara Holland has written several books, including Bingo Night at the Fire Halls, Wasn't the Grass Greener?, The Joy of Drinking, When All the World Was Young: A Memoir, and Endangered Pleasures: In Defense of Naps, Bacon, Martinis, Profanity, and Other Indulgences where this essay, "Naps," appears. In "Naps," Holland argues for our right to take an afternoon nap like most of the rest of the "civilized" world, claiming "Americans are afraid of naps."

DUSTBIN OF HISTORY AND CULTURE

L'ÉCLUSIÈRE: Ecluse is French for lock.
COOLIDGE: Calvin Coolidge, 30th president of the United States (1923–1929).
MILTON: John Milton (1608–1674): considered one of the greatest of English poets, Milton, a Puritan, wrote his epic *Paradise Lost*, while blind, dictating to his daughter.
WINSTON CHURCHILL: Sir Winston Churchill (1874–1965) was prime minister (1940–1945 and 1951–1955) of Britain during WWII (1939–1945).
MORPHEUS: God of dreams, son of Sleep.

1   In France, on a rented canal boat, my friends and I gazed in despair at the closed oaken gates of the lock. We'd come to them only seconds after the witching hour of noon, but we were too late. There was no one to open the lock for us; *l'éclusiére* was at lunch, and after lunch she would lay herself down, close her eyes, and nap. At two, but not before, she would emerge refreshed from her square granite house and set the great cogs in motion.

2   We tied the boat up to a spindly bush beside the towpath and waited. And waited. It was high haying season, but the fields lay empty of farmers. The roads lay empty of trucks. France lunched, and then slept. So did Spain. So did much of the civilized world.

3   If we'd been differently nurtured we too would have taken a nap, but we were Americans, condemned from the age of four to trudge through our sleepless days. Americans are afraid of naps. Napping is too luxurious, too sybaritic, too unproductive, and it's free; pleasures for which we don't pay make us anxious. Besides, it seems to be a

natural inclination. Those who get paid to investigate such things have proved that people deprived of daylight and their wristwatches, with no notion of whether it was night or day, sink blissfully asleep in midafternoon as regular as clocks. Fighting off natural inclinations is a major Puritan virtue, and nothing that feels that good can be respectable.

4   They may have a point there. Certainly the process of falling asleep in the afternoon is quite different from bedtime sleep. Whether this is physiological or merely a by-product of guilt, it's a blatantly sensual experience, a voluptuous surrender, akin to the euphoric swoon of the heroine in a vampire movie. For the self-controlled, it's frightening—*how far down am I falling? will I ever climb back?* The sleep itself has a different texture. It's blacker, thicker, more intense, and works faster. Fifteen minutes later the napper pops back to the surface as from time travel, bewildered to find that it's only ten of two instead of centuries later.

5   Like skydiving, napping takes practice; the first few tries are scary.

6   The American nap is even scarier because it's unilateral. Sleeping Frenchmen are surrounded by sleeping compatriots, but Americans who lie down by day stiffen with the thought of the busy world rushing past. There we lie, visible and vulnerable on our daylit bed, ready to cut the strings and sink into the dark, swirling, almost sexual currents of the impending doze, but what will happen in our absence? Our stocks will fall; our employees will mutiny and seize the helm; our clients will tiptoe away to competitors. Even the housewife, taking advantage of the afternoon lull, knows at the deepest level of consciousness that the phone is about to ring.

7   And of course, for those of us with proper jobs, there's the problem of finding a bed. Some corporations, in their concern for their employees' health and fitness, provide gym rooms where we can commit strenuous exercise at lunchtime, but where are our beds? In Japan, the productivity wonder of the industrialized world, properly run companies maintain a nap room wherein the workers may refresh themselves. Even in America, rumor has it, the costly CEOs of giant corporations work sequestered in private suites, guarded by watchpersons, mainly so they can curl up unseen to sharpen their predatory powers with a quick snooze. A couple of recent presidents famous for their all-night energies kept up the pace by means of naps. Other presidents, less famous for energy, slept by day *and* night; woe to the unwary footstep that wakened Coolidge in the afternoon.

8   This leaves the rest of us lackeys bolt upright, toughing it out, trying to focus on the computer screen, from time to time snatching our chins up off our collarbones and glancing furtively around to see if we were noticed. The modern office isn't designed for privacy, and most of our cubicles have no doors to close, only gaps in the portable partitions. Lay our heads down on the desk at the appropriate hour and we're exposed to any passing snitch who strolls the halls enforcing alertness. It's a wonder they don't walk around ringing bells and blowing trumpets from one till three. American employers do not see the afternoon forty winks as refreshing the creative wellsprings of mere employees. They see it as goofing off.

9   Apparently most of us agree. Large numbers of us are, for one reason or another, home-bound, but do we indulge in the restorative nap? Mostly not. Even with no witness but ourselves, we're ashamed to. It would mean we weren't busy. We tell ourselves we have a million urgent things to do and our lives are so full and exciting we couldn't possibly lie down by daylight. Never mind that our heads are no particular use in midafternoon and half the work we do may need to be redone in the cold light of tomorrow morning. Oozing virtue and busyness, we flog ourselves on till evening.

10   In the evening, at least according to the cartoons, American men fall asleep on the couch, after dinner, a-flicker with light from the television screen. They are home from work, the day's toil accomplished, and they're free to doze, though if they'd napped at the biologically appointed time they wouldn't need to now, and at this hour it's not so much a nap as an awkward preview of the night's sleep, possibly leading to four-a.m. insomnia. Women, on the other hand, are never home from work unless it's someone else's home; home for them is simply different work, and naps are not an option.

11   It's time to rethink the nap from both the corporate and the personal viewpoint.

12   Those CEOs who find their own naps such an asset to productivity might consider what they'd do for the rest of us. They could hire consultants to conduct productivity studies, dividing us into teams of sleepers and wakers. When the results were in, they might even decide to mandate naps, as naps were mandated in nursery school, when we each unfolded a name-tagged blanket and spread it on the floor and lay down and shut up for a while. Granted we can't all have office suites, or even couches, and it would be unseemly to have us stacked up like firewood on the conference table, but we could

use futons, stored discreetly under the desk, or folding cots, or sleeping bags. The phones could be left to their answering devices, the faxes could pile up in the hopper, and the sales reps could pound in vain on the door as they'd find themselves doing in France.

13   Those of us at home, with beds at hand, should take pleasure as well as productivity into account. Consider the cat. A perfectly healthy cat can nap through the entire month of February and wake feeling all the better for it. The house may be simply pattering with uncaught mice, but no twitch of guilt quivers the whiskers of the napping cat. In summer he stretches out to full length, preferably in a breezy doorway where he's rather in the way, and sometimes on his back, looking dead enough to alarm the chance visitor, and drapes his arm over his eyes. Swiftly and easily he lowers himself into sleep, sensuous, fur-lined sleep, the sleep of the untroubled conscience. Nothing tells him he ought to be rushing about his various occupations. Sleep, for a cat, is a worthy occupation in itself.

14   Let us consider the cat and go to bed. Bed the haven, the motherly lap, the downy nest. Bed, from which Earth with its fuss and fidgeting shrinks to the size of Pluto, visible only by telescope. We should loosen or remove some of our clothing, close the curtains, and lie down flat, allowing the vital forces to circulate through the brain and restore its muscle tone.

15   Bed is *not* a shameful, shiftless place to be by day, nor is it necessary to run a fever of 102 to deserve it. Bed can even be productive. The effortless horizontal body and the sensory deprivation of the quiet bedroom leave the mind free, even in sleep, to focus, to roam, sometimes to forge ahead. Knotty problems can unknot themselves as if by magic. Creative solutions can tiptoe across the coverlet and nestle onto the pillow of the napper, even while the black velvet paws of Morpheus lie closely over his eyes. He may wake half an hour later with the road ahead laid clear.

16   Creativity doesn't come a-running to those who toil and slave for her; she's as much the daughter of rest and play as of effort; just because we're uncomfortable doesn't mean we're productive; just because we're comfortable doesn't mean we're lazy. Milton wrote *Paradise Lost* in bed. Winston Churchill, a prodigious producer, wrote all those large important histories in bed, brandy bottle at the ready. No doubt when inspiration flagged and his thoughts refused to marshal, he took a nip and a nap. Now, there was a man who knew a thing or two about a good day's work.

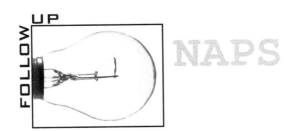

Exploring Language

compatriot: a person from your own country.
euphoric: a feeling of great happiness, joy, ecstasy, well-being.
furtively: slyly or secretively.
lackey: servant; footman.
mandate: command or authorize.
prodigious: extraordinary in size; enormous, huge.
spindly: long, thin, and frail.
sybaritic: luxurious.
unilateral: one-sided.
Note: For pronunciation, go to dictionary.com, search the word, and click on the speaker icon.

Thinking and Talking Points

1. Are Americans—in general—afraid of naps, as Holland claims? Is there a prejudice against naps? What evidence does she present for this claim? What is your experience with nap prejudice?

2. Holland claims that "pleasures for which we don't pay make us anxious." Do you agree? Can you think of examples? How does she defend this statement?

3. Holland uses a light-hearted tone in her essay. What word choices convey this tone? How do we know she is serious about her topic?

4. Examine phrases like "civilized world" (paragraph #2), "proper jobs," and "properly run companies" (paragraph #8). What are the underlying implications of these statements? What do they tell us about her opinions?

5. Examine the last and first sentences of each paragraph, and discuss how Holland links the essay through strong **transitions**, tying each paragraph to the next with careful word choices.

Styling

One style technique you might be familiar with is **alliteration**, the repetition of sounds close to one another, creating rhythm. Some examples from Holland's essay include "consider the cat," "deprived of daylight" and "snitch who strolls." Notice that the words in each pair begin with the same letter or sound.

PRACTICE   First, find at least three other pairs of words close together that create alliteration in Holland's essay.

YOU TRY IT   Choose a topic and brainstorm five pairs of words that contain alliteration. Some ideas for topics might be candy (jelly beans and juju bees), descriptions of your favorite meal (simply sublime), your pet (perky poodle), favorite song or poet (melancholy musician). Using your brainstorming list, write five sentences. Apply this technique to your next essay.

Teaming Up

1. **Warm-up for Writing Ideas #1 and #2.** Everyone in the group jot down a list of jobs they've had (even babysitting or mowing lawns), and then under each job, list the positives and negatives. Compare lists. Co-write a paragraph that discusses what benefits would be available in the ideal job.

2. **Warm-up for Writing Idea #3.** Brainstorm your guilty pleasure, what it is and why you like it. Everyone pass their paper to their right. On your peer's paper, brainstorm all the reasons why the activity might be objectionable to others (or yourself). After you get your paper handed back to you, write a defense next to each objection. Now you have a good start on Writing Idea #3.

Writing Ideas

1. Research companies in another country and their work habits. How much vacation time is typical? What about overtime? Do they provide child care? Exercise rooms? Meals? Nap rooms? What other perks might be offered? Write an essay that compares those benefits to a typical benefit package in the United States.

2. Research two companies in the same field, perhaps Microsoft and Google. What benefits do they offer employees? Which company

seems more progressive in providing for employees? Which one needs to improve? You might write your essay in letter format to the company you think needs improvement, comparing them to the superior company, questioning and advising them on their practices.

3. Everyone has a guilty or "endangered" pleasure, an innocent pastime (not illegal) that others complain or nag about, or frown upon. Write an essay that defends your innocent pleasure. Some ideas might be shopping, eating junk food, playing video games, chocolate, reading silly novels, or watching mindless television shows, or spending hours on Facebook or Twitter.

Essay Connections

Essays that analyze culture include an excerpt from "The Culture of Celebrity" by Joseph Epstein, "About Men," by Gretel Ehrlich, and "Somebody's Baby" by Barbara Kingsolver.

PRINCE

The Fargodome
Fargo, North Dakota
December 8, 1997

Chuck Klosterman

Chuck Klosterman's work has appeared in Esquire, GQ, Spin, New York Times Magazine, and The Washington Post. He's the author of several essay collections, including Fargo Rock City, Sex, Drugs, and Cocoa Puffs, and Killing Yourself to Live. The essay "Prince" appears in "The Show I'll Never Forget: 50 Writers Relive Their Most Memorable Concertgoing Experience," where he expresses his admiration of Prince as a genius, which he defines as "considerably more gifted and creative than almost everyone else who aspires to do the things he does best."

DUSTBIN OF HISTORY AND CULTURE

BYZANTINE: Eastern half of the Roman empire, which survived after the rest of Rome fell; it was eventually overrun by the Ottomans in 1453.

CORINTHIANS (Paul's first letter to): Also known as the Epistle of St. Paul (first and second letters are now the seventh and eighth books of the New Testament). The first letter was written about 53 or 54 CE, addressed to the Christian community of Corinth, Greece, which he had founded; it deals with the problems of the early church.

BIOSPHERE II: A self-contained ecological system in Arizona; Biosphere I is the earth.

TAFKAP: acronym for "The Artist Formerly Known as Prince."

1   I loved Prince when I was thirteen, and that was humiliating. It was among my darkest secrets. Seven hours before the first day of junior high, I laid in bed and listened to my sister's *Purple Rain* cassette, mortified by my own womanliness. "This will destroy me," I privately thought. "People will see right through me. I am a pussy." At the time, the only other artists I loved were Mötley Crüe, Ratt, KISS, and Ozzy. As far as I could tell, these were the only artists any intelligent, heterosexual male could (or would) love. While much of

"Prince, The Fargodome, Fargo, North Dakota, December 8, 1997" by Chuck Klosterman excerpted from *The Show I'll Never Forget: 50 Writers Relive Their Most Memorable Concertgoing Experience,* edited by Sean Manning, (Da Capo, 2007). Reprinted by permission of Chuck Klosterman.

1985 America may have secretly appreciated "Round and Round," I was a deeply closeted Prince fanatic, unwilling to tell even my friends and family. I listened to the solo on "Let's Go Crazy," and my creeping fears were instantaneously validated: Prince was a better guitar player than Warren DeMartini. It was true, and I could not deny it. When I watch *Before Stonewall,* this is the experience I relate to.

2   Twelve years later, I had to review a Prince concert for the *Forum* newspaper in Fargo, North Dakota. By then, I had been "out" as a Prince person for seven or eight years. The only problem was that I didn't really care anymore: Prince was working through his preposterous TAFKAP period and was slowly releasing long-awaited records that mostly sucked. Oddly, I found myself lying about Prince again, but now the context was reversed: I kept finding myself saying things like, "A bad record by Prince is still better than 90 percent of the albums that will come out this year, because he is a genius. A bad Prince record is still better than anything by the Crystal Method." Which was true, I suppose, but really only proved that MTV's *Amp* appeared to be inventing a dystopic future.

3   So ANYWAY, I went to this show cautiously pessimistic. I suspected it might be embarrassing, or devoid of familiar material, or punctuated by Prince walking onto the stage and wordlessly holding up four inexplicable fingers for the duration of the evening. However, my main trepidation involved time: I had to file my review by 11:10 P.M. that night, and that deadline was inflexible. The site of the concert (the Fargodome!) was a ten-minute drive from the *Forum* office, and this was the pre-laptop era. All the radio stations claimed the show would begin at eight, but everybody knew Prince usually played long and never played on time; at his club in Minneapolis, he would (supposedly) begin impromptu rock sets at 3:45 A.M. in the middle of the week. Nonetheless, I would need to exit the Dome parking lot by 10:15—this would give me fifty minutes to write a fifteen-inch, seven hundred-word review (plus or minus five minutes to self-edit the copy before sending it to the Night Desk). If Prince played two hours, I would almost certainly miss the encore; this is a common problem for anyone who has ever covered music for a daily newspaper. I think I saw three encores in eight years.

4   I arrived at the Dome around 7:30, pleasantly surprised to find I was directly in front of the stage (reviewers are usually relegated to the side of the arena, but not tonight). My friend Ross and I idly chatted about which songs might or might not be performed. (Ross was pulling

hard for "Housequake" and "Pussy Control," if I recall correctly.) We also snickered about the smallness of the crowd; while more than twenty thousand people had showed up to the Dome for Elton John, there were only 7,114 people in the building for TAFKAP. Prince had implemented a Byzantine anti-scalping policy where he would only announce a show two weeks before the actual date, and then everyone had to purchase vouchers that could only be exchanged for tickets at the door; I believe it was modeled after the method in which citizens of communist Russia were able to attain bread. Prince has been a goofball his entire life, but the middle nineties were truly the apex of his insanity. He was so crazy in 1997 that most people didn't even notice.

5   So . . . 7,114 of us sat there and waited. And waited. I was not surprised Prince didn't go on at eight, but I grew a little irritated at 8:30. And then—off in the distance, at the rear of the auditorium—there emerged the sound of a bass drum. "Aha!" we collectively thought. "This is it. Prepare for Prince!" The drum grew louder as it moved toward the stage; the beat emanated from (what looked like) a substantial marching band (the kind of band that might perform at halftime during the annual Grambling/Southern football game). We all searched for rock's purple elf within the melee. Was he leading the pack? No. Was he hidden among their broad shoulders and flamboyant outfits? No. Was he inside the bass drum, like the Lucky Charms leprechaun? Nay.

6   He was not there.

7   He was not there, because this was actually Larry Graham and Graham Central Station. Now, I have attended many shows where the audience was unfamiliar with the opening act. However, this was the only major concert I've ever attended where every single member of the audience was completely unaware that an opening act was appearing. There had been no publicity about this whatsoever. Everybody—including myself—immediately assumed this had to be Prince's entourage. I mean, I had no fucking idea what Larry Graham looked like; I hadn't seen a picture of him since the seventies. They took the stage and tried to bury us with funk, but we all kept waiting for Prince to come out. "This is rather curious," I thought. "Why is the backing band performing 'Thank You (Falettin Me Be Mice Elf Agin)' in its *totality*?" Twenty minutes passed before we finally concluded that this was, in fact, a group relatively unrelated to Prince. And they were excellent, but they played a long time; their set was over an hour. It was now 9:45, and—for all I knew—Prince wasn't even in

Fargo. He was probably sitting inside Biosphere II, talking to a puppet and thinking about Paul's First Letter to the Corinthians.

8   It now seemed plausible that this concert might not begin before eleven, which would turn my seven hundred–word review into a less-nuanced four-word review: "Prince is a jerk." This was a real problem; there are no journalistic alternatives for covering an event that doesn't exist. Ross found this scenario increasingly comical. But then—at 9:59—a certain kind of existence began; this tiny, capricious freak walked onstage and started making rock music. And it was so goddamn mesmerizing that I remember almost none of it.

9   I initially recall thinking, "Okay, I can maybe watch five songs, and then I have to go write this stupid story." But I have no idea how many songs I experienced, or what most of these songs were, or if any of them were "Housequake" or "Pussy Control." I had a notebook, but I didn't take any notes. There may have been a medley that included "Little Red Corvette," "Raspberry Beret," and "I Could Never Take the Place of Your Man," but that might have actually occurred at a Prince concert I would see in Cleveland three years later. He was just so amazingly good at *everything*. There was a sixty-second span where he played a keyboard, a bass, and a guitar in immediate succession, and I think he played each individual instrument better than anyone ever had played them before, anywhere, during any historical period over the past eleven thousand years. *And Prince didn't even care.* He didn't look happy, and he didn't look bored. He didn't even look focused. It seemed completely spontaneous, yet it wouldn't have mattered if he had rehearsed those specific sixty seconds for eight or nine months; the experience would have been exactly the same. And what I learned at this concert—and what I suspect can only be learned through seeing Prince live—is that all the moronic bullshit I made up about Prince's bad records and the Crystal Method was completely true: Prince is a genius. I was completely right. I just didn't know what "being right" meant.

10   Prior to this concert, what I actually meant when I said, "Prince is a genius," was that, "Prince is considerably more gifted and creative than almost everyone else who aspires to do the things he does best." By this criteria, there are a handful of other musicians who would qualify as geniuses: John Lennon and Paul McCartney, Jimmy Page, Donald Fagan and Walter Becker, Tony Iommi, Ike Turner, Lindsey Buckingham, Kevin Shields, and probably twenty-five other very famous people I can't recall at the moment I'm writing this particular

sentence. For anecdotal purposes, this definition of "genius" is usually acceptable. But those artists are not geniuses; they are simply very, very, very good at a vocation they have selected. That difference became weirdly lucid whenever Prince did anything onstage, including his attempt to have sexual intercourse with a piano. Eddie Van Halen plays guitar like a genius, but that is something he *figured out* how to do. He *turned himself into a genius,* and that isn't the same thing.

11   I suppose it's possible that Prince has worked harder at his music than any of his peers; I know almost nothing about his life that hasn't been fictionalized for his semi-autobiographical movies. This is not an attempt to discredit his work ethic, or to suggest he's lazy. However, this singular Fargo concert forces me to believe that the degree to which he has (or hasn't) worked on his craft is almost completely irrelevant. Prince doesn't really deserve credit for being a genius because he is not a normal human. His ability to create and perform music is so inherent and instinctual that it cannot really be measured against normal criteria; the only other rock musicians in this class are Jimi Hendrix and (maybe) Bob Dylan. And I only realized this by *seeing* Prince from a distance of twenty-five feet. His transcendence is not accurately felt through his songs or his albums, because a lot of those songs and records aren't especially good. Some of them are semi-terrible. But bad Prince records are still valuable because *he made them.* They are like triptychs from Stonehenge.

12   I do not know what time I exited the show, but it was not even half over. I know I arrived at the *Forum* office at 10:50 and wrote 492 bland words that did not reflect the experience in any meaningful way (and this review does not mention any specific song Prince played). According to my best calculations, I probably saw forty minutes of that concert. Which were thirty-nine more than I needed.

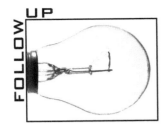

Exploring Language

apex: top or highest point.

capricious: given to sudden and/or unpredictable changes in mood or behavior.

dystopic: imaginary place or society where everything is bad; opposite of utopia.

emanate: radiate or spread out from.

entourage: a group of people who follow around and/or assist an important or famous person.

inexplicable: unexplainable.

melee: a mass of disorderly or unruly people; a group of people in a confused fight.

nuance: a slight difference, especially in sound or meaning.

transcendence: rising above the ordinary, often associated with a spiritual experience.

trepidation: fear or nervousness.

triptychs: three paintings or carved panels hinged together; or hinged tablet made of three leaves, used in ancient Rome.

Note: For pronunciation, go to dictionary.com, search the word, and click on the speaker icon.

USAGE   Write a sentence containing three of the above words.

Thinking and Talking Points

1. What is Klosterman's main point or thesis? What evidence does he use to support his view?

2. Usually, students are taught to avoid repetition, but sometimes repetition creates style. Notice at the end of paragraph #5, "He was not there," is set off as its own paragraph, and then repeated in the first line of the next paragraph. What effect is Klosterman trying to achieve?

3. The essay contains so-called "cuss" words and slang. Why might this language be appropriate in the context of this piece of writing? Can

you think of other writing situations where it might be necessary and acceptable? In what writing situations would it not be appropriate?

4. Find areas in the essay where the writer uses exaggeration. How is this technique used to his advantage?

5. Klosterman makes a distinction between being a genius and turning yourself into one. What is that distinction? What is his definition of a genius?

Styling

One style technique you might be familiar with is **alliteration**, the repetition of sounds close to one another, creating rhythm. Some examples from Klosterman's essay include "specific sixty seconds" (s), "Prepare for Prince" (p), and "preposterous period" (p).

PRACTICE   Find at least three other pairs of words close together that create alliteration in Klosterman's essay.

YOU TRY IT   Choose a topic and brainstorm five pairs of words that contain alliteration. Some ideas for topics might be candy (jelly beans and juju bees), descriptions of your favorite meal (simply sublime salmon), your pet (perky poodle) or favorite song or poet (melancholy musician). Using your brainstorming list, write five sentences containing alliterations.

Teaming Up

1. The "You Try It" in the "Styling" section easily adapts to a group activity. It can be done as a round robin exercise, where each person writes down an object (like the ones above), passes it to the right, and then the next person must tag on another word, perhaps an adjective, that contains alliteration. If done in groups of three, then each word winds up with two tagged on alliterations. The best of the bunch can be made into sentences.

2. **Warm-up for Writing Idea #3.** Bring in lyrics to a song you think stands up to the elements of poetry: imagery, tone and rhythm (for example **alliteration** and **assonance**), **symbol** and/or **allegory**, figurative language (**metaphor, simile, personification**). Read each set of lyrics and choose the one that best exemplifies poetry. (See the glossary for words in bold.)

Writing Ideas

1. Write an essay about the best (or worst) live show you've ever attended. It can be a concert, play, musical—as long as it was live. Describe when and where it took place and what was going on in your life during that time. Use sensory detail to describe the surroundings, the crowd, the music. Your essay should reflect the tone of the show being the best or worst in your experience.

2. Compare and/or contrast two music concerts in the same **genre** (either ones you have attended or seen on DVD). Examples of genres might be country western, classical, rock, hip-hop, or rap. Argue for one artist being superior to the other in that genre. Be specific about what areas the artist excels. Reread Klosterman's essay for ideas.

3. Compare the theme in a song that you think qualifies as poetry to a poem of the same theme. Consider researching a literature data base in your school library (if available or try your public library) and type in search terms like "poetry themes." Write an essay comparing the themes as well as other literary devices, illustrating the universality of such themes. Some themes to consider might be teen depression, anger, war, suffering, guilt, betrayal, love, philosophy, politics, jealousy, solitude, nature. For comparing elements of poetry, here is a list to consider: imagery, tone and rhythm (alliteration, assonance), symbol and/or allegory, figurative language (metaphor, simile, personification).

Essay Connections

Other essays in this book with music themes include "Monster Mash" by Jack Kroll and "A Voice for the Lonely" by Stephen Corey. Clayton Collins discusses the impact of music on the brain, in "Musical Awakenings."

ROLL OVER BACH, TOO!

Jack Kroll

Jack Kroll was an award-winning journalist and drama critic for Newsweek. He died at age 74 on June 8, 2000. This essay on the Beatles attempts to explain the group's special appeal, claiming, "For many, Sgt. Pepper was an epochal event, the matriculation of rock into high art though some may not be fans of the music, most should find a connection with his enthusiasm for this group of music icons."

DUSTBIN OF HISTORY AND CULTURE

BUSTER KEATON: (1895–1966) An American silent film star and popular comic actor.

CHARLIE CHAPLIN: (1889–1977) Actor, director, producer, mostly of silent films. Though English, he moved to America, where he got his start in film.

DUKE ELLINGTON: (1899–1974) American jazz musician, credited with bringing jazz into concert halls.

LOUIS ARMSTRONG: (1900–1971) Also known as Satchmo. American jazz musician who often performed in films and was an international celebrity.

T. S. ELIOT: (1888–1965) One of the most influential poets of the 20th century; his most famous and controversial work is "The Waste Land."

1   Were you there? If not, you really can never know. Amazement must be experienced first-hand, and the coming of the Beatles was an amazement. Girls screamed; the captions in *Newsweek*'s Feb. 24, 1964, cover story read: "eeeeeeeeeeeee . . . E E E E E E E E E E E E . . . *EEEEEEEEEEEE!*" and the London *Times* music critic praised the Beatles' "pandiatonic clusters" and "flat-submediant key-switches." Both reactions were perfectly appropriate; the Beatles were blowing minds and nervous systems. And cash registers. On their first U.S. tour, two entrepreneurial types bought the pillowcases on which the four mop-tops had reposed in a Kansas City hotel and sliced them into 160,000 tiny squares, which they sold for a dollar each.

2   The girls were screaming not at key-switches (which the Beatles, who could not read music, arrived at instinctively) but at things like the

"Yeah, yeah, yeahs," in "She Loves You," delivered by Paul McCartney and George Harrison. But what linked the screechers and the scholars was a sense of something new, an absolute freshness that the Beatles manifested musically and personally. Those early songs—"I Want to Hold Your Hand," "Please Please Me"—were both sexy and innocent. Like those two "pleases," the first a polite supplication, the second a verb vibrating with sexual possibility. A British writer described the band as "beat-up and depraved in the nicest possible way."

3   That's a perfect description of rock-and-roll charisma. But what made the Beatles the key pop artists of the '60s was the synthesis that they made out of almost every conceivable pop element. Both John Lennon and Ringo Starr hailed their hometown of Liverpool as a crucible, a port city that brought together Irish, blacks, Chinese and sailors coming from America with blues records. Clubs and pubs jumped with the sounds of country and Western, British music-hall songs and rural folk tunes. The classical composer and critic Wilfrid Mellers said that the Beatles, like "other geniuses such as Bach, Mozart and Beethoven, knew the right time and place to be born."

4   Out of all these elements, plus the influence of pioneer rockers like Chuck Berry and Little Richard, the Beatles created a unique multifaceted music. It rocked hard, it glinted with irony, it sang with poignant melancholy, as in "Yesterday," McCartney's anthem of loss, in which he sings solo and turns his guitar into the heart-strings of loneliness. The Lennon-McCartney songs were minidramas that evoked a wide spectrum of emotion. McCartney's "Penny Lane" and Lennon's "Strawberry Fields Forever" (coupled on one amazing single) conjured up their lost worlds of childhood, Paul's a "very strange" Utopia, John's a place where "nothing is real / and nothing to get hungabout."

5   In less than five years the Beatles produced a series of albums of increasing complexity, notably *A Hard Day's Night, Rubber Soul, Revolver* and *Sgt. Pepper's Lonely Hearts Club Band*. The album's climactic number, "A Day in the Life," is the Beatles' peak achievement. "I read the news today oh boy," sings Lennon, with a sweet hopelessness. Recounting news items of death, war and absurdity, John's refrain, "I'd love to turn you on," fuses the Beatles' drug experience with the desire to transcend the horrors of a foundering civilization. The number ends with the now legendary gigantic crescendo, played by a 41-piece orchestra, that wells up like a groan from the anguished heart of the city.

6   For many, *Sgt. Pepper* was an epochal event, the matriculation of rock into high art. Kenneth Tynan called it a decisive moment in the

history of Western civilization. But some critics thought that high art was exactly what rock shouldn't be. "What's so great about Art?" demanded critic Nik Cohn, insisting that the Beatles "have flown away into limbo." In a review I compared "A Day in the Life" to T. S. Eliot's apocalyptic poem "The Waste Land." In his illuminating survey of the Beatles' career, *Revolution in the Head,* Ian MacDonald rejects the comparison. He says of "A Day in the Life": "The fact that it achieves its transcendent goal via a potentially disillusioning confrontation with the 'real' world is precisely what makes it so moving." But that splendid sentence is also a succinct summation of "The Waste Land."

7   What the Beatles did in the '60s remains the most thrilling surge of creativity in the history of pop culture. They obliterated distinctions of high and low, like Chaplin, like Buster Keaton, like Louis Armstrong and Duke Ellington. They made it clear that if art is to survive in the techno-millennium that looms ahead, it must be hooked into the realities and redemptions in the days of our lives.

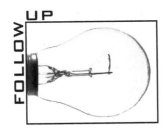

ROLL OVER
BACH, TOO!

Exploring Language

apocalyptic: prophetic of the world's future, usually a doomed or
threatened vision.

crucible: a melting pot; in this context, a place where those of
different backgrounds and styles meet, influencing change.

entrepreneurial: striking out on one's own in business or other
ventures.

epochal: memorable or very significant.

matriculation: enrollment or signing up; admission to a group.

multifaceted: having many sides or appearances.

poignant: touching or moving.

redemption: atonement or making up for something.

succinct: brief, compact.

supplication: a plea or request.

synthesis: a blend or fusion.

transcend: to rise above, often used in a spiritual context.

Note: For pronunciation, go to dictionary.com, search the word, and
click on the speaker icon.

USAGE Look up *crucible* in the dictionary and notice its different meanings. Use the word in at least two sentences, each with a different meaning.

Thinking and Talking Points

1. What is Kroll's thesis? Examine the examples Kroll uses to support each of his paragraphs. How well does he support his point? How does he explain his examples and tie them back to his thesis?

2. Kroll, in paragraph #6, quotes critics who disagree with his comparison of the Beatles' work to high art and comparison of "A Day in the Life" to a famous poem by T.S. Eliot, "The Waste Land." Why does he bring in critics who disagree with him? How does he turn it to his advantage?

3. Read the section in paragraph #3 where Kroll quotes critic Mellers comparing the Beatles to famous classical composers. Do you agree with this assessment? Can you think of other music groups that might be compared to classical "geniuses"?

4. Kroll writes in paragraph #4, "The Lennon-McCartney songs were minidramas that evoked a wide spectrum of emotion." Listen to one of the songs he discusses—or find the lyrics—and explain how the song is a minidrama.

Styling

An opening that hooks the reader is an important ingredient in any writing. Jack Kroll opens his essay with a simple question, "Were you there?" Asking a question arouses the reader's curiosity. He or she usually wants an answer. In her essay "No Wonder They Call Me a Bitch," Ann Hodgman spends the entire introduction—with the exception of the first line—asking questions. When you're stuck for a good opening line, think about your essay, what questions you address, and try to come up with a short question.

PRACTICE   Write a short question for each of these topics: hockey, hunting, jazz, snakes, art.

YOU TRY IT   Open your next essay with a question or series of questions.

Note: See the titles section for more introduction ideas.

Teaming Up

1. **Warm-up for Writing Idea #1.** Have someone in the group bring in the lyrics to "A Day in the Life" by the Beatles (available with the CD *Sgt. Peppers Lonely Hearts Club Band*). Now compare the verses from "The Waste Land" (the entire poem is too long to reprint here). What similarities in theme do you notice? What makes both of these pieces "apocalyptic"? How are they "hooked into the realities and redemptions in the days of our lives"?

2. **Warm-up for Writing Idea #2.** Bring in lyrics to a song you think is "hooked into the realities and redemptions in the days of our lives." Compare in your group, explaining why your choice is a mini-drama, how it fits Kroll's quote above. Now you have a start on Writing Idea #2.

Writing Ideas

1. Find the lyrics to another Beatles' song Kroll mentions in paragraph #4. Analyze the lyrics, and write an essay explaining how the song is a mini-drama, how it's "hooked into the realities and redemptions in the days of our lives."

2. Analyze a song of your own choice, possibly from Teaming Up #2, and write an essay comparing it to one of the Beatles' songs, explaining how both are "apocalyptic."

3. Research photos of the Beatles, one from their early days when Kroll says their music was "both sexy and innocent" and the other from the later years when Kroll says "the Beatles produced a series of albums of increasing complexity." Now listen to songs from both periods. Compare. Write an essay that attempts to answer this question: what does the change in appearance and the change in tone of the lyrics and music say about changes in our culture?

Essay Connections

The essay "Musical Awakenings" by Clayton S. Collins examines music's ability to heal; in "A Voice for the Lonely," Stephen Corey writes a memoir about music's impact on the senses while paying a tribute to singer Roy Orbison of "Pretty Woman" fame. The essay "Prince" by Chuck Klosterman praises him as a genius.

From "The Waste Land" by T. S. Eliot

April is the cruelest month,
breeding Lilacs out of the dead land, mixing
Memory and desire, stirring
Dull roots with spring rain.
Winter kept us warm, covering
Earth in forgetful snow, feeding
A little life with dried tubers.

* * *

Unreal City,
Under the brown fog of a winter dawn,
A crowd flowed over London Bridge, so many,
I had not thought death had undone so many.
Sighs, short and infrequent, were exhaled,
And each man fixed his eyes before his feet.
Flowed up the hill and down King William Street,
To where Saint Mary Woolnoth kept the hours

With a dead sound on the final stroke of nine.
There I saw one I knew, and stopped him, crying: "Stetson!
"You who were with me in the ships at Mylae!
"That corpse you planted last year in your garden,
"Has it begun to sprout? Will it bloom this year?
"Or has the sudden frost disturbed its bed?
"O keep the Dog far hence, that's friend to men,
"Or with his nails he'll dig it up again!"

MYLAE: where a battle was fought between Rome and Carthage in 260 B.C. Rome
    won.
SAINT MARY WOOLNOTH: a church in London.

Questions for Interpretation

1. April is springtime, a time of rebirth and resurrection. Why, then, does Eliot call it the "cruelest month"?
2. What does the brown fog represent?
3. People are walking across the London Bridge like the living dead, eyes fixed and staring, uttering sighs. Why does Eliot present such a picture of humans?
4. What commentary is Eliot making about war?

SOMEBODY'S BABY

Barbara Kingsolver

Born in 1955 in Kentucky, Barbara Kingsolver has won numerous awards for her novels, short stories, and essays: The Poisonwood Bible *was a finalist for the Pulitzer Prize, and* The Lacuna *won Britain's coveted Orange Prize for Fiction in 2010. Other works include* Animal Dreams, The Bean Trees, *and* High Tide in Tucson: Essays from Now or Never, *where "Somebody's Baby" appears; Kingsolver points out the difference in cultural attitudes concerning children, contrasting her experiences in Spain to America.*

DUSTBIN OF HISTORY AND CULTURE

SUBJUNCTIVE TENSE: a grammar term referring to the "mood" of a verb when used in conditional or hypothetical statements or questions, like "I wish I were taller" rather than "I wish I was taller." Though not used as extensively as in the past, the subjunctive still persists.

GUAPA: pretty; guapo means handsome.

1   As I walked out the street entrance to my apartment, a kid in maroon high-tops and a startling haircut approached, saying "Hi gorgeous." Three weeks ago, I would have assessed the degree of malice and made ready to run or tell him to bug off, depending. Today, instead, I smile, and so does my 4-year-old daughter, because after dozens of similar encounters I understand that he doesn't mean me but *her*.

2   This is not the United States.

3   For most of the year my daughter was four we lived in Spain, in the warm southern province of the Canary Islands. I struggled with dinner at midnight and the subjunctive tense, but my only genuine culture shock has reverberated from this earthquake of a fact: people there like kids. They don't just say so, they do. Widows in black, buttoned-down c.e.o.'s, purple-sneakered teen-agers, the butcher, the baker, all have stopped on various sidewalks to have little chats with my daughter. Yesterday, a taxi driver leaned out his window to shout "Hola, guapa!" My daughter, who must have felt my conditioned

flinch, looked up at me wide-eyed and explained patiently, "I like it that people think I'm pretty." With a mother's keen myopia, I would tell you, absolutely, my daughter is beautiful enough to stop traffic. But in Santa Cruz de Tenerife, I have to confess, so is every other person under the height of one meter. Not just those who agree to be seen and not heard. When my daughter gets cranky in a restaurant (and really, what do you expect at midnight?), the waiters flirt and bring her little presents and nearby diners look on with that sweet, wistful gleam of eye that before now I have only seen aimed at the dessert tray. Children are the meringues and eclairs of this culture. Americans, it seems to me now, sometimes regard children as a sort of toxic-waste product: a necessary evil, maybe, but if it's not their own they don't want to see it or hear it or, God help us, smell it.

4   If you don't have children, you think I'm exaggerating. But if you've changed a diaper in the last decade, you know exactly the toxic-waste glare I mean. It goes far beyond diapers. In the United States, I have been told in restaurants: "We come here to get away from kids." (This for no infraction on my daughter's part that I could discern, other than being visible.) On an airplane, I heard a man tell a beleaguered woman whose infant was bawling (as loudly as I would, to clear my aching ears, if I couldn't manage chewing gum): "If you can't keep that thing quiet, you should keep it at home."

5   Air travel, like natural disasters, throws strangers together in unnaturally intimate circumstances. Think how well you got to know the bald spot on the guy who reclined in front of you on some long flight. As a consequence, I think of airplanes as a splendid cultural magnifying glass. On my family's recent voyage from New York to Madrid, we weren't assigned seats together. I shamelessly begged my neighbor—a forty-something New Yorker traveling alone—if she would take my husband's seat in another row so our air-weary and plainly miserable daughter could stretch out across our laps. My fellow traveler snapped: "No, I have to have the window seat, just like you had to have that baby."

6   As simply as that, a child with needs (and ears) became an inconvenient thing, for which I was entirely to blame. The remark left me stunned and, as always happens when someone is remarkably rude to me, momentarily guilty. Yes, she's right, conceiving this child was a rash, lunatic moment of selfishness, and now I had better be prepared to pay the price.

7   In the U.S.A., where it's said that anyone can grow up to be President, we parents are left pretty much on our own when it comes to the little Presidents-in-training. Our social programs for children are the hands-down worst in the industrialized world, but apparently that is just what we want as a nation. It took a move to another country to make me realize how thoroughly I had accepted my nation's creed of every family for itself. Whenever my daughter crash-landed in the playground, I was startled at first to see a sanguine, Spanish-speaking stranger pick her up and dust her off. And if a shrieking bundle landed at my feet, I'd furtively look around for the next of kin. But I quickly came to see this detachment as perverse when applied to children, and am wondering how it ever caught on in the first place.

8   My grandfathers on both sides lived in households that were called upon, after tragedy struck close to home, to take in orphaned children and raise them without a thought. In an era of shortage, this was commonplace. But one generation later that kind of semipermeable household had vanished, at least among the white middle class. It's horrifying thought, but predictable enough, that the worth of children in America is tied to their dollar value. Children used to be field hands, household help, even miners and factory workers—extensions of a family's productive potential and so, in a sense, the property of an extended family. But precious property, valued and coveted. Since the advent of child-labor laws, children have come to hold an increasingly negative position in the economy. They're spoken of as a responsibility, a legal liability, an encumbrance—or, if their unwed mothers are on welfare, a mistake that should not be rewarded. The political shuffle seems to be about making sure they cost us as little as possible, and that their own parents foot the bill. Virtually every program that benefits children in this country, from Sesame Street to free school lunches, has been cut back in the last decade—in many cases, cut to nothing. If it takes a village to raise a child, our kids are knocking on a lot of doors where nobody seems to be home.

9   Taking parental responsibility to extremes, some policymakers in the U.S. have seriously debated the possibility of requiring a license for parenting. I'm dismayed by the notion of licensing an individual adult to raise an individual child, because it implies parenting is a private enterprise, like selling liquor or driving a cab (though less lucrative). I'm also dismayed by what it suggests about innate fitness

or nonfitness to rear children. Who would devise such a test? And how could it harbor anything but deep class biases? Like driving, parenting is a skill you learn by doing. You keep an eye out for oncoming disasters, and know when to stop and ask for directions. The skills you have going into it are hardly the point.

10   The first time I tried for my driver's license, I flunked. I was sixteen and rigid with panic. I rolled backward precariously while starting on a hill; I misidentified in writing the shape of a railroad crossing sign; as a final disqualifying indignity, my VW beetle—borrowed from my brother and apparently as appalled as I—went blind in the left blinker and mute in the horn. But nowadays, when it's time for a renewal, I breeze through the driver's test without thinking, usually on my way to some other errand. That test I failed twenty years ago was no prediction of my ultimate competence as a driver, anymore than my doll-care practices (I liked tying them to the back of my bike, by the hair) were predictive of my parenting skills (heavens be praised). Who really understands what it takes to raise kids? That is, until after the diaper changes, the sibling rivalries, the stitches, the tantrums, the first day of school, the overpriced-sneakers standoff, the first date, the safe-sex lecture, and the senior prom have all been negotiated and put away in the scrapbook?

11   While there are better and worse circumstances from which to launch offspring onto the planet, it's impossible to anticipate just who will fail. One of the most committed, creative parents I know plunged into her role through the trapdoor of teen pregnancy; she has made her son the center of her life, constructed a large impromptu family of reliable friends and neighbors, and absorbed knowledge like a plant taking sun. Conversely, some of the most strained, inattentive parents I know are well-heeled professionals, self-sufficient but chronically pressed for time. Life takes surprising turns. The one sure thing is that no parent, ever, has turned out to be perfectly wise and exhaustively provident, 1,440 minutes a day, for 18 years. It takes help. Children are not commodities but an incipient world. They thrive best when their upbringing is the collective joy and responsibility of families, neighborhoods, communities, and nations.

12   It's not hard to figure out what's good for kids, but amid the noise of any increasingly antichild political climate, it can be hard to remember just to go ahead and do it: for example, to vote to raise your school district's budget, even though you'll pay higher taxes. (If you're earning enough to pay taxes at all, I promise, the school needs those

few bucks more than you do.) To support legislators who care more about afterschool programs, affordable health care, and libraries than about military budgets and the Dow Jones industrial average. To volunteer time and skills at your neighborhood school and also the school across town. To decide to notice, rather than ignore it, when a neighbor is losing it with her kids, and offer to baby-sit twice a week. This is not interference. Getting between a ball player and a ball is interference. The ball is inanimate.

13   Presuming children to be their parents' sole property and responsibility is, among other things, a handy way of declaring problem children to be someone else's problem, or fault, or failure. It's a dangerous remedy; it doesn't change the fact that somebody else's kids will ultimately be in your face demanding now with interest what they didn't get when they were smaller and had simpler needs. Maybe in-your-face means breaking and entering, or maybe it means a Savings and Loan scam. Children deprived—of love, money, attention, or moral guidance—grow up to have large and powerful needs.

14   Always there will be babies made in some quarters whose parents can't quite take care of them. Reproduction is the most invincible of all human goals; like every other species, we're only here because our ancestors spent millions of years refining their act as efficient, dedicated breeders. If we hope for only sane, thoughtful people to have children, we can wish while we're at it for an end to cavities and mildew. But unlike many other species we are social, insightful, and capable of anticipating our future. We can see, if we care to look, that the way we treat children—all of them, not just our own, and especially those in great need—defines the shape of the world we'll wake up in tomorrow. The most remarkable feature of human culture is its capacity to reach beyond the self and encompass the collective good.

15   Its an inspiring thought. But in mortal fact, here in the U.S. we are blazing a bold downhill path from the high ground of "human collective," toward the tight little den of "self." The last time we voted on a school-budget override in Tucson, the newspaper printed scores of letters from readers incensed by the very possibility: "I don't have kids," a typical letter writer declared, "so why should I have to pay to educate other people's offspring?" The budget increase was voted down, the school district progressed from deficient to desperate, and I longed to ask that miserly nonfather just whose offspring he expects to doctor the maladies of his old age.

16   If we intend to cleave like stubborn barnacles to our great American ethic of every nuclear family for itself, then each of us had better raise and educate offspring enough to give us each day, in our old age, our daily bread. If we don't wish to live by bread alone, we'll need not only a farmer and a cook in the family but also a home repair specialist, an auto mechanic, an accountant, an import-export broker, a forest ranger, a therapist, an engineer, a musician, a poet, a tailor, a doctor, and at least three shifts of nurses. If that seems impractical, then we can accept other people's kids into our lives, starting now.

17   It's not so difficult. Most of the rest of the world has got this in hand. Just about any country you can name spends a larger percentage of its assets on its kids than we do. Virtually all industrialized nations have better schools and child-care policies. And while the U.S. grabs headlines by saving the occasional baby with heroic medical experiments, world health reports (from UNESCO, USAID, and other sources) show that a great many other parts of the world have lower infant mortality rates than we do—not just the conspicuously prosperous nations like Japan and Germany, but others, like Greece, Cuba, Portugal, Slovenia—simply because they attend better to all their mothers and children. Cuba, running on a budget that would hardly keep New York City's lights on, has better immunization programs and a higher literacy rate. During the long, grim haul of a thirty-year economic blockade, during which the United States has managed to starve Cuba to a ghost of its hopes, that island's child-first priorities have never altered.

18   Here in the land of plenty a child dies from poverty every fifty-three minutes, and TV talk shows exhibit teenagers who pierce their flesh with safety pins and rip off their parents every way they know how. All these punks started out as somebody's baby. How on earth, we'd like to know, did they learn to be so isolated and selfish?

19   My second afternoon in Spain, standing on a crowded bus, as we ricocheted around a corner and my daughter reached starfish-like for stability, a man in a black beret stood up and gently helped her into his seat. In his weightless bearing I caught sight of the decades-old child, treasured by the manifold mothers of his neighborhood, growing up the way leavened dough rises surely to the kindness of bread.

20   I thought then of the woman on the airplane, who was obviously within her rights to put her own comfort first, but whose withheld generosity gave my daughter what amounted to a sleepless, kicking,

squirming, miserable journey. As always happens two days after someone has spoken to me rudely, I knew exactly what I should have said: Be careful what you give children, for sooner or later you are sure to get it back.

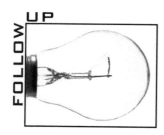

SOMEBODY'S BABY

Exploring Language

advent: arrival, beginning.

beleaguered: harassed, pestered, bothered.

cleave: in this context, stick to, cling to.

coveted: desired or wished for.

creed: belief, system, or doctrine.

discern: to recognize as distinct or different; perceive.

encumbrance: a burden or hindrance.

flinch: to draw back or shrink from; recoil.

furtively: slyly or secretly; underhandedly.

impromptu: spontaneous, improvised; spur-of-the-moment; prepared suddenly, in haste.

incensed: made angry or provoked.

incipient: just starting to be or exist; beginning.

innate: natural, inborn; existing in a being from birth as in innate talent for art.

lucrative: profitable, moneymaking.

maladies: in this context, illness, sickness, or disease.

manifold: numerous and varied; many.

myopia: shortsighted, though not in the physical sense (in this context, Kingsolver's "mother's keen myopia" refers to mothers all thinking their children are beautiful, regardless; can also mean narrow-minded or lacking understanding, in addition to referring to the vision condition of not being able to see things that are far away).

perverse: determined to go against what is right, expected, or desired; persistent or obstinate in what is wrong.

provident: in this context, cautious or prudent; also showing foresight.

retrospect: to look on the past with thought; reflecting on the past.

reverberate: returned or echoed repeatedly.

sanguine: optimistic, confident; or a reddish complexion.

semipermeable: from the word *permeate*, meaning to saturate or pervade; permeable means capable of being saturated or pervaded; semi, meaning partially or somewhat.

wistful: yearning, longing; wishful, often in a mournful or melancholy manner.
Note: For pronunciation, go to dictionary.com, search the word, and click on the speaker icon.

USAGE Write one sentence using *sanguine* to mean a reddish complexion; write a second sentence using the definition confident or optimistic.

Thinking and Talking Points

1. What is Kingsolver's thesis? What evidence does she use for support and how convincing is it?
2. How does she use contrast to her advantage?
3. The author writes that the idea of requiring a license for parenting would harbor "deep class biases." Give examples of what class biases she might mean.
4. Kingsolver claims that the United States has an "increasingly antichild political climate." List her support. To what extent to you agree or disagree? Support your view with examples that either agree with or counter her point.
5. What, according to Kingsolver, accounts for this cultural difference in attitudes toward children?
6. To read that one child dies from poverty in the United States every fifty-three minutes might come as a surprise or shock—what might account for this grim statistic? How might the problem be solvable?

Styling

"Somebody's Baby" opens the argument with a personal illustration—a narrative—of a larger social issue (see the "Introduction" section in this text). Brainstorm social or political topics—perhaps neglect of the elderly, the treatment of animals, the plight of schools, etc.—and choose one to use in a narrative introduction.

PRACTICE Write a brief story introduction that illustrates the problem.

YOU TRY IT Use this technique in an essay.

Teaming Up

1. Brainstorm a list of social programs for children. Divide the group, half bringing in articles in favor of the program, half researching the opposite view. Make a list of points from each side, and write a summary for each view. Discuss which side has the strongest argument (not necessarily the side you agree with).

2. List Barbara Kingsolver's points (her main reasons for her view). Next to each point list a counter-argument (a point that refutes the claim). Personal views are irrelevant for the exercise; it's good practice in critical thinking to be able to argue both sides of an issue.

Writing Ideas

1. Write an essay that contrasts another cultural or social difference between the United States and another country, or between different parts of the U.S. (East Coast versus West Coast, California and New York, Oregon and California, Louisiana and Chicago, or two counties in your area, etc.). The essay must have a point or argument. Use the narrative technique in the introduction.
2. Write an essay about another group that suffers neglect or bias; avoid the obvious stereotypes, striving for an out-of-the-ordinary topic (see Gretel Ehrlich's "About Men" for ideas).

Essay Connections

"About Men" by Gretel Ehrlich argues against the cultural stereotype of the American cowboy (and men in general); Ken Chen travels to China in "City Out of Breath."

THE CHEMIST'S WAR

Deborah Blum

Award-winning science writer Deborah Blum teaches journalism at the University of Wisconsin-Madison. In 1992, she won the Pulitzer Prize for her series "Monkey Wars," for the Sacramento Bee (now a book), examining the ethics and dilemmas surrounding primate research. Other books include Sex on the Brain: Biological Differences Between Men and Woman; A Field Guide for Science Writers *(2005);* Love at Goon Park: Harry Harlow and the Science of Affection *(2004);* The Poisoners Handbook *(2010), and* Ghost Hunters: William James and the Search for Scientific Proof of Life After Death. *She has also published articles in numerous magazines, newspapers, anthologies, and journals:* The Los Angeles Times, The Boston Globe, The New York Times, Discover Magazine, Psychology Today, The Utne Reader, Best American Science and Nature Writing, *including* Slate *where "The Chemist's War" first appeared.*

DUSTBIN OF HISTORY AND CULTURE

PROHIBITION: The period from 1920 (Volstead Act passed in 1919 to enforce the Eighteenth Amendment) to 1933 forbidding the sale and manufacture of alcoholic beverages. In 1933, the Twenty-first Amendment repealed the law.
BOOTLEGGED: illegally made, transported, or sold alcohol.
SPEAKEASIES: nightclubs and saloons selling illegal alcohol during Prohibition.

1   It was Christmas Eve 1926, the streets aglitter with snow and lights, when the man afraid of Santa Claus stumbled into the emergency room at New York City's Bellevue Hospital. He was flushed, gasping with fear: Santa Claus, he kept telling the nurses, was just behind him, wielding a baseball bat.

2   Before hospital staff realized how sick he was—the alcohol-induced hallucination was just a symptom—the man died. So did another holiday partygoer. And another. As dusk fell on Christmas, the hospital staff tallied up more than 60 people made desperately ill by alcohol and eight dead from it. Within the next two days, yet another 23 people died in the city from celebrating the season.

3   Doctors were accustomed to alcohol poisoning by then, the routine of life in the Prohibition era. The bootlegged whiskies and so-called gins often made people sick. The liquor produced in hidden stills frequently came tainted with metals and other impurities. But

this outbreak was bizarrely different. The deaths, as investigators would shortly realize, came courtesy of the U.S. government.

4   Frustrated that people continued to consume so much alcohol even after it was banned, federal officials had decided to try a different kind of enforcement. They ordered the poisoning of industrial alcohols manufactured in the United States, products regularly stolen by bootleggers and resold as drinkable spirits. The idea was to scare people into giving up illicit drinking. Instead, by the time Prohibition ended in 1933, the federal poisoning program, by some estimates, had killed at least 10,000 people.

5   Although mostly forgotten today, the "chemist's war of Prohibition" remains one of the strangest and most deadly decisions in American law-enforcement history. As one of its most outspoken opponents, Charles Norris, the chief medical examiner of New York City during the 1920s, liked to say, it was "our national experiment in extermination." Poisonous alcohol still kills—16 people died just this month after drinking lethal booze in Indonesia, where bootleggers make their own brews to avoid steep taxes—but that's due to unscrupulous businessmen rather than government order.

6   I learned of the federal poisoning program while researching my new book, The Poisoner's Handbook, which is set in jazz-age New York. My first reaction was that I must have gotten it wrong. "I never heard that the government poisoned people during Prohibition, did you?" I kept saying to friends, family members, colleagues.

7   I did, however, remember the U.S. government's controversial decision in the 1970s to spray Mexican marijuana fields with Paraquat, an herbicide. Its use was primarily intended to destroy crops, but government officials also insisted that awareness of the toxin would deter marijuana smokers. They echoed the official position of the 1920s—if some citizens ended up poisoned, well, they'd brought it upon themselves. Although Paraquat wasn't really all that toxic, the outcry forced the government to drop the plan. Still, the incident created an unsurprising lack of trust in government motives, which reveals itself in the occasional rumors circulating today that federal agencies, such as the CIA, mix poison into the illegal drug supply.

8   During Prohibition, however, an official sense of higher purpose kept the poisoning program in place. As the Chicago Tribune editorialized in 1927: "Normally, no American government would engage in such business. ... It is only in the curious fanaticism of Prohibition that any means, however barbarous, are considered justified." Others, however, accused lawmakers opposed to the poisoning plan of being in cahoots with criminals and argued that bootleggers and their law-breaking alcoholic customers deserved no sympathy. "Must Uncle Sam guarantee safety first for souses?" asked Nebraska's *Omaha Bee.*

9   The saga began with ratification of the 18th Amendment, which banned the manufacture, sale, or transportation of alcoholic beverages in the United States. High-minded crusaders and anti-alcohol organizations had helped push the amendment through in 1919, playing on fears of moral decay in a country just emerging from war. The Volstead Act, spelling out the rules for enforcement, passed shortly later, and Prohibition itself went into effect on Jan. 1, 1920.

10   But people continued to drink—and in large quantities. Alcoholism rates soared during the 1920s; insurance companies charted the increase at more than 300 percent. Speakeasies promptly opened for business. By the decade's end, some 30,000 existed in New York City alone. Street gangs grew into bootlegging empires built on smuggling, stealing, and manufacturing illegal alcohol. The country's defiant response to the new laws shocked those who sincerely (and naively) believed that the amendment would usher in a new era of upright behavior.

11   Rigorous enforcement had managed to slow the smuggling of alcohol from Canada and other countries. But crime syndicates responded by stealing massive quantities of industrial alcohol—used in paints and solvents, fuels and medical supplies—and redistilling it to make it potable.

12   Well, sort of. Industrial alcohol is basically grain alcohol with some unpleasant chemicals mixed in to render it undrinkable. The U.S. government started requiring this "denaturing" process in 1906 for manufacturers who wanted to avoid the taxes levied on potable spirits. The U.S. Treasury Department, charged with overseeing alcohol enforcement, estimated that by the mid-1920s, some 60 million gallons of industrial alcohol were stolen annually to supply the country's drinkers. In response, in 1926, President Calvin Coolidge's government decided to turn to chemistry as an enforcement tool. Some 70 denaturing formulas existed by the 1920s. Most simply added poisonous methyl alcohol into the mix. Others used bitter-tasting compounds that were less lethal, designed to make the alcohol taste so awful that it became undrinkable.

13   To sell the stolen industrial alcohol, the liquor syndicates employed chemists to "renature" the products, returning them to a drinkable state. The bootleggers paid their chemists a lot more than the government did, and they excelled at their job. Stolen and redistilled alcohol became the primary source of liquor in the country. So federal officials ordered manufacturers to make their products far more deadly.

14   By mid-1927, the new denaturing formulas included some notable poisons—kerosene and brucine (a plant alkaloid closely related to strychnine), gasoline, benzene, cadmium, iodine, zinc, mercury salts,

nicotine, ether, formaldehyde, chloroform, camphor, carbolic acid, quinine, and acetone. The Treasury Department also demanded more methyl alcohol be added—up to 10 percent of total product. It was the last that proved most deadly.

15   The results were immediate, starting with that horrific holiday body count in the closing days of 1926. Public health officials responded with shock. "The government knows it is not stopping drinking by putting poison in alcohol," New York City medical examiner Charles Norris said at a hastily organized press conference. "Yet it continues its poisoning processes, heedless of the fact that people determined to drink are daily absorbing that poison. Knowing this to be true, the United States government must be charged with the moral responsibility for the deaths that poisoned liquor causes, although it cannot be held legally responsible."

16   His department issued warnings to citizens, detailing the dangers in whiskey circulating in the city: "Practically all the liquor that is sold in New York today is toxic," read one 1928 alert. He publicized every death by alcohol poisoning. He assigned his toxicologist, Alexander Gettler, to analyze confiscated whiskey for poisons—that long list of toxic materials I cited came in part from studies done by the New York City medical examiner's office.

17   Norris also condemned the federal program for its disproportionate effect on the country's poorest residents. Wealthy people, he pointed out, could afford the best whiskey available. Most of those sickened and dying were those "who cannot afford expensive protection and deal in low grade stuff."

18   And the numbers were not trivial. In 1926, in New York City, 1,200 were sickened by poisonous alcohol; 400 died. The following year, deaths climbed to 700. These numbers were repeated in cities around the country as public-health officials nationwide joined in the angry clamor. Furious anti-Prohibition legislators pushed for a halt in the use of lethal chemistry. "Only one possessing the instincts of a wild beast would desire to kill or make blind the man who takes a drink of liquor, even if he purchased it from one violating the Prohibition statutes," proclaimed Sen. James Reed of Missouri.

19   Officially, the special denaturing program ended only once the 18th Amendment was repealed in December 1933. But the chemist's war itself faded away before then. Slowly, government officials quit talking about it. And when Prohibition ended and good grain whiskey reappeared, it was almost as if the craziness of Prohibition—and the poisonous measures taken to enforce it—had never quite happened.

Exploring Language

cahoots: "in cahoots" means to be in league, partnership, or conspiracy with one or more others, usually in a secretive manner.

clamor: an outcry, uproar, or loud noise.

denaturing: in this context, to make alcohol unfit for drinking.

disproportionate: out of proportion in size or number.

fanaticism: irrational or excessive devotion or enthusiasm.

potable: drinkable.

ratification: formal approval or consent.

rigorous: harsh, severe, demanding.

saga: the informal use refers to a story or series of events over a long period; in literature, a saga is a medieval narrative (story) that tells of the adventures or deeds of a hero.

souse: to be drenched with or immersed in liquid (in this instance alcohol); the term has come to refer to a drunk.

Note: For pronunciation, go to dictionary.com, search the word, and click on the speaker icon.

USAGE Choose three of the words from the list and write a sentence for each.

Thinking and Talking Points

1. Who is at "war" in the essay? What language does Blum use that fits with the idea of war? List specific words or sentences.
2. Does Blum have a specific thesis or is her point implied? What is her opinion about the decisions the government made during Prohibition? Examine words choices that convey her tone and list them.
3. Reread the first two paragraphs. Is this narrative opening a good hook? How does it contrast with the revelation at the end of paragraph three?
4. After hitting the reader with the surprise that the government poisoned alcohol in the 1920's, Blum reveals another plan by the government to poison marijuana with the herbicide Paraquat in the

1970's—a plan they dropped after public outcry. Why does Blum include this incident? Does it strengthen her point? What claim does she make about the incident's effect today?

5. What other details does she provide about Prohibition that might not be common knowledge? What statistics come as a surprise?

6. Despite the poisoning program and resulting deaths, people continued to drink, a phenomenon of human nature Gore Vidal attempts to explain in his essay "Drugs," written in the sixties. Read that short essay and explain his point concerning people wanting what is forbidden them. What else do these two essays have in common?

Styling

Blum uses an introduction narrative technique, almost fable-like in its tone, though she does not rely on her own experience but uses newspaper articles from the twenties, creating a factual opening that reads like a story (read more on narrative openings in the "Introductions" section of your text).

PRACTICE   Brainstorm a list of issues that concern or intrigue, either current or historical, and search your college's newspaper and periodicals data base for information and editorials on one, especially articles that have a human interest slant (ideas: Paraquat, animal shelters, the economy, marijuana clinics).

YOU TRY IT   Using the articles, **in your own words**, write a narrative introduction implying an opinion about the topic. The first line should have a story-like appeal, as Blum's does: "It was Christmas Eve 1926 . . ." or "Once there was . . ."

Teaming Up

1. The Styling exercise works well in groups: reading the articles together, brainstorming ideas for the narrative introduction, co-writing the paragraph, and revising and editing.

2. Choose at least five words from the "Exploring Language" list and use them to co-write a paragraph, either narrative (telling a mini-story), descriptive (perhaps a character sketch), or argument. The paragraph can be humorous but must follow general paragraph guidelines, sticking to the same subject.

Writing Ideas

1. Write an opinion essay that examines a government policy, action, or law. Use the story introduction technique from the Styling, or another option from the "Introductions" section in the text. The letter format with Frederick Douglas's "Letter to His Master" is another approach to expressing an opinion of a government policy or action.

2. Compare/Contrast "The Chemist's War" to "Drugs" by Gore Vidal, examining style, content, and relevance to today's concerns over these issues. Does one writer have a stronger point or style?

Essay Connections

"Drugs" by Gore Vidal is an obvious choice for another essay questioning government policy or human behavior; "Modern Times" by Lawrence Weschler, though dated, comments on Desert Storm, but remains relevant, questioning war fought with technology. "How to Drive Fast" by P.J. O'Rourke satirizes drugs, drinking, and driving.

LETTER TO HIS MASTER

Frederick Douglass

Frederick Douglass—an American slave known as Frederick Augustus Washington Bailey—escaped to Massachusetts, becoming a famous writer and lecturer, speaking out against the evils of slavery, and advising Abraham Lincoln. In this eloquent letter, Douglass writes to his former master, demanding to know the fate of his family, still owned by Thomas Auld.

DUSTBIN OF HISTORY AND CULTURE

WILLIAM LLOYD GARRISON: (1805–1879) American abolitionist who founded *The Liberator*, an anti-slavery newspaper.

1 Thomas Auld:

2   Sir—The long and intimate, though by no means friendly relation which unhappily subsisted between you and myself, leads me to hope that you will easily account for the great liberty which I now take in addressing you in this open and public manner. The same fact may possibly remove any disagreeable surprise which you may experience on again finding your name coupled with mine, in any other way than in an advertisement, accurately describing my person, and offering a large sum for my arrest. In thus dragging you again before the public, I am aware that I shall subject myself to no inconsiderable amount of censure. I shall probably be charged with an unwarrantable, if not a wanton and reckless disregard of the rights and proprieties of private life. There are those North as well as South who entertain a much higher respect for rights which are merely conventional, than they do for rights which are personal and essential. Not a few there are in our country, who, while they have no scruples against robbing the laborer of the hard earned results of his patient industry, will be shocked by the extremely indelicate manner of bringing your name before the public. . . .

3   I have selected this day on which to address you, because it is the anniversary of my emancipation; and knowing of no better way I am led to this as the best mode of celebrating that truly important event. Just ten years ago this beautiful September morning, yon bright sun beheld me a slave—a poor, degraded chattel—trembling at the sound of your voice, lamenting that I was a man, and wishing myself a brute.

The hopes which I had treasured up for weeks of a safe and success-ful escape from your grasp, were powerfully confronted at this last hour by dark clouds of doubt and fear, making my person shake and my bosom to heave with the heavy contest between hope and fear. I have no words to describe to you the deep agony of soul which I expe-rienced on that never to be forgotten morning—(for I left by daylight). I was making a leap in the dark. The probabilities, so far as I could by reason determine them, were stoutly against the undertaking. The preliminaries and precautions I had adopted previously, all worked badly. I was like one going to war without weapons—ten chances of defeat to one of victory. One in whom I had confided, and one who had promised me assistance, appalled by fear at the trial hour, deserted me, thus leaving the responsibility of success or failure solely with myself. You, sir, can never know my feelings. As I look back to them I can scarcely realize that I have passed through a scene so try-ing. Trying however as they were, and gloomy as was the prospect, thanks be to the Most High, who is ever the God of the oppressed, at the moment which was to determine my whole earthly career. His grace was sufficient, my mind was made up. I embraced the golden opportunity, took the morning tide at the flood, and a free man, young, active and strong, is the result. . . .

4   Since I left you, I have had a rich experience. I have occupied stations which I never dreamed of when a slave. Three out of the ten years since I left you, I spent as a common laborer on the wharves of New Bedford, Massachusetts. It was there I earned my first free dollar. It was mine. I could spend it as I pleased. I could buy hams or herring with it, without asking any odds of any body. That was a pre-cious dollar to me. You remember when I used to make seven or eight, or even nine dollars a week in Baltimore, you would take every cent of it from me every Saturday night, saying that I belonged to you, and my earnings also. I never liked this conduct on your part—to say the best, I thought it a little mean. I would not have served you so. But let that pass. I was a little awkward about counting money in New England fashion when I first landed in New Bedford. I like to have betrayed myself several times. I caught myself saying phip, for fourpence; and at one time a man actually charged me with being a runaway, whereupon I was silly enough to become one by running away from him, for I was greatly afraid he might adopt measures to give me again into slavery, a condition I then dreaded more than death.

5   I soon, however, learned to count money, as well as to make it, and got on swimmingly. I married soon after leaving you: in fact, I was engaged to be married before I left you; and instead of finding my companion a burden; she was truly a helpmeet. She went to live at service and I to work on the wharf, and though we toiled hard the first winter, we never lived more happily. After remaining in New Bedford for three years, I met with Wm. Lloyd Garrison, a person of whom you have *possibly* heard, as he is pretty generally known among slaveholders. He put it into my head that I might make myself serviceable to the cause of the slave by devoting a portion of my time to telling my own sorrows, and those of other slaves which had come under my observation. This was the commencement of a higher state of existence than any to which I had ever aspired. I was thrown into society the most pure, enlightened and benevolent that the country affords. Among these I have never forgotten you, but have invariably made you the topic of conversation—thus giving you all the notoriety I could do. I need not tell you that the opinion formed of you in these circles, is far from being favorable. They have little respect for your honesty, and less for your religion.

6   But I was going on to relate something of my interesting experience. I had not long enjoyed the excellent society to which I have referred, before the light of its excellence exerted a beneficial influence on my mind and heart. Much of my early dislike of white persons was removed, and their manners, habits and customs, so entirely unlike what I had been used to in the kitchen-quarters on the plantations of the South, fairly charmed me, and gave me a strong disrelish for the coarse and degrading customs of my former condition. I therefore made an effort so to improve my mind and deportment as to be somewhat fitted to the station to which I seemed almost providentially called. The transition from degradation to respectability was indeed great, and to get from one to the other without carrying some marks of one's former condition, is truly a difficult matter. I would not have you think that I am now entirely clear of all plantation peculiarities, but my friends here, while they entertain the strongest dislike to them, regard me with that charity to which my past life somewhat entitles me, so that my condition in this respect is exceedingly pleasant. So far as my domestic affairs are concerned, I can boast of as comfortable a dwelling as your own. I have an industrious and neat companion, and four dear children—the oldest a girl of nine years and three fine boys, the oldest eight, the next six, and the

youngest four years old. The three oldest are now going regularly to school—two can read and write, and the other can spell with tolerable correctness words of two syllables. Dear fellows! they are all in comfortable beds, and are sound asleep, perfectly secure under my own roof. There are no slaveholders here to rend my heart by snatching them from my arms, or blast a mother's dearest hopes by tearing them from her bosom. These dear children are ours—not to work up into rice, sugar and tobacco, but to watch over, regard, and protect, and to rear them up in the nurture and admonition of the gospel—to train them up in the paths of wisdom and virtue, and, as far as we can to make them useful to the world and to themselves. Oh! sir, a slaveholder never appears to me so completely an agent of hell, as when I think of and look upon my dear children. It is then that my feelings rise above my control. I meant to have said more with respect to my own prosperity and happiness, but thoughts and feelings which this recital has quickened unfit me to proceed further in that direction. The grim horrors of slavery rise in all their ghastly terror before me, the wails of millions pierce my heart, and chill my blood. I remember the chain, the gag, the bloody whip, the death-like gloom overshadowing the broken spirit of the fettered bondman, the appalling liability of his being torn away from wife and children, and sold like a beast in the market. Say not that this is a picture of fancy. You well know that I wear stripes on my back inflicted by your direction; and that you, while we were brothers in the same church caused this right hand, with which I am now penning this letter, to be closely tied to my left, and my person dragged at the pistol's mouth, fifteen miles, from the Bay side to Easton to be sold like a beast in the market for the alleged crime of intending to escape from your possession. All this and more you remember, and know to be perfectly true, not only of yourself, but of nearly all of the slaveholders around you.

7   At this moment, you are probably the guilty holder of at least three of my own dear sisters, and my only brother in bondage. These you regard as your property. They are recorded on your ledger, or perhaps have been sold to human flesh mongers, with a view to filling your own ever-hungry purse. Sir, I desire to know how and where these dear sisters are. Have you sold them? or are they still in your possession? What has become of them? are they living or dead? And my dear old grandmother, whom you turned out like an old horse, to die in the woods—is she still alive? Write and let me know all about them. If my grandmother be still alive, she is of no service to you, for

by this time she must be nearly eighty years old—too old to be cared for by one to whom she has ceased to be of service, send her to me at Rochester, or bring her to Philadelphia, and it shall be the crowning happiness of my life to take care of her in her old age. Oh! she was to me a mother, and a father, so far as hard toil for my comfort could make her such. Send me my grandmother! that I may watch over and take care of her in her old age. And my sisters, let me know all about them. I would write to them, and learn all I want to know of them, without disturbing you in any way, but that, through your unrighteous conduct, they have been entirely deprived of the power to read and write. You have kept them in utter ignorance, and have therefore robbed them of the sweet enjoyments of writing or receiving letters from absent friends and relatives. Your wickedness and cruelty committed in this respect on your fellow-creatures, are greater than all the stripes you have laid upon my back, or theirs. It is an outrage upon the soul—a war upon the immortal spirit, and one for which you must give account at the bar of our common Father and Creator. . . .

8   I will now bring this letter to a close, you shall hear from me again unless you let me hear from you. I intend to make use of you as a weapon with which to assail the system of slavery—as a means of concentrating public attention on the system, and deepening their horror of trafficking in the souls and bodies of men. I shall make use of you as a means of exposing the character of the American church and clergy—and as a means of bringing this guilty nation with yourself to repentance. In doing this I entertain no malice towards you personally. There is no roof under which you would be more safe than mine, and there is nothing in my house which you might need for your comfort, which I would not readily grant. Indeed, I should esteem it a privilege, to set you an example as to how mankind ought to treat each other.

9   I am your fellow man, but not your slave.

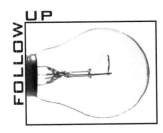
LETTER TO HIS MASTER

Exploring Language

censure: to criticize or reprimand.

chattel: personal possession or property.

deportment: manners, conduct.

disrelish: dislike or distaste.

notoriety: fame, usually with negative implications, like a "notorious criminal."

providentially: luckily or timely opportunity, sometimes referring to divine interference.

subsist: to exist; to keep alive or provide food for.

unwarrantable: unjustifiable, indefensible.

wanton: cruel or malicious; mischievous.

Note: For pronunciation, go to dictionary.com, search the word, and click on the speaker icon.

USAGE Look up the word wanton and study its different meanings. Write two sentences that use different meanings of the word.

Thinking and Talking Points

1. What examples in the essay illustrate the effects of slavery? How do these examples evoke sympathy?

2. What tone does the letter take? Is he respectful to Auld? Does he tell him off?

3. Douglass writes that refusing to allow slaves to read and write is more cruel than "all the stripes you have laid upon my back, or theirs." Why?

4. In the opening, Douglass writes, "I shall probably be charged with an unwarrantable, if not a wanton and reckless disregard of the rights and proprieties of private life." Read the rest of the paragraph. Is he being ironic or mocking? If so, how?

5. How does the letter refute the justification made by slaveholders that slaves were less intelligent and therefore less human than the slaveholders?

Styling

Douglass, like all good writers, uses a variety of sentence styles and lengths. Short sentence: "It was mine." Medium sentence: "Since I left you, I have had a rich experience." Long sentence:

> The same fact may possibly remove any disagreeable surprise which you may experience on again finding your name coupled with mine, in any other way than in an advertisement, accurately describing my person, and offering a large sum for my arrest.

Like many of Douglass's long sentences, this one uses a **loose** structure, but it does so in a unique way: after the first statement, each clause focuses in on a detail in the clause before it. He begins with a complete sentence: "The same fact may possibly remove any disagreeable surprise which you may experience on again finding your name coupled with mine."

The next phrase is dependent (in English grammar jargon), a prepositional phrase focusing on *coupled,* giving a closer detail: "in any other way than in an advertisement."

The next dependent group of words gives a detail about the advertisement: "accurately describing my person."

The last dependent group of words gives another detail about the advertisement, linking it to the previous one with a conjunction, and: "and offering a large sum for my arrest."

Note: The conjunction *and* is an option. The sentence would be correct without it. Here's a student example based on the Douglass model:

> The lightning flashed incandescently across the storm-troubled sky, illuminating the skeletal limbs of the maple grove that whipped violently back and forth in the fierce wind, casting shadows resembling nightmarish monsters against the sodden ground.

Notice that each dependent grouping provides a detail about the clause before it, getting closer each time, moving from the sky, to the limbs of the trees, and finally to the ground.

PRACTICE   Fill in the blanks below with dependent word groups, each time focusing in closer to the object or place. I've completed the first element for you.

The fog comes in at night like an uninvited guest, *creeping through the quiet streets*, _____, _____.

A hawk bolted from the mountain, *soaring into the valley below,* _____, _____.

YOU TRY IT Write five sentences in this structure. Use this sentence style in your next writing assignment.

Teaming Up

1. **Warm-up for Writing Idea #2.** Have each member of the group bring in a current newspaper or magazine article about someone in the public eye he or she disagrees with on moral or ethical grounds. Pick out one article you all agree would make a good target, and make a list in the following order:

    a. Explain what the person or group has done that's wrong.
    b. Explain what's wrong with the behavior.
    c. Explain how the behavior hurts others.
    d. Invite the person or group to respond to the allegations.

    Draft a letter to this person or group. Have each member of the group take a copy of the letter home to revise and edit. At the next class period, choose the best revision to read to the class.

    For more on this type of argument, see *Adios, Strunk and White* by Gary and Glynis Hoffman.

2. **Warm-up for Writing Idea #3.** Have one person research and bring in a copy of a Douglass speech. The other members of the group will bring in information on free speech and censorship. Compare the issues to those Douglass brings up. What similarities do you find in the defense of free speech? Which ones do you agree or disagree with? Have the arguments changed since Douglass wrote his speech?

Writing Ideas

1. Imagine what it would be like to be denied the right to read and write. Write an essay as if you're talking to someone who has the power to grant you this right, arguing why you should be allowed to learn.
2. Write an essay to a public figure you think has committed a moral or ethical outrage on society. Follow the format in Teaming Up activity #1.
3. Research and read a speech by Douglass on free speech, then compare it to current arguments on the topic. What principles in the Douglass speech apply today? Are there any that don't? Write an essay comparing these issues, giving your opinion on the free speech debate.

Essay Connections

Another Frederick Douglass essay in this book, "Learning to Read and Write," focuses in depth on the denial of this right to slaves. Both of these essays—and his autobiography—are important historical documents, as well as moving accounts of slavery. Shelby Steele's "The Content of Our Character" focuses on current problems in the African-American community.

ADVICE TO YOUTH

Mark Twain

Mark Twain (1835–1910), real name Samuel Longhorn Clemens, American writer and humorist, is best known for The Adventures of Huckleberry Finn and Tom Sawyer, but he wrote many other novels, short stories, and essays. In "Advice to Youth," an address to students, he satirizes the arrogance of youth who lie, manipulate parents, and think they're superior.

DUSTBIN OF HISTORY AND CULTURE

GATLING GUN: A machine gun invented by Richard J. Gatling.
INNOCENTS ABROAD: A book by Mark Twain (see Teaming Up #2).
ROBERTSON: Frederick Robertson (1816–1853), English Anglican clergyman (see Teaming Up #2).
SAINT'S REST: A work written by English Puritan clergyman Richard Baxter (1615–1691) (see Teaming Up #2).

1   Being told I would be expected to talk here, I inquired what sort of a talk I ought to make. They said it should be something suitable to youth—something didactic, instructive, or something in the nature of good advice. Very well. I have a few things in my mind which I have often longed to say for the instruction of the young: for it is in one's tender early years that such things will best take root and be most enduring and most valuable. First, then, I will say to you, my young friends—and I say it beseechingly, urgingly—

2   Always obey your parents, when they are present. This is the best policy in the long run, because if you don't they will make you. Most parents think they know better than you do, and you can generally make more by humoring that superstition than you can by acting on your own better judgment.

3   Be respectful to your superiors, if you have any, also to strangers, and sometimes to others. If a person offends you, and you are in doubt as to whether it was intentional or not, do not resort to extreme measures; simply watch your chance and hit him with a brick. That will be sufficient. If you shall find that he had not intended any offense, come out frankly and confess yourself in the wrong when you struck him; acknowledge it like a man and say you didn't mean to. Yes, always avoid violence; in this age of charity and kindliness, the time has gone by for such things. Leave dynamite to the low and unrefined.

4   Go to bed early, get up early—this is wise. Some authorities say get up with the sun; some others say get up with one thing, some with another. But a lark is really the best thing to get up with. It gives you a splendid reputation with everybody to know that you get up with the lark; and if you get the right kind of a lark, and work at him right, you can easily train him to get up at half past nine, every time— it is no trick at all.

5   Now as to the matter of lying. You want to be very careful about lying; otherwise you are nearly sure to get caught. Once caught, you can never again be, in the eyes of the good and the pure, what you were before. Many a young person has injured himself permanently through a single clumsy and ill-finished lie, the result of carelessness born of incomplete training. Some authorities hold that the young ought not to lie at all. That, of course, is putting it rather stronger than necessary; still, while I cannot go quite so far as that, I do maintain, and I believe I am right, that the young ought to be temperate in the use of this great art until practice and experience shall give them that confidence, elegance, and precision which alone can make the accomplishment graceful and profitable. Patience, diligence, painstaking attention to detail—these are the requirements; these, in time, will make the student perfect; upon these, and upon these only, may he rely as the sure foundation for future eminence. Think what tedious years of study, thought, practice, experience, went to the equipment of that peerless old master who was able to impose upon the whole world the lofty and sounding maxim that "truth is mighty and will prevail"—the most majestic compound fracture of fact which any of woman born has yet achieved. For the history of our race, and each individual's experience, are sown thick with evidence that a truth is not hard to kill and that a lie told well is immortal. There in Boston is a monument of the man who discovered anesthesia; many people are aware, in these latter days, that that man didn't discover it at all, but stole the discovery from another man. Is this truth mighty, and will it prevail? Ah no, my hearers, the monument is made of hardy material, but the lie it tells will outlast it a million years. An awkward, feeble, leaky lie is a thing which you ought to make it your unceasing study to avoid; such a lie as that has no more real permanence than an average truth. Why, you might as well tell the truth at once and be done with it. A feeble, stupid, preposterous lie will not live two years—except it be a slander upon somebody. It is indestructible, then, of course, but that is no merit of yours. A final word; begin your practice of this gracious

and beautiful art early—begin now. If I had begun earlier, I could have learned how.

6   Never handle firearms carelessly. The sorrow and suffering that have been caused through the innocent but heedless handling of firearms by the young! Only four days ago, right in the next farm-house to the one where I am spending the summer, a grandmother, old and gray and sweet, one of the loveliest spirits in the land, was sitting at her work, when her young grandson crept in and got down an old, battered, rusty gun which had not been touched for many years and was supposed not to be loaded, and pointed it at her, laughing and threatening to shoot. In her fright she ran screaming and pleading toward the door on the other side of the room; but as she passed him he placed the gun almost against her very breast and pulled the trigger! He had supposed it was not loaded. And he was right—it wasn't. So there wasn't any harm done. It is the only case of that kind I ever heard of. Therefore, just the same, don't you meddle with old unloaded firearms; they are the most deadly and unerring things that have ever been created by man. You don't have to take any pains at all with them; you don't have to have a rest, you don't have to have any sights on the gun, you don't have to take aim, even. No, you just pick out a relative and bang away, and you are sure to get him. A youth who can't hit a cathedral at thirty yards with a Gatling gun in three-quarters of an hour, can take up an old empty musket and bag his grandmother every time, at a hundred. Think what Waterloo would have been if one of the armies had been boys armed with old muskets supposed not to be loaded, and the other army had been composed of their female relations. The very thought of it makes one shudder.

7   There are many sorts of books; but good ones are the sort for the young to read. Remember that. They are a great, an inestimable, an unspeakable means of improvement. Therefore be careful in your selection, my young friends; be very careful; confine yourselves exclusively to Robertson's Sermons, Baxter's *Saint's Rest, The Innocents Abroad,* and works of that kind.

8   But I have said enough. I hope you will treasure up the instructions which I have given you, and make them a guide to your feet and a light to your understanding. Build your character thoughtfully and painstaking upon these precepts, and by and by, when you have got it built, you will be surprised and gratified to see how nicely and sharply it resembles everybody else's.

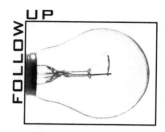

ADVICE TO YOUTH

Exploring Language

didactic: intended to teach, but often refers to teaching in a preachy, moralistic manner.

eminence: fame or prominence.

temperate: mild, moderate.

Note: For pronunciation, go to dictionary.com, search the word, and click on the speaker icon.

USAGE Locate the sentences where Twain uses these Exploring Language words in paragraphs #1 and #5, and study their usage. Here's a challenge: use all three of these words in one sentence.

Thinking and Talking Points

1. In this type of satirical humor, writers say one thing but mean the opposite. Find examples in the essay that illustrate that Twain isn't advocating lying, feeling superior, or shooting one's grandmother. How effective is this type of humor?
2. Why do you think Twain gives satirical advice to students in his address rather than instructive advice as he claims?
3. Why does Twain write that slander is indestructible? Do you agree? Is this type of lie worse than other lies Twain mentions?
4. What is Twain's view of youth? To what extent do you agree with his view? Is his "advice" relevant today?
5. What point does he make in the last line of the essay?

Styling

Though satire has a unique style, good humorists also use strong writing techniques such as sentence variety. Notice that Twain uses some very long sentences, some very short, others medium. Sentence variety keeps the reader alert, like a song with varying beats and tones. Because you know how to write short and medium sentences, practice modeling one of Twain's longer sentences:

Only four days ago, right in the next farmhouse to the one where I am spending the summer, a grandmother, old and gray and sweet, one of the loveliest spirits in the land, was sitting at her work, when her young grandson crept in and got down an old, battered, rusty gun which had not been touched for many years and was supposed not to be loaded, and pointed it at her, laughing and threatening to shoot.

Don't let long sentences intimidate you; they're just short sentences dressed up. If you analyze Twain's sentence, you'll find the short sentence:

Only four days ago a grandmother was sitting at her work.

The rest of the sentence consists of word groups that dress up this simple sentence, describing and giving more information. Twain could have split some of this information into separate sentences, but he knew a well-written long sentence gives what English teachers refer to as "flow" to an essay. Examine the rest of the word groups to determine their purpose. The first one is an interrupter placed between "ago" and "a grandmother," giving extra information about Twain's whereabouts: right in the next farmhouse to the one where I am spending the summer.

Notice that the word group is **dependent**—it can't stand alone as its own sentence. The next two dependent word groups come after "grandmother," describing her:

old and gray and sweet

one of the loveliest spirits in the land

The next series of dependent word groups provides action—read them again (in the complete sentence above), writing them out separately on a sheet of paper, noticing that they, too, are dependent.

PRACTICE Fill in the blank in the simple sentence below, adding a dependent clause that describes the teller:

Last week a bank teller, _____, sat innocently at her window.

Next, replace the period after window with a comma, and add a dependent clause describing what the teller is doing:

Last week a bank teller, _____, sat innocently at her window, _____.

Now, give a series of action clauses:

Last week a bank teller, _____, sat innocently at her window, _____, when _____, _____, and _____, and _____.

YOU TRY IT   Write three more sentences based on the above model. Use this structure in your next writing assignment.

Caution: Don't get discouraged if you commit comma splices at first. Writing correct long sentences sometimes takes several practice tries.

Teaming Up

1. In groups of three or four members, decide on a topic that might lend itself to satirical advice, like cheating. Brainstorm a list of satirical reasons advocating the topic. Choose one of the reasons to develop into a paragraph, and then co-write the paragraph.

2. Have each group member do a little research on the works Twain recommends students read: *The Innocents Abroad,* Frederick Robertson's *Sermons*, and Richard Baxter's *Saint's Rest* (the latter two available on the Web). You should be able to find enough information in a good encyclopedia to give you clues. In your group, discuss the findings and why Twain suggests young people should read works like these exclusively.

    Note: Try Britannica Online rather than unreliable sites. Most college libraries subscribe to Britannica Online or other reputable encyclopedias.

Writing Ideas

1. Write an essay about an experience you had with lying or slander, either by you or aimed at you, explaining the situation and the damage caused.

2. Write an essay that gives advice, either serious or satirical. You can give moral or ethical advice, as Twain does, or write a "how to" piece, a type of essay English teachers call Process Analysis: see the 'Writing Strategies' section for instructions.

3. Visit a library that has an online periodicals database and research political campaign slander. Write an essay arguing for or against this type of campaign strategy, not only whether it works, but its moral

and ethical implications. Use the research to provide examples in the essay. For more on writing research papers, see the Research Section Six.

Essay Connections

P. J. O'Rourke's "Driving Fast" satirizes teen behavior. "Turbulence" by David Sedaris is a humorous account of behavior he has encountered. Jonathon Swift's "A Modest Proposal" is easy to find on the Web. Just use a good search engine—like google.com—and type in Swift Modest Proposal.

ABOUT MEN

Gretel Ehrlich

Writer, rancher, documentary film maker, Gretel Ehrlich has several books to her credit, includ-ing *This Cold Heaven*, *The Solace of Open Spaces*, *Questions of Heaven*, *John Muir: Nature's Visionary*, and *The Future of Ice*. In "About Men," from *Solace of Open Spaces*, Ehrlich debunks the myth of the American cowboy, claiming that those Marlboro ads have it all wrong: "Instead of the macho, trigger-happy man our culture perversely wants him to be, the cowboy is more apt to be convivial, quirky, and softhearted."

DUSTBIN OF HISTORY AND CULTURE

CHISHOLM TRAIL: A cattle trail that ran between San Antonio, Texas and Abilene, Kansas (exact trail unknown); it was used for about twenty years after the Civil War (1861–1865) until the expansion of the railroad made it no longer useful.

HOBBLES: Restraints used mostly on horses (though sometimes on dogs or humans), placed on the front legs to restrict movement.

1   When I'm in New York but feeling lonely for Wyoming I look for the Marlboro ads in the subway. What I'm aching to see is horseflesh, the glint of a spur, a line of distant mountains, brimming creeks, and a reminder of the ranchers and cowboys I've ridden with for the last eight years. But the men I see in those posters with their stern, humor-less looks remind me of no one I know here. In our hellbent earnest-ness to romanticize the cowboy we've ironically disesteemed his true character. If he's "strong and silent" it's because there's probably no one to talk to. If he "rides away into the sunset" it's because he's been on horseback since four in the morning moving cattle and he's try-ing, fifteen hours later, to get home to his family. If he's "a rugged individualist" he's also part of a team: ranch work is teamwork and even the glorified open-range cowboys of the 1880s rode up and down the Chisholm Trail in the company of twenty or thirty other riders. Instead of the macho, trigger-happy man our culture has perversely wanted him to be, the cowboy is more apt to be convivial, quirky, and softhearted. To be "tough" on a ranch has nothing to do with conquests

and displays of power. More often than not, circumstances—like the colt he's riding or an unexpected blizzard—are overpowering him. It's not toughness but "toughing it out" that counts. In other words, this macho, cultural artifact the cowboy has become is simply a man who possesses resilience, patience, and an instinct for survival. "Cowboys are just like a pile of rocks—everything happens to them. They get climbed on, kicked, rained and snowed on, scuffed up by wind. Their job is 'just to take it,'" one old-timer told me.

2   A cowboy is someone who loves his work. Since the hours are long—ten to fifteen hours a day—and the pay is $30 he has to. What's required of him is an odd mixture of physical vigor and maternalism. His part of the beef-raising industry is to birth and nurture calves and take care of their mothers. For the most part his work is done on horseback and in a lifetime he sees and comes to know more animals than people. The iconic myth surrounding him is built on American notions of heroism: the index of a man's value as measured in physical courage. Such ideas have perverted manliness into a self-absorbed race for cheap thrills. In a rancher's world, courage has less to do with facing danger than with acting spontaneously—usually on behalf of an animal or another rider. If a cow is stuck in a boghole he throws a loop around her neck, takes his daily (a half hitch around the saddle horn), and pulls her out with horsepower. If a calf is born sick, he may take her home, warm her in front of the kitchen fire, and massage her legs until dawn. One friend, whose favorite horse was tying to swim a lake with hobbles on, dove under water and cut her legs loose with a knife, then swam her to shore, his arm around her neck lifeguard-style, and saved her from drowning. Because these incidents are usually linked to someone or something outside himself, the westerner's courage is selfless, a form of compassion.

3   The physical punishment that goes with cowboying is greatly underplayed. Once fear is dispensed with, the threshold of pain rises to meet the demands of the job. When Jane Fonda asked Robert Redford (in the film *Electric Horseman*) if he was sick as he struggled to his feet one morning, he replied, "No, just bent." For once the movies had it right. The cowboys I was sitting with laughed in agreement. Cowboys are rarely complainers; they show their stoicism by laughing at themselves.

4   If a rancher or cowboy has been thought of as a "man's man"— laconic, hard-drinking, inscrutable—there's almost no place in which the balancing act between male and female, manliness and femininity, can be more natural. If he's gruff, handsome, and physically fit

on the outside, he's androgynous at the core. Ranchers are midwives, hunters, nurturers, providers, and conservationists all at once. What we've interpreted as toughness—weathered skin, calloused hands, a squint in the eye and a growl in the voice—only masks the tenderness inside. "Now don't go telling me these lambs are cute, one rancher warned me the first day I walked into the football-field-sized lambing sheds. The next thing I knew he was holding a black lamb. "Ain't this little rat good-lookin'?"

5   So many of the men who came to the West were southerners— men looking for work and a new life after the Civil War—that chivalrousness and strict codes of honor were soon thought of as western traits. There were very few women in Wyoming during territorial days, so when they did arrive (some as mail-order brides from places like Philadelphia) there was a stand-offishness between the sexes and a formality that persists now. Ranchers still tip their hats and say, "Howdy, ma'am" instead of shaking hands with me.

6   Even young cowboys are often evasive with women. It's not that they're Jekyll and Hyde creatures—gentle with animals and rough on women—but rather that they don't know how to bring their tenderness into the house and lack the vocabulary to express the complexity of what they feel. Dancing wildly all night becomes a metaphor for the explosive emotions pent up inside, and when these are, on occasion, released, they're so battery-charged and potent that one caress of the face or one "I love you" will peal for a long while.

7   The geographical vastness and the social isolation here make emotional evolution seem impossible. Those contradictions of the heart between respectability, logic, and convention on the one hand, and impulse, passion, and intuition on the other, played out wordlessly against the paradisical beauty of the West, give cowboys a wide-eyed but drawn look. Their lips pucker up, not with kisses but with immutability. They may want to break out, staying up all night with a lover just to talk, but they don't know how and can't imagine what the consequences will be. Those rare occasions when they do bare themselves result in confusion. "I feel as if I'd sprained my heart," one friend told me a month after such a meeting.

8   My friend Ted Hoagland wrote, "No one is as fragile as a woman but no one is as fragile as a man." For all the women here who use "fragileness" to avoid work or as a sexual ploy, there are men who try to hide theirs, all the while clinging to an adolescent dependency on women to cook their meals, wash their clothes, and keep the ranch

house warm in winter. But there is true vulnerability in evidence here. Because these men work with animals, not machines or numbers, because they live outside in landscapes of torrential beauty, because they are confined to a place and a routine embellished with awesome variables, because calves die in the arms that pulled others into life, because they go to the mountains as if on a pilgrimage to find out what makes a herd of elk tick, their strength is also a softness, their toughness, a rare delicacy.

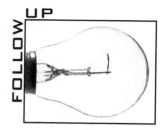

ABOUT MEN

Exploring Language

androgynous: having both masculine and feminine characteristics.
convivial: friendly, agreeable.
disesteemed: made unfavorable.
evasive: avoiding a direct response to a verbal challenge; elusive is
used when the avoidance is physical.
immutability: unchangeable.
inscrutable: not easily understood; mysterious.
laconic: using few words.
stoicism: repressing emotion and physical pain.
Note: For pronunciation, go to dictionary.com, search the word, and
click on the speaker icon.

USAGE   Write two sentences, one using *elusive* and the other *evasive*.

Thinking and Talking Points

1. How does Ehrlich debunk the myth of the American cowboy? Which
   examples best support her point? Do any weaken it? Which ones surprise you the most? How does America "romanticize" the cowboy?
2. Examine the stories and quotes about and from cowboys. How does
   each one support a topic sentence in the paragraph?
3. What does Ehrlich's essay imply about stereotypes in general? What
   other not-so-obvious stereotypes exist in our culture?
4. How does Ehrlich use contrast to her advantage? Examine each one
   and comment on whether or not it works.
5. In paragraph #5, she examines the origins of the cowboy's standoff-
   ishness. What is the significance of her analysis? Does it adequately
   explain the cowboys' relationships with women?

Styling

If you've ever been told that your essay doesn't flow, the problem might
be lack of **transitions**. Though many things contribute to flow in an

essay—correct grammar and punctuation, sentence variety, organization—if proper transition doesn't exist between paragraphs, the piece will sound too abrupt, as if you're changing ideas without signaling your reader. You might have been taught simple transitions like however, therefore, first of all, secondly, and so on, but to bump your writing up to a more college-level style, transitions should be more subtle than these worn-out examples.

Examine the last and first sentences of each paragraph in Ehrlich's essay. She carefully shifts ideas by using the same word in a different form (*emotions* and *emotional* in paragraphs #6 and #7); words that have similar meanings or connotations (*job* and *work* in paragraphs #1 and #2); or seeming opposites (*compassion* and *physical punishment* in paragraphs #2 and #3). Though there are more sophisticated transitions, these three should get you started.

PRACTICE   For each word in the list, think of a similar word, an opposite, or use the same word in a different form: friendly, melancholy, sincere, evil, cynical, water, writer, surfer, computer, plastic.

YOU TRY IT   Examine an essay you have written to see if you've used strong transition. If not, edit the essay, using the above styles of transition.

Note: See the transition ideas in Section Five.

Teaming Up

1. **Warm-up for Writing Idea #3.** As a group, brainstorm ideas on other topics that are often advertised, and have each person bring in at least three ads so you'll have nine to twelve ads on the same topic. Some ideas might be pet food, blue jeans, surf wear, moms, make-up, toys. Examine the ads for stereotypes and list them. Discuss how each stereotype might be untrue.

2. Using the list from Teaming Up #1, co-write a paragraph using "if" to debunk the myths in one of the stereotypes. For help, examine paragraph #2 in the essay and use it for a model.

3. **Warm-up for Writing Idea #2.** Have each group member write down a figure from popular culture that he or she admires or loathes. The icon can be from the past or present as long as it fits the definition of an icon. An icon is a representative image, in this case a body of cultural assumptions; for example, Marilyn Monroe is seen as an

icon of American beauty, and with that comes a set of assumptions about beauty in America. As a group, brainstorm the assumptions you make about what each image represents. Co-write a paragraph describing the icon and the assumptions you listed.

Writing Ideas

1. Write an essay that debunks a common misconception (or misconceptions) about a personality trait such as sentimentality, altruism, shyness, loneliness, individualism. Explain how there might be more sides to this character trait than our clichéd thinking usually allows. For example how might sentimentality be a negative quality? Is an individualist hiding a selfish nature? Does an altruist have an egoist alter ego? Follow the Writing Strategies for Defining Terms in Section Five.
2. The Marlboro Man might be seen as an American icon, embodying our cultural assumptions about the American cowboy. Explore another icon and write an essay that debunks our widely held assumption about that icon. You can choose from the art world, music, television, film, cereal boxes, advertising, Disney—almost anything is open for analysis.
3. Examine ads on another topic—blue jeans, toys, make-up, pet food, anything that's often advertised—and write an essay that explores the stereotypes hidden in these ads and debunk each stereotype. Describe each ad in detail.

Essay Connections

In "Somebody's Baby," Barbara Kingsolver discusses cultural attitudes about children in different countries. Joseph Epstein lambastes American's obsession with celebrity.

FROM THE CONTENT OF OUR CHARACTER

Shelby Steele

Shelby Steele is a writer and educator who has many published essays and books to his credit. In this excerpt from his book, Steele argues that despite still-existing racism, overall, there is "a remarkable range of opportunity if we are willing to pursue it." African Americans, according to Steele, need to stop focusing on a victim-based identity and take advantage of what mainstream America has to offer.

DUSTBIN OF HISTORY AND CULTURE

JEAN-PAUL SARTRE: (1905–1980) French philosopher and writer and leading proponent of existentialism.

RALPH ELLISON: (1914–1994) American novelist and essayist who wrote *The Invisible Man.*

EXISTENTIAL: See "Thinking and Talking Points" #5

1   There are many profound problems facing black America today: a swelling black underclass; a black middle class that declined slightly in size during the Eighties; a declining number of black college students; an epidemic of teenage pregnancy, drug use, and gang violence; continuing chronic unemployment; astoundingly high college and high school dropout rates; an increasing number of single-parent families; a disproportionately high infant mortality rate; and so on. Against this despair it might seem almost esoteric for me to talk about the importance of individual identity and possibility. Yet I have come to believe that despite the existing racism in today's America, opportunity is the single most constant but unexploited aspect of the black condition. The only way we will see the advancement of black people in this country is for us to focus on developing ourselves as individuals and embracing opportunity.

2   I have come to this conclusion over time. In the late Sixties, I was caught up in the new spirit of black power and pride that swept over black America like one of those storms that change the landscape. I

will always believe this storm was inevitable and, therefore, positive in many ways. What I gained from it was the power to be racially unapologetic, no mean benefit considering the long trial of patience that blacks were subjected to during the civil rights movement. But after a while, by the early Seventies, it became clear that black power did not offer much of a blueprint for how to move my life forward; it told me virtually nothing about who I was as an individual or how I might live in the world as myself. Of course, it was my mistake to think it could. But in the late Sixties, "blackness" was an invasive form of collective identity that cut so deeply into one's individual space that it seemed also to be an individual identity. It came as something of a disappointment to realize that the two were not the same, that being "black" in no way spared me the necessity of being myself.

3   In the early Seventies, without realizing it, I made a sort of bargain with the prevailing black identity—I subscribed in a general way to its point of view so that I could be free to get on with my life. Many blacks I knew did the same.

4   And what were we subscribing to? Generally, I think it was a form of black identity grounded in the spirit of black power. It carried a righteous anger at and mistrust of American society; it believed that blacks continued to be the victims of institutional racism, that we would have to maintain an adversarial stance toward society, and that a right racial unity was necessary both for survival and advancement. This identity was, and is, predicated on the notion that those who burned you once will burn you again, and it presupposes a deep racist reflex in American life that will forever try to limit black possibility.

5   I think it was the space I cleared for myself by loosely subscribing to this identity that ultimately put me in conflict with it. It is in the day-to-day struggle of living on the floor of a society, so to speak, that one gains a measure of what is possible in that society. And by simply living as an individual in America—with my racial-identity struggle suspended temporarily—I discovered that American society offered me, and blacks in general, a remarkable range of opportunity if we were willing to pursue it.

6   In my daily life I continue to experience racial indignities and slights: This morning I was told that blacks had too much musical feeling (soul, I suppose) to be good classical musicians; yesterday I passed two houses with gnomish black lawn jockeys on their front porches; my children have been called "nigger," as have I; I wear a tie and carry a briefcase so that my students on the first day of class will know I'm the professor; and so on. I also know that actual racial discrimination

persists in many areas of American life. I have been the victor in one housing-discrimination suit, as were my parents before me. My life is not immune to any of this, and I will never endure it with élan. Yet I have also come to realize that, in this same society, I have been more in charge of my fate than I ever wanted to believe and that though I have been limited by many things, my race was not foremost among them.

7   The point is that both realities exist simultaneously. There is still racial insensitivity and some racial discrimination against blacks in this society, but there is also much opportunity. What brought me into conflict with the prevailing black identity was that it was almost entirely preoccupied with the former to the exclusion of the latter. The black identity I was subscribing to in the Seventies—and that still prevails today—was essentially a "wartime" identity shaped in the confrontational Sixties. It saw blacks as victims even as new possibilities for advancement opened all around.

8   Why do we cling to an adversarial, victim-focused identity and remain preoccupied with white racism? Part of the reason, I think, is that we carry an inferiority anxiety—an unconscious fear that the notion that we are inferior may, in fact, be true—that makes the seizing of opportunity more risky for us, since setbacks and failures may seem to confirm our worst fears. To avoid this risk we hold a victim-focused identity that tells us there is less opportunity than there actually is. And, in fact, our victimization itself has been our primary source of power in society—the basis of our demands for redress. The paradoxical result of relying on this source of power is that it rewards us for continuing to see ourselves as victims of a racist society and implies that opportunity itself is something to be given instead of taken.

9   This leaves us with an identity that is at war with our own best interests, that magnifies our oppression and diminishes our sense of possibility. I think this identity is a burden for blacks, because it is built around our collective insecurity rather than a faith in our human capacity to seize opportunity as individuals. It amounts to a self-protective collectivism that focuses on black unity instead of individual initiative. To be "black" in this identity, one need only manifest the symbols, postures, and rhetoric of black unity. Not only is personal initiative unnecessary for being "black," but the successful exercise of initiative—working one's way into the middle class, becoming well-off, gaining an important position—may, in fact, jeopardize one's "blackness," make one somehow less black.

10   This sort of identity is never effective and never translates into the actual uplift of black people. Though it espouses black pride, it is actually a repressive identity that generates a victimized self-image, curbs individualism and initiative, diminishes our sense of possibility, and contributes to our demoralization and inertia. Uplift can only come when many millions of blacks seize the possibilities inside the sphere of their personal lives and use them to move themselves forward. Collectively we can resist oppression, but racial development will always be, as Ralph Ellison once put it, "the gift" of individuals.

11   There have been numerous government attempts at remedying the list of problems I mentioned earlier. Here and there a program has worked; many more have been failures. Clearly, we should find the ones that do work and have more of them. But my deepest feeling is that, in a society of increasingly limited resources, there will never be enough programs to meet the need. We black Americans will never be saved or even assisted terribly much by others, never be repaid for our suffering, and never find that symmetrical, historical justice that we cannot help but long for.

12   As Jean-Paul Sartre once said, we are the true "existential people." We have always had to create ourselves out of whole cloth and find our own means for survival. I believe that black leadership must recognize the importance of this individual initiative. They must preach it, tell it, sell it, and demand it. Our leadership has looked at government and white society very critically. Now they must help us look at ourselves. We need our real problems named and explained, otherwise we have no chance to overcome them. The impulse of our leaders is to be "political," to keep the society at large on edge, to keep them feeling as though they have not done enough for blacks. And, clearly, they have not. But the price these leaders pay for this form of "politics" is to keep blacks focused on an illusion of deliverance by others, and no illusion weakens us more. Our leaders must take a risk. They must tell us the truth, tell us of the freedom and opportunity they have discovered in their own lives. They must tell us what they tell their own children when they go home at night: to study hard, to pursue their dreams with discipline and effort, to be responsible for themselves, to have concern for others, to cherish their race and at the same time build their own lives as Americans. When our leaders put a spotlight on our victimization and seize upon our suffering to gain us ineffectual concessions, they inadvertently turn themselves into enemies of the truth, not to mention enemies of their own people.

13   I believe that black Americans are freer today than ever before. This is not a hope; this is a reality. Racial hatred has not yet left the American landscape. Who knows how or when this will occur. And yet the American black, supported by a massive body of law and, for the most part, the goodwill of his fellow citizens, is basically as free as he or she wants to be. For every white I have met who is a racist, I have met twenty more who have seen me as an individual. This, I am not ashamed to say, has been my experience. I believe it is time for blacks to begin the shift from a wartime to a peacetime identity, from fighting for opportunity to seizing it. The immutable fact of late-twentieth-century American life is that it is there for blacks to seize. Martin Luther King did not live to experience this. But then, of course, on the night before he died, he seemed to know that he would not. From the mountaintop he had looked over and seen the promised land, but he said, "I may not get there with you." I won't say we are snuggled deep in the promised valley he saw beyond the mountain; everyday things remind me that we are not. But I also know we have it better than our greatest leader. We are on the other side of his mountaintop, on the downward slope toward the valley he saw. This is something we ought to know. But what we must know even more clearly is that nothing on this earth can be promised except a chance. The promised land guarantees nothing. It is only an opportunity, not a deliverance.

FROM THE CONTENT OF OUR CHARACTER

Exploring Language

collectivism: the theory or practice of group ownership and control, especially over production, distribution, and land.

élan: spirit or enthusiasm.

esoteric: limited to or understood by a smll group.

espouse: to support or advocate.

ineffectual: not producing the intended effect.

Note: For pronunciation, go to dictionary.com, search the word, and click on the speaker icon.

USAGE Look up *élan* in a thesaurus and discover other lively words that have similar connotations.

Thinking and Talking Points

1. What is Steele's thesis?
2. What is Steele defining?
3. What strategies does Steele use to develop his definition?
4. Steele's book, *The Content of Our Character,* has been both praised and condemned. From reading this excerpt, what do you think makes it so controversial?
5. Look up the word *existential.* What does Steele mean when he uses this term?

Styling

Reread paragraph #1 and study the list Steele writes to underscore the problems facing black America. He uses a complete sentence and a colon followed by a list of problems separated by semicolons. Though semicolons usually separate complete sentences, they can be used to separate items in a series when too many commas might confuse the reader.

There are many profound problems facing black America today: a swelling black underclass; a black middle class that declined slightly in size during the Eighties; a declining number of black college students; an epidemic of teenage pregnancy, drug use, and gang violence; continuing chronic unemployment; astoundingly high college and high school dropout rates; an increasing number of single-parent families; a disproportionately high infant mortality rate; and so on.

The phrase *an epidemic of teenage pregnancy, drug use, and gang violence* contains a mini-list requiring commas; if Steele had used commas instead of semicolons after *a declining number of black college students* and after *gang violence,* the reader might be confused, not knowing which items went with which phrase.

PRACTICE   Fill in the blank after the colon with a list of items separated by semicolons, one containing internal commas.

Ryota filled the stereo with his favorite CDs: _____
_____

YOU TRY IT   Write three complete sentences followed by colons and lists separated by semicolons, with at least one of the phrases in each sentence containing a mini-list requiring commas.

Teaming Up

1. In your group, make a list of support Steele uses in his argument. Next, make a list of arguments and examples from an opposing view and discuss the results.

2. **Warm-up for Writing Idea #1.** Before class, brainstorm a list of qualities that define you. Type the list, but don't put your name on it. In your group, collect all the responses and shuffle them, redistributing one to each member (if you get your own, shuffle again). Read the lists aloud, trying to guess whose list you have. How accurate were your guesses? Did you learn anything new about your group members?

Writing Ideas

1. Using your list from Teaming Up activity #2, write an essay that defines you, telling what experiences shaped who you are today, and how you arrived at your list.

2. Choose a quality or personality trait and write an extended definition. Some ideas: loneliness, earnestness, depression, serenity, kindness, anger, pity, shame, indignation.

Essay Connections

"About Men" by Gretel Ehrlich busts the stereotype of the American cowboy and men in general. Barbara Kingsolver blasts American attitudes concerning children in contrast to other cultures. Paul Solotaroff illustrates our misunderstanding of people with Asperger's syndrome, a mild form of autism.

THE CULTURE OF CELEBRITY

Joseph Epstein

Among Joseph Epstein's (former editor of American Scholar) books are Snobbery: The American Version, Friendship: an Expose, and In a Cardboard Belt!: Essays Personal, Literary, and Savage. His essays have appeared in Harper's, Atlantic Monthly, The New Yorker, and Best American Essays. This excerpt from "The Culture of Celebrity" appeared in Best American Essays 2006; it reflects on our obsession with the lives of famous people simply because they are famous.

DUSTBIN OF HISTORY AND CULTURE

FLAUBERT, GUSTAVE (1821–1880): French writer best known for *Madame Bovary;* the French government charged Flaubert with immorality because of the novel's content.

MACHIAVELLIAN: Refers to Niccolo Machiavelli (1469–1527), an Italian Renaissance statesman and writer of *The Prince,* among other works; the term *Machiavellian* has come to be associated with deception and dishonesty.

ANDY WARHOL (1928–1987): American pop artist who painted mundane objects like Campbell's soup cans and Coca-Cola bottles, as well as portraits of celebrities.

SID AND MERCEDES BASS: Wealthy oil tycoons known for lavish parties; in 2006 they donated $25 million to The Metropolitan Opera.

AHMET AND MICA ERTEGUN: Ahmet Ertegun, son of a Turkish diplomat, founder and former chairman of Atlantic records, died in 2006; Mica is his widow.

TED WILLIAMS (1918–2002): Played with the Boston Red Sox from 1939–1960.

ADONIS: In mythology, a handsome young man loved by Venus; when he is killed by a wild boar, she changes his blood into a flower.

OLIVER GOLDSMITH (1730–1774): Irish born novelist, essayist, poet, and dramatist, best known for his humorous and bawdy—and still popular—play, *She Stoops to Conquer.*

FRANK MUIR (1920–1998): British writer and broadcaster of radio and television shows like *Till Death Do Us Part* and *Steptoe and Son.*

From "The Culture of Celebrity" by John Epstein as appeared in *The Weekly Standard,* October 17, 2005, Vol. 11, Issue 5. An earlier version of this essay was published in "Celebrity Culture" the Spring 2005 issue of *The Hedgehog Review: Critical Reflections on Contemporary Culture,* published by the Institute for Advanced Studies in Culture at the University of Virginia (www.virginia.edu/iasc/). Reprinted by permission.

MARCEL PROUST (1871–1922): French novelist, his best known work being *Swann's Way.*

W. H. AUDEN (1907–1973): British born poet and critic who became a U.S. citizen in 1939; poems include "The Unknown Citizen," "Lullaby," and "In Memory of W.B. Yeats."

PHILIP LARKIN (1922–1985): British poet whose collections include *The Whitsun Weddings* and *High Windows;* a novel (*Jill* and *A Girl in Winter*); he was also a jazz critic.

LENNY BRUCE (1925–1966): Comedian whose comedy was seen as obscene and outrageous; Bruce was arrested, but his controversial comedy act is seen to have been groundbreaking, opening the way for those who followed.

SEAMUS HEANEY: A native of Northern Ireland, Heaney was born in 1939, and won the Nobel Prize in Literature in 1995. In addition to his numerous poems, he translated the Old English elegiac narrative *Beowulf.*

1   Celebrity at this moment in America is epidemic, and it's spreading fast, sometimes seeming as if nearly everyone has got it. Television provides celebrity dance contests, celebrities take part in reality shows, perfumes carry the names not merely of designers but of actors and singers. Without celebrities, whole sections of the *New York Times* and the *Washington Post* would have to close down. So pervasive has celebrity become in contemporary American life that one now begins to hear a good deal about a phenomenon known as the Culture of Celebrity.

2   The word "culture" no longer, I suspect, stands in most people's minds for that whole congeries of institutions, relations, kinship patterns, linguistic forms, and the rest for which the early anthropologists meant it to stand. Words, unlike disciplined soldiers, refuse to remain in place and take orders. They insist on being unruly, and slither and slide around, picking up all sorts of slippery and even goofy meanings. An icon, as we shall see, doesn't stay a small picture of a religious personage but usually turns out nowadays to be someone with spectacular grosses. "The language," as Flaubert once protested in his attempt to tell his mistress Louise Colet how much he loved her, "is inept."

3   Today, when people glibly refer to "the corporate culture," "the culture of poverty," "the culture of journalism," "the culture of the intelligence community"—and "community" has, of course, itself become another of those hopelessly baggy-pants words, so that one hears talk even of "the homeless community"—what I think is meant by "culture" is the general emotional atmosphere and institutional

character surrounding the word to which "culture" is attached. Thus, corporate culture is thought to breed selfishness practiced at the Machiavellian level; the culture of poverty, hopelessness and despair; the culture of journalism, a taste for the sensational combined with a short attention span; the culture of the intelligence community, covering-one's-own-behind viperishness; and so on. Culture used in this way is also brought in to explain unpleasant or at least dreary behavior. "The culture of NASA has to be changed" is a sample of its current usage. The comedian Flip Wilson, after saying something outrageous, would revert to the refrain line "The debbil made me do it." So, today, when admitting to unethical or otherwise wretched behavior, people often say, "The culture made me do it."

4   As for "celebrity," the standard definition is no longer the dictionary one but rather closer to the one that Daniel Boorstin gave in his book *The Image; or, What Happened to the American Dream:* "The celebrity," Boorstin wrote, "is a person who is well-known for his well-knownness," which is improved in its frequently misquoted form as "A celebrity is someone famous for being famous." The other standard quotation on this subject is Andy Warhol's "In the future everyone will be world-famous for fifteen minutes," which also frequently turns up in an improved misquotation as "Everyone will have his fifteen minutes of fame."

5   But to say that a celebrity is someone well known for being well known, though clever enough, doesn't quite cover it. Not that there is a shortage of such people who seem to be known only for their well-knownness. What do a couple named Sid and Mercedes Bass do, except appear in boldface in the *New York Times* Sunday Styles section and other such venues (as we now call them) of equally shimmering insignificance, often standing next to Ahmet and Mica Ertegun, also well known for being well known? Many moons ago, journalists used to refer to royalty as "face cards"; today celebrities are perhaps best thought of as bold faces, for as such do their names often appear in the press (and in a *New York Times* column with that very name, "Bold Face").

6   The distinction between celebrity and fame is one most dictionaries tend to fudge. I suspect everyone has, or prefers to make, his own. The one I like derives not from Aristotle, who didn't have to trouble with celebrities, but from the career of Ted Williams. A sportswriter once said that he, Williams, wished to be famous but had no interest in being a celebrity. What Ted Williams wanted to be famous for was his hitting. He wanted everyone who cared about baseball to

know that he was—as he believed and may well have been—the greatest pure hitter who ever lived. What he didn't want to do was to take on any of the effort off the baseball field involved in making this known. As an active player, Williams gave no interviews, signed no baseballs or photographs, chose not to be obliging in any way to journalists or fans. A rebarbative character, not to mention often a slightly menacing s.o.b., Williams, if you had asked him, would have said that it was enough that he was the last man to hit .400; he did it on the field, and therefore didn't have to sell himself off the field. As for his duty to his fans, he didn't see that he had any.

7   Whether Ted Williams was right or wrong to feel as he did is of less interest than the distinction his example provides, which suggests that fame is something one earns—through talent or achievement of one kind or another—while celebrity is something one cultivates or, possibly, has thrust upon one. The two are not, of course, entirely exclusive. One can be immensely talented and full of achievement and yet wish to broadcast one's fame further through the careful cultivation of celebrity; and one can have the thinnest of achievements and be talentless and yet be made to seem otherwise through the mechanics and dynamics of celebrity creation, in our day a whole mini- (or maybe not so mini) industry of its own.

8   Or, another possibility, one can become a celebrity with scarcely any pretense to talent or achievement whatsoever. Much modern celebrity seems the result of careful promotion or great good luck or something besides talent and achievement: Mr. Donald Trump, Ms. Paris Hilton, Mr. Regis Philbin, take a bow. The ultimate celebrity of our time may have been John F. Kennedy Jr., notable only for being his parents' very handsome son—both his birth and good looks factors beyond his control—and, alas, known for nothing else whatsoever now, except for the sad, dying-young-Adonis end to his life.

9   Fame, then, at least as I prefer to think of it, is based on true achievement; celebrity on the broadcasting of that achievement, or the inventing of something that, if not scrutinized too closely, might pass for achievement. Celebrity suggests ephemerality, while fame has a chance of lasting, a shot at reaching the happy shores of posterity.

10   Oliver Goldsmith, in his poem "The Deserted Village," refers to "good fame," which implies that there is also a bad or false fame. Bad fame is sometimes thought to be fame in the present, or fame on earth, while good fame is that bestowed by posterity—those happy shores again. (Which doesn't eliminate the desire of most of us, at

least nowadays, to have our fame here and hereafter, too.) Not false but wretched fame is covered by the word "infamy"—"Infamy, infamy, infamy," remarked the English wit Frank Muir, "they all have it in for me"—while the lower, or pejorative, order of celebrity is covered by the word "notoriety," also frequently misused to mean noteworthiness.

11   Leo Braudy's magnificent book on the history of fame, *The Frenzy of Renown,* illustrates how the means of broadcasting fame have changed over the centuries: from having one's head engraved on coins, to purchasing statuary of oneself, to (for the really high rollers— Alexander the Great, the Caesar boys) naming cities or even months after oneself, to commissioning painted portraits, to writing books or having books written about one, and so on into our day of the publicity or press agent, the media blitz, the public relations expert, and the egomaniacal blogger. One of the most successful of public relations experts, Ben Sonnenberg Sr., used to say that he saw it as his job to construct very high pedestals for very small men.

12   Which leads one to a very proper suspicion of celebrity. As George Orwell said about saints, so it seems only sensible to say about celebrities: they should all be judged guilty until proven innocent. Guilty of what, precisely? I'd say of the fraudulence (however minor) of inflating their brilliance, accomplishments, worth, of passing themselves off as something they aren't, or at least are not quite. If fraudulence is the crime, publicity is the means by which the caper is brought off.

13   Is the current heightened interest in the celebrated sufficient to form a culture—a culture of a kind worthy of study? The anthropologist Alfred Kroeber defined culture, in part, as embodying "values which may be formulated (overtly as mores) or felt (implicitly as in folkways) by the society carrying the culture, and which it is part of the business of the anthropologist to characterize and define." What are the values of celebrity culture? They are the values, almost exclusively, of publicity. Did they spell one's name right? What was the size and composition of the audience? Did you check the receipts? Was the timing right? Publicity is concerned solely with effects and does not investigate causes or intrinsic value too closely. For example, a few years ago a book of mine called *Snobbery: The American Version* received what I thought was a too greatly mixed review in the *New York Times Book Review.* I remarked on my disappointment to the publicity man at my publisher's, who promptly told me not to worry: it was a full-page review, on page 11, right-hand side. That, he said, "is

very good real estate," which was quite as important as, perhaps more important than, the reviewer's actual words and final judgment. Better to be tepidly considered on page 11 than extravagantly praised on page 27, left-hand side. Real estate, man, it's the name of the game.

14 We must have new names, Marcel Proust presciently noted—in fashion, in medicine, in art, there must always be new names. It's a very smart remark, and the fields Proust chose seem smart, too, at least for his time. (Now there must also be new names, at a minimum, among movie stars and athletes and politicians.) Implicit in Proust's remark is the notion that if the names don't really exist, if the quality isn't there to sustain them, it doesn't matter; new names we shall have in any case. And every sophisticated society somehow, more or less implicitly, contrives to supply them.

15 I happen to think that we haven't had a major poet writing in English since perhaps the death of W. H. Auden or, to lower the bar a little, Philip Larkin. But new names are put forth nevertheless—high among them in recent years has been that of Seamus Heaney—because, after all, what kind of a time could we be living in if we didn't have a major poet? And besides there are all those prizes that, year after year, must be given out, even if so many of the recipients don't seem quite worthy of them.

16 Considered as a culture, celebrity does have its institutions. We now have an elaborate celebrity-creating machinery well in place— all those short-attention-span television shows (*Entertainment Tonight, Access Hollywood, Lifestyles of the Rich and Famous*); all those magazines (beginning with *People* and far from ending with the *National Enquirer*). We have high-priced celebrity-mongers—Barbara Walters, Diane Sawyer, Jay Leno, David Letterman, Oprah—who not only live off others' celebrity but also, through their publicity-making power, confer it and have in time become very considerable celebrities each in his or her own right.

17 Without the taste for celebrity, they would have to close down the whole Style section of every newspaper in the country. Then there is the celebrity profile (in *Vanity Fair, Esquire, Gentlemen's Quarterly;* these are nowadays usually orchestrated by a press agent, with all touchy questions declared out-of-bounds), or the television talk-show interview with a star, which is beyond parody. Well, *almost* beyond: Martin Short in his parody of a talk-show host remarked to the actor Kiefer Sutherland, "You're Canadian, aren't you? What's that all about?"

18   Yet we still seem never to have enough celebrities, so we drag in so-called It Girls (Paris Hilton, Cindy Crawford, other super-models), tired television hacks (Regis Philbin, Ed McMahon), back-achingly boring but somehow sacrosanct news anchors (Walter Cronkite, Tom Brokaw). Toss in what I think of as the lower-class punditi, who await calls from various television news and chat shows to demonstrate their locked-in political views and meager expertise on major and cable stations alike: Pat Buchanan, Eleanor Clift, Mark Shields, Robert Novak, Michael Beschloss, and the rest. Ah, if only Lenny Bruce were alive today, he could do a scorchingly cruel bit about Dr. Joyce Brothers sitting by the phone wondering why Jerry Springer never calls.

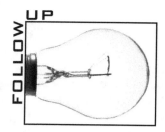

THE CULTURE OF CELEBRITY

Exploring Language

congeries: a collection or mass.

ephemerality: short-lived; lasting only a short period of time.

glibly: offhand; without thought or preparation; with ease.

inept: awkward or clumsy; without skill.

mores: accepted attitudes and customs of a culture.

notoriety: the quality of being unfavorably known; well-known for the wrong reasons; infamous.

pejorative: belittling or derogatory.

posterity: future generations.

presciently: to know things before they happen; foresight.

pundit: an authority or expert; a critic; Epstein created his own word with punditi.

rebarbative: repellent or irritating.

sacrosanct: sacred; above criticism.

Note: For pronunciation, go to dictionary.com, search the word, and click on the speaker icon.

USAGE Reread paragraph #3. Which definition of "glibly" is Epstein using? Write two sentences, one using glibly as meaning without thought or preparation and the other meaning with ease.

Thinking and Talking Points

1. What evidence does Epstein use for his comment, "Celebrity at this moment in America is epidemic . . ."? Do you agree? Why or why not?
2. How does the essay distinguish celebrity from fame?
3. How does Epstein define the word *culture,* the way it's used today versus the past?
4. What is the essay's main point? What is Epstein's view of "the culture of celebrity"? What are his objections to the use of the word *community?*
5. Epstein claims that celebrities are guilty of fraudulence. How does he support this statement? Do you agree? Why or why not?

Styling

Many good writer's create their own adjectives by hooking together words that are not always adjectives—perhaps nouns or verbs—with hyphens. You might be familiar with such words that have become standard, like deep-rooted, stay-at-home moms, or close-knit. The trick is to not rely on these standards but write fresh ones of your own.

Epstein uses this technique several times: "baggy-pants words," "covering-one's-own-behind viperishness," and "dying-young-Adonis end." **Notice that the noun being described is not connected to the new adjective.**

Until you master this technique, you might be more successful if you stick to using nouns and verbs in your hyphenated words to describe another noun. If, for example, you want to describe a cat's fur, you wouldn't hook together a string of adjectives like black-silky-shiny-gleaming fur. It doesn't quite work. Instead, write something like gleams-in-the-light fur. Here you've got the verb, (gleams), a preposition and two articles (in, the) and a noun (light).

In "Bully Pulpit," Amy Dickinson could have written "the time I vomited on my sneakers," but instead chose to hyphenate, creating vomiting-on-my-sneakers incident.

Note: Be sure when you're typing to use **hyphens**, not **dashes**. Type one short line (-) for a hyphen, two (--) for a dash. Otherwise, you'll confuse your reader.

PRACTICE   Rewrite the sentence below using new, hyphenated adjectives to describe the subject (noun).

> There was one time when I slipped in the cafeteria with a tray full of food and dumped it on a popular football jock.

YOU TRY IT   Write three sentences of your own using hyphenated words to describe a subject.

Teaming Up

1. **Warm-up for Writing Idea #1.** Make a list of words you think are overused (to save time, you can use the words in Writing Idea #1). Write at least three sentences for each overused word. Be specific so that the context is clear. Give a specific incident as an example. Next, replace each overused word with a fresh one.

2. **Warm-up for Writing Idea #3.** Choose a category from Writing Idea #3 and list several examples. Next, describe three of the examples in some detail. Discuss why these shows (or the merchandise) are popular and why you think stars participate.

Writing Ideas

1. Write an essay tracing the history of a word that you think is overused. Discuss the origin of the word, its previous meaning, and how it is used today. See Writing Strategies for Defining Terms in Section Five. Some ideas might be the words miracle, awesome, or history (as in "That's ancient history").

2. Write an essay that analyzes the difference between the words *icon* and *celebrity*. Look up the origin of each word and their definitions. Use the Writing Strategies for Defining Terms in Section Five.

3. In his introduction, Epstein complains, "Television provides celebrity dance contests, celebrities take part in reality shows, perfumes carry the names not merely of the designers but of actors and singers." Choose one of these categories—dance contests, reality shows, or designer merchandise—and analyze the content. Describe each show or type of merchandise in detail. Attempt to answer why celebrities participate and why people watch these shows or buy these products. Does your analysis end up supporting or refuting Epstein's claim that celebrity is an epidemic?

Essay and Film Connections

Other essays that analyze culture include "About Men," by Gretel Ehrlich and "Naps" by Barbara Holland.

Pico Iyer

*Travel writer and globe trotter Pico Iyer—born in England—grew up in California, received a King's Scholarship to Eton, has two masters' degrees, writing and literature, from Harvard where he taught for two years, and lives in Japan. Published in an exhausting number of magazines—*The New York Review of Books, Salon, Time, The Conde Nast Traveler, *and* Harper's, *among them—Iyer has also written numerous books on a variety of topics, his latest* The Man within my Head, *an interior exploration of his connection to Graham Greene. Others include* The Global Soul, The Sun After Dark, Tropical Classical, *and* The Open Road: The Global Journey of the Fourteenth Dalai Lama. *"The Writing Life: the Point of the Long and Winding Sentence" appeared in January 08, 2012, edition of* The Los Angeles Times, *where he defends the beauty of the long sentence to capture nuances and battle the short sound bites of the too-much-quick-information era.*

DUSTBIN OF HISTORY AND CULTURE

SALMAN RUSHDIE (1947–): Novelist (born in Bombay, India) sentenced to die in 1989 by the Ayatollah Khomeini—political and religious leader of Iran—for having written *The Satanic Verses.* Other works include *Midnight's Children* and *Shame.* (He's alive and still writing after having gone into hiding for several years).

DON DELILLO (1936–): American author whose work includes the popular *White Noise, Americana,* and *Players.*

ANNIE DILLARD (1945–): American nature writer, novelist, artist, poet; works include *The Pilgrim at Tinker Creek* (nonfiction and winner of the Pulitzer Prize), *Teaching a Stone to Talk* (nonfiction), and *The Maytrees* (novel).

WILLIAM GASS (1925–): American novelist, short story writer, critic, teacher, and proponent of long and winding sentences in his book of essays Life Sentences; his novels are *The Tunnel* and the *Omensetter's Luck.*

SIR THOMAS BROWN (1605–1682): English author, physician, and philosopher, best known for his book of reflections, *Religion Medici.*

ORHAN PAMUK (1952–): Turkish novelist, born in Istanbul, who won the Novel Prize in literature, 2006.

RSS FEEDS: an acronym for Really Simply Syndication, also known as web feeds; RSS feeds deliver content, publishing in more than one place on the web.

1   "Your sentences are so long," said a friend who teaches English at a local college, and I could tell she didn't quite mean it as a compliment. The copy editor who painstakingly went through my most recent book often put yellow dashes on-screen around my multiplying clauses, to ask if I didn't want to break up my sentences or put less material in every one. Both responses couldn't have been kinder or more considered, but what my friend and my colleague may not have sensed was this: I'm using longer and longer sentences as a small protest against—and attempt to rescue any readers I might have from —the bombardment of the moment.

2   When I began writing for a living, my feeling was that my job was to give the reader something vivid, quick and concrete that she couldn't get in any other form; a writer was an information-gathering machine, I thought, and especially as a journalist, my job was to go out into the world and gather details, moments, impressions as visual and immediate as TV. Facts were what we needed most. And if you watched the world closely enough, I believed (and still do), you could begin to see what it would do next, just as you can with a sibling or a friend; Don DeLillo or Salman Rushdie aren't mystics, but they can tell us what the world is going to do tomorrow because they follow it so attentively.

3   Yet nowadays the planet is moving too fast for even a Rushdie or DeLillo to keep up, and many of us in the privileged world have access to more information than we know what to do with. What we crave is something that will free us from the overcrowded moment and allow us to see it in a larger light. No writer can compete, for speed and urgency, with texts or CNN news flashes or RSS feeds, but any writer can try to give us the depth, the nuances—the "gaps," as Annie Dillard calls them—that don't show up on many screens. Not everyone wants to be reduced to a sound bite or a bumper sticker.

4   Enter (I hope) the long sentence: the collection of clauses that is so many-chambered and lavish and abundant in tones and suggestions, that has so much room for near-contradiction and ambiguity and those places in memory or imagination that can't be simplified, or put into easy words, that it allows the reader to keep many things in her head and heart at the same time, and to descend, as by a spiral staircase, deeper into herself and those things that won't be squeezed

into an either/or. With each clause, we're taken further and further from trite conclusions—or that at least is the hope—and away from reductionism, as if the writer were a dentist, saying "Open wider" so that he can probe the tender, neglected spaces in the reader (though in this case it's not the mouth that he's attending to but the mind).

5   "There was a little stoop of humility," Alan Hollinghurst writes in a sentence I've chosen almost at random from his recent novel "The Stranger's Child," "as she passed through the door, into the larger but darker library beyond, a hint of frailty, an affectation of bearing more than her fifty-nine years, a slight bewildered totter among the grandeur that her daughter now had to pretend to take for granted." You may notice—though you don't have to—that "humility" has rather quickly elided into "affectation," and the point of view has shifted by the end of the sentence, and the physical movement through the rooms accompanies a gradual inner movement that progresses through four parallel clauses, each of which, though legato, suggests a slightly different take on things.

6   Many a reader will have no time for this; William Gass or Sir Thomas Browne may seem long-winded, the equivalent of driving from L.A. to San Francisco by way of Death Valley, Tijuana and the Sierras. And a highly skilled writer, a Hemingway or James Salter, can get plenty of shading and suggestion into even the shortest and straightest of sentences. But too often nowadays our writing is telegraphic as a way of keeping our thinking simplistic, our feeling slogan-crude. The short sentence is the domain of uninflected talk-radio rants and shouting heads on TV who feel that qualification or subtlety is an assault on their integrity (and not, as it truly is, integrity's greatest adornment).

7   If we continue along this road, whole areas of feeling and cognition and experience will be lost to us. We will not be able to read one another very well if we can't read Proust's labyrinthine sentences, admitting us to those half-lighted realms where memory blurs into imagination, and we hide from the person we care for or punish the thing that we love. And how can we feel the layers, the sprawl, the many-sidedness of Istanbul in all its crowding amplitude without the 700-word sentence, transcribing its features, that Orhan Pamuk offered in tribute to his lifelong love?

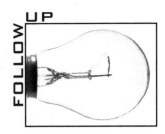

FOLLOW UP

THE WRITING LIFE

Exploring Language

affectation: pretension; attempting to appear to have a quality, trait, or manner not actually possessed.

ambiguity: without clear-cut meaning or definition.

elide: omit (usually refers to a vowel or syllable); ignore or pass over; from Latin 'to crush out.'

labyrinthine: like a labyrinth (a maze or tunnel of complicated paths).

legato: smooth and connected.

nuances: slight differences in meaning or expression; subtle.

reductionism: simplifying a complex idea, distorting it; a theory that states any complexity can be reduced to its simplest parts and understood.

subtle: in this context, hard to grasp, mysterious, as in *subtle distinction.*

uninflected: in this context, not modulating or changing the tone or pitch of voice.

Note: For pronunciation, go to dictionary.com, search the word, and click on the speaker icon.

Thinking and Talking Points

1. Iyer writes that his use of longer and longer sentences is a protest and a rescue; explain his meaning.

2. Throughout the essay, Iyer gives examples of what we lose when we rely on fast information bites that assault our senses. List his examples.

3. In paragraph #6, Iyer writes, "The short sentence is the domain of uninflected talk-radio rants and shouting heads on TV who feel that qualification or subtlety is an assault on their integrity (and not, as it truly is, integrity's greatest adornment)." Explain how qualification or subtlety is "integrity's greatest adornment."

4. Study some of Iyer's long sentences. How do they help support his point? Be specific by pointing out sentences and analyzing their content for complex thoughts or nuances that would be lost in shorter sentences.

5. How does the example out of Hollinghurst's work in paragraph #5 help exemplify Iyer's point about the need for long sentences?

280

Styling

Copy the first sentence of paragraph #5. Break it down, writing each individual clause (between the commas) on a separate line, leaving space to write your own clauses underneath.

PRACTICE   First, write a sentence with a colon that will require clauses as explanation. Underneath each of Iyer's clauses, write your own material to match your sentence, modeling each of Iyer's clauses, the length and punctuation, making sure each clause is **dependent**.

YOU TRY IT   Put your clauses together in one long sentence. Check it for run-ons and **parallelism**. Write three more sentences in this style.

Teaming Up

1. Have two or three other peers read your sentences to check for errors and logic (that the sentences stays on subject and don't wander into a different topic).
2. Read and analyze the long sentence below from *A Wizard of Earthsea* by Ursula LeGuin (isolate the main sentence and the descriptive clauses). Choose a topic to describe—a lavish meal, a place, a messy room (or an overly neat room), or anything else the group agrees upon. Brainstorm the details and, modeling LeGuin's sentence, write a one-paragraph description consisting of just one sentence.

   So to Ged who had never been down from the heights of the mountain, the Port of Gont was an awesome and marvelous place, the great houses and towers of cut stone and waterfront of piers and docks and basins and moorages, the seaport where half a hundred boats and galleys rocked at quayside or lay hauled up and overturned for repairs or stood out at anchor in the roadstead with furled sails and closed oarports, the sailors shouting in strange dialects and longshoremen running heavy-laden among barrels and boxes and coils of rope and stacks of oars, the bearded merchants in furred robes conversing quietly as they picked their way along the slimy stones above the water, the fishermen unloading their catch, coopers pounding and shipmakers hammering and clamsellers singing and shipmasters bellowing, and beyond all the silent, shining bay.

Note: While writing every sentence in an essay this long might become tedious, it's good practice in grammar and punctuation, and will help make writing your own long sentences easier if you can sustain correctness throughout one of this length.

Writing Ideas

1. Find a passage from a Hemingway short story or novel and one from either Orhan Pamuk or William Gass and analyze and compare/contrast the style.
2. Watch and read some of the "news flashes or RSS feeds" and other sound bites and bumper sticker-esque language that bombard us. Analyze and argue what we lose and/or gain, using quotes from the sources and from Pico Iyer's essay.

Writing Strategies

WRITING BASIC COLLEGE ESSAYS

Most essays combine **rhetorical modes** (strategies that help organize material): a process/analysis might also be an argument; a narrative might also compare and contrast; a compare and contrast might have paragraphs of cause and effect; most essays have description, and so on. The best writers don't rely on the five-paragraph format, though it helps to know how to compose in that format before moving on to other, more complex styles. The strategies in this section have been broken down into their basic rhetorical modes for clarity. It's up to the writer to decide which strategies need combining (in college, often the prompt will indicate the required format).

Getting Started with Prewriting

Most writers have trouble getting started, but the temptress Procrastination can wreak havoc with grades, so resist the appeal of American Idol, Facebook, and Twitter. Traditional brainstorming techniques are outlined below for those who need a reminder. The standard ideas don't work for everyone, so use a method you deem comfortable, whether it's listing, clustering, freewriting, or simply writing notes on scrap paper as ideas occur throughout the day. Sometimes, it only takes determination to get something down on paper. Ernest Hemingway, in *A Moveable Feast*, wrote, "But sometimes when I was starting a new story and I could not get it going, I would sit in front of the fire and squeeze the peel of the little oranges into the edge of the flame and watch the sputter of blue that they made. I would stand and look out over the roofs of Paris and think, 'Do not worry. You have always written before and you will write now. All you have to do is write one true sentence.'" If you write one sentence, another will usually follow.

Traditional Brainstorming

FREEWRITING Freewriting, a simple but useful technique, can help unstick you. Write down any weird or not-so-weird ideas buzzing about in your head, without any thought to structure, grammar, or spelling. Just write nonstop. Don't even think. Just write, write, write. Though most of what comes out might look like alien messages from deep space, a brilliant idea or two might be lurking, waiting for you to discover and develop it.

CLUSTERING Write your topic in the center of a piece of paper and draw a circle around it. Draw lines out from your topic, like spokes of a wheel, and draw bubbles, like balloons, at the end of each line. Fill in each bubble with one thing that pops into your mind about your topic. Repeat this technique for each bubble.

LISTING If you're the type of person who likes to make daily lists, here's the brainstorming technique for you. Simply write your topic at the top of a sheet of paper and list whatever flashes into your head about that topic. A list might look like this:

Children

no free time to play

too many structured activities

what happened to playing baseball in the park with no adults?

need to learn independence

too much pressure

don't learn decision making

can't solve their own problems

must have some supervision and guidance, of course

Next, choose three or four interesting ideas from the list and write them at the top of a sheet of paper:

independence	*problem solving*	*decisions*
wimps	can't fix things	which college
too afraid	run to mom and dad	which major
live at home	disagreements	which job
can't grow up		

You could keep this up into infinity, but you only need to keep listing until you feel you have some solid ideas to start your essay. What you now have is an idea for a thesis and three developmental paragraphs and ideas for examples to support each idea.

Basic Try-Not-to-Rely-on-It Five-Paragraph Format

This format works well as a first draft or perhaps on an in-class essay to help keep thoughts organized under time pressure, and it's a good place to start for novice writers, though once you master this basic strategy, it's time to move on to other rhetorical modes and blending styles. Basic essays consist of an introduction with a hook and a thesis, plan of development, three body paragraphs with topic sentences, and a conclusion.

THESIS STATEMENTS

A thesis can occur anywhere in a paper: some writers lead up to their thesis at the end of an essay; others use a transition paragraph after the introduction, and occasionally a writer will sneak the thesis in somewhere in the middle of the paper, but traditional essays usually have the thesis stated at the end of the introduction. Before beginning to write an essay, it helps to have a working thesis in mind—a preliminary statement that might change as you think through ideas or research a topic.

Thesis statements control the essay; everything in the paper should relate to the thesis. It is the main point, often expressed as an opinion. Though not all papers require a thesis, most college writing does. There are a few rules to keep in mind when writing a thesis:

1. A thesis cannot be a fact. It should express a point of view or opinion. The statement "Television ads supporting presidential candidates often denigrate the opponent" is a fact, not a thesis.
2. A thesis should not be too broad: "There are many controversies surrounding televised presidential campaign ads" needs to be nar-

rowed to a specific issue. This statement also breaks the first rule: it's a fact.

3. A thesis should not announce its topic: avoid phrases like "I will discuss," "this essay will show," "this essay will analyze," or "I think, I believe, it is my opinion." The first three don't express an opinion, and the last three are generally considered weak style and a way of avoiding taking a strong stand. It's a you-can't-attack-my-opinion strategy. "This essay will analyze the controversy surrounding televised presidential campaigns" is not an appropriate thesis: it is too broad and doesn't express an opinion.

1. To build a strong thesis, start with a broad topic:
American politics

2. Narrow the topic by carving out a special area, perhaps through brainstorming:
Television's coverage of presidential campaigns.

3. Take a stand on the topic in a rough thesis (using a should/because construction in steps three and four will help determine if the statement has an opinion and plan of development):
Television's coverage of presidential campaigns **should be** limited.

4. Add your plan of development—your reasons for your opinion that will be used in topic sentences: presidential campaigns **should be** limited **because** the media's bias for or against a candidate misleads the public, avoids the issues, and gives the media too much power over the outcome of elections.

This thesis, though roughly worded, has a clear focus, makes a statement rather than announcing the topic, and expresses an opinion (an opponent could argue against it).

5. Recast the thesis, smoothing out the basic wording:
Although many might argue that limiting television coverage of presidential campaigns violates the idea of free press and free speech, the media's bias for or against a candidate takes focus away from the issues, misleading and unfairly influencing the public's view, granting the press too much power over the outcome of elections.

Plan of Development and Topic Sentences

Like a thesis statement controls the ideas in the essay, the topic sentences control the ideas in the body paragraphs. Key words in the topic sentence can help keep the paragraph from wandering off topic. Looking at the plan of development in the above thesis—the three reasons stated at the end of the statement—**the first body paragraph** would focus on the media's ability to sway elections by taking focus away from the issues; **the second body paragraph** would discuss misleading and influencing the public's view; **the last reason** would argue the power of the press. Notice that each reason is discussed in the order it appears in the thesis.

This type of organizational strategy usually saves the strongest or most important reason for the last body paragraph, pyramiding paragraphs on top of each other, least to most important.

Example Topic Sentence: Though claiming objectivity, the mainstream media often has its own agenda, unfairly misleading the public about a candidate's views by focusing on personal rather than the political issues.

BODY PARAGRAPHS

In addition to topic sentences, body paragraphs contain evidence—specific examples, supporting facts, statistics, explanations, personal experience, and description; if it's an argument essay (like the above topic) it might also incorporate refuting the opposition (see the "Writing Strategies for Argument"). In the topic on media bias, body paragraphs might contain examples of news broadcasts, perhaps contrasting interviews with two candidates that illustrate the types of questions the interviewer asked that helped the candidate avoid the issues, or description of misleading ads, and perhaps researched facts on how much air time candidates received in the last election, or supporting quotations.

Use numerous examples to support each point. A paragraph that relies on one or two examples weakens the stand, failing to sway many readers that you have a reasonable, balanced essay.

Concluding Strategies for Body Paragraphs

Body paragraphs—and all other paragraphs—contain **concluding statements**, a last sentence that finishes off the paragraph, wrapping up the idea before transitioning into the next point. Writers use different strategies for concluding a paragraph, depending on their purpose.

1. Outrage Dressed as Statistic

Deborah Blum's essay "The Chemist's War" uses a bald, shocking statistic at the end of paragraph #4. Her essay recounts events during Prohibition when the federal government poisoned industrial alcohol manufactured in the United States to discourage people from drinking bootleg liquor. The statistic, stated matter-of-factly, outrages readers who, like Blum, were unaware that the government had gone to such lengths to enforce this law:

> Frustrated that people continued to consume so much alcohol even after it was banned, federal officials had decided to try a different kind of enforcement. They ordered the poisoning of industrial alcohols manufactured in the United States, products regularly stolen by bootleggers and resold as drinkable spirits. The idea was to scare people into giving up illicit drinking. **Instead, by the time Prohibition ended in 1933, the federal poisoning program, by some estimates, had killed at least 10,000 people.**

Calling it "the federal poisoning program" and dangling the number of deaths at the end of the paragraph, neatly concludes the point, giving the reader cause to pause at the sheer callousness of the federal government, tying to the topic sentence in her next paragraph, "Although mostly forgotten today, the 'chemist's war of Prohibition' remains one of the strangest and most deadly decisions in American law-enforcement history." (The word "deadly" transitions to "killed," and "chemist's war"' to "poisoning program".)

2. Provocative Questions

Though many handbooks and instructors advise students to avoid asking questions in an essay, professional writers use questions successfully, knowing that sometimes a provocative question can leave a reader thinking and feeling, lingering over the paragraph or anxious to move on to the next. In "The Surfing Savant" by Paul Solotaroff, an essay about a gifted surfer, Clay Marzo, with Asperger's syndrome, a form of high-functioning autism, he begins the second body paragraph describing all of the things that Marzo—though elegant, confident, and graceful on a surfboard—has trouble doing on land. Toward the end of this paragraph, he writes:

In middle school, Marzo was treated so badly that his mother, Jill, had to pull him out and teach him at home, where he wouldn't be punched for staring at wannabe thugs. His agonizing shyness has fractured his family and sparked ugly set-tos with his father, Gino, an old-school hard-hat striver who accused him of flaking off and screwing up his shot at stardom. **That charge hurts Clay more than the others combined: when your own father misconceives you so badly, how can you hope that strangers will understand?**

That question tugs at the readers' minds and hearts, hopefully evoking compassion for those afflicted with such a difficult and misunderstood disorder.

Bernard Cooper, in "Burl's," uses two questions at the end of a body paragraph that illustrate the conflict he felt as a young boy struggling with his sexual identity. In this paragraph, his parents have sent him to gymnastics class to try to "tilt" him toward the male side of his nature:

When the first day of gymnastics class arrived, my mother gave me money and a gym bag and sent me to the corner of Hollywood and Western to wait for a bus. The sun was bright, the traffic heavy. While I sat there, an argument raged inside my head, the familiar, battering debate between the wish to be like other boys and the wish to be like myself. **Why shouldn't I simply get up and go back home, where I'd be left alone to read and think? On the other hand, wouldn't life be easier if I liked athletics, or learned to like them?**

These questions illustrate the battering debate, his struggle to reconcile his desire to be himself with what others wanted and expected him to be—indeed, a battering debate.

In "Nourishing Awareness in Each Moment," Zen monk Thich Nhat Hanh ends paragraph #2 with a series of questions that are statements in disguise:

Do you ever find yourself watching an awful TV program, unable to turn it off? The raucous noises, explosions of gunfire, are upsetting. Yet you don't get up and turn it off. Why do you torture yourself in this way? Don't you want to close your windows? **Are you frightened of solitude—the emptiness and the loneliness you may find when you face yourself alone?**

These questions accuse the reader with the words *torture* and *frightened*; most will have to admit to occasionally falling into this TV trap.

3. Concluding Quotation

Though generally you want to lead in and out of quotations, sometimes they are more affective left on their own at the end of a paragraph, with just the lead-in.

In the second paragraph of "The Culture of Celebrity," Joseph Epstein, after discussing the unruliness of words, how they seem to capriciously change meanings, their refusal to "remain in place and take orders," he ends with a famous quote, **"'The language,' as Flaubert once protested in his attempt to tell his mistress Louise Colet how much he loved her, 'is inept.'"**

4. A Short Sentence for Impact

Sometimes brevity speaks louder than a lengthy sentence or other technique. In paragraph #5 of "Joyas Voladoras," Brian Doyle writes:

Mammals and birds have hearts with four chambers. Reptiles and turtles have hearts with three chambers. Fish have hearts with two chambers. Insects and mollusks have hearts with one chamber. Worms have hearts with one chamber, although they may have as many as eleven single-chambered hearts. Unicellular bacteria have no hearts at all; but even they have fluid eternally in motion, washing from one side of the cell to the other, swirling and whirling. No living being is without interior liquid motion. **We all churn inside.**

That short, impactful sentence, loaded with meaning, shifts the seemingly scientific discussion to his real point—heartbreak, both literally and metaphorically, leading into his beautiful, specific conclusion about the joys and agonies of the human heart.

Clayton Collins, in his essay on the neurologist Oliver Sacks and his work with music, quotes Sacks:

> Sacks remembers a woman with Parkinson's who would sit perfectly still until "activated" by the music of Chopin, which she loved and knew by heart. She didn't have to hear a tune played. "It was sometimes sufficient to give her an opus number," Sacks says. "You would just say 'Opus 49,' and the F-minor *Fantasy* would start playing in her mind. **And she could move.**"

The remarkable fact that a woman frozen with Parkinson's can suddenly move upon hearing a scrap of music is best stated briefly, startling and emphatic.

Joyce Carol Oates, knowing the value of the short sentence, at the end of paragraph #3 in "On Boxing," after describing the beauty of the sport, simply writes **"All is Style."**

STRATEGIES FOR CREATING TITLES

Many titles—whether films, essays, novels, songs, or plays—often seem familiar, a where-have-I-heard-that-before refrain. Writers forage through history, literature, pop culture, music, film, almost every conceivable place, for snappy titles. A title is the first part of the essay readers see; don't bore them with one of those my-summer-vacation titles: "Animal Rights" or "Comparison Essay" or "Essay #1." Why title an essay "Animal Rights" when you can use something provocative that jumps off of a bumper sticker and gives it a little twist like "Save the Whales, Screw the Shrimp" by Joy Williams?

With electronic devices like iPhones and iPads, iPods and laptops, it's easy to have quick access to sources to pillage for titles. Scroll through the iPod for song titles to borrow; look at the Netflix list for films; google a dictionary of quotations for a famous quote and snag a few words that fit the topic; visit Amazon.com or the Barnes and Noble website for book and magazine titles; pick a favorite TV station and peruse the film show titles. *The History Channel, Animal Planet, Discovery* can also be ravaged. Much old literature—poems, plays, short stories, even novels—can be found on the web. It shouldn't take long browsing to find a title that fits your topic. Below are a few categories with examples from numerous writers who have pillaged other sources for strong titles. Writers borrow from a wide range of sources, including from each other.

Literature (novelists borrowing from poetry, essays, and the Bible).

Of Mice and Men by John Steinbeck: from a line in a poem by Robert
Burns called "To a Mouse."

East of Eden by John Steinbeck from Genesis 4:16.

Tender Is the Night by F. Scott Fitzgerald from "Ode to a Nightingale" by
John Keats.

For Whom the Bell Tolls by Ernest Hemingway from "Meditation" 17 by
John Donne.

Brave New World by Aldous Huxley from Shakespeare's play *The Tempest.*

No Country for Old Men by Cormac McCarthy from a line in the poem
"Sailing to Byzantium" by William Butler Yeats.

I Know Why the Caged Bird Sings by Maya Angelou from a line in the
poem "Sympathy" by Paul Lawrence Dunbar.

Where Angels Fear to Tread by E.M. Forester from "Essay on Criticism" by
Alexander Pope.

Music and Film (essayists, novelists, and filmmakers borrowing from
music and film)

"Somebody's Baby" by Barbara Kingsolver, from the song "Somebody's
Baby" by Jackson Browne.

"A Voice for the Lonely" essay by Stephen Corey, a twist on "Only the
Lonely" by Roy Orbison.

"Roll Over Bach, Too!" essay by Jack Kroll, a twist on "Roll Over,
Beethoven" by the Beatles.

"Monster Mash" essay by Jack Kroll, from the song of the same title by
Bobby Pickett.

She's Come Undone by Wally Lamb, from the song of the same title by The
Guess Who.

Stand by Me film, title borrowed from the song "Stand by Me" by Ben E. King.

Sweet Home Alabama film, title from the song "Sweet Home Alabama" by
Lynyrd Skynrd.

"Modern Times" essay by Lawrence Weschler from the silent Charlie
Chaplin film *Modern Times.*

History and Pop Culture

The Big Bang Theory TV series, borrowing from science.

One Potato, Two Potato: The Folklore of American Children a book by Mary
and Herbert Knapp borrowing a line from a children's rhyme.

"Got Corn?" an essay in the April 2012 *Smithsonian* magazine from the "Got Milk?" ads.

Batteries Not Included title of a film borrowed from the disclaimer on the side of electronics boxes. Student Juan Diaz titled a paper on cereal icons "Milk Not Included."

"Fiddling While Africa Starves" an essay by P.J. O'Rourke, borrowed from history, the Emperor Nero who, it is said, fiddled while Rome burned.

"Name That Tone" by Louis Menand, the title a play on an old game show, Name That Tune. Brainstorm a list of game show titles and change a word to fit your topic. (This idea works well as a group activity.)

HOOKS, INTRODUCTIONS, AND CONCLUSIONS

Numerous standard tricks for hooking the reader work well: tell a mini-story, describe a scene, ask a question, use a startling remark or statistic, a quotation—but taking these standard tips and reinventing them can generate more lively hooks and introductions. These same techniques—with a little reworking—can be used in either introductions or conclusions, with a few exceptions, noted below.

Storytelling—The Personal Anecdote

This standard often works best, depending on the topic or the experience. Barbara Kingsolver, in "Somebody's Baby," begins her essay on Americans' callous treatment of children not their own, with an anecdote that contrasts Spain's loving treatment of her four-year-old daughter with the surliness of the Americans:

> As I walked out the street entrance to my newly rented apartment, a guy in maroon high-tops and a skateboard haircut approached, making kissing noises and saying, "Hi, gorgeous." Three weeks earlier, I would have assessed the degree of malice and made ready to run or tell him to bug off, depending. But now, instead, I smiled, and so did my four-year-old daughter, because after dozens of similar encounters I understood he didn't mean me but her.

> This was not the United States.

In her defense of "Naps," Barbara Holland opens her essay by recounting an incident in France, being stranded on her boat in the canal because the gatekeeper was taking a nap.

> In France, on a rented canal boat, my friends and I gazed in despair at the closed oaken gates of the lock. We'd come to them only seconds after the witching hour of noon, but we were too late. There was no one to open the lock for us; l'eclusiere was at lunch, and after lunch she would lay herself down, close her eyes, and nap. At two, but not before, she would emerge refreshed from her square granite house and set the great cogs in motion.

She uses this mini-story to illustrate that other countries take a rest in the middle of the day, unlike Americans who toil on in the afternoon, getting very little done as a result of skipping naps.

Storytelling—The Not-So-Personal Anecdote

Often, writers will borrow stories from history, the news, or other sources. (When using excavated stories, it's best to put them in your own voice rather than quoting.) In "The Chemist's War," Deborah Blum begins her essay on the government alcohol poisoning program during Prohibition with a harrowing news story from history illustrating the results of this misguided idea.

> It was Christmas Eve, 1926, the streets aglitter with snow and lights, when the man afraid of Santa Claus stumbled into the emergency room at New York City's Bellevue Hospital. He was flushed, gasping with fear: Santa Claus, he kept telling the nurses, was just behind him, wielding a baseball bat.

> Before hospital staff realized how sick he was—the alcohol-induced hallucination was just a symptom—the man died. So did another holiday partygoer. And another. As dusk fell on Christmas, the hospital staff tallied up more than sixty people made desperately ill by alcohol and eight dead from it. Within the next two days, yet another twenty-three people died in the city from celebrating the season.

(Yes, it is acceptable to have two paragraphs for an introduction either for emphasis or to break up an otherwise too-long paragraph.)

Storytelling—Borrowing from Myth, Fable, Fairy Tale, and Legend

With so many of these stories available online (an education website is usually the best source), it's easy to forage for a story with a theme that complements a topic, and they work for either **introductions or conclusions**. Summarize and rewrite them rather than copying and quoting; also lead in and out of these stories to connect them to the thesis (see "Paraphrasing" and "Summarizing"). Libraries have numerous books like *Bullfinch's Mythology, Native American Myths and Legends, Irish Folk Tales,* and many multicultural collections of fairy tales.

These sources spark endless ideas: a psychology paper on narcissistic personality disorder with the Greek myth of Narcissus, the beautiful young man who fell in love with his own reflection, thinking it a beautiful nymph; a paper on sleep disorders paired with the god of sleep and dreams, Morpheus; an essay on too much drinking amongst college students with a story of Bacchus or Dionysus; mothers jealous of their daughters with the Grimm's "Snow White"; a definition essay on pride with Grimm's "Godfather Death."

Aesop's Fables uses animal characters as stand-ins for humans, reflecting on human nature, so they make good fodder for a number of topics: definition papers on different human qualities like anger ("The Farmer and the Dog"), ingratitude or parental neglect ("The Cuckoo, The Hedge-Sparrow, and the Owl"), hypocrisy ("The Fox and the Cat"). These fables also work in essays on animals, for example "The Crow and the Pitcher," to illustrate the intelligence of the crow.

Making Use of Symbolism

Writers often glean material from symbol dictionaries for introductions, body paragraphs, or conclusions.   In "Mute Dancers: How to Watch a Hummingbird," Diane Ackerman uses the Aztec symbolism of the hummingbird as a resurrection bird to illustrate its importance to that culture: warriors thought if they died in battle, they'd be reincarnated as hummingbirds due to the tiny creature's "brazen" behavior and sword-like beak. In "Hair," she blends the symbolism of hair, its meaning to different cultures, into her essay.   Gordon Grice in "Black Widow" discusses the symbol of this misunderstood arachnid, how we "project our archetypal terrors" onto the spider.   (At this writing, online symbolism dictionaries have not proven useful as they mostly relate to dream symbolism.)

Famous Quotations and Literary Openings

Dictionaries of quotations, another language resource to plunder, usually alphabetized by topic, are easy to navigate and contain a wide range of subjects with several quotations for each entry by people ranging from Shakespeare to politicians, scientists, and philosophers—people ancient and modern, with widely different views.

Snippets of poems can also help build an introduction. Jack Kroll opens his essay with lines from Homer's *Illiad* to illustrate our long fascination with horror:

> Then his teeth flew out; from two sides, blood came to his eyes; the blood that from lips and nostrils he was spilling, open-mouthed; death enveloped him in its black cloud.

Joyce Carol Oates opens her essay "On Boxing" with a quote by Irish featherweight champion Barry McGuigan:

> Why are you a boxer, Irish featherweight champion Barry McGuigan was asked.
>
> He said, "I can't be poet. I can't tell stories."

If a dictionary of quotations doesn't turn up a perfect quote, check the internet for old poetry and lines from plays and stories (similar to the advice under the "Titles" section).

See Section Five for advice on blending quotations.

Startling Remarks and Comparisons A short, startling sentence in the first line of an introduction or an appropriate comparison will usually get the reader's attention:

> "A lot of hummingbirds die in their sleep." Diane Ackerman
>
> "I hunt black widow." Gordon Grice.
>
> "Oliver Sacks danced to the dead." Clayton S. Collins
>
> "I loved Prince when I was thirteen, and that was humiliating." Chuck Klosterman
>
> "Were you there?" Jack Kroll
>
> "A turtle is a kind of bird with the governor turned low." Edward Hoagland

Writers build on these remarks and comparisons to flesh out their introductions (see the essays for the complete introductions).

Riddles

Professional writers use this versatile technique for topics ranging from animals, archaeology, and icons, to fairy tale characters, television personalities, and mental disorders. One sample appears with "Teaming Up" #1 following Diane Ackerman's "Mute Dancers: How to Watch a Hummingbird."

Riddles can be tricky; they need to be challenging enough to intrigue the reader but not so difficult that they're impossible to guess.

Many instructions for writing riddles appear on the web, though mostly for poetry writing. Prose riddles leave more options as they don't have to rhyme. These basic guidelines use a student riddle by Sarah Cabbell in a fundamentals of composition course to exemplify some steps for creating riddles:

1. **After deciding on a topic, list the unique and significant details**: tentacles with suckers, no skeleton, is difficult to spot because it blends in with the rocks, people think it's deadly, it squirts ink, lives in the ocean.
   If Sarah had written this list up as it is, the answer would be too obvious and spoil the riddle.
2. **Disguise obvious clues, using simile, metaphor, synonyms or antonyms**: instead of "it squirts ink" she compares it to a magician; tentacles become a skirt, and so on.
3. **Use the third person he, she, it, or they.** Sarah chose "it."
4. **Use simple or compound sentences (two sentences joined with a conjunction) to create interesting juxtapositions (the relationship of objects, perhaps ones that seem like contradictions but have enough truth to make them work)**: "It has an excessive number of legs but is unable to walk."
5. **Build clues from the least obvious to the final clues that will help the reader guess, but not too easily:**
   It is found throughout the world but can be hard to spot. It lives in the largest habitat on earth but makes its home in the smallest of places. It is thought to be deadly because of its legendary reputation from tall tales, but that is a misconception. Like a magician, it can perform a disappearing act. It seems to always wear a skirt, but because of its introverted personality, it never shows it off. It has an excessive number of legs but is unable to walk. It would be safe to say it is a real sucker.
6. **Reveal the answer in a second paragraph**. Sarah began her second paragraph with this **transition** sentence: "The octopus is one of the most misunderstood and mysterious animals in the ocean."

Personification Applying human characteristics to an object challenges critical thinking, forcing the writer and the reader to think more complexly about a topic in order to find its not-so-obvious qualities. In an essay titled "It's All in the Implications" (*Los Angeles Times*, 02/13/06), Pico Iyer personifies the word implication:

> Once upon a time, there was a spirit called Implication. He didn't get picked very often when the other kids were choosing teams, and he tended to live in the shadows. But he always had a sense of pride, deep down, because he knew that people would call on him in their most important moments: in bed beside someone they loved, or while on their knees whispering to what—or who—they believed in. Life wasn't black or white, he knew; Implication was a friend of all the colors.

He continues the essay, with Implication being first blacklisted, becoming an outcast, then a fugitive when he walks into the post office and finds his name on the "10 Most Wanted List" along with Subtlety, Ambiguity, Diplomacy, and Mischief, a clever but grim commentary on the demise of language, lost to a world of quick sound bites.

Personification can make an **introduction** pop; it can also be combined with the riddle style. Think of a personification as a character sketch. Below is a list of details—a brainstorming list—that Ruth Gendler might have used for her personification of the quality "truth" (complete essay in the text).

Guidelines for Personifying

1. Choose an object or human personality trait: **"Truth."**
2. Assign a gender: **Male.**
3. Decide what the object or trait would look like if it were a person. No need to be detailed, but try to give it some physical characteristics: **Tall, unconventional looking, golden hair, short beard, spacious shoulders**.
4. What other qualities or objects would it have as friends or relatives: **Certainty and Uncertainty.**
5. Consider what type of job, hobbies, or activities would fit the personality profile: **Employed as a thief stealing illusions. Fascinated with X-rays, photographs of cells, and the history of plants. Studies mime. Gentle nature, not sarcastic. Wrote film reviews but quit when he found his quotes taken out of context.**

6. Set the details up in a mini-story: **See the finished product in the text.**

Extended Comparisons or Analogies

Though this technique works anywhere in an essay, it often makes a memorable conclusion. In Mark Twain's essay "Reading the River," he details what he gained and lost by becoming a river boat pilot on the Mississippi, concluding by comparing his inability to view the river simply for its beauty to a doctor who treats beautiful women only to see the disease:

> No, the romance and beauty were all gone from the river. All the value any feature of it had for me now was the amount of usefulness it could furnish toward compassing the safe piloting of a steamboat. Since those days, I have pitied doctors from my heart. What does the lovely flush in a beauty's cheek mean to a doctor but a "break" that ripples above some deadly disease? Are not all her visible charms sown thick with what are to him the signs and symbols of hidden decay? Does he ever see her beauty at all, or doesn't he simply view her professionally and comment upon her unwholesome condition all to himself? And doesn't he sometimes wonder whether he has gained most or lost most by learning his trade?

Try breaking down a social or political system to compare: In his research problem/solution paper, freshman composition student Robert Olswang compares the emperor penguin's social structure to socialism, drawing direct parallels, "His success and survival is due to a social cohesiveness that is not besieged by a systematic hierarchy where everyone is equal: where one goes, they all go." He builds on his comparison, using tenets of the socialist system to describe the penguins' actions. For the same assignment, another student used Zen Buddhism to compare to an egret.

Over the years, students have illustrated diverse, remarkable comparisons in their conclusions: a listing of abuse to a pair of old ballet slippers, that in the end, still have worth, can still dance; a daughter's relationship with her mother to a designer bag, an accessory for her mother to show off; a thorn tree to a father's anger. With a small bit of research and some thought, writing memorable endings to essays becomes less of a struggle and banishes the tired restate-the-thesis conclusions teachers dread. With a few examples and some outside resources, imagination thrives.

TRANSITIONS

An organized, well-written essay needs transitions between paragraphs and between ideas within paragraphs. Though writers use different strategies to transition, generally, the concluding line of one paragraph should have a link to a word or phrase in the first line of the next paragraph. Avoid high school transitions such as "first of all," "secondly," "however," and "in conclusion." There are stronger ways to transition:

Using a different form of the same word to begin a new idea:

Barbara Holland uses "napper" and "napping" to transition between paragraphs #4 and #5:

"Fifteen minutes later the **napper** pops back to the surface as from time travel, bewildered to find that it's only ten of two instead of centuries later.

Like skydiving, **napping** takes practice; the first few tries are **scary**."

After this one-line paragraph, she moves into six, picking up the word "scary" and turning it into "scarier":

"The American nap is even **scarier** because it's unilateral."

Using words that mean the opposite:

In "Nourishing Awareness in Each Moment," Thich Nhat Hanh ends his first paragraph with this line:

"Then I started a fire in the fireplace, and soon the crackling logs brought warmth back to the room."

He builds on this idea of warmth in the first line of paragraph #2, steering the reader into another idea, using the opposite of warmth:

"Sometimes in a crowd we feel tired, **cold**, and lonely."

He moves from physical warmth to emotional cold.

Using words with similar meanings:

Diane Ackerman, in "Mute Dancers: How to Watch a Hummingbird," writes at the end of the first paragraph:

> "By day's end, wrung-out and **exhausted**, a hummingbird rests near **collapse**."

In the first line of paragraph #2, she links "exhausted" and "collapse" with "zombielike" and "torpor."

> "In the dark night of the hummingbird, it can sink into a **zombielike** state of **torpor**; its breathing grows shallow and its wild heart slows to only 36 beats a minute."

In "A Voice for the Lonely," Stephen Corey uses the word "dawn" at the end of paragraph #1 with "early riser" in the beginning of paragraph #2; "transistor radio" at the end of #2, linked to "music" in paragraph #3.

Using the same word:

Joseph Epstein uses the same word at the end of paragraph #13 and the first sentence in #14, though the plural form in #14:

> "Real estate, man, is the **name** of the game."

> "We must have new **names**, Marcel Proust presciently noted—in fashion, in medicine, in art, there must always be new **names**."

For more on transitions, see the "Styling" with "About Men" by Gretel Ehrlich and "Strategies for Writing the Personal Essay" for time transitions.

Once finished with the big changes, work on editing for fragments, run-on sentences, punctuation, and other errors. It helps to read the paper aloud or have someone else read it. Reading the essay in reverse—beginning with the last sentence of the essay—isolates sentences, making it easier to spot mistakes.

POINT OF VIEW

There are three points of view to write from:

First Person (I)

Second Person (you)

Third Person (he, she, it, or they)

Most narratives call for the **first person** point of view, or "I" perspective.

Second person is used in process/analysis essays or command form style, or anytime the writer wants to create intimacy with the reader. David Huddle uses the second person in "Museum Piece":

> "Jan Vermeer's *Girl With the Red Hat* always appealed to you because of that hat."

Sometimes writers use the **command** form, dropping the obvious use of "you," implying it by giving commands. In "What Really Happened," Madge McKeithen writes a personal essay about confronting a friend's killer in prison, but using second person, relying mostly on commands, brutally taking the reader through the painful step-by-step process of visiting the murderer to grieving, and seeing her dead friend's son at a wedding many years later:

> Receive the hundreds of pages of letters he sends over the next six months. Save them for a while. Keep thinking of her. (That part is not hard.) Write from her son's perspective. Write it as fiction. Write from her perspective. Listen.
>
> Ask. *Where are her words?*
>
> Shred his.
>
> Wait several years. Attend a wedding. Be sociable. Hear the charming man next to you talk about his four children, his wife, that his father killed his mother when he was small, his career, his hopes for his children, his love for the grandmother who raised him.

Third person, though often presented as the objective point of view, still contains the writer's opinion and is no more objective than first or second. Whether a writer writes "I think drugs should be legalized" or

"Drugs should be legalized," both statements express the same opinion, neither one more objective than the other. Many college essays require third person because of its formality.

Note: Whether using first, second, or third person, stay consistent. Shifting is grammatically wrong:

Error: Students in the tutoring center can practice **their** writing skills. **You** can get help on an essay or work on grammar at a computer.

The shift from the plural, third person in the first sentence shifts to second person in the second sentence.

Corrections

> **Students** in the tutoring center can practice **their** writing skills. **They** can get help with an essay or work on grammar at a computer.

Or

> In the tutoring center, **you** can practice **your** writing skills. **You** can get help with an essay or work on grammar at a computer.

Revising and Editing

It's midnight the night before the paper is due. You've written a draft, so you're in good shape, right? Wrong. Most students think that having a draft means they can just hit spell check on the computer and then print. I admit that occasionally a student can pull this tactic off, but for the rest of us, we've only just begun. Writing means rewriting, rewriting, and more rewriting.

First, revise the paper. Revising means big changes, like adding or deleting information, reorganizing the essay, rewriting sentences, checking that the ideas are fully developed. Here's a list of questions to ask yourself about each developmental paragraph of your essay:

1. Can I add another example?
2. Can I add more information?
3. Can I describe something and make it more vivid for the reader?
4. Can I add a statistic or quote as evidence to strengthen my claim?
5. Can I explain a quote so the reader is clear on why I used it?

6. Have I related all of the material to my thesis statement or topic sentence?

7. Are there terms my reader may not understand (for example, surfing jargon) that I need to define?

All of these questions may not apply to every paper, but most of them will. You can always add an example or more information or description, and check to make sure that all of the material relates to the thesis or topic sentence.

STRATEGIES FOR WRITING PERSONAL ESSAYS

Storytelling comes naturally. You tell stories almost every day. When trying to tell a story in writing, keep in mind that the reader can't ask questions. It's up to you to hold the reader's attention, make a point, keep to the story, and evoke a sense of time and place.

Purpose

Why are you writing this story, sharing this memory? Though your purpose might be implied rather than stated directly, that purpose should be clear. Are you trying to inform, explain, teach, warn? Would the topic interest a general audience? Stories about car accidents or the horror of finding a significant other cheating don't offer much to the reader, even those who might have had the same experience. What kind of point can you offer that won't sound worn out? Don't drink and drive, or watch out for deceptive boyfriends or girlfriends, husbands or wives? David Sedaris's personal story about a conflict with a woman on an airplane who wanted to change seats comments on conflict/resolution. In "Mortality" by Bailey White, her car becomes a metaphor for aging. Bernard Cooper's "Burl's" explores not only sexual identity but an epiphany he has that reality is not always what it seems. Have a thought-provoking purpose or the story falls flat.

Zooming In

Most narratives zoom in on a small time period, and most writing books advise sticking to a 24-hour time period or less. For beginning writers, that's generally very good advice. Trying to write a life's story in a three-page essay, won't leave much room for detail and description. While experienced writers do sometimes flash forward or backward in time, like Edward Hoagland does in "The Courage of Turtles," many good narratives zoom in tight, like Lawrence Weschler's "Modern Times," which takes place in a few minutes in his office at work. The idea is to focus on a slice of life, to capture a meaningful moment in time. If you go much outside the 24-hour time frame, you could get into trouble with chronological order or confuse your reader by jumping in time without the proper transition.

Time Transitions

Transitions—words or phrases that help you move smoothly from one idea to another—are crucial in narrative. When writing from memory, you make automatic adjustments in time in your head, but if you leap in time without informing your reader, confusion results. When you move your story in time, let the reader know with phrases like *later that day* or *the following morning*. If you do decide to make big leaps in time, use proper transition, time indicators like "When I was five" or "After I entered high school" to help the reader travel in time with you so the reader isn't confused, thinking a small child is doing something like driving a car.

Evoking Senses

Another crucial element in writing memories is creating a vivid picture through description and sensory detail. You want the reader to hear, smell, taste, feel, see the experience. In "A Voice for the Lonely" Stephen Corey, instead of just telling the reader that it was quiet in the early mornings when he delivered newspapers, writes, "I recall stopping my brisk walk sometimes, especially in winter when every step squeaked and crunched on the snow that nearly always covered the ground, and marveling at how there were no sounds except those of my own making." He uses sound—squeaked and crunched—to show the silence. In "Burl's," Bernard Cooper describes the "medicinal odor of mothballs" that permeated his father's closet in paragraph #20, contrasting the smell of his mother's closet, "the air ripe with perfume" in #22; the sense of touch, "But no matter how much I wanted them to fit, those shoes were as cold and hard as marble" and "I was seared by a gust of heat" in paragraph #5; sight, "In the periphery of my vision, the shelf of wigs looked like a throng of kindly bystanders"; taste, "tasted Tobasco sauce" in #4. For more on using strong description and senses, flip through the Styling sections in this book, or look in the index under senses.

WRITING STRATEGIES FOR EXPLAINING AND EXPLORING IDEAS

For many essays that attempt to explain a concept or explore an idea, you can use the basic structure discussed in the section on Writing Basic College Essays. Sometimes, though, you may be attempting to compare, show a cause-effect relationship, define a term, or explain a process. Keep in mind that most good essays rely on a clear purpose, organized paragraphs with strong examples, vivid description, sentence variety, and specific details. It's wise to have a snappy title and a hook introduction.

Good essays often blend modes: a comparison essay might begin with a personal narrative, a cause-effect essay might contain a definition paragraph, and a process essay might rely heavily on description. You can combine any of these strategies.

Comparison and Contrast

In a comparison or contrast essay, you're attempting to hold one thing up to another to make a point. In Pauline Kael's review of *The Little Mermaid,* she contrasts Disney's film version to the original story by Hans Christian Andersen to illustrate the inferiority of the Disney cartoon. Comparison shows similarities to make a point, while contrast focuses on differences. For beginning writers, it's sometimes easier to make a point by writing about differences, so the example illustrates a contrast.

There are two basic methods of organization for writing a comparison or contrast paper: one side at a time or point by point. In the one-side-at-a-time method—sometimes called the block method—the first half of the essay discusses one topic and the second half compares or contrasts the other topic. A paper like Kael's "The Little Mermaid," contrasting Disney's *Cinderella* film with the old folktale from Grimms,' might be organized like this:

Paragraph 1:	I. Introduction and Thesis
Paragraph 2:	II. Disney Film
	a. Weak charcterization
	b. Beauty wins as a primary lesson
	c. Spiritual element reduced to ninny fairy godmother
Paragraph 3:	III. Grimms' Story
	a. Strong characterization
	b. Beauty comes from within
	c. Spiritual element in form of dead mother's spirit
Paragraph 4:	IV. Conclusion

Notice that the same points are covered for both versions. If you were to write in the second method, point by point, you would organize the essay this way:

Paragraph 1:	I. Introduction and Thesis
Paragraph 2:	II. Characterization
	a. Disney: weak
	b. Grimm: strong
Paragraph 3:	III. Beauty
	a. Disney: beauty wins is primary lesson
	b. Grimm: beauty comes from within
Paragraph 4:	IV. Spiritual Element
	a. Disney spiritual element reduced to ninny fairy godmother
	b. Grimm spiritual element in form of dead mother's spirit.
Paragraph 5:	V. Conclusion

Paragraphs don't always lay out so neatly into this formula. If paragraphs get too long, they might need broken up. For example, in the point-by-point method, break Characterization into two paragraphs: one for Disney and one for Grimm.

When comparing or contrasting, it's important to let the reader know which subject you're discussing by using transitions. Here's a list of transitions commonly used in comparison and contrast essays: *on the other hand, by contrast, similarly, by comparison.*

CAUTION Don't just show how two things are alike or different. There's no point to your essay if you fail to have an opinion. Why are you comparing? To show one's superiority over the other? To warn the reader? To promote understanding of an idea? You must have a **thesis statement**.

Cause and Effect

Why do some young girls mutilate themselves? Why did the Anasazi Indians live in the remote cliffs and resort to cannibalism? What's causing the failure of our educational system? What caused the Los Angeles riots? Does excess television cause obesity in children? Cause and effect essays attempt to explain why something happens—causes—and the results of incidents—effects.

Usually results have many causes, so you want to examine your topic closely for hidden reasons. After the Los Angeles riots, many people blamed the failure of our court system to convict the police officers involved in the Rodney King beating, and while that event certainly triggered the riots, the causes are much more complex, rooted in many years of police brutality and poverty, among other things. If you're going to blame television for obesity in children, you'd better examine the children's eating habits and social lives. It could be that children who watch television and eat excessively do so because of another problem like being picked on in school or trying to escape painful family problems or abuse. It's rare that you can say "this caused that."

There's no one organizational strategy for writing cause and effect essays, but generally writers explain the problem and then examine the causes. For example, the causes of self-mutilation are complex: pressures of adolescence, self-blame, shame, anger, feelings of abandonment. To neglect one of these causes of this serious problem would result in simplistic thinking.

Often, in a short essay on a large event, it's better to narrow to a **specific cause**, though letting the reader know that many causes contributed to the event. The economic crash of 2008 had numerous causes, but the essay might focus on one contributor, the banking industry. The paper would focus more on the **effects**, though explaining in the first couple of paragraphs the problems with the banking industry followed by paragraphs discussing the results: unemployment, foreclosures, increase in homelessness and the amount of people on welfare, adults with children moving back in with parents.

A cause and effect essay on cheating in school might be first outlined for causes and effects:

"Cheating in School"

Causes	Effects
Peer pressure	Not being prepared for the next level course
Parental pressure	Getting caught cheating and kicked out of school
Laziness	Difficulty getting accepted at another college
Lack of ethics	Not having the skills necessary for the job market
Belief that everyone cheats	

Explaining a Process

Process Analysis essays break down a subject into its steps and explain to the reader how to do something: develop a roll of film, watch an animal in the wild, run a marathon, grow tomatoes, tile a floor, or more serious topics like visit someone in prison. Often process essays take the command form **point of view** (see Point of View). Speech classes sometimes have students explain to the class how to do something in process analysis format.

Explaining or analyzing a process in writing isn't much different from explaining it to a friend or to a class, though in writing, friends or peers cannot ask questions. Be aware of the audience by writing clear step-by-step instructions and considering the audience's level of expertise. In an essay on how to grow orchids, a general reader—like your peers in a Speech class or an English teacher—will need more details and explanation than a gardening group that already has some experiencing tending plants.

In her essay "What Really Happened," Madge McKeithen takes the reader through the detailed process of visiting a murderer in prison (one who murdered his wife, a friend of hers), from how to find the correctional institution in which the offender is incarcerated, through speaking with the lawyer who defended him, writing the request to visit, choosing a date, renting a car, checking into the facility, talking with the offender, receiving the hundreds of letters he sends over subsequent months, but most importantly, remembering her—the victim.

WRITING STRATEGIES FOR DEFINING TERMS

Words can be slippery. They change meaning, wear disguises, take on new personas depending on who's using them. Charity wears many masks, kindness one day, an insult to pride the next, sometimes a veil for greed. What determines greed for one person constitutes ambition for another. Words are master chameleons.

Purpose

When writing a definition essay, the job is to rip off the masks, expose secrets; don't be content with worn out definitions. Don't write what everyone already knows about the word. For a more interesting paper, look at the side of the word nobody talks about. If you're writing a paper defining the word *lonely*, don't fall into the pity-all-the-lonely-people trap; you won't offer your reader anything new; if, on the other hand, you take the road less traveled, as one student did, and write, "Loneliness doesn't deserve pity or guilt. It deserves to be crushed in the street, crumpled under tires like dead leaves, crunched like a paper bag. Maybe then, like the Phoenix that goes up in flames and rises from its own ashes, the lonely will create their own lives, stop hermiting themselves, learn to paint or take a dance class, volunteer for meals-on-wheels, join a singles club, and quit tormenting the rest of us with their sorrowful lives." This thesis shocks the reader out of complacency.

Language Resources

Finding a new angle for a thesis can be a difficult task, but looking up the word in various language resources can help you find an edge. Many language resources are available online and in the library or a bookstore. While a standard dictionary might be helpful, other, more exciting sources abound: dictionaries of quotations, dictionaries of slang, a thesaurus, and *The Oxford English Dictionary.* If you do decide to use a standard dictionary like *Webster's,* avoid boring phrases like "According to *Webster's* . . ." These phrases numb the mind, and the reader will be reluctant to read further. For the paper on loneliness, the student first used a dictionary of quotations to discover what others have said about the term, finding a quote by Paul Elmer More stating that people "hold themselves aloof in chosen loneliness of passion," giving her the idea to focus on loneliness as self-pitying, self-inflicted isolation. She uses this quote in her essay as part of her conclusion.

Next, she visited a thesaurus, finding a bonanza of words to string together, creating an engaging inventory to underscore her point: "Loneliness is self-abandonment, icy isolation, me and my shadow, me-myself-and-I narcissism; single, solo, solitary, stag, I-travel-light baby; unescorted, unaccompanied, unaided, unassisted, pride run rampant." Notice the thoughtful word arrangement. Rather than repeating a list from the thesaurus, she braids them—except for the first string—with **alliteration**, chaining together words beginning with *s,* following with a string of *u* words, using a semicolon to separate the strings. Both strands end with a punch, a more-than-one-word phrase breaking the monotony of a single-word list, emphasizing her notion that most people choose their loneliness. The first strand—notice the complete sentence—contains some alliteration (*m*), but mostly establishes the cold, selfish aspect of the term.

To further defend her definition, the student investigated *The Oxford English Dictionary* (or OED), a several volume set chronicling the history of the English language. She discovered that the word *lonely* derives from *alone,* which stems from Middle English, a combination of *all* plus *one,* or all one. From there she reasoned that *all one* has a selfish, me-me-me implication, further validating her view.

Examples

In addition to a purpose for defining the word, the definition needs numerous examples. In the essay on loneliness, the student gives specific examples of sorrowful lives: the lonely business man, married to his job; the housewife stuck in an unhappy marriage; the whore on Harbor Boulevard. The student discusses each example, showing how most lonely people bring about their own loneliness, admitting that some loneliness results from mental illness, "but most lonely people wear their isolation like a crown of thorns." She also harvests examples from pop culture, using the Beatles' album *Sergeant Pepper's Lonely Heart's Club Band,* citing song lyrics that express America's frenzy of pity for the lonely. Without specific, thoroughly discussed examples, the reader wouldn't be convinced of such an unconventional point of view.

Debunking Misconceptions and Preconceived Ideas

Don't just rely on the obvious when writing a definition; be original. One strategy to argue from negation, or what a word is not. In his essay "Charm," from *I Can't Stay Long,* Laurie Lee writes, "Certainly, charm is not a question of learning palpable tricks, like wrinkling your nose, or having a laugh in your voice, or gaily tossing your hair out of your dancing eyes and twisting your mouth into succulent love-knots." He busts the standard view of charm, following with specifics defining charm: "Charm can't withhold, but spends itself willingly on young and old alike, on the poor, the ugly, the dim, the boring, on the last fat man in the corner."

Learning to write strong extended definitions is an important writing and thinking skill. Whether writing an essay defining Romanticism for art history, existentialism for philosophy, or Puritanism for religious studies, learning to capture elusive words and make them concrete challenges your mind, your assumptions, broadening your view of the world.

WRITING STRATEGIES FOR ARGUING

Standing up to the high school bully. Wondering whether technology keeps us too much in touch. Deciding if we've lost the war on drugs. Rethinking the value of television talk shows. Opinions on these topics—and many others—form the basis for argument. The trick, though, when writing an argument essay is to support opinion with solid evidence. The goal is persuasion—don't just spout an opinion. To convince a reader—

especially one who doesn't agree—state the point clearly, back it up with proof, and refute points from the other side.

Stating the Point

The point is the **thesis statement**, the writer's opinion on the topic. "Drugs should be legalized because we've already lost the war" states an opinion without using *I*. Generally, in college argument essays, avoid using *I*. First, it's redundant: if you state it, then it is your opinion, no *I* needed. Second, it's considered weak, wishy-washy to write *I think* or *I believe*. It's akin to saying, "It's only my opinion, so don't take me that seriously." Stand up for your convictions with a forceful statement. Notice, too, that the above statement contains *should* and *because*. Those two words signal your opinion—*should*—and your reasons for that opinion—*because*. As you become more practiced at writing thesis statements, you'll want to drop the obvious use of should and because, writing your statement in a more polished manner, as Gore Vidal does in "Drugs": "It is possible to stop most drug addiction in the United States within a very short time. Simply make all drugs available and sell them at cost." Of course, if Vidal doesn't support that statement with solid evidence, we'd simply ignore him.

Supporting Your Point

Support a point in an argument essay the same way as in any essay (see the section on Writing Basic College Essays), with strong examples, statistics, quotes, details. Know the topic, by researching. Explore both sides of the issue in order to refute the other side.

Refuting the Opposition

Know the other side's objections to the argument and respond, showing how they might be wrong or misguided. One approach is to bring up their objections, either in the form of a quote or paraphrase, and then respond: "Those who oppose legalizing drugs claim that legalization will lead to more drug addiction. Not so. People who are going to take drugs will do so, legal or not. During Prohibition, when alcohol was illegal, the law didn't stop alcoholism or drinking; it just turned it into a criminal activity." This strategy states the other side's view and then refutes it. The key is to be sure the reader knows when you are presenting an opposing view. Use phrases like "Opponents believe," to avoid confusing the reader.

Organization

Though a basic organization—introduction with thesis, body paragraphs, conclusion—works for arguments, almost any mode can be used or blended with other modes for a hybrid: a contrast or comparison essay might begin with a narrative and then argue one side over another or a cause and effect might use a definition in the opening or body. It depends on the paper's purpose. For addressing the opposition, use statements from the opponent's view as topic sentences and refute them. Another strategy spends three or four paragraphs discussing the writer's views, and then presents the opposition's views in one or two paragraphs, refuting them as they're presented.

WRITING STRATEGIES FOR CLASSIFICATION

When visiting Disneyland or Disney World, visitors find their way around by looking at a map divided into different areas, classified according to time or place: Frontierland, Tomorrowland, Fantasyland, Adventureland, Main Street USA, Critter Country, and so on. These classifications orient them to the park and let them know what to expect. Even a first-time visitor will probably figure out that Space Mountain is in Tomorrowland, not Frontierland. The descriptive names make sense of an otherwise chaotic place. A divided and classified closet: summer clothes, work attire, winter wardrobe; a pantry: canned goods, spices and baking supplies, breakfast items, boxed foods; a notebook: science, English, math, history, geology. If a hardware store heaped the paint in with the garden tools, the faucets in with the tulip bulbs, shoppers would walk out.

Writers often classify to make sense of a complex topic, poke fun or satirize, explain a comparison involving more than two subjects. A student might be asked to write a paper for a sociology class discussing parenting styles; periods of art in an art history class; types of earthquakes in a geology class. Classification can be useful for many topics.

In her essay "Friends, Good Friends—and Such Good Friends" (not in this book), Judith Viorst classifies her friends into seven categories: convenience friends, special-interest friends, historical friends, crossroads friends, cross-generational friends, part-of-a-couple friends, men who are friends. Viorst follows good rules of classification to write her essay:

Purpose

1. Make a point. If you write an essay classifying teenagers according to high school cliques, and you just list the types, you aren't

doing your reader a service. Anyone can make a list of types. The classification needs a thesis. Is it trying to warn the reader about a certain type of clique? Argue that cliques are detrimental to student learning? Illustrate that strict conformity leads to problems later in life? In Viorst's essay, she doesn't just discuss the types of friends; she makes a point:

> I once would have said that a friend is a friend all the way, but now I believe that's a narrow point of view. For the friendships I have and the friendships I see are conducted at many levels of intensity, serve many different functions, meet different needs and range from those as all-the-way as the friendship of the soul sisters mentioned above to that of the most nonchalant and casual playmates.

She then discusses each class of friends, pointing out how the class fits into her definition of friendship. Notice that she busts the standard view of friendship as being the no-matter-what kind.

Ruling Principle

2. Tie each category back to the thesis. For Viorst, it's the level of intimacy that ties the essay together. In English teacher jargon, this would be called the "Ruling Principle of Classification," how the topic is divided. Should a classification of rocks be by size, color, shape, composition? Pick one ruling principle and stick to it. If Viorst suddenly threw in a class of friends and didn't mention the intimacy factor, we would wonder why she added that category. If you classified Adventure films according to character types and then discussed a group by dialogue, the essay would be straying from the ruling principle, and would not stick together. The ruling principle is the glue of the essay.

Support

3. Use numerous examples. Every essay needs strong examples. In her category on Convenience friends, after defining what she means by convenience, Viorst lists the types of things these women do for each other: "Convenience friends are convenient indeed. They'll lend us their cups and silverware for a party. They'll drive our kids to soccer when we're sick. They'll take us to pick up our car when we need a lift to the garage. They'll even take our cats when we go on vacation." Listing specific good-

neighbor chores gives her point weight. She goes on to give examples of what she would and would not discuss with a convenience friend, the intimacy factor, gluing her essay back to its point.

4. Avoid simplifying. Acknowledge that the topic may be more complex than the classification covers. Admit the generalization and mention possible exceptions to the categories. In a paper on high school cliques, admit that not every student fits neatly into one of these groups. The conclusion might be a good place to write a disclaimer.

Labels

5. Label the groups. Notice that Viorst has descriptive labels that hint at the topic and give it flavor. The reader can tell by the label what to expect. When brainstorming a list of high school cliques, one class came up with the following groups: Rah Rahs (jocks and cheerleaders), Bandos (students in the band), Brains (formerly referred to as nerds), Misfits (students who dress and act in opposition to the rest of the crowd), Stoners (speaks for itself), Clubbies (students who always join clubs or run for office).

Organization

6. Organize the paper. There are many ways to organize material for classification, depending on the topic, but here are two common methods: chronological and emphatic order. If classifying historical time periods, consider organizing chronologically—time order—in the order the events occurred in time. If organizing friends, use emphatic order—least important category or shortest category first, and the most important or longest last.

SUMMARIZING

A summary is a restatement—in your own words—of another writer's work. In college, you might be asked to summarize a chapter in a textbook, summarize an article and then respond in an essay to the writer's ideas, or summarize to demonstrate understanding in a reading class. Learning to summarize helps you absorb material for tests, improve reading comprehension, and learn to identify key points. To summarize correctly, follow these steps:

1. Read the article through once to get the general idea.
2. Read a second time, highlighting key ideas—or taking notes if you don't want to defile your book.
3. Then—without looking at the text—write one-sentence summaries for each paragraph of the writer's main ideas.
4. Now write a draft of the summary from the sentences, providing examples from each paragraph that support the main ideas.
5. Check the summary against the author's work, making sure your writing is in your own words. When using any of the author's original words, put them in quotation marks. It's okay to put quotation marks around parts of a sentence to distinguish the writer's words from your own. For example, if you are summarizing Shelby's Steele's piece from his book *The Content of Our Character*, you might write a sentence like this:

> Although Steele concedes that prejudice against blacks is still a problem in America, overall, he thinks "there is also much opportunity."

Note: See the Paraphrasing section for information on how to paraphrase correctly.

TIPS FOR WRITING SUMMARIES

1. A summary should be about one-quarter the length of the article being summarized. If the summary is longer than one page, you may have to break it into paragraphs. A good rule is to change paragraphs when beginning to summarize a new idea.
2. Do not give an opinion in a summary. Save your views for critiques.
3. Always give the title of the text being summarized as well as the author's name in the introduction of the summary. Don't just write the title of the piece at the top of the page. Introduce the writer and the work:

> In the article "Drugs" by Gore Vidal, the author argues in favor of legalizing all drugs.

Notice that this opening sentence introduces the title, the author, and the author's thesis.
4. Be sure to paraphrase correctly (see below).

PARAPHRASING

Paraphrasing—simply put—means rewording. When taking an in-class essay examination based on material from a text, you repeat the material on the test in your own words. You're not quoting from the text but writing what you remember. You might use paraphrasing in a research paper to liven up another writer's words by using your own style, replacing a style that might otherwise sound dry.

A direct quote would look like this (the number in parentheses is the page number where the original statement is found):

> Joseph Verrengia reports, "Laboratory tests on some of the artifacts, including a piece of human excrement, have revealed traces of a human protein that scientists say is the first direct evidence of cannibalism among the Anasazi" (15).

A paraphrase of the above quote might look something like this:

> According to Joseph Verrengia, science has proven—using tests on human waste left at the scene of the crime—that the Anasazi did, indeed, chow down on their brethren, slicing and dicing, roasting and toasting their own kind, a grisly banquet for reasons unknown (15).

Notice that the source is given in both instances. While it is not necessary to cite every line of a paraphrase when writing a summary—the summary already told the reader that it is rewording another writer's work—you do have to give credit to other writers when using their ideas or words when paraphrasing in an essay. It doesn't matter that you've reworded it. You still must give the source. Otherwise, you're guilty of **plagiarism**.

Be sure to *completely* reword the material or put quotation marks around partially quoted material. When using any of the writer's original words, put quotation marks around them. If in the Verrengia example above the writer had written "piece of human excrement" instead of "human waste" and didn't put quotation marks around Verrengia's words, it would be considered plagiarism. See #5 under Summarizing.

PLAGIARISM AND GENERAL ADVICE FOR USING SOURCES

"This above all: To thine own self be true."

—William Shakespeare

Many students come to college with mistaken or vague definitions of **plagiarism**. Most know that it's wrong to download a paper off the Internet or borrow another student's work and present it as their own—a revolting practice—but knowing when to document a source can sometimes be confusing. Though most students have integrity and wouldn't plagiarize on purpose, some students pillage sources unintentionally, unaware that they are plagiarizing. You must give credit to every source. This is tricky business. However, if you remember some general guidelines, you'll be safe.

1. Always give an in-text citation showing the source of the material. See the section on Basic Documentation for information on how to correctly cite material within an essay.

2. If information is common knowledge, or something you already know, you do not have to cite a source because *you* are the source. In a paper on AIDS, it's not necessary to cite a source on the transmission of the virus. For most people, that's common knowledge. If you're a saltwater aquarium hobbyist writing an essay on how to start an aquarium, then you're probably an expert on many aspects of this exotic pastime, so you don't have to cite that information unless it's something you have to look up.

3. Avoid overquoting or overparaphrasing—stringing material together with little of your own writing. Instead, comment on material, giving your own opinion. Ask yourself, "Do I agree with this writer? What do I think? How does the quote or paraphrase support or refute my own opinion? Is the material logical? Helpful to the reader?"

4. Blend quotes smoothly. Don't just leave them dangling. See the Basic Documentation section for how to blend quotes. The Summarizing section, above, also has ideas for blending quotes.

5. Make sure you've interpreted the quote correctly and that it's relevant to your point.

6. Be fair to the writer when quoting or paraphrasing. To partially quote someone is okay as long as the partial quote doesn't change the meaning and you put quotation marks around the quoted material. Political commercials sometimes partially quote a rival, intentionally misrepresenting his or her ideas. That's shoddy practice.

Research

When writing college essays, you will probably be required to do some research and incorporate it into your own writing. If you use researched material, you must document it correctly. Remember that any words or ideas that are not your own must be documented (see Plagiarism). This section illustrates how to find materials, site information within an essay, and assemble Works Cited pages using the MLA (Modern Language Association) style of documentation. Not every school or department uses MLA format, but most English Departments do. Other styles include APA (American Psychological Association) and Chicago Manual of Style. If a teacher requires a style other than the MLA, visit the library or search the reference section of a reliable web site. One site that can help you with your works cited page is EasyBib.com.

BASIC SOURCES

The library is king of information. Libraries pay for services and databases that you cannot get for free on the Web. Infotrac, for example, contains articles from periodicals like magazines and journals and specific newspaper databases. You can search for hours on the Web and find nothing reliable on a topic or spend ten minutes in your library databases and find a bonanza of materials. And the library has librarians to help. You won't find that kind of service on the Web (see "The Internet" below).

The library has a book catalogue, usually on computer, where you can instantly find books on any topic. They also have reference materials like dictionaries and encyclopedias specific to a subject: art dictionaries, symbol dictionaries, reptile dictionaries. They have copy machines, computers, and access to other libraries.

Don't limit a search to books or the Web. Use a variety of sources to ensure you've found the best information on your topic. Interview people, experts in the field. For example, if you're writing an essay on reptiles, phone the local zoo and speak to the keeper of the reptile house. If writing about a social or community issue, write to or call city officials like parole officers and social workers. Talk to professors in colleges who are experts in their fields.

Don't forget that grab bag, the television. Proceed with caution, as with the Web. Avoid talk shows—unless you're writing a paper on the intellectual deterioration of America and want to use talk shows for examples. Rely on PBS stations that show quality programs. Stations with a focus on history, animals, and science generally have reliable information, but again, be cautious: these shows might also have a bias.

THE INTERNET

While the Internet is a great tool that has quick access to information, it also contains a lot of false or biased material. Junk clutters the information superhighway. Anyone can put up a Web page, so be certain to use valid sites. In general, *only use databases that the school library subscribes to.* College libraries pay a lot of money to provide students access to academic, valid research. Take advantage of that privilege. Most databases can be accessed from home, even when the library is closed. Ask your school's librarian for help if you're not familiar with these services. Keep in mind this simple rule: if it's not paid for by a college library, proceed with caution. Even if it's an online encyclopedia, it can contain wrong information. Legitimate online encyclopedias—like Britannica Online—charge for the service.

Evaluating Internet Sites and Other Sources

There's a T-shirt/bumper sticker slogan that states, "Question Authority, But Raise Your Hand First." Use this as your **mantra** when evaluating sources, whether from a library, periodical database, interview, television program, film, radio, or the Internet. Again, be especially cautious using the Internet. It's not considered academic to rely on the Internet instead of books or periodicals. But if you do use an Internet site, evaluate sources critically and respectfully. Here are a few guidelines:

1. Is the source trustworthy? Can the site be counted on for accurate, up-to-date information? Find out what organization or individual runs the site. Consider asking the school's librarian.

2. Does the site contain a **bias**? Most do, so don't necessarily rule out an Internet source for this reason, but try to determine whether the information is too far out of the mainstream to be credible. A source that claims the Holocaust didn't happen would not be considered dependable. A website maintained by a political group—Republican, Democratic, Libertarian—will have a distinct bias.

3. Don't rely on only one source. If you're writing a paper on the medical use of marijuana and only rely on a Web page sponsored by medical marijuana advocates, your essay will not be thoroughly researched. Use a variety of sources on both sides of the issue.

4. Always cite the Internet source correctly. See the Basic Documentation section.

5. Does the source provide new, interesting information you hadn't considered that will add to your essay?

6. What is the writer's style? Is the **tone** too emotional? Does the writer rely on **jargon**? Are the ideas clear?

BASIC DOCUMENTATION

This section provides the basics of MLA documentation, covering the most commonly used sources, so if a source documentation problem is not discussed here, the library should have a copy of *The MLA Handbook for Writers of Research Papers* or the *MLA Style Manual,* which provide more in-depth documentation information.

Format

Do not use a title page for your research paper unless specifically requested to by your teacher. Instead, in the upper left corner of the page, put your name, the teacher's name, the class, and the date. In the upper right corner, put your last name and the page number. Put your last name and page number on every page of your document, but the left corner information goes only on the first page. (See the sample at the end of the documentation section.)

Double space the entire document. Do not put extra spaces between paragraphs. Indent the first line of each paragraph.

Use one-inch margins all around your paper, and use a standard type size like 12 point. If you use huge type, it will look like you've run out of things to say and are trying to take up space by using big type.

Parenthetical References

Within an essay, a parenthetical reference is brief information about a source provided in parentheses. When writing a paper using information and quotes from books, magazines, journals, newspapers, interviews, the Internet, or other sources, give a parenthetical reference next to the quote or information. Generally, use the writer's last name and the page number.

Do not use a comma to separate the author's name from the page number, nor should you write *p.* for page. Cite the source just like the examples below. If using the writer's name to introduce the quote, then only the page number is required in parentheses. Keep parenthetical references as brief as possible, saving detailed information for the Works Cited pages. Here's an example of blending a quote with your own writing:

Fairy tales teach children about the real world. We grow up to find out, "As we had suspected, the fairy tales had been right all along—the world was full of hostile, stupid giants and perilous castles and people who abandoned their children in the nearest forest" (Lurie 18).

Notice that the period goes outside the parentheses. The following example uses the writer's name to introduce the quote:

Fairy tales teach children about the real world. According to Alison Lurie, we grow up to find out, "As we had suspected, the fairy tales had been right all along—the world was full of hostile, stupid giants and perilous castles and people who abandoned their children in the nearest forest" (18).

Because the writer's name introduces the quote, there's no need to repeat it in the parenthetical reference, only the page number.

If two people wrote the work, use both names in parentheses: (Brown and Smith 44). For three authors, follow the same strategy: (Brown, Smith, and Diaz 44). When a source has three or more authors, use the last name of the first author listed followed by *et al.* (and others): (Brown et al. 44).

If the source doesn't list an author, then abbreviate the title instead. A book titled *Medicines of the Rain Forest* with no author would be cited like this: (*Medicines* 32).

When using a quote of more than three typed lines, set the quote off by indenting *two* tab spaces, eliminating the quotation marks, and putting the period before the parenthetical reference:

```
Fairy tales teach children about the real world,

how to cope with problems, be kind, and have hope. We

grow up to find out:

        As we had suspected, the fairy tales had been

    right all along—the world was full of hostile,

    stupid giants and perilous castles and people

    who abandoned their children in the nearest for-

    est. To succeed in this world you needed some

    special skill or patronage, plus remarkable

    luck; and it didn't hurt to be very good-look-

    ing. (Lurie 18)
```

Warning: Keep long quotations to a minimum or it looks like you're not doing your own thinking and writing, stringing together others' ideas instead.

Citing Online Sources within an Essay

When citing online sources—whether web pages or online data bases—within an essay, treat them the same as print sources if they have authors and page numbers. Without the author or page number, sometimes it's better to mention the article title, web page creator, or web site in the text and not use a parenthetical reference. **Do not** use a web address in the essay or in a parenthetical reference; it clutters the text. That information belongs on the works cited page. Keep the essay clean, only giving brief information in parentheses. When using a parenthetical reference for an online source with no author or page number, cite the article title in quotation marks, if available, or an abbreviated title of the web page in italics, but provide enough information to clearly identify the source on the works cited page.

An article cited: ("Killdeer").

When two articles share a title, identify the source as well in italics:

("Killdeer" *Britannica*).

("Killdeer" *Science Resource Center*).

Works Cited

The works cited section at the end of the paper lists in alphabetical order— by author, article title, or source title, in that order—information about the sources cited in the essay, corresponding to the parenthetical references within the text, making it easy for the reader to find.   When available, always use the author's last name.   A works cited page begins on a **separate sheet of paper** but is numbered in sequence with the rest of the essay.   If the paper is five pages long, then page six would become the works cited page.   The writer's last name and page six go at the top of the page in the right hand corner (see the sample works cited page).

BOOKS   To cite a book, use the following information in this order: author's last name, followed by the first name; the title of the book, in italics; the city; publisher and the publication year; and the word "Print" for print editions (most of this information can be located on the copyright page):

Bettelheim, Bruno. *The Uses of Enchantment*. New York:

Random House, 1975. Print.

When an entry takes up more than one line, use one tab space to indent the second line of the entry.   Use a period after each section and space twice, as indicated in the sample; add a colon after the city, a comma after the publisher, a period after the year, and type two spaces before the word "Print" followed by a period.

Tomlinson, Carl M. and Carol Lynch-Brown. *The*

Essentials of Children's Literature. 2nd ed.

Needham Heights: Allyn and Bacon, 1996. Print.

The first name on the list is alphabetized with last name first, while the other authors names are listed with first name followed by last name. If there is an edition number listed on the book, place it after the book title.

For books with **three authors**, cite all three:

Darigan, Daniel L., Michael O. Tunnell, and James S.

Jacobs. *Children's Literature: Engaging Teachers*

and Children in Good Books. Upper Saddle River:

Pearson, 2002. Print.

When more than three authors are listed, use the first author listed followed by the abbreviation et al. (and others):

Beechy, Michael et al. *1,000 Symbols*. New York: The

Ivy Press, 2002. Print.

If a book has been translated, give the translator's name after the title:

Beowulf. Trans. Seamus Heany. New York: Farrar,

Straus and Giroux, 2002. Print.

ENCYCLOPEDIA ARTICLES   When citing articles from encyclopedias, use the author's last name (if available), the article title in quotation marks, the encyclopedia title in italics, the edition, and print:

"Killdeer." *Grizmek's Animal Encyclopedia*. 2004 ed.

Print.

MAGAZINE ARTICLES   For magazines, use the author, title of the article, title of the magazine, the day and month, the year, and the page numbers the article runs through:

Swartz, Mimi. "You Dumb Babies!" *New Yorker* 30 Nov.

1998: 60-67. Print.

Notice that the day goes before the month, and a colon after the year. The article title is in quotation marks and the magazine title in italics. Multiple authors would be written the same as for books. Notice the pages the article runs through are after the year with no *p.* or *page.* For magazines published monthly, leave out the day.

NEWSPAPER ARTICLES   Again start with the author's last name, the title of the article in quotation marks, followed by the newspaper title in italics or underlined. Because newspapers have sections, give the section and page. If the newspaper has an early and late edition, specify which one the article came from. An entry with only one edition would look like this:

> Dillow, Gordon. "'Our Kids' Really Can't Be Saved."
>
> *Orange County Register* 20 Feb. 2000, L3. Print.

Here's an example of an entry specifying an edition:

> Brown, Sylvia. "Budget Crimes." *Los Angeles Times* 20
>
> March 1997, late ed.: D1 +. Print.

The + sign indicates the article is on more than one page; the *1* is the page number; the *D* is the section.

SCHOLARLY JOURNALS   What's the difference between a magazine and a journal? Magazines are aimed at the average reader and usually come out weekly or monthly. Journals—although some are published monthly—usually come out quarterly, biannually, or annually and tend to be specific to a field of study, like the *Shakespeare Quarterly*. If you're not sure if it's a magazine or journal, check the front and inside cover; you should be able to find the term *journal*.

Treat a journal article like a magazine article, with a couple of exceptions: the volume number and possibly issue number, determined by whether or not the journal has continuous pagination. If, for example, issue 3 of a journal begins on page 232 instead of page 1, then the journal is paginated continuously and does not need the issue number. Usually this type of pagination covers a year and starts over with page 1 in the new volume in the next year. If each issue starts with page 1, then use the issue number.

Another quirk about citing journals: put parentheses around the year, followed by a colon and the page numbers. Here is an example of an entry without an issue number:

> Yolen, Jane. "American's Cinderella." *Children's*
>
> *Literature in Education* 8 (1977): 21-29. Print.

The *8* stands for the volume number. Put quotation marks around the article title and underline or italicize the journal title. Here's an example of an entry with an issue number:

> Hearn, Michael Patrick. "Happily, Ever After: The
>
> Resilience of the Fairy Tale." *Tall: Teaching and*
>
> *Learning Literature with Children and Young Adults*
>
> 8.1 (1998): 85-98. Print.

The *8* stand for the volume number and the *1* for the issue number. Notice a period separates the volume and issue.

INTERVIEWS Always begin an interview citation with the name of the person interviewed. If you're interviewing an individual in person, cite the interview like this:

> Roberts, Julia. Personal Interview. 27 July 1999.

If you interviewed the person over the phone, Phone Interview would replace Personal Interview.

If you're citing an interview published in a magazine or newspaper, it would look like this:

> Roberts, Julia. Interview. *New York Times* 18 Jan.
>
> 1999, late ed.: D22. Print.

Cite a television or radio interview similar to the above, but give the interviewer's name when available and the title of the program, underlined or in italics:

> Roberts, Julia. Interview with Barbara Walters. *Sixty*
>
> *Minutes*. NBC. New York. 18 Jan. 1999.

FILMS Generally, cite a film by giving the title first, followed by the director, major actors, studio, and year of release:

> *Lone Star*. Dir. John Sayles. Perf. Kris
>
> Kristofferson, Matthew McConaughey, Chris Cooper,
>
> and Elizabeth Pena. Columbia Tristar, 1996.

Perf. is an abbreviation for Performers.

TELEVISION SHOWS   Usually for a television program, you will need the title of the episode (if there is one) in quotation marks, the title of the show (in italics), name of the network, call letters and city of the local station—if any—and the date the show aired:

> *Pythons: A Predator's Perspective*. DSC. 15 July 2008.

ELECTRONIC SOURCES AND THE WEB   **Note:** The MLA no longer requires the URL, so only add it if required by the instructor. The URL goes in brackets after the date of access. Generally, electronics sources and web sites are treated like their paper counterparts with a couple of exceptions: the online source and the date of access. Cite the page numbers if available. If not, use the abbreviation n. pag. indicating no page. For an article in an **online data base**, use the author's name (if available), the article title in quotations marks, periodical title in italics, the data base title, Web and date of access:

> Greji, Eldon.   "Water Carriers."   *Birder's World* June
>
> 2009. n. pag.   Science Resource Center. Web.   22
>
> March 2012.

For scholarly journals, add the volume and issue number after the periodical title, just as you would in a journal article:

> Dolby, Nadine. "Research in Youth Culture and Policy:
>
> Current Conditions and Future Directions." *Social*
>
> *Work and Society: The International Online-Only*
>
> *Journal* 6.2 (2008): n. pag.   Web.   20 May 2012.

For an encyclopedia like *Britannica*, cite the author (if available), article title, publication date, source, and date of access:

> Robertson, Clinton and Charles.   "Killdeer."
>
> *Encyclopedia Britannica* 2004 ed.   Web.   5 May
>
> 2012.

For Web sites, give the author (if any), title of the page (if it's part of a larger site), the title of the web page in italics, the publisher of the web site, date the site was last updated, source (Web), and date of access:

```
"Cinderella."  The Cinderella Project.  Ed. Michale

    N. Saida.  University of Southern Mississippi,

    October 2005.  Web.  15 May 2012.
```

Works Cited Example

Study the following Works Cited sample. Notice the title. It's no longer called a bibliography because that term refers to books and you use a variety of sources. Follow these guidelines:

1. Do not number the entries.
2. Double space the entire section. Resist the temptation to put extra spaces between each entry or between the title of the section and the first entry.
3. Place article titles in quotation marks and italicize or underline book, magazine, and periodical titles.
4. When the entry runs more than one line, indent one tab space for following lines.
5. Put your last name and page number in the upper right corner of the page.
6. Alphabetize by author's last name. If no author is listed for a work, alphabetize the work by title.
7. Place a period at the end of each entry.
8. Use the punctuation shown in the sample entries.

Works Cited

Beechy, Michael et al. 1,000 *Symbols*. New York: The Ivy
    Press, 2002. Print.

Greji, Eldon. "Water Carriers." *Birders World* June 2009.
    n. pag. Science Resource Center. Web. 22 March 2012.

"Killdeer." *Grizmek's Animal Encyclopedia*. 2004 ed.
    Print.

Robertson, Clinton and Charles. "Killdeer." *Encyclopedia
    Britannica*. 2004 ed. Web. 5 May 2012.

Wheelwright, Jeff. "Attack of the Flying Carp." *Discover*
    March 2012: 60-66. Print.

Example First Page of a Research Paper

Smith 1

Jane Smith

Professor Diaz

English 100

6 Sept. 2009

Title

Begin typing the first line here. Don't forget to indent.
Notice there are no extra spaces between the title and the
first line or between the class information and the title.
Resist the temptation to include extra spaces.

Also, notice that there are no extra spaces between paragraphs. Just indent one tab space, double space your entire
document, and use one-inch margins all around.

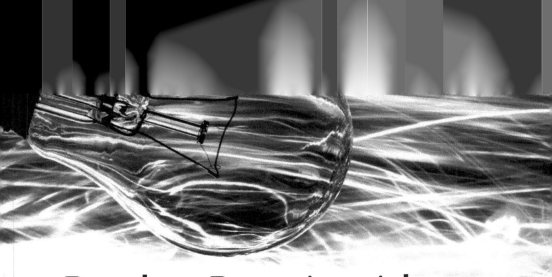

Basic Punctuation Rules and Practice

Though not intended as a workbook or comprehensive manual, this section covers common errors many beginning writers make, with exercises for reinforcement to help with style practice throughout the text.

COMMAS

Commas with Items or Actions in a Series

When several items or actions occur in a row, they require commas.

Example:
Blouses, jeans, t-shirts, socks, and shoes littered the bedroom.

Note: Some manuals say to leave the comma out before the "and," but for clarity's sake, put the comma before the conjunction (but, or, yet, so, for, and, nor*) when there are more than two items. Otherwise, the last two items become linked and might confuse the reader.

If there are only two items, omit the comma:

Example:
Socks and shoes littered the hallway.

***Tip**: To remember conjunctions, memorize the acronym BOYSFAN.

But
Or
Yet
So
For
And
Nor

Practice: Insert commas where needed. One sentence is correct.

1. The Cocker Spaniel bolted to its feet growled and threw itself against the window at the mailman.

2. Dorothy cocked the shotgun sighted the target and pulled the trigger.

3. William Steig wrote and illustrated numerous children's picture books.

4. The Border Collie can retrieve ropes balls keys shoes and many other items on command.

5. Scones lemon bars brownies cupcakes decorated for Halloween and a variety of over-sized cookies filled the bakery shop window.

6. The Volkswagon careened down the hill hit a boulder flipped over rolled several times and landed in the ditch.

7. Scientists now know that animals have better memories can reason more complexly live more socially complex lives have more complex understanding of others and have more self-awareness than was previously thought.

8. Maria competed in the long jump the 500 meter race the pole vault and the relay.

9. Her favorite hobbies include raising turtles painting landscapes decorating cakes growing orchids surfing with her friends and watching black and white movies.

10. The coffee shop owner worked the breakfast rush helped clean up the aftermath interviewed a perspective employee and chatted with customers in the lull of the afternoon.

Commas with Lead-in (or Introductory) Material

When an incomplete word group (dependent clause, phrase, or single word) introduces a subject, the introduction takes a comma before the subject. Some words signal that there might be a comma needed before the subject. Watch for words like while, since, when, because, words ending in "ing," and prepositions (above, around, beneath, beyond, below, over, under, in, into, upon, and many others).

Example:
While driving down the highway in her new Volkswagen convertible, she felt completely free from the stress of her first college semester.

"While driving down the highway in her new Volkswagen convertible" leads into (or introduces) the subject "she."

Warning: To avoid modifier errors, check that the lead-in material refers directly to the subject. For example, in the following sentence, the introductory material refers to a subject not stated in the sentence, momentarily confusing the reader:

Aiming the rifle, the quail flew into the tree.

Is the quail aiming the rifle?

Note: Check that lead-in clauses or phrases beginning with "ing" are not the subjects of sentences. If they function as the subject, don't use the comma.

Example:
Painting landscapes is her favorite hobby.

"Painting" is the subject of the sentence, not part of a lead-in. The following sentence requires the comma because the "ing" word group introduces the subject, Juan.

Example:
Carrying his fishing rod, Juan headed for the lake.

Another common error is using a comma after words like "although" and "because." Be sure the comma goes at the end of the lead-in.

Wrong:
Although, the injured player was never able to play hockey again he became a famous sportscaster.

Correct:
Although the injured player was never able to play hockey again, he became a famous sportscaster.

Reminder: The subject of the sentence, or noun, is a person, place, or thing.

Practice: Insert commas where needed.

1. To protect your skin from skin cancer you should wear sunscreen of SPF 50 or higher.

2. If you're allergic to milk you can try dairy products like ice cream and cheese made of soy.

3. During the holidays students often forget many of the punctuation rules they learned in English class.

4. With strong winds over 50 miles per hour the storm blew debris all over the road.

5. In an ice storm power lines often break under the weight of the ice.

6. To justify his decision the president went on national TV to argue that his plan would create new jobs.

7. Because the electricity went out during the storm several students were unable to finish their term papers.

8. While doing her usual Monday morning online banking she noticed suspicious activity and immediately called the bank.

9. When running a marathon it is important to stay hydrated.

10. Since the robbery the bank has increased security.

Commas with Interrupters

Often writers use material that is not necessary to the meaning of the sentence but provides additional information or description. If you removed the material from the sentence, it would still make sentence sense:

Example:
The vinyl seat, sticky from the heat, clung to her skin.

The word group "sticky from the heat" interrupts the sentence "The vinyl seat clung to her skin." Don't put commas around elements in a sentence unless they interrupt.

Example:
Her job at the bank provided a good income.

The word group "at the bank" is a prepositional phrase, not an interrupter. Interrupters often go between the subject and verb.

With Appositives

Appositives rename or give more information about a noun right next to them. Treat them as interrupters and put commas on **both** sides of them.

Example:
Jerry, her acupuncturist, moved to Thailand.
"Her acupuncturist" renames the noun Jerry.

Example:
The dog, a small terrier, slept in the corner of his pen at the rescue center.

"A small terrier" renames the dog.

Dashes can be used with appositives, though it isn't usually necessary and can seem overdone. Commas are often the best choice.

Practice: Insert commas around interrupting material.

1. Marilyn Monroe even with all of the adulation she received was unhappy.

2. Tommy's ex-girlfriend the one who relentlessly stalked him was finally arrested.

3. Sarah, who has red hair, brought her pet bearded dragon to class.

4. Barry, an excellent musician, played the bass guitar in a rock band.

5. Jose's brother, the competitive one, always burst into a rage if Jose beat him at basketball.

6. Orangutans, thought by some to be smarter than chimpanzees, have a complex social structure with cultural traditions.

7. Alex, a smart African gray parrot, helped prove that animals can grasp abstract concepts.

8. Many paintings by the artist Jan Lievens, a contemporary of Rembrandt's, are often attributed to Rembrandt.

9. The two great painters, studying under the same master, knew each other and even modeled for one another.

10. Mansfield Correctional Facility, now an historical site in Ohio, was used in the film *The Shawshank Redemption*.

Commas Between Two Complete Sentences Joined with a Conjunction

See the tip with comma rule number one, items in a series. When two complete sentences are joined together with a conjunction creating a compound sentence, a comma is required.

Example:
Mai wanted to study creative writing, but her parents wanted her to study medicine and become a doctor.

Note: A comma is required after "writing" because there is a complete sentence after "but": "Her parents wanted her to study medicine" can stand on its own as a sentence. No comma comes after "medicine" even though there is a conjunction because "become a doctor" is not a complete sentence.

Exception: When two sentences joined with a conjunction are short, a comma is not necessary:

Example:
Go to work and don't be late. (These short commands–though complete sentences–don't require commas.)

Note: Don't mistake "then" for a conjunction. Two complete sentences joined with "then" need a semicolon, a period, or a conjunction with a comma. A comma alone won't do the job and creates an error called a comma splice.

Wrong:
She ran in the marathon, **then** she won the pole vault.

Correct:
She ran in the marathon, **and then** she won the pole vault.
She ran in the marathon; **then** she won the pole vault.
She ran in the marathon. **Then** she won the pole vault.

Tip: Check the word groups on both sides of the conjunction for a complete sentence before adding a comma.

Practice: If the conjunction joins two sentences, add a comma. Two are correct.

1. Miranda earned a 4.0 GPA in high school but she could not get into the college of her choice.

2. The refrigerator needed cleaning and the garbage reeked of an unpleasant odor.

3. Joshua passed his final exam in history with an A but he still failed the class because he didn't turn in his research essay.

4. Numerous children's films have been based on quality picture books but the films lack the literary and artistic value of the originals.

5. The picture book *Jumanji* by Chris Van Allsburg has stunning drawings but the movie added silly scenes and dialogue.

6. She turned on the radio and listened to a football game to keep from falling asleep at the wheel.

7. Writer David Sedaris finds humor in odd situations and his newest book, *When You Are Engulfed in Flames,* is sure to be a hit.

8. Plastic is a marvelous invention but it may cause cancer as well as problems in landfills.

9. You should never use plastic to cook food in the microwave nor put hot beverages in plastic cups.

10. Many people think they eat healthy yet most don't get the recommended five servings of fruits and vegetables.

Commas Between Two or More Words that Describe (Adjectives)

When two or more adjectives describe the same subject (noun), they require commas.

Example:

Sylvester collects smooth, shiny pebbles which he thinks have magical powers.

"Shiny" and "smooth" both describe the pebble. A simple test to see if adjectives require commas is to switch their places in the sentence and see if it still makes sense. If it does, then add a comma; if not, leave the comma out.

Sylvester collects shiny, smooth pebbles which he thinks have magical powers.

For a second test, put "and" between them. If it makes sense, use the comma; if it doesn't, then leave the comma out.

Sylvester collects **smooth and shiny** pebbles which he thinks have magical powers.

Note: Don't use a comma between the adjective and the subject.

Wrong:

Sylvester collects smooth, shiny, pebbles.

Practice: Place commas between two or more adjectives that describe the same subject.

1. Her tattered dirty coat could not keep out the piercing cold.

2. The sultry record-breaking heat sent thousands of people to California's southland beaches.

3. Cobwebs blanketed the musty damp rotting cellar.

4. Brutal windy weather kept shivering Missourians indoors.

5. The orchids grew in an orchestra of exotic colorful shapes.

6. Ramon ran through the quiet fog-shrouded streets of San Francisco.

7. The sunset looked eerie through the dark smoky atmosphere caused by the wildfire.

8. Black widow spiders construct messy tangled webs that are surprisingly efficient.

9. Tantalizing sweet nectar attracted orioles as well as hummingbirds.

10. Nutritious tasty meals can be made in thirty minutes or less.

Commas with Dates

Set off the year with commas on both sides with a month *and* a date:
January 1, 2000, scared many people who thought the millennium would bring a catastrophe.

Don't use commas with the month and the year:
Many people celebrated the millennium in January 2001.

COLONS

There are two basic ways to use colons: with a list or an explanation. One rule to remember is to always use a complete sentence before you use a colon.

Example with a list:
The many foods that triggered her allergies flitted through her mind as she looked at the restaurant menu: peanuts, shrimp, crab, wheat, milk, eggs, and soy.

Example with an explanation:
Virginia couldn't decide which pet in the animal shelter she wanted most: the white kitten with the big blue eyes or the sad mutt with the oversized ears that no one seemed to want.

The puppy and kitten examples explain her decision.

Tip: Never use a colon after such as, like, or for example. A colon replaces these overused phrases. Notice that using a colon with such as or for example breaks the use-a-complete-sentence-first rule.

Practice: Add a colon where needed with a list or an explanation. One sentence is correct.

1. Orchids come in many varieties:lady slippers, butterfly orchids, cymbidiums, cattelyas, and many other species.

2. Both jobs had advantages:one providing great health coverage but the other with more opportunities for advancement.

3. Regina mulled over her opportunities:stay in school and finish her education or take the acting job that might lead to fame and fortune.

4. There are three types of drivers that irritate me:the most parking spot hogs who steal spaces or park across two spots, impatient people who honk at the elderly, and those with road rage who weave in and out of traffic, screaming and making rude gestures to other drivers.

5. Many types of seashells washed up on the beach:scallops, mussels, conch shells, clams, sea urchins, and others I couldn't identify.

6. Science can now accomplish many things that were once considered science fiction:cloning, regenerating tissue, replacing joints, and using DNA to diagnose genetic disorders, among others.

7. Many new drugs have been invented to improve brain functions like:memory, alertness, attention span, and mental illness.

8. Researchers think they have solved the puzzle as to why we need to sleep maintaining the immune system.

9. Many bird species are disappearing from North America : nighthawks, whip-poor-wills, barn swallows, flycatchers, and many others.

10. Some spices not only enhance the flavor of food but also provide antioxidants for better health:cinnamon, ginger, red pepper, and curry belong on the top of the list of antioxidant rich spices.

RUN-ONS, COMMA SPLICES, AND SEMICOLONS

There are two basic ways to use the semicolon: to connect two complete sentences in place of a comma and conjunction and to separate items in a list when commas would create confusion.

The sentences should illustrate a close connection in thought, contrast, or comparison. In this instance, the semicolon acts as a stop sign signaling the reader to apply the brakes rather than slow down and yield like a comma.

Example
She loved her boyfriend; his mother was another matter.

The semi-colon is a good choice, more dramatic than a comma and a conjunction, creating tone, emphasizing the relationship friction between the mother and the girl.

Run-on Sentences
Two sentences put together without the proper connection are called run-ons. Semicolons provide one way to fix a run-on or a fused sentence. Many people think any long sentence qualifies as a run-on, but in college, most teachers want varied structure with some long sentences—if they're correct. A run-on can occur in short sentences:

Example:
She loved her boyfriend his mother was another matter.

Though short, without a period and a capital, a semicolon, or comma with a conjunction, it's a run-on sentence. Writers sometimes attempt to connect two sentences with a comma, creating another error called a **comma splice.** A comma alone doesn't fix a run-on. To correct run-ons and comma splices, use either a semicolon, a comma with a conjunction, a period and a capital, or recast the sentence to make one clause dependent:

She loved her boyfriend; his mother was another matter.
She loved her boyfriend, **but** his mother was another matter.
She loved her boyfriend. **H**is mother was another matter.
Though she loved her boyfriend, his mother was another matter.

Semicolons also connect complete sentences joined by the words however, moreover, nevertheless, nonetheless, therefore, and other transitional words (called conjunctive adverbs or adverbial conjunctions). When these words interrupt a sentence rather than join two, put commas around them.

Example connecting two sentences:
The coyotes harassed the alley cat for over an hour as it hid under the truck; however, they finally gave up and went to look for easier prey.

Note that a comma goes after the however.

Example interrupting one sentence:
The coyotes, however, did not give up easily.

Tips: Check both sides of the word for a complete sentence. If there is a complete sentence on either side, then you need the semicolon and the comma. "The coyotes" is not a complete sentence; it's only a subject. Don't use the semicolon. Treat it as an interrupter. When you take out the however, there is one sentence, not two: The coyotes did not give up easily.

Practice: Use a semicolon, a comma with a conjunction, a period and a capital, or recast to correct the following run-on sentences. Use a variety of these methods.

1. Gardening can be an enjoyable and profitable hobby however you shouldn't garden if you're allergic to bees.

2. Taking precautions however can allow you to enjoy the outdoors despite this deadly allergy.

3. Vincent Van Gogh painted sunlit landscapes in the south of France he also painted lively nighttime scenes that some critics say merge fantasy and reality.

4. Spotted owls in Oregon have struggled to survive now they're being bullied by a new neighbor, the barred owl.

5. She enjoys making homemade lasagna her favorite thing to cook is salmon in salsa verde.

6. The band gave a performance almost identical to the one several years ago fans still felt they got their money's worth.

7. Jamal became an artist despite his father's protests; now Jamal has his own art studio and earns a six figure income.

8. Hurley is shy and overweight nevertheless; he finally got up the nerve to ask the blond psychologist on a picnic.

9. Joel dribbled the ball down the court; he slipped past players twice his size to make the basket.

10. Jonah earned a 4.0 GPA; he still couldn't get into the college of his choice.

11. Most people think orchids are difficult to grow; however, they thrive quite nicely with minimal care.

12. Internet hackers are almost impossible to stop; banks won't prosecute because it's too expensive.

13. People usually think of illegal drugs when they hear about drug abuse; prescription drug abuse, though, is on the rise among teens.

Practice:
Fix any run-on or comma splice errors in the following paragraph with one of the four methods discussed.

In Victorian England, people were obsessed with rare, difficult-to-find orchids. Orchid hunters, men paid by nurseries to find these exotic flowers, faced danger and death in places like Panama, Madagascar, India, and Peru. The men were tough and smart; they were willing to risk their lives for the large sums of money nurseries paid them to find these rare plants. Some died of disease, some died of accidents. They even murdered each other. Owning wild orchids was outlawed in 1975; however, thieves still smuggle and steal orchids from backyards and poach them from the wild in places like Florida. Orchid thieves walk for miles through swamps for orchids like the ghost orchid; an endangered species that may soon be gone. Orchid mania thrives despite the laws, which thieves know are difficult to enforce.

Semicolons: separate items in a list when commas would create confusion. Objects and their details can crash into each other in a sentence if not properly distinguished from one another:

Example:

The art teacher posted a list of supplies to bring to the next class meeting: one set of graphie pencils, preferably the turquoise ones; a set of Prismacolor pencils; two types of charcoal, vine and compressed; two stomps for blending, one for charcoal and one for graphite; a pad of 400 series drawing paper, size 18 X 24; a drawing board to hold the pad of paper; an Exacto knife; and an artist's box to keep all of the materials organized.

Without a semicolon, the reader—unless familiar with art supplies—would have difficulty knowing which detail goes with which object. For consistency, use a semicolon before each new object as well as before the conjunction (and). Usually a semicolon replaces a conjunction between two sentences, but in this instance, the semicolon makes it clear the Exacto knife is a separate item, not connected to the artist's box.

Note: Also see the "Styling" with Shelby Steele's "On the Content of Our Character."

DASHES

Dashes can be used three ways: Replace commas with dashes to set off an interrupter. Dashes draw attention; only use them to emphasize an interrupter. They're also used to set off elements at the end of a sentence for emphasis and for a list that interrupts a sentence because the commas would be confusing **(see the "Styling" accompanying Gordon Grice's "Black Widow" for more instruction)**. Dashes—visually shouting at the reader for attention—can help create a tone or make the reader more carefully consider something in the sentence that would be toned down by commas or parentheses.

Examples:

At the end of the sentence with add-on material (nonessential elements):

In "A Voice for the Lonely," Stephen Corey writes about music's emotional impact on the listener:

"And in an even more strange way, a song we love goes silent as we 'listen' to it, leaving us in that rather primitive place where all the sounds are interior ones—sounds which can't be distinguished from feelings, from pulsings and shiverings, from that gut need to make life stronger than death for a least a few moments."

Corey could have used a comma after "interior ones," but he chose the dash so the reader will pay more attention to his explanation of the sounds.

Sometimes writers will reverse this strategy, placing the complete sentence after the dash rather than before it, as Lawrence Weschler does in "Modern Times":

"On the ground, the carnage of war, the gore, the frantically desperate attempts at rescue, the bitterly expiring hopes—**they're all the same as they've ever been.**"

This strategy creates a sense of anticipation leading up to the main idea.

A dash can also be used to set off a list at the end of a sentence in place of a colon.

With an interrupter:
In "Burl's" by Bernard Cooper, he describes what he thinks, at first, are two women walking toward him on the hot sidewalk outside a restaurant when he was a child:

"The silky fabric—one dress was purple, the other pink—accentuated their breasts and hips and rippled with insolent highlights."

The colors highlight the men's attempts at femininity.

With a list that interrupts a sentence:
Edward Hoagland, in "The Courage of Turtles," describes how turtles cope with their plight:

"They don't feel that the contest is unfair; they keep plugging, rolling like sailorly souls—a bobbing, infirm gait, a brave sealegged momentum—stopping occasionally to study the lay of the land."

And the tough role of frogs in the food chain:

"Frogs' tasty legs are the staff of life to many animals—herons, raccoons, ribbon snakes—though they themselves are hard to feed."

The commas might confuse a reader if the dashes didn't enclose the entire interrupter. When using this technique, check to see the sentence would be grammatically correct without the list.

Practice:
Use the practice exercise under "Commas with Interrupters," but replace the commas with dashes.

QUOTATION MARKS AND UNDERLINING/ITALICS

Note: Quotation marks used when citing sources in a research paper or on a works cited page are covered in Section Six of your textbook. Quotation marks are used to set off dialogue in writing, signaling when a new speaker is speaking; see the "Styling" exercise with David Sedaris's "Turbulence."

As a general rule, use italics—most writers consider underlining outdated—when referring to the major work, like a book, magazine, newspaper, journal, play, film, television show, or CD. Material *within* the major source takes quotation marks: book chapters, magazine article titles, newspaper article titles, journal articles, a particular episode of a television show, or a song on a CD.

Examples:

Major Work in Italics	**Article Titles, Songs, TV Episodes Use Quotation Marks**
New York Times Magazine	"The Global-Warming Heretic"
The Smithsonian (magazine)	"Dinosaur Wars: Who Owns America's Fossils?"
The Orange County Register	"The Dow Drops 500 Points"
Sparks: A Reader to Energize Writing	"Contemplations: Essays that Explain and Explore"
Hamlet	Quotations marks around lines from the play.
The Big Bang Theory	"The Bad Fish Paradigm" (TV episode title)
Tragic Kingdom (No Doubt Band)	"Just a Girl" (song on a CD)

Note: Place Semi-colons or colons **outside** the quotation marks, commas and periods inside.

FRAGMENTS

The word fragment means "piece," so a sentence fragment is a piece of a sentence, a job left undone by the writer who has either left out a subject, a verb, or not expressed a complete thought. Often, fragments can be attached to a complete sentence with a comma or combined in other ways.

Example:
Wrong:
Some scientists are on the verge of creating a half-dinosaur, half chicken hybrid. By adding dinosaur DNA to a chicken egg.

The second sentence is a fragment and needs to be combined with the first sentence.

Correct:
Some scientists are on the verge of creating a half-dinosaur, half-chicken hybrid by adding dinosaur DNA to a chicken egg.

Some scientists are on the verge of creating a half-dinosaur, half-chicken hybrid—by adding dinosaur DNA to a chicken egg.

By adding dinosaur DNA to a chicken egg, some scientists are on the verge of creating a half-dinosaur, half-chicken hybrid.

Note: Fragments can be used for emphasis though with caution.

Practice:
Correct the following fragments by either attaching them to an existing sentence or completing the thought by adding missing words.

1. During WWII, women took on many roles vacated by men. Roles flying planes and working in factories on assembly lines.

2. Women were trained as pilots. In a program called WASP, an acronym for Women Airforce Service Pilots.

3. Many male pilots resented the women. Because they felt their jobs were threatened.

4. People were skeptical of women pilots. Thinking they were too high strung.

5. Working hard and persevering, The women pilots became as good or even better than men.

6. Wearing men's khaki jumpsuits they dubbed zoot suits.

7. Having no opportunity to prove themselves in combat because the war ended, Women were not considered veterans.

8. Though they had earned wings, They received no recognition for their part in the war effort.

9. Keeping in touch, launching a campaign, and hoping for full military recognition.

10. Congress passed a bill in 1977 and By 1979 considered women veterans.

Underline fragments in the following paragraph and then correct them.

Edgar Allan Poe, was born in Boston in 1809. His parents were actors in traveling shows. His father died in 1810 and his mother in 1811, Leaving Edgar penniless. A merchant, John Allan, from Virginia, took Edgar in and raised him, Though he mistreated young Edgar. When Edgar went to college, the wealthy John Allan refused to pay for tuition or support Edgar. Edgar left the University of Virginia after a short time and turned to drinking and gambling, Moving to Boston to begin his career as a writer, He published his first book, a volume of poetry, in 1827, but it didn't find many readers. Finally, in 1833, Edgar received payment for a short story, drawing the attention of a publisher who liked Edgar's work And gave him a job as an editor. He lost the job due to his drinking. He soon married his cousin, Virginia Clemm, Who was thirteen years old. Edgar gained success publishing short stories and poems, establishing his brilliance as a writer with his poem "The Raven." He died of alcoholism in 1849 at the age of forty, Three years after the death of his wife, Virginia, who died of tuberculosis in 1846.

COMPREHENSIVE QUIZ

Add punctuation and fix fragments, run-ons, or comma splices where needed. Some sentences will need more than one type of punctuation.

1. Ben and Jerry's ice cream comes in many flavors Chunky Monkey Cherry Garcia Peppermint Stick and plain vanilla to name a few.

2. Her cat Mo serenely watches fish in the aquarium, her other cat Picasso likes to pry open the lid and try to catch the fish.

3. Geoffrey the goldfish swims luxuriously in his big tank however he darts with agitation when Picasso decides to use Geoffrey's home as a kitty entertainment center.

4. Most days however Picasso sleeps in his cat tower in the window.

5. Scholars once thought of the Anasazi Indians as peaceful hunters and gatherers evidence has proven that they participated in cannibalism.

6. Running down the quiet foggy trail startled by two deer that appeared out of the mist.

7. Walking down the street in her new glasses Rose says that she loves Wonder Woman and her grandmother she doesn't mention the rest of her family.

8. When the school bell rang for the last day of the year happy students streamed out of classrooms and into the beginning of summer vacation.

9. Those flowers tulips daisies snapdragons and marigolds won't grow in that soil.

10. An abundance of shoes cluttered the hallway sneakers Uggs sandals flip flops strappy heels and cowgirl boots.

11. The television show Gilmore Girls her daughter's favorite finally ended after seven years.

12. Her favorite episodes are Cinnamon's Wake, That Damned Donna Reed, and They Shoot Gilmores, Don't They?

13. The whale shark is a slow-moving polka-dotted deep-diving shark.

14. Weighing up to several tons whale sharks are also notable for their markings unique spots that help scientists identify individual fish.

15. Whale sharks feeding mostly on plankton are named for their great size and diet.

16. Snorkeling with whale sharks a popular tourist pastime.

17. There are a few rules to remember when swimming with whale sharks only two divers at one time in the water no flash photography and no physical contact with the fish.

18. The red-tailed hawk a magnificent bird is abundant in Missouri

19. Neil LaBute is a witty playwright and screenwriter but some people call him a misogynist jerk.

20. When you finish reading Harry Potter you should read Ursula LeGuin's A Wizard of Earthsea, it's a better book.

ANSWERS

Commas with Items or Actions in a Series

1. The Cocker Spaniel bolted to its feet, growled, and threw itself against the window at the mailman.

2. Dorothy cocked the shotgun, sighted the target, and pulled the trigger.

3. William Steig wrote and illustrated numerous children's picture books. **Correct**

4. The Border Collie can retrieve ropes, balls, keys, shoes, and many other items on command.

5. Scones, lemon bars, brownies, cupcakes decorated for Halloween, and a variety of over-sized cookies filled the bakery shop window.

6. The Volkswagon careened down the hill, hit a boulder, flipped over, rolled several times, and landed in the ditch.

7. Scientists now know that animals have better memories, can reason more complexly, live more socially complex lives, have more complex understanding of others, and have more self-awareness than was previously thought.

8. Maria competed in the long jump, the 500 meter race, the pole vault, and the relay.

9. Her favorite hobbies include raising turtles, painting landscapes, decorating cakes, growing orchids, surfing with her friends, and watching black and white movies.

10. The coffee shop owner worked the breakfast rush, helped clean up the aftermath, interviewed a perspective employee, and chatted with customers in the lull of the afternoon.

Commas with lead-in (or introductory) material:

1. To protect your skin from skin cancer, you should wear sunscreen of SPF 50 or higher.

2. If you're allergic to milk, you can try dairy products like ice cream and cheese made of soy.

3. During the holidays, students often forget many of the punctuation rules they learned in English class.

4. With strong winds over 50 miles per hour, the storm blew debris all over the road.

5. In an ice storm, power lines often break under the weight of the ice.

6. To justify his decision, the president went on national TV to argue that his plan would create new jobs.

7. Because the electricity went out during the storm, several students were unable to finish their term papers.

8. While doing her usual Monday morning online banking, she noticed suspicious activity and immediately called the bank.

9. When running a marathon, it is important to stay hydrated.

10. Since the robbery, the bank has increased security.

Commas with Interrupters

1. Marilyn Monroe, even with all of the adulation she received, was unhappy.

2. Tommy's ex-girlfriend, the one who relentlessly stalked him, was finally arrested.

3. Sarah, who has red hair, brought her pet bearded dragon to class.

4. Barry, an excellent musician, played the bass guitar in a rock band.

5. Jose's brother, the competitive one, always burst into a rage if Jose beat him at basketball.

6. Orangutans, thought by some to be smarter than chimpanzees, have a complex social structural with cultural traditions.

7. Alex, a smart African gray parrot, helped prove that animals can grasp abstract concepts.

8. Many paintings by the artist Jan Lievens, a contemporary of Rembrandt's, are often attributed to Rembrandt.

9. The two great painters, studying under the same master, knew each other and even modeled for one another.

10. Mansfield Correctional Facility, now an historical site in Ohio, was used in the film *The Shawshank Redemption*.

Commas with Two Sentences Joined by a Conjunction

1. Miranda earned a 4.0 GPA in high school, but she could not get into the college of her choice.

2. The refrigerator needed cleaning, and the garbage reeked of an unpleasant odor.

3. Joshua passed his final exam in history with an A, but he still failed the class because he didn't turn in his research essay.

4. Numerous children's films have been based on quality picture books, but the films lack the literary and artistic value of the originals.

5. The picture book *Jumanji* by Chris Van Allsburg has stunning drawings, but the movie added silly scenes and dialogue.

6. She turned on the radio and listened to a football game to keep from falling asleep at the wheel. **Correct**

7. Writer David Sedaris finds humor in odd situations, and his newest book, *When You Are Engulfed in Flames,* is sure to be a hit.

8. Plastic is a marvelous invention, but it may cause cancer as well as problems in landfills.

9. You should never use plastic to cook food in the microwave nor put hot beverages in plastic cups. **Correct**

10. Many people think they eat healthy, yet most don't get the recommended five servings of fruits and vegetables.

Commas Between Words that Describe (Adjectives)

1. Her tattered, dirty coat could not keep out the piercing cold.

2. The sultry, record-breaking heat sent thousands of people to California's southland beaches.

3. Cobwebs blanketed the musty, damp, rotting cellar.

4. Brutal, windy weather kept shivering Missourians indoors.

5. The orchids grew in an orchestra of exotic, colorful shapes.

6. Ramon ran through the quiet, fog-shrouded streets of San Francisco.

7. The sunset looked eerie through the dark, smoky atmosphere caused by the wildfire.

8. Black widow spiders construct messy, tangled webs that are surprisingly efficient.

9. Tantalizing, sweet nectar attracted orioles as well as hummingbirds.

10. Nutritious, tasty meals can be made in thirty minutes or less.

Colons

1. Orchids come in many varieties: lady slippers, butterfly orchids, cymbidiums, cattelyas, and many other species.

2. Both jobs had advantages: one providing great health coverage but the other with more opportunities for advancement.

3. Regina mulled over her opportunities: stay in school and finish her education or take the acting job that might lead to fame and fortune.

4. There are three types of drivers that irritate me the most: parking spot hogs who steal spaces or park across two spots, impatient people who honk at the elderly, and those with road rage who weave in and out of traffic, screaming and making rude gestures to other drivers.

5. Many types of seashells washed up on the beach: scallops, mussels, conch shells, clams, sea urchins, and others I couldn't identify.

6. Science can now accomplish many things that were once considered science fiction: cloning, regenerating tissue, replacing joints, and using DNA to diagnose genetic disorders, among others.

7. Many new drugs have been invented to improve brain functions like memory, alertness, attention span, and mental illness. **Correct**

8. Researchers think they have solved the puzzle as to why we need to sleep: maintaining the immune system.

9. Many bird species are disappearing from North America: nighthawks, whip-poor-wills, barn swallows, flycatchers, and many others.

10. Some spices not only enhance the flavor of food but also provide antioxidants for better health: cinnamon, ginger, red pepper, and curry belong on the top of the list of antioxidant rich spices.

Run-ons, Comma Splices, and Semicolons: Answers will vary.

1. Gardening can be an enjoyable and profitable hobby; however, you shouldn't garden if you're allergic to bees. (Or period and a capital)

2. Taking precautions, however, can allow you to enjoy the outdoors despite this deadly allergy.

3. Vincent Van Gogh painted sunlit landscapes in the south of France; he also painted lively nighttime scenes that some critics say merge fantasy and reality. (Or period and a capital)

4. Spotted owls in Oregon have struggled to survive; now they're being bullied by a new neighbor, the barred owl. (Or period and capital or comma with conjunction "and")

5. She enjoys making homemade lasagna, **but** her favorite thing to cook is salmon in salsa verde. (Or semicolon or period and capital)

6. The band gave a performance almost identical to the one several years ago, **but** fans still felt they got their money's worth. (Or period and capital or semicolon)

8. <u>Though they had earned wings</u>, they received no recognition for their part in the war effort.

9. <u>They kept</u> in touch, launching a campaign, hoping for full military recognition.

10. Congress passed a bill in 1977, and by 1979, they <u>considered women veterans</u>.

One possible solution (answers may vary).

<u>Edgar Allan Poe was born in Boston in 1809</u>. His parents were actors in traveling shows. His father died in 1810 and his mother in 1811, <u>leaving Edgar penniless</u>. A merchant, John Allan from Virginia, took Edgar in and raised him, <u>though he mistreated young Edgar</u>. When Edgar went to college, the wealthy John Allan refused to pay for tuition or support Edgar. Edgar left the University of Virginia after a short time and turned to drinking and gambling. He moved<u> to Boston to begin his career as a writer</u>. He published his first book, a volume of poetry, in 1827, but it didn't find many readers. Finally, in 1833, Edgar received payment for a short story, drawing the attention of a publisher who liked Edgar's work <u>and gave him a job as an editor</u>. He lost the job due to his drinking. He soon married his cousin, Virginia Clemm, <u>who was thirteen years old</u>. Edgar gained success publishing short stories and poems, establishing his brilliance as a writer with his poem "The Raven." He died of alcoholism in 1849 at the age of forty, <u>three years after the death of his wife, Virginia, who died of tuberculosis in 1846.</u>

Comprehensive Quiz (Answers may vary)

1. Ben and Jerry's ice cream comes in many flavors: Chunky Monkey, Cherry Garcia, Peppermint Stick, and plain vanilla, to name a few.

2. Her cat, Mo, serenely watches fish in the aquarium; her other cat, Picasso, likes to pry open the lid and try to catch the fish. (Or period and capital or comma with conjunction; or make a dependent clause with the world "while" after aquarium)

3. Geoffrey, my goldfish, swims luxuriously in his big tank; however, he darts with agitation when Picasso decides to use Geoffrey's home as a kitty entertainment center. (Or period and capital)

4. Most days, however, Picasso sleeps in his cat tower in the window.

5. Scholars once thought of the Anasazi Indians as peaceful hunters and gatherers. Evidence has proven that they participated in cannibalism. (Or semicolon or comma with conjunction; or make the first clause dependent by adding "Although" before scholars with a comma after "gatherers")

6. Running down the quiet, foggy trail, **she was** startled by two deer that appeared out of the mist.

7. Walking down the street in her new glasses, Rose says that she loves Wonder Woman and her grandmother, but she doesn't mention the rest of her family. (Or semicolon or period with capital)

8. When the school bell rang for the last day of the year, happy students streamed out of classrooms and into the beginning of summer vacation.

9. Those flowers—tulips, daisies, snapdragons, and marigolds—won't grow in that soil.

10. An abundance of shoes cluttered the hallway: sneakers, Uggs, sandals, flip flops, strappy heels, and cowgirl boots.

11. The show *Gilmore Girls,* her daughter's favorite, finally ended after seven years.

12. Her favorite episodes are "Cinnamon's Wake," "That Damned Donna Reed," and "They Shoot Gilmores, Don't They?"

13. The whale shark is a slow-moving, polka-dotted, deep-diving shark.

14. Weighing up to several tons, whale sharks are also notable for their markings, unique spots that help scientists identify individual fish.

15. Whale sharks, feeding mostly on plankton, are named for their great size and diet.

16. Snorkeling with whale sharks **is** a popular tourist pastime.

17. There are a few rules to remember when swimming with whale sharks: only two divers at one time in the water, no flash photography, and no physical contact with the fish.

18. The red-tailed hawk, a magnificent bird, is abundant in Missouri. (or dashes)

19. Neil LaBute is a witty playwright and screenwriter, but some people call him a misogynist jerk.

20. When you finish reading ***Harry Potter,*** you should read Ursula LeGuin's ***A Wizard of Earthsea.*** It's a better book. (Or semicolon after the book title)

Glossary

adjective   a word that describes or modifies a noun: "Children's dirty faces peered in the candy shop window." The word *dirty* describes *faces*.

adverb   a word that describes or modifies a verb, an adjective, or another adverb: "The girl longingly peered through the shutters." The word *longingly* describes how the girl peered.

alliteration   using words close together that begin with the same letter or sound: *feasting* and *flying* both begin with *f*.

allusion   an indirect or implied reference; don't confuse with *illusion,* meaning deceptive appearance or delusion.

annotating   adding notes or explanation; critical commentary.

anthropomorphizing   assigning human characteristics or personality traits to animals.

appositive   a word or phrase that renames, describes, or gives more information about a noun (subject) and helps eliminate clunky clauses using *who* and *which.* "The orchids, *cymbidiums,* grew splendidly in the greenhouse." *Cymbidiums* renames *orchids* and is much cleaner than writing *which are cymbidiums*.

assonance   repetition of vowel sounds; resemblance of sound between words.

bias   a tendency or preference; sometimes prejudice.

chronological order   organization by time order, or order in which events happened.

classification   organizing an essay by grouping ideas or objects according to type or characteristic; an essay classifying high school students might be organized according to the group they associate with: jocks, cheerleaders, band members, nerds, brains, etc.

cliché   worn-out phrases such as *drinks like a fish, light as a feather,* or *not playing with a full deck.* General rule: if you've heard it before, don't use it in your writing.

comma splice   a writing error in which you join two sentences with a comma. Comma splices can be fixed with a semicolon, a comma with a conjunction, or a period and a capital.

>   *Incorrect:* That cat is a Persian, her name is Cleopatra.
>   *Correct:* That cat is a Persian; her name is Cleopatra.
>   *Correct:* That cat is a Persian, and her name is Cleopatra.
>   *Correct:* That cat is a Persian. Her name is Cleopatra.

Sometimes a comma splice can be fixed by making one of the clauses dependent.

>   *Incorrect:* I waited in line for tickets to the Dave Matthews Band concert, a storm broke out and it began to rain.
>   *Correct:* As I waited in line for tickets to the Dave Matthews Band concert, a storm broke out and it began to rain.

The word *as* makes the first clause dependent.

complete sentence   a statement that can stand on its own; it expresses a complete thought. See **fragment**.

conjunction   a connecting word: *for, and, nor, but, or, yet, so.* In an informal essay, you can begin a sentence or paragraph with a conjunction, but do so sparingly.

connotation   a suggestion or implication: "Her words had sinister connotations."

criticism   in the context of this book, criticism refers to essays or articles by professionals commenting on or critiquing the work of others, whether it's film, art, or literature.

definition In the context of this book, definition refers to a type of essay called extended definition where the entire essay focuses on defining one word in depth. See "Writing Strategies for Defining."

dependent clause a clause that cannot stand on its own as a sentence; it is depending on another complete sentence. See **independent clause**.

> *Dependent clause:* When she ice skates
> *Dependent clause introducing an independent clause:* When she ice skates, the crowd roars with applause.

emphatic order organization according to which points are the most important or most developed, saving the strongest or most in-depth discussion for the end of the essay right before the conclusion.

figurative language metaphor, simile, personification, analogy.

first person the *I* point of view.

fragment, sentence fragment the word *fragment* means a piece, so a sentence fragment is a piece of a sentence—it's missing something, either a subject or verb, or it has both of these but doesn't express a complete thought.

freewrite a warm-up or prewriting exercise where you write on your topic without stopping to think, disregarding organization, grammar, spelling, or punctuation.

genre the largest category for classifying the arts. Film genres would include science fiction, drama, comedy, and western.

hyphen a punctuation symbol that joins words together to make one, like *deep-rooted*. Don't confuse hyphens with dashes: a hyphen is shorter than a dash, so when you're typing dashes, use two hyphens.

incomplete sentence see **fragment**.

independent clause a group of words that could stand on its own as a complete sentence; it forms a complete thought. See **dependent clause**.

interrupter a word or phrase that interrupts a sentence, requiring commas, dashes, or parentheses: "I told you, Binh, that the essay was due today." *Binh* interrupts the sentence "I told you that the essay was due today."

interrupting clause a group of words that interrupts a sentence, requiring commas, dashes, or parentheses: "Crystal's hair, cut Winona Ryder style, glistened with auburn highlights." The clause *cut Winona Ryder style* interrupts the sentence "Crystal's hair glistened with auburn highlights." If you want the clause to get more attention, use dashes; if you want it to be less noticeable, use parentheses.

introductory clause a dependent clause that introduces the main sentence: "When I work in my garden, I feel serene." The main sentence is "I feel serene"; *when I work in my garden* introduces the sentence. Use a comma after introductory clauses or phrases.

jargon language used by a particular group, often not understood by the general population: computer jargon, English teacher jargon (some of the terms in this glossary are English teacher jargon).

loose sentence a sentence structure that begins with a complete sentence followed by a series of clauses or phrases that add description or information. See **periodic sentence**.

mantra a word or sound you repeat to help you concentrate during meditation.

metaphor a direct comparison between two objects not using *like* or *as*. "She is a poem." See **simile**.

narrative an essay or work of fiction told in story form.

noun a person, place, or thing.

opposition in an argument essay, the opposition is the other side; the opposite view.

periodic sentence a sentence that begins with a series of dependent clauses or phrases describing or giving more information about the main sentence, which comes at the end. See **loose sentence**.

personification giving human qualities to inanimate objects: "The chair *sulked* in the corner."

plagiarism presenting someone else's words or ideas as your own—a serious academic offense. Always give credit to the proper source.

point of view (see First, second, third person).

preposition a word that links words or phrases by showing relationship, direction, or position: *of, from, by, after, through, in,* etc.

prewriting   the process of figuring out what you want to write about and which direction your writing will take. See the Getting Started and Traditional Brainstorming sections of this book.

rationale   an explanation or reason.

refute   to deny or prove wrong. In an argument essay, you should refute your opposition by presenting the other side's views and discussing how their thinking is illogical or misguided.

run-on sentence, fused sentence   two complete sentences that are run together but should be separated with a period, semicolon, or comma with a conjunction: "That cat is a Persian her name is Cleopatra." Don't try to fix a run-on with a mere comma. That's like yielding at a stop sign and creates another error called a **comma splice**. Fix a run-on the same way you would a comma splice.

second person   you (a more intimate way to address the reader). *Caution:* Don't use "you" in the general sense, meaning "anyone."

semicolon   a mark of punctuation (;) used to join two complete sentences when the thoughts are closely related. Do not use a semicolon with conjunctions; it replaces them.

sentence variety   using many different sentence styles in your essay rather than repeating the same structure.

simile   a comparison that uses *like* or *as*. "She moves like a poem." See **metaphor**.

specific details, specific examples   details or examples that are not vague words or phrases. Instead of *flower,* write *daisy; beer* becomes *Budweiser; oak* replaces *tree.*

subtext   an underlying meaning or message in a piece of writing, not directly stated but inferred.

thesis statement   the controlling idea or argument of an essay. A thesis should be specific, contain an opinion rather than fact, and not just announce your topic.

third person   someone else, not *I* (first person) or *you* (second person): *students* are; *she* writes; *researchers* believe.

tone   your writer's voice; the emotional or intellectual attitude, style, or manner of expression in your writing: sarcastic, ironic, comic, nostalgic are examples of tone.

transitions   words or phrases that help move sentences or paragraphs smoothly from one idea to the next. Some common transitions are conjunctive adverbs like *however, moreover, nevertheless, therefore;* phrases like *in addition, on the other hand;* single words like *thus, also, first, second, third, finally.* A more sophisticated trick for transitions is to pick up a word or idea at the end of one paragraph and use it in the beginning of the next one. See the Writing Strategies section for more on transitions.

verb   a word that expresses action (*jumped, went, made, drank, ran*) or state of being (*is, are, was, were, be, being, been, am*).

Index